Beatles For Sale to Help!

Compiled by Bruce Spizer

With additional contributions by

Bill King,
Al Sussman,
Frank Daniels,
Piers Hemmingsen
and other Beatles fans

498 Productions, L.L.C.
935 Gravier Street, Suite 707
New Orleans, Louisiana 70112
Phone: 504-299-1964
email: 498@beatle.net

The Billboard, Cash Box and Record World chart data used in this book was taken from books published by Record Research, including Billboard Pop Album Charts 1965-1969, The Comparison Book 1954-1982, and Top R&B Singles. Photo credits: Zack Smith Photography (page vi); Alamy (pages 44-tickets in upper right corner, 242-photo); Beatles Book Photo Library (pages 67, 221, 224, 225, 231-photo, 234, 245-lower left, 249, 251-left, 252, 257); Popperfoto/ Getty Images (page 241); Getty Images (page 245-top left & top right); and Marc Weinstein photo (page 259). Images by Heritage Auctions, HA.com: pages 41, 95-lower right, 98-posters, 101, 169-book covers. The Canadian images on pages 119 and 121 were provided by Piers Hemmingsen. Most of the other collectibles shown in the book are from the collections of Bruce Spizer, Frank Daniels, Jeff Augsburger, Jay Benjamin, Gary Hein and Perry Cox.

Print edition ISBN 979-8-9863190-9-4 Library of Congress Control Number: 2025907237
Printed in U.S.A.
1 2 3 4 5 6 7 8 9 0

Every Little Thing

Growing up in the 1960s, I was fascinated by every little thing about the Beatles. It started the instant I heard "I Want To Hold Your Hand" on the Newman School bus radio for the first time in early January 1964. I remember hearing "She Loves You" and "Please Please Me" on WTIX leading up to the group's appearance on The Ed Sullivan Show. Shortly thereafter, my mother took me to Studio A and bought me *Meet The Beatles!*

I constantly listened to WTIX to hear the latest Beatles songs and learn about the group's activities. In 1964, the station ran reports from George's sister, Louise Harrison Caldwell, and had jingles that incorporated bits of Beatles songs such as "I want to hold your hand and listen to the Beatles on WTIX." I'm sure their rival New Orleans Top 40 station WNOE played a lot of Beatles music, but I was a loyal WTIX listener and never departed from The Mighty 690 and their Boss Jocks. And while the girls in my class bought magazines about the Beatles, I did not do so. My allowance was used to buy comic books, with my favorites being The Flash, Batman, Green Lantern, Justice League of America, Superman, Spider-Man, Thor, and Daredevil.

Around Thanksgiving 1964, I remember hearing "I Feel Fine" and "She's A Woman" on the radio. I had no idea what caused that weird sound at the beginning of "I Feel Fine," but I thought it was really cool. I also didn't know that the Capitol album *Beatles '65* was only part of the British *Beatles For Sale* LP. *Beatles '65* had an eye-catching cover with John, Paul, George and Ringo holding umbrellas in the main panel plus three smaller pictures of the group. At the time, I did not realize that the cover represented the four seasons.

Although I studied the photographs and read the liner notes on the back cover, the main attraction was the music. In addition to having both sides of the latest single, *Beatles '65* was full of other great songs, with my favorites being "No Reply," "I'll Follow The Sun" and "I'll Be Back."

That holiday season, my parents took me and my older sisters to see our first James Bond film, *Goldfinger*. I thought it was terrific movie. I loved the chase scene with Bond's car and thought Oddjob was an interesting villain. A few weeks later, I wrote a short essay on the film for a fourth-grade assignment. It turned out to be my first movie review!

I was becoming nearly as interested in Bond as the Beatles–something about those British chaps! One weekend, my mom took me to the book store at Tulane University and bought me a few James Bond novels. I doubt she knew how sexy they were. But, as was the case with my reading comic books and Mad magazine, she was delighted that I was reading something!

I began hearing another great Beatles song on WTIX in mid-February, "Eight Days A Week." It was a catchy sing-along tune with highly effective handclaps. I felt no need to buy the new single as it was constantly being played on the radio. This was followed about two months later with "Ticket To Ride." I loved the guitar riff, John's slightly hoarse voice, Ringo's drumming and the change-of-pace ending. The label contained the exciting news of a new Beatles movie, "Eight Arms To Hold You."

That summer I went to camp at Lookout Mountain, Tennessee and then on a family vacation. Once again, I was out of town and missed the Beatles movie. Ouch!

Shortly after starting fifth grade, I heard two new Beatles songs on WTIX. One was a country & western song sung by Ringo titled "Act Naturally." The other, "Yesterday," was a tender ballad with Paul singing over guitar and strings. It had a hauntingly beautiful melody and was my favorite of the two. A few days later, the Beatles were on The Ed Sullivan Show. In addition to playing their new single, the group performed the hits "I Feel Fine," "Ticket To Ride" and "Help!," plus the wild rocker "I'm Down." I was mesmerized by the pair of three-song segments featuring the Beatles.

That fall, I ordered an album titled *The Incredible World Of James Bond*, which contained musical highlights from the first three Bond films. I played the disc whenever I read my growing collection of James Bond novels. I also remember taking the bus downtown with my cousin Barry to see the James Bond double feature *Dr. No/From Russia With Love*. It was the first time our parents let us go downtown on our own. Now I had seen all three James Bond films but had yet to see the Beatles on the big screen! When I finally got to see *Help!*, I enjoyed the James Bond aspects of the plot, the beautiful colors of the Alps and the Bahamas, and the parodies of Bond's car and Oddjob's deadly derby.

Although I did not purchase the *Help!* soundtrack album when it first came out, I added it to my record collection in the summer of 1968. At the time, I was at Camp Zakelo in Harrison, Maine. My cabin took a road trip to Montreal, Canada. While there, I went to a department store that had a record section. I picked up a copy of the Capitol *Help!* LP and was quite surprised to see a few Beatles albums shown on the back cover that I had never heard of, *Beatlemania! With The Beatles*, *Twist And Shout* and *Long Tall Sally*. Of course, I had to buy the LP. By then, I had read the Hunter Davies biography on the Beatles, so I was aware of the British albums. After learning that Canada had different records as well, I realized the group's record catalog varied throughout the world. I found that fascinating.

In writing, compiling and editing this book, I was reminded how great the music and pop culture was in 1965: Beatles, Bond and beyond. As I listened to the LPs and singles covered in this book over and over again, I heard every little thing in the recordings. These albums don't get enough recognition. They fall between the first phase of Beatlemania and the brilliance of *Rubber Soul* and *Revolver*. However, these records represent what I love about the Beatles music: Every...Little...Thing.

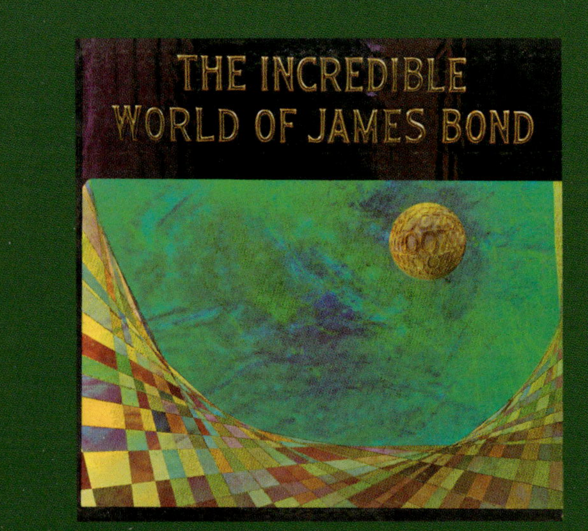

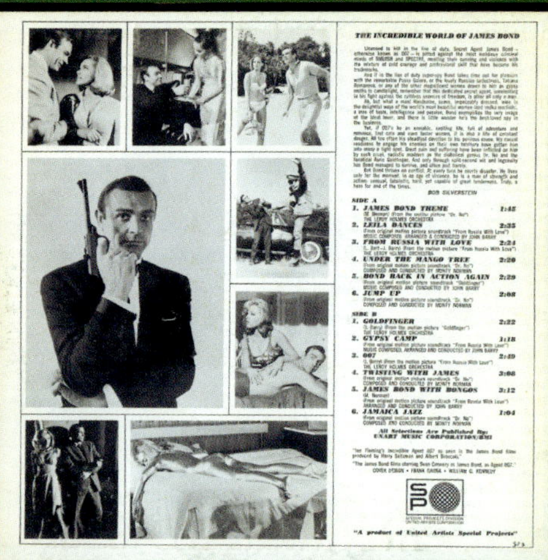

Eight Days A Week

Welcome to the ninth and final book in my Beatles Album Series. What started off as a single book to mark the 50th anniversary of *Sgt. Pepper's Lonely Hearts Club Band* from a fan's perspective turned into nine books. The basic format was there from the beginning. Explore the album from a historical perspective as to how the music was marketed and received in the United Kingdom, the United States and Canada at the time of its release. Add a chapter on what was going on in the world to place it all in context. Throw in chapters on the packaging of the album and the recording of the songs. Have a section of personal fan recollections on what the music meant to and how it affected them.

As the series moved forward, the format evolved and expanded. Chapters on music and film were added, as were different special features such as this book's chapter on the connection between the Beatles and James Bond. With these additions, the later books have increased page counts. Some books have supplemental material available in the digital edition or as a separate and free download at www.beatle.net.

While the series started with the *Sgt. Pepper* book, I recommend that the books be shelved in chronological order that follows the album release dates rather the book publication dates. The proper order is: *The Beatles Please Please Me to With The Beatles*; *The Beatles A Hard Day's Night & More*; *Beatles For Sale to Help!*; *The Beatles Rubber Soul to Revolver*; *The Beatles and Sgt. Pepper: A Fans' Perspective*; *The Beatles Magical Mystery Tour and Yellow Submarine*; *The Beatles White Album and the Launch of Apple*; *The Beatles Get Back to Abbey Road*; and *The Beatles Finally Let It Be*.

I am very proud (and fortunate) to have assembled the same team of contributors for all nine books in the series. Beatlefan editor Al Sussman contributed two chapters on what was happening in 1965 in the news and in music to place the Beatles music in historical context. Piers Hemmingsen provided the Canadian perspective. Frank Daniels added a chapter on the Beatles and James Bond. Beatlefan publisher Bill King returned with more fan notes and more of his interview with film producer Walter Shenson.

As always, we were treated to dozens of wonderful Fan Recollections. Once again, we received more Fan Recollections than we could fit in the book. The surplus is contained in the digital supplement, which also has fun facts that we just couldn't fit into the print edition.

On the technical side, Diana Thornton worked her magic to make the book look terrific as always. She has been an integral part of all 17 books I have published spanning 28 years! Proof readers included Diana, Frank, Al, Beatle Tom Frangione and Tom Brennan. In the tradition, my thanks to my family, Sarah, Eloise, Barbara, Trish, Big Puppy and others too numerous and crazy to name. Mark Lewisohn provided his expertise. Finally, I must thank the thousands of Beatles fans who have purchased my books over the years.

I currently have no plans to write additional books on the Beatles, but to borrow a title from a James Bond film, *Never Say Never Again*. I may work with Diana to prepare digital editions of hardcover books that sold out. And for those wondering how I have been able to practice law full time and write books on the Beatles, I don't need a lot of sleep and work eight days a week.

About Author

Bruce Spizer is a native and lifelong resident of New Orleans, Louisiana, who was eight years old when the Beatles invaded America. He began listening to the radio at age two and was a die-hard fan of WTIX, a top forty AM station that played a blend of New Orleans R&B music and top pop and rock hits. His first two albums were *The Coasters' Greatest Hits*, which he permanently "borrowed" from his older sisters, and *Meet The Beatles!*, which he still occasionally plays on his vintage 1964 Beatles record player.

During his high school and college days, Bruce played guitar in various bands that primarily covered hits of the sixties, including several Beatles songs. He wrote numerous album and concert reviews for his high school and college newspapers, including a review of *Abbey Road* that didn't claim Paul was dead. He received his B.A., M.B.A. and law degrees from Tulane University. His legal and accounting background have proved valuable in researching and writing his books.

Bruce is considered one of the world's leading experts on the Beatles. A "taxman" by day, Bruce is a Board Certified Tax Attorney with his own practice. A "paperback writer" by night, Bruce is the author of 17 critically acclaimed books on the Beatles, including *The Beatles Are Coming! The Birth of Beatlemania in America,* a series of six books on the group's American record releases, *Beatles For Sale on Parlophone Records,* which covers all of the Beatles records issued in the U.K. from 1962- 1970, and his series of nine books on the Beatles albums. His articles have appeared in Beatlefan, Goldmine and American History magazines. He wrote the questions for the special Beatles edition of Trivial Pursuit. He maintains the popular website www.beatle.net.

Bruce has been a speaker at numerous Beatles conventions and at the Grammy Museum, the Rock 'N' Roll Hall of Fame & Museum and the American Film Institute. He has been on ABC's Good Morning America and Nightline, CBS's The Early Show, CNN, Fox and morning shows in New York, Chicago, Los Angeles, New Orleans and other cities, and is a frequent guest on radio shows, including NPR, BBC and the Beatles Channel.

Bruce serves as a consultant to Universal Music Group, Capitol Records and Apple Corps Ltd. on Beatles projects, including writing the essays for the *1964 U.S. Albums In Mono*. He has an extensive Beatles collection of American, Canadian and British first issue records, promotional items and concert posters.

contents

Record Mirror

Largest selling colour pop weekly newspaper
No. 194 Week ending November 28, 1964
Every Thursday 6d. Registered at the G.P.O. as a newspaper

INSIDE THIS WEEK

Pet Clark, Marvin Gaye, & Rockin' Berries colours. Gene Pitney exclusive.

LESS BEATLES FOR BRITAIN

SO it is to be "Less Beatles" during 1965! Shame, shame, shame . . . so say the fans. But it was only to be expected. The fabulous foursome have been under extreme pressure for a long time and the news that they are to cut down on their personal appearances in Britain is no surprise.

But the boys are still doing, as ever, their best for the fans. They are, of course, making their second feature-length movie — for 12 weeks as from February 22. This is the comedy thriller, with Ringo on the run from a potential killer. Story is by American Mark Vahm. Foint is that this film will enable the Beatles to be seen by millions of their fans throughout the world.

They are doing more. They are filming two television spectaculars, which again will go through the world. First is expected to be made in London, soon after their filming is over; the second will be in America. Some of the top figures in world show business are being sought to co-star with the Liverpool lads. It is expected that the Beatles will figure in sketches and acting sequences as well as providing the music.

That they are cutting down on actual personal appearances, once their Christmas season at the Hammersmith Odeon is over, is no surprise. Brian Epstein is anxious that the Beatles should not be over-exposed, or over-worked. Certainly they are not losing the zest for touring packages, but they equally certainly have to start thinking of cutting down.

THE BEATLES — a new colour pic of the team taken by EMI photographer John Dove during their last recording session. The Beatles new disc "I Feel Fine" looks like being a cert number one hit in Britain and the States—but in Britain it has competition with the Rolling Stones biggie "Little Red Rooster." Despite the current big beat slump there's no chance of sales falling for the fabulous foursome. Watch out soon for more news of the next film from the Beatles, and of course their LP "Beatles For Sale" should be in the shops any day now.

Beatles For Sale in the U.K. in 1965

As 1964 headed to an end, Beatles fans in the U.K. could look back at another fabulous year of excitement generated by the Fab Four. The year started off with the last ten nights of the 1963 Beatles Christmas Show held at the Astoria Cinema in Finsbury Park, London. At the time, the group held down the top two spots on the album charts with their first album, *Please Please Me*, at number two, and their latest, *With The Beatles*, at number one. "I Want To Hold Your Hand" was topping the singles charts, with "She Loves You" still hanging around and not far behind.

In mid-January, the group departed for Paris, where they would perform for 20 days and nights at the Olympia Theatre as part of a 10-artist program. This was followed by the Beatles first U.S. visit. With Beatlemania at fever pitch, the group drew a record-breaking 73 million viewers with their debut on The Ed Sullivan Show and played to thousands of screaming fans at sold-out performances at the Washington Coliseum and New York's prestigious Carnegie Hall. The British music weeklies provided extensive coverage of both the Paris and U.S. trips.

During the spring and summer, the Beatles released a pair of singles, "Can't Buy Me Love" and "A Hard Day's Night," the exciting *Long Tall Sally* EP, and *A Hard Day's Night*, an album consisting entirely of 13 Lennon-McCartney originals. They starred in their own feature film, the critically acclaimed *A Hard Day's Night*. British fans also had many opportunities to see the band perform live and on TV. After headlining at the New Musical Express Annual Poll-Winners' All-Star Concert at Empire Pool in Wembley on April 26, the band played shows in Edinburgh and Glasgow, Scotland and at the Prince of Wales Theatre in London. This was followed by a world tour with shows in Denmark, the Netherlands, Hong Kong, Australia and New Zealand. Afterwards, the group was back in the U.K. performing in Brighton, Blackpool, Bournemouth, Scarborough and London (with a quick trip to Stockholm, Sweden thrown into the mix). The Beatles also embarked on a triumphant and record-breaking tour of the United States and Canada in August and September. The boys' world-wide and American success was a source of British pride, but it inevitably meant "LESS BEATLES FOR BRITAIN" in 1965, as headlined and explained in the November 28, 1964 Record Mirror.

The September 1964 issue of The Beatles Book (No. 14) reported on an August 11 session during which the boys ran over "several new titles for their next single." The Beatle News item indicated that the group would not pick a song for the single until after their North American tour. The next month the magazine had an in-person report on the session from Billy Shepherd (the pen name used by Record Mirror reporter Peter Jones), who was accompanied to EMI Studios (later named Abbey Road Studios) by photographer Leslie Bryce. Although not mentioned by name, the song recorded that night was "Baby's In Black," which Shepherd incorrectly assumed would be the group's next single.

When the boys arrived at Studio Two, they encountered a nearly dark room–a practical joke by producer George Martin who was, in effect, teasing the group for their previous praise of the "subdued lighting" they saw at Pye recording studios. Shepherd was impressed with the way the group experimented. "They'd try all sorts of ad-lib ideas, vocally and instrumentally," picking up new ideas "as quick as a flash." After playing the song for Martin, with Paul singing and John and George working out an initial arrangement, the group ran through a few performances of the song before heading up to the control room to hear their work on tape. The group returned to the studio floor for a few more run-throughs before Martin thought they were ready for a proper take: "Shall we try one right now, boys?" After a bit of clowning around, the group settled down, recording several takes of the song. During the playback in the control room, Peter Asher of Peter and Gordon arrived to see the boys. Shortly before 11:00 PM, Martin was ready to call it a day, telling the group that they had done very well. Although John was full of energy and wanted to keep going, Martin told him engineer Norman Smith was tired, so they would "go on later in the week."

After an August 14 session, the group embarked on their first North American tour. The September 12 Disc reported that the group would get back to the studio upon their return, hoping to issue a new single and LP before Christmas. In an interview with Penny Valentine, Martin indicated there was a problem finding material to record. "They are literally living hand-to-mouth because anything they write is snapped up by other people. It's not easy to write good material all the time and they won't record anything they don't think comes up to standard." For this reason, the album would have songs written by the group along with "more standard material, rather like the first two albums." Martin added that the Beatles would not be recording a Christmas album as it wasn't their "cup of tea."

CHRISTMAS SHOW

THE BEATLES Christmas Show will start at the Hammersmith Odeon on Thursday, December 24, and run until Saturday January 16. The box office will open on Monday September 7.

Artistes appearing with the Beatles are Freddie and The Dreamers, The Yardbirds, Sounds Incorporated, Jimmy Savile, Elkie Brooks, Michael Haslan and The Mike Cotton Sound.

CHANGING GUITARS

I wonder how many Beatle People notice that George changes his guitars several times during a performance. He prefers to use his Gretch on numbers like "All My Loving", "She Loves You", "Things We Said To Day" and "Beethoven" but switches to his twelve string Rickenbacker for "A Hard Day's Night", "Twist And Shout" and "You Can't Do That". And at long last one manufacturer is planning to make a special guitar which will be named after him.

George checks his American dollars.

GUITARIST RINGO

Yes, the Beatles will soon have FOUR guitarists. Ringo has been playing about with the other's guitars for a long time now and can play fairly well. George recently took on the role of tutor and promises to produce a reserve player by Christmas. That'll complete the doubling up because all the Beatles can get by on drums.

New Single Session

The boys had a special recording session on August 11 to run over several new titles for their next single. But they do not expect to settle on a number befor[e] they return from their Ame[rican] and Canadian trip.

BILL AGREES TO D[...] JOHN'S ROLL[...]

'Big' Bill Corbe[tt] has been the driv[er] boys Austin Prince by a hire car firm ed to become [...] feur and driv[e] Rolls Royce [...] recently.

PAUL AND GEORGE PLAY PRACTICAL JOKE

During the drive back to London after their Bournemouth concert on August 2 the boys stopped their car outside a transport cafe in a small town. It was after midnight and it was the only place to get a cup of tea. While road manager Neil got the cups Paul and George got out to stretch their legs. Suddenly Paul started to tear up and down the main street pretending he was a mod gone crazy. George immediately took on the role of rocker and started chasing him. Lights were flashed on in bedrooms and several passing cars slowe[d] [...]wn to have a look. Very soon [...] [p]olice car roared up to s[...] [...]d rocker war tha[...] [...]. They su[...] [...] and st[...]

Printed by Wembley Press Limited, 13 Aintree Ro[...]
Distributors: Surridge, Dawson & Co. Ltd., 136-14[...]

THE Beatles BOOK No. 15 OCT. 1964

Millions of fans throughout the world wait breathlessly for the results of any Beatles' recording session. But few get to hear where the boys are cutting discs, or when. Certainly reporters aren't invited along to pick up the secrets—the boys usually like privacy.

BUT—a really BIG "but"—I did wangle an invitation from John, Paul, Ringo and George for the last one. The session that produced the Beatles' newest single. And to say it's a session I'll never forget is to put it very mildly indeed.

Care to join *Beatles Book* photographer Leslie Bryce and I on that rather steamy evening at EMI's Abbey Road Studios, near London's West End? Right then, off we go, through the forecourt into the main building.

Practical Joke

Inside, through to Studio Two. Push the door open. And immediately you get the impression something has gone very wrong. No usual blaze of lights with hectic activity. Wrong night? Surely not . . .

There are just three red lights—one big one, two small. And a tiny little light in the control room.

George lets us into the secret of the lack of lighting. Seems John, Paul, George and Ringo had looked in at the Pye recording studios and were impressed with the "subdued lighting" there. So George Martin had laid on this elaborate practical joke for them. And cellotaped up the light switches in the studio in case a Beatle thought to try and put matters right

Eventually George Harrison turned up, parking his E-Type Jag. Came in, blinked with amazement, said: "What's all this?"

Then John arrived with Ringo and Cynthia Lennon. John and Ringo went straight through to the control room. The gag clicked with John first.

"It's our George having us on about our subdued lighting," he said with a laugh.

Paul was last to arrive—in a taxi. John and Ringo had turned up in the Jaguar Mark 7, chauffeured by Bill Corbett.

Mad Session

And so, eventually, half-an-hour late, the session started. Mad session? Of course it was. John and Paul kept up a run of non-stop antics during most of the proceedings.

Fantastic thing for me was the way they experimented. They'd try all sorts of ad-lib ideas, vocally and instrumentally. They pick up new ideas as quick as a flash.

And there's seldom any music lying about. Usually it's just a piece of paper with the lyrics written on it and with (maybe) some guitar chords noted by the side.

On this occasion, Paul had written the words on the back of a fan-letter he'd been reading. Which makes that particular fan-letter a very important document indeed.

George Martin held up that piece of paper while the boys did a first run-through of the song, John and George Harrison working out a rough initial arrangement as Paul sang the words. Then big Malcolm Evans, the road manager, burst in through the doors with mugs of steaming hot tea. Tea plays a big part in a Beatle recording session. In fact, he had a lot of comings and goings during the evening.

The October 16 New Musical Express ("NME") reported that the Beatles next single was "surrounded by mystery," adding that although "I'm A Loser" was the choice, this was "almost certain to change" before the disc's probable release date of November 6. The next week George Harrison told Andy Gray of NME that two of the tracks recently recorded by the group were for the next single, but he couldn't disclose the title yet. John added: "State secret." That week Disc ran an article in its October 24 issue on the single in which Paul told Alan Walsh "the secret behind the choice." Walsh reported that "after demolishing a meal of steak and chips" in the Beatles dressing room at the ABC Cinema in Ardwick, Manchester on Wednesday, October 14, Paul said that the group was hoping to have their next single out by November 27. He indicated that the band had recorded five or six tracks before the start of their tour, but thought they would settle on a song that had a "big and really distinctive intro," adding: "We wanted to do a number which had a start as distinctive as the chord at the beginning of 'A Hard Day's Night' and we decided to do a fast drum roll with a guitar phrase over it. When we did it in the studio, we kept doing the roll wrong and we'll probably re-record this one before the disc comes out." The song Paul referred to was most likely "What You're Doing," which opens with a distinctive drum pattern and guitar riff played by George on his 12-string Rickenbacker. The group initially recorded the song on September 29-30 and did a remake on October 26. Although "What You're Doing" was not selected for the single, the song eventually chosen for the single would have a "big and really distinctive intro."

Beatles fans first learned of the titles of the group's upcoming record releases in the October 31 music weeklies. The new single, set for November 27, featured a pair of songs written by John and Paul, "I Feel Fine" and "She's A Woman." The next week, Disc reported in its November 7 issue that the Beatles next single "I Feel Fine" and album *Beatles For Sale* each had advance orders of over half a million. These sales resulted from the recent announcement of the new releases, with an EMI spokesman adding that "the avalanche was increasing." The boys would promote the new single with TV appearances on Thank Your Lucky Stars (November 21) and Top Of The Pops (December 3).

In that same issue, Don Nicholl gave five of five stars to the reissue of the 1961 Bobby Parker single "Watch Your Step," writing that "all rhythm 'n' blues enthusiasts ought to raise a cheer" to the news, calling the record an "outstanding disc of its kind with the vocal building in wild fashion out front after a gentle start." He added that the "rhythmic accompaniment is fervent and features some of the best drum-guitar-mouth organ work you'll ever hear in the blues sector." At the time Nicholl praised the song, he had no idea that the Beatles next single, "I Feel Fine," was heavily influenced by the disc (as detailed on page 236). The October 31 Record Mirror ran an ad touting the single: "'Watch Your Step' opens with a pounding guitar intro, before Bobby Parker's wildly exciting vocalising takes over in front of a wailing band. The record is pure dynamite from start to finish, and literally compelling in making one want to get up and dance." That same issue's review listed the disc as a Top Fifty Tip. "A long rock-blues instrumental intro on this fast beater, and a Ray Charles styled vocal starts wailing after a while. Certainly one of the wildest vocals we've heard for quite a while. Great dancing beat and loads of all-around appeal." Despite all this praise, the record did not chart.

Paul and John discussed "I Feel Fine" with Ray Coleman in the November 7 Melody Maker. Paul warned: "Don't be put off by the opening noise. It was a laugh. John was playing his Jumbo guitar as we did the final run-through before recording, and when the red light came on for the actual session he played it, unintentionally. The result's a sound of feedback, and after a bit of thought we decided to leave it in. It's the biggest gimmick thing we've ever used." John added: "The selling part of the song, commercially, is the phrase 'I Feel Fine' and the guitar run that follows it. George and I play the same bit on guitar together on the record. I suppose it has a bit of a country-and-western feel about it, but then so have a lot of our songs. The middle-eight is the most tuneful part, to me, because it's a typical Beatles bit." Paul believed the line "I'm in love with her and I feel fine" would be the catch phrase that helped sell the record. John sarcastically said that reviewers would say that bit will "set your feet a tapping." Paul said that the group also liked the B-side, "She's A Woman," adding: "This is the first real rocker we've written, and we're glad. We played it to Mary Wells [a black American R&B singer and Motown recording artist who was on their 1964 Autumn U.K. tour] and said to her, 'Listen, it's the coloured sound.'" John indicated that the group was "really pleased with the record."

The industry trade magazine Record Retailer reviewed the single in its November 26 issue. "A strange buzz opens this and some intricate guitar work follows on, leading up to some typical Beatles vocal work. It's their most out-of-rut song to date and has a solid sound that veers more towards country-and-western than rhythm-and-blues." The flip side was described as "a pounding bluesy beater, one solo voice and almost as much appeal as a top side."

Don Nicholl told the story of the new single in the November 28 Disc, writing that a couple of tracks on the Beatles new LP nearly became the new single, "Eight Days A Week" and "I'm A Loser." But as the group didn't like putting album tracks out as singles, they kept hoping that "something else would turn up for the single." This happened when John came to the studio and said, "I think I've got the answer." John played "I Feel Fine" to Paul, who liked the tune and lyrics, and worked on the harmonies. George came up with his guitar solo, and the song was complete for recording. When the group was ready to tape the number, there was an "electronic accident" when someone "plonked a guitar string" causing a "buzzing effect that could have been edited out." However, "the boys worked on it to make the distinctive start which now will be one of the disc's big features!" Paul indicated that the group could reproduce the sound on stage, adding that they don't do anything on discs that they can't achieve on stage. [That would begin to change in 1965.] While John wrote and sang the A-side, Paul wrote and sang the B-side. Nicholl noted that it was becoming a habit for "either John or Paul to sing their own songs."

John claimed that there wasn't any animosity over which song would be the A-side. "The fact that one of us may have done the lion's share of writing a particular song has nothing to do with it. We pick them on merit." John stated that these days he and Paul seemed to be doing more individual writing in the way that the songs on the single happened. "One of us gets the idea and works the song up until near-completion before taking it to the other for criticisms and final suggestions."

Nicholl then gave his verdict of the song, noting it would have been a hit even if the Beatles weren't known. "After the intriguing jew's harp kind of noise for the opening, 'I Feel Fine' moves along with a youthful zest that's going to make it one of The Beatles' most-repeated numbers...John sings it happily and the guitar sound throughout is first-class." Nicholl found it interesting "to see John Lennon's preoccupation with 'diamond rings' popping up in the lyric once more!" [Although Paul wrote and sang "I'll buy you a diamond ring my friend" in "Can't Buy Me Love."] Nicholl was less enthusiastic about the B-side. "Paul chants 'She's A Woman' with a rather desperate manner that builds towards the finish. Nearest thing to an out-and-out rhythm 'n' blues raver which the group has ever had among their originals. Guitar work is less imaginative on this half, however, and there's a very fine line between simplicity and boredom."

Derek Johnson reviewed the new single in the November 27 NME for those who "haven't already heard it on the radio, or are not one of the million-odd fans who placed an advance order for it." Johnson wrote: "A REAL gas!... After a startling, reverberating opening, it develops into a happy-go-lucky mid-tempo swinger. There's a tremendous rhythm and a really catchy melody, mainly featuring John on vocal with Paul and George harmonising. One of the boys' best yet!" The flip side "She's A Woman" had a "similar tempo, but a pounding and instant beat...with Paul lending a bluesy feel to the vocal." The song was "arresting and ear-catching." Record Mirror praised the disc in its November 28 issue. "Electronic buzzes and some sensational Carl Perkins' type guitar open this latest one from the Beatles. It's a fast tuneful number with a lot of underlying depth, and a basic rock 'n' roll approach. Vocal is more distinctive than on their previous couple of discs. Rather a haunting sound." The magazine was less enthusiastic about "She's A Woman," calling it a "blues-tinged number with a clean sound" and a "solid beat all way through," but "without the magic of the top side." The November 28 Melody Maker gave the new single front page coverage with the headline "Beatles Feeling Just Fine." The magazine did not run a proper review of the disc, instead printing Mick Jagger's comments on the single. "I like 'I Feel Fine,' I like the backing more than anything–I reckon they must have spent eight days of the week working that out because it's very good. I don't like the lyrics all that much. But the backing is excellent. I dare say I'll buy it! There's nothing striking about 'She's A Woman,' but I like the way Paul sings it. The tune is not that much, but like all their records, you can play the other side just as much as the A side and like it."

Peter Aldersley reviewed "I Feel Fine" in the November 28 Pop Weekly, writing: "From the arresting gimmick of the guitar opening, right through to the fadeout ending all the hallmarks are there. Once again, though, it is a song which will grow on you...there is no immediate melodic impact but spin it a few times and it will be with you—or you'll be 'with it'! It is a happy, bouncing rhythm and the overall sound is just that one we know so well now." Beat Instrumental praised the disc in its December issue, noting that the group "got clean away from the usual Beatles sound" with a "Country and Western flavour." "I Feel Fine" opened with a very odd sound (feedback noises) followed by a guitar riff played in harmony by John and George. John's double-tracked vocal added to the weirdness of the song, while George's lead guitar phrases were "the best he has ever done." Paul's "She's A Woman" was an "out-and-out rocker." The disc demonstrated that the Beatles were "one of the best long-term recording combinations in the world."

Melody Maker

December 5, 1964 9d. weekly

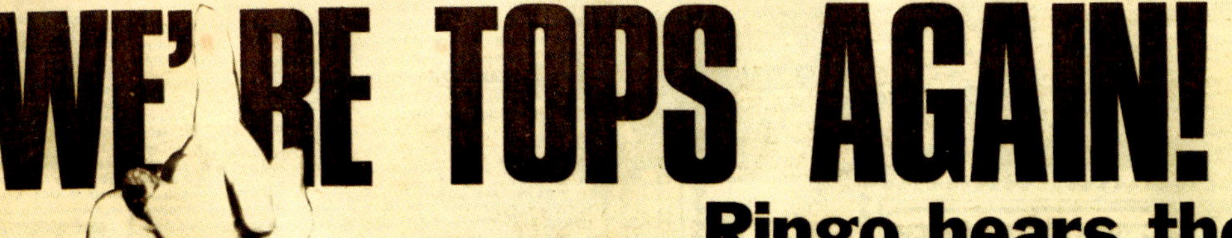

WE'RE TOPS AGAIN!

Ringo hears the good news in the MM office

THE Melody Maker Pop Fifty this week became one of the hottest talking points in show business as the Beatles sailed to yet another top position—on first entry—with "I Feel Fine".

Ringo Starr visited the MM office in London to watch the final count-down after a massive operation had established the Beatles as top of the chart.

Daily Mirror pop writer Patrick Doncaster was there, and told the graphic story of how the Pop Fifty is compiled. His full-page article appeared in the Mirror on Tuesday.

For Ringo, it was a day of elation 24 hours before entering London's University College Hospital for a tonsils operation. "I Feel Fine—in fact I'm made up!" said the drummer.

The planning of the Pop Fifty is a giant task every week. This week, with the release last Friday of the new Beatles single, a special plan was implemented to ensure that Britain's most authoritative hit parade was assessed with the greatest speed and accuracy. The chart bureau was augmented.

Record shop managers throughout Britain co-operated magnificently in rushing their returns to the MM, express post.

It started at 6.50 am and ended when results were announced at 12.10 pm.

Monday was OPERATION BEATLES Day. The day's drama is reflected in pictures by Mirror cameraman Bob Hope on page 3.

I FEEL FINE!

Ringo in the MM office—'I'm made up,' he said when he heard the number one news

JAZZ ON A WINTER'S DAY page twelve

LENNON'S BLIND DATE centre pages

"I Feel Fine" entered the Britain's Top 50 chart published by Record Retailer on December 3 at number six while the Rolling Stones were on top with their blues disc "Little Red Rooster," a cover of the Howlin' Wolf single written by Willie Dixon and issued by Chicago-based Chess Records in 1961. The following week "I Feel Fine" moved to number one, where it remained for five weeks, holding off Petula Clark's "Downtown" before being replaced by Georgie Fame's "Yeh, Yeh." The Beatles new single charted for 13 weeks, including eight in the top ten. Although Record Retailer was aimed at the music industry, its charts reached a larger audience through their appearance in Record Mirror.

The December 5 Melody Maker featured an article on how "I Feel Fine" went straight to the top of its weekly Pop 50 chart based solely on sales from its first day in record shops (Friday, November 27). The magazine tallied the sales on the following Monday as part of "Operation Beatles," which began at 6:50 AM at London's General Post Office with the collection of mailed-in sales information from record shops, and ended later that morning at the magazine's office with sales totals confirmed on an adding machine. When Ringo dropped by at 12:10 that afternoon, he was told the good news and responded, "We didn't expect it–we just hoped." The magazine's cover features Ringo holding a placard saying "I FEEL FINE!" as he signals the song's number one position with his finger. The single held down the top spot in Melody Maker for six straight weeks, charting for 13 weeks, including eight in the top ten. "I Feel Fine" also debuted at number one in the Top Thirty charts of NME (on December 4) and Disc (on December 5), remaining at number one for six of its ten weeks on the charts. The single topped the BBC chart.

"I Feel Fine" had advance orders of over 750,000 copies prior to its release on November 27, with 50,000 more sold the following Monday. With sales well in excess of 250,000 units, Disc awarded a Silver Disc award to the Beatles for the new single in its December 5 issue. It was the ninth Silver Disc given to the group by the magazine. The following week, sales were reported at 900,000. The December 19 Melody Maker reported that sales of the single had passed one million copies, giving the Beatles their fourth British Gold Disc award, joining "She Loves You," "I Want To Hold Your Hand" and "Can't Buy Me Love." The magazine observed that "I Feel Fine" had "proved to be the most successful Beatles single as far as sales are concerned because it has achieved the million mark within a fortnight [two weeks] of release."

As detailed on page 2, George Martin and the Beatles held recording sessions at EMI Studios in August prior to the start of the group's North American tour. In the August 22 Melody Maker, Martin explained: "It was just a case of getting things in the can before they went away to the States." The magazine's September 22 edition reported that the Beatles were back in England, aiming to place a new single on the charts and record a new LP. The band planned to have the single and album completed prior to the start of its U.K. tour on October 9 so that the album could be released in time for the Christmas trade.

The October 3 Melody Maker informed readers that the Beatles were recording a new single during night sessions at EMI Studios but details were secret. A spokesman for NEMS added that "the boys are also making a new LP." In an interview with Ray Coleman in the magazine's October 10 edition, Harrison talks about the current sessions. "We're just recording things as fast as John and Paul write them." He indicated that the group was dissatisfied with its first three albums. "We thought they were okay at the time, but on hearing them over and over we noticed where we could get things better here and there." Accordingly, the band wanted to "take it easy with the LP." They had completed about six tracks. The next week, John admitted to Melody Maker that the group was "looking for old songs we used to know and sing, because we're running out of good stuff to put on LPs. Material's becoming a hell of a problem."

The group discussed its most recent [Sunday, October 18] recording session with Andy Gray in the October 23 NME. Paul told Gray: "We put six tracks on tape. Not as fast as we used to, but we take more time now. Got to keep getting better...We've done 13 tracks of our next album." George added: "Two of the tracks recreate the sound we had when we were at the Cavern...We've only one track to go...Ringo's." When asked by Gray why his song was last, Ringo replied: "'Cause I haven't learnt it yet. But I'm thinking about it." James Craig reported on a recent recording session in the October 31 Record Mirror. Craig observes that the group doesn't show signs of "the regimental discipline of the lesser groups," adding that the Beatles "act on instinct, on improvisation." John and Paul work on the vocals, while George is "coaxing out intricate solo phrases" on guitar. Ringo sits away from the others, drumming "sharp beat-patterns...using his hands on his knees." When recording, the boys are perfectionists, ironing out minor details and leaping up to the control room for play-backs. Their new song "moves with excitement and verve."

THE BEATLES STUDIO SECRETS!

EMI PIX BY JOHN DOVE STORY BY JAMES CRAIG

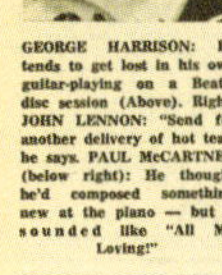

GEORGE HARRISON: He tends to get lost in his own guitar-playing on a Beatle disc session (Above). Right: JOHN LENNON: "Send for another delivery of hot tea," he says. PAUL McCARTNEY (below right): He thought he'd composed something new at the piano — but it sounded like "All My Loving!"

THE BEATLES trail into the recording studios of EMI in London's Abbey Road. Not together . . . to expect all the Beatles to turn up at the same time is to expect a miracle. Recording manager **George Martin**, tall and easy-to-meet, no longer believes in miracles.

Paul arrives in his own car. So **does George. John** and **Ringo** come by the group's limousine. They're late. But then George Martin often calls a session half-an-hour earlier than he wants because it means getting a prompter start.

Neil Aspinall and **Malcolm Evans**, the road managers, line up the equipment. A fast job of work—both are experts after months of world travel. The Beatles huddle together and chat over an arrangement. Voices are raised. The atmosphere, one feels, is starting to warm up.

John and Paul work out their vocal touches by one microphone. George sits, clutching his guitar, coaxing out intricate solo phrases. Ringo sits quietly, away from the others. He drums, sharp beat-patterns, but quietly . . . using his hands on his knees.

INSTINCT

It looks as if nothing is organised. But that's the way the Beatles prefer to work. The regimental discipline of many of the lesser groups doesn't appeal. The Beatles act on instinct, on improvisation.

Up in the control-room, George Martin watches patiently. He sees Paul McCartney refer to a tatty scrap of paper, apparently mouthing some words. Not to worry. Paul often puts the finishing touches to a new set of lyrics on an envelope or empty cigarette packet. Spur-of-the-moment stuff, again. Yet those words, so carelessly jotted down, will be worth many thousands of pounds.

John announces that the boys have made a decision. George Martin and the engineer perk up. "We need some tea," says John. Malcolm Evans, quietly reading in a corner of the studio, is leaping out towards the "char-machine" in the corridor. "You get to be a

★★★★★★★★★★★★

mind-reader in this business," he says.

Everything stops for tea with the Beatles. Yet hardly anything had happened yet! After the best part of half-an-hour. Suddenly a Beatle shouts: "OK George, let's try one." Tapes spin and the Beatles launch into a very energetic version of a new McCartney-Lennon number.

MIMING

Thumbs-up signs from the control-room, but the boys are perfectionists. They've noticed something not quite *right*. They get together, ironing out a minor section of phrasing. For no apparent reason, John indulges in some riotous miming gestures. An all-in-wrestler? Maracca-shaker? Difficult to tell, but everybody smiles broadly.

Another take. Then another. The boys leap up to the control-room for the play-backs. George grimaces at a middle-eight play-back but the others mumble that "It's great, just right, George." George Martin looks pleased. So do the handful of visitors . . . people like **Jane Asher**, or **Peter and Gordon**, or **Brian Epstein** often drop in.

John asks if they can do just one more "take." They've had an idea to change, and improve, one small bit of the introduction. Back to the studio floor, Ringo reaching his drum kit by a series of Groucho Marx-like steps, head bent well forward.

Lighthearted banter from all sides. George Martin restores order with a polite: "Let's REALLY get one this time, boys." Suddenly, in a split-second, the Beatle-ragging is turned off . . . and the serious business of getting a final tape of a new single is undertaken. The song (title has to be kept secret as yet) really moves with excitement and verve. Somehow it is easier, in the studio, to pick out MORE of the boys' individual instrumental contributions. But then there is no screaming, no yelling. Just a Beatle Sound.

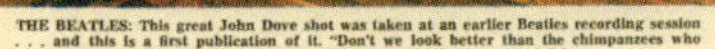

THE BEATLES: This great John Dove shot was taken at an earlier Beatles recording session . . . and this is a first publication of it. "Don't we look better than the chimpanzees who drink this sort of char on telly-commercials?" enquired John.

RINGO STARR: Beatle song-publisher Dick James once had a hit with "Robin Hood." "I defy you to wear a feather in THAT hat," roared Ringo.

The above interior two-page spread from the October 31, 1964 Record Mirror features James Craig's report on "The Beatles Studio Secrets!" describing a session for the *Beatles For Sale* LP attended by music publisher Dick James (shown upper right with Ringo). The session he attended was most likely the one held on September 30, 1964. The pictures were taken for EMI by John Dove. The photos of George on his Rickenbacker 12-string electric guitar (upper left), John framed by a pair of legs (second from left) and Paul on piano (below the other photos) appear on the back cover of Capitol's *Beatles VI* album either cropped or expanded (see page 212). The caption pertaining to Paul states: "He thought he'd composed something new on the piano–but it sounded like 'All My Loving!'"

The November 13 NME reported advance sales of 550,000 units for *Beatles For Sale*, due out on December 4. Derek Johnson provided a track-by-track review, telling readers the Liverpool quartet's latest package was "rip-roaring, infectious stuff, with the accent on beat throughout" and "worth every penny asked." It featured eight new Lennon-McCartney tunes and six cover songs that "reflect the early years of the group" as "numbers that raised screams at the Cavern in Liverpool." The album is "overflowing with absorbing and distinctive Beatles trade-marks."

"No Reply" is a melodic number "with tremendous thumping chords and falsettos" that, "after alternate soft passages...explodes into violent frenzy." It would have been a great single. "I'm A Loser" has a "wistful and bluesy feel despite the pounding and infectious beat" along with a wailing harmonica solo. "Baby's In Black" is unusual and moody, with "startling and unexpected chords" and sombre lyrics. Chuck Berry's "Rock And Roll Music" is "bubbling with excitement" and has John, Paul and George Martin on piano. [Johnson misidentifies Paul as the lead vocalist on this track sung by John.] "I'll Follow The Sun" features "positively captivating harmonies" with "John and Paul at their most tuneful" blending sentimental lyrics with a "hummable melody...set to a steady and infectious rhythm" featuring Ringo playing the top of a packing case. "Mr. Moonlight" really stands out with its "earthy sound," organ and John's "blues-shouting" vocal with "forceful and raucous ensemble vocalising off-setting his solo."

"Kansas City" is a "completely uninhibited performance, with screaming and falsettos" and "ample scope for joining in with the Beatles in the 'hey-hey-hey-hey' answering-back routine." "Eight Days A Week" is a "bouncy hand-clapper" that "drives along at a compulsive pace, aided by frantic cymbal-bashing from Ringo." John and Paul inject a "happy-go-lucky feel into the vocal." Buddy Holly's "Words Of Love" is a "mid-tempo harmony with a snappy beat" with "attractive guitar figure" from George, and Ringo on conga drum. Carl Perkins' "Honey Don't," previously sung by John, has Ringo on vocal over a "walking-pace rhythm." "Every Little Thing" has a "rumbling, strident backing, with reverberating drum rolls" and a catchy melody sung predominately by John joined by "harmony falsettos" from Paul. "I Don't Want To Spoil The Party," one of Johnson's favorite tracks, is a "story-in-song" whose "plaintive lyric belies the driving, bounding beat." "What You're Doing" boasts a "shattering all-enveloping sound, with Paul's voice shining through the walloping, thumping beat." Carl Perkins' "Everybody's Trying To Be My Baby" spotlights George on vocal.

BEATLES next album

JUST three weeks from today, the new Beatles album will be available in your local record store—in fact, it will be a case of " Beatles For Sale " on December 4. And, believe me, the latest package from the Liverpool quartet is worth every penny asked. It's rip-roaring, infectious stuff, with the accent on beat throughout.

By DEREK JOHNSON

There are 14 tracks, including eight new Lennon-McCartney compositions. Numbers by Chuck Berry, Carl Perkins, Buddy Holly and the Lieber-Stoller team complete the composing credits.

These non-Beatles tracks are included for a purpose: they reflect the early years of the group because they were mostly numbers that raised screams at the Cavern in Liverpool. Nowadays, the Beatles don't get much chance to play them. The LP is overflowing with absorbing and distinctive Beatle trade-marks.

I've just been given a pre-hear of the album. Here's a brief run-down on the titles. **Indicates a Lennon-McCartney composition.

NO REPLY** is a melodic mid-tempo item, with tremendous thumping chords and falsettos. It's mainly a duet, but with John's voice prominent. After alternate soft passages, it suddenly explodes into violent frenzy. Can't help thinking this would've have made a great single !

I'M A LOSER** very nearly was a single—I know it was considered for their next release. Featuring John soloing, with the others joining in the harmony passages, it has a wistful and bluesy feel despite the pounding and infectious beat. Wailing harmonica solo, too.

BABY'S IN BLACK** is a most unusual number with a shuffle rhythm. Moody with startling and unexpected chords, the lyric is as sombre as the title implies. Baby's in black, it seems, because "he's gone and won't come back." Rather different from what we expect of the boys.

ROCK AND ROLL MUSIC, the standard down-to-earth Chuck Berry rocker, showcases Paul in his more frenzied mood. This one really moves—it's bubbling with excitement. The piano work is by John, Paul and George Martin.

I'LL FOLLOW THE SUN** is rather more subdued, and features some positively captivating harmonies. This is John and Paul at their most tuneful. The sentiment of the lyric is blended with a hummable melody, and set to a steady and infectious rhythm. The rhythm sounds unusual here—it's Ringo playing the top of a packing case !

MR. MOONLIGHT is perhaps the most ear-catching track on the LP. It has a predominantly earthy sound, with John blues-shouting in passages, with forceful and raucous ensemble vocalising off-setting his solo. Organ, which takes a solo half-way through, adds to the fullness—and there are some strident bass tones. Yes, this really stands out.

KANSAS CITY, the Lieber-Stoller evergreen, needs no introduction from me. This is a completely uninhibited performance, with screams and falsettos—the lot ! And there's ample scope for joining in with the Beatles in the "hey-hey-hey-hey" answering-back routine.

EIGHT DAYS A WEEK**, a bouncy hand-clapper, drives along at a compulsive pace, aided by frantic cymbal-bashing from Ringo, which he maintains throughout. This is a typical happy John-and-Paul song, with both boys injecting a happy-go-lucky feel into the vocal.

WORDS OF LOVE, a mid-tempo harmony vocal with a snappy beat going in the background, is the familiar Buddy Holly composition. I found it particularly outstanding for George's attractive guitar figure behind the vocal. Ringo is on conga drum this time—he's worked very hard on the LP.

Songs . . . PAUL and JOHN

Rhythm . . . RINGO and GEORGE

HONEY DON'T was written by Carl Perkins, with Ringo handling the repetitive and compulsive lyric, set to a strumming, walking-pace rhythm with electronic plucking. The girls will love Ringo's spoken instructions to George—"Walk on, George . . . for Ringo ! " John used to sing this.

EVERY LITTLE THING** has a rumbling, strident backing, with reverberating drum rolls—altogether a fascinating sound, plus a catchy melody. John is prominent in the vocal, with harmony falsettos from Paul.

I DON'T WANT TO SPOIL THE PARTY** is one of my favourite tracks. The plaintive lyric belies the driving, bounding beat. It's virtually a story-in-song, performed with absorbing counter-harmonies. Here again the melody content is strong, and George is in top form.

WHAT YOU'RE DOING** boasts a shattering all-enveloping sound, with Paul's voice shining through the walloping, thumping beat. The tune is not so infectious here, but it's the rhythm and overall sound which matter.

EVERYBODY'S TRYING TO BE MY BABY is the Carl Perkins number which you may have heard the boys work on stage. A medium-fast shaker spotlighting George as vocalist, as well as in solo guitar passage, it has an insistent rhythm.

Readers of the November 14 Disc learned even more about *Beatles For Sale* in a Nigel Hunter article titled "Paul Reveals the Secrets of The Beatles LP." Hunter wrote that the LP would be the "best value for money yet from the Beatles." The 14-song album had eight new compositions by John and Paul and came in a specially-designed sleeve. Paul added: "We got 14 tracks into the record, which is about as much as you can fit in. We're pleased about this because we don't like to give short measure, and we felt a bit bad about the 'Hard Day's Night' album having only 13 numbers." When asked if he and the others had a particular favorite among the new tracks, Paul said: "We like them all. If there was something we weren't keen on after we'd recorded it, we would scrap it or do something else." [Paul failed to disclose that the band had rejected a cover of Little Willie John's "Leave My Kitten Alone" (see page 237).] The six songs that weren't written by John and Paul were numbers that "the boys used to play and enjoy during their early Cavern days in Liverpool." McCartney indicated that there were "some interesting sounds in the LP" and provided comments on each of the songs in their running order.

John sang lead on "No Reply," with Paul adding vocal harmony. "We tried to give it different moods, starting off quietly with a sort of vaguely bossa nova tempo, building up to a straight beat crescendo in the middle, and then tailing off quietly again." "I'm A Loser" was a "folk song gone pop" sung mostly by John, who adds some nice harmonica. Paul felt the need to explain "Baby's In Black." "The story is about a girl who's wearing black because the bloke she loves has gone away forever. The feller singing the song fancies her, too, but he's getting nowhere. We wrote it originally in a waltz style, but it finished as a mixture of waltz and beat." For Chuck Berry's "Rock And Roll Music," the group "tried for that old-type clipped down-in-the-valley echo" sound. "There's some piano going on, too. George Martin, John and I on the keyboard all at once!" He and John wrote "I'll Follow The Sun" a while ago, but changed the middle eight before recording it. "John and I sing it, and Ringo played the top of a packing case instead of his drums this time. Just for a change, you know!" "Mr. Moonlight" was the B-side to "Dr. Feelgood" [by Dr. Feelgood and the Interns], and, like "Rock And Roll Music," another number the group played at the Cavern. "I play a bit of organ softly in the background, and John and I do the singing. Ringo got hold of a horn-shaped sort of conga drum for this with good effect." "Kansas City" was another old one from the Cavern Club that the group had been asked to record. "I do most of the singing this time and some piano playing, and John and George join in on the vocal bit."

Paul revealed how "Eight Days A Week" came about. "I got the title for this once when I was being driven over to visit John. The chauffeur was talking away to me, saying how hard his boss worked the staff–so hard they seemed to do eight days a week. We've altered the plot a bit for the song, of course. The bloke loves the girl for eight days a week." He and John sing the song. "Words Of Love" is a Buddy Holly song from the Cavern days. "There was a fabulous guitar bit on the Holly disc, sounding almost like bells. George took the same riff and double-tracked it, and sounds just as good." "Honey Don't" is "Ringo's solo piece, a simple and sweet piece which he handles as well vocally as he does his drum kit." Another Cavern number, only John sang it back then. "Every Little Thing" was written in Atlantic City during the group's U.S. tour. John plays the guitar riff, while George is on acoustic guitar. "Ringo bashes some timpani drums for the big noise you'll hear." John and Paul went after a "real Country and Western flavour" when they wrote "I Don't Want To Spoil The Party." They sing it in that style, and George "takes a real country solo on guitar." "What You're Doing" was also written in Atlantic City. "Ringo does a nice bit of drumming decoration in the introduction, and I double-track on the vocal as well as playing some piano." "Everybody's Trying To Be My Baby" is a Carl Perkins tune. "We've got that clipped tape echo effect....It's a swinging end to the album, and George has a good solo again."

Nigel Hunter gave readers his thoughts on the album. "Their best yet...There's an enormous amount of variety and contrast in all respects, and the boys don't limit their tempos to the medium kind like they did for most of 'A Hard Day's Night.'" Hunter listed the highspots as: "the mixture of bossa and beat for 'No Reply;' John's wailing harmonica in 'I'm A Loser;' the knockout harmonies of the waltzy beater 'Baby's In Black;' the vocal riot in 'Kansas City;' Ringo's solo vocal in 'Honey Don't;' and the country and western spirit of the Party."

Chris Welch reviewed *Beatles For Sale* in the November 14 Melody Maker, predicting the LP would "sell, sell, sell." The album was up to the group's standard and would "knock out pop fans, rock fans, R&B and Beatle fans." It was real value for money, with 14 tracks, including some excellent new Lennon-McCartney originals and "belting rockers by Carl Perkins and Chuck Berry." Welch's favorites were "I Don't Want To Spoil The Party," "Honey Don't" and "Rock And Roll Music." All numbers were winners, with the "possible exception" of "Mr. Moonlight," with "Mexican overtones and an occasional un-tuned tom tom beat." The album opener, "No Reply," has a "typical so-sad unison vocal and could be a hit single." "I'm A Loser" is a swinging tune with harmonica, followed by the slow rocker "Baby's In Black." John powerfully sings "Rock And Roll Music," while "I'll Follow The Sun" is a "pleasant ballad but not exceptional." Side One closes with "Mr. Moonlight" and Paul in his "best blues shouting form" on "Kansas City." The second side opens with "Eight Days A Week," a "hand-clapping stomper" and the Buddy Holly song "Words Of Love." Ringo sings lead on "Honey Don't," with "great guitar boogie going on." This is followed by "Every Little Thing" and "I Don't Want To Spoil The Party," which has "a great country and western beat with amusing, wry lyrics, a good solo by George, and solid, swinging drums by Ringo." "What You're Doing" has introductory drums. The album closes with "Everybody's Trying To Be My Baby," which Welch views as "more hit single material." Although double-tracking is used on the album, there are no gimmicks. He concludes: "The music is honest and again displays the Beatles' success formula–talent."

Record Mirror's Barry May, among the first to hear the new LP on Monday, November 9, gave his report in the magazine's November 14 issue in an article titled "Holly song on Beatles album." He described the album's gate-fold sleeve as "open out book-form, with colour pictures on the front and back, and black and white shots inside." The front cover was "an arty shot of John, Paul, George, and Ringo, in Hyde Park."

For the most part, May does little more than provide the very basics of the album's selections in their running order. 'No Reply" features "John on lead vocal, joined later by Paul, with George's earthy 12 string guitar very much to the forefront." "I'm A Loser" has John on lead vocal and a "wild bluesy mouth-harp in between." Lennon and McCartney's "Baby In Black" has a "Country and Western feel about it," while Chuck Berry's "Rock And Roll Music" gets into a "fantastic rock beat with hard rock piano played by John, Paul and recording manager George Martin." The second side opens "with a fade-in guitar intro on 'Eight Day's A Week.'" After noting that the "weird and wonderful sounds of the guitar are further exploited for Buddy Holly's 'Words Of Love,'" May quickly sums up the remaining songs.

Peter Jones reviewed the album the next week in the November 21 Record Mirror. After stating that the remarkable foursome has provided "all the value-for-money anybody could expect," Jones again "marvels at the virtuosity and versatility of the boys," citing the abundance of George's 12-string guitar, Paul playing organ on one track, and the trio of John, Paul and George Martin joining on piano for the Chuck Berry rocker "Rock And Roll Music." Jones praises the singing of all four, observing that "if John is the actual 'voice' of the Beatles, then Paul's vocal touches improve all the way." Ringo "ain't half bad" on "Honey Don't," while George is "in great form" on Carl Perkins' "Everybody's Trying To Be My Baby." "Fiery vocal work, adamantly furious instrumental material, positive personality stamped on every track" lead Jones to conclude that *Beatles For Sale* is "an album which will probably go down in pop posterity."

Beatles For Sale entered the 20-position Britain's Top LPs chart compiled Record Retailer (and also published in Record Mirror) at number four on December 10, 1964. The following week it replaced *A Hard Day's Night* at number one, where it remained for seven straight weeks before being bumped to number two by *Rolling Stones Number Two*. The Beatles LP charted for 46 weeks, including 11 at number one, 12 in the second spot and 31 in the top five. The album entered Melody Maker's Top Ten LPs chart on December 12 at number one, remaining there for nine straight weeks. It charted for 37 weeks, including 15 at number one, 10 at number two and 29 in the top five. The disc entered NME's 10-position Best Selling LPs in Britain chart on December 11 at number one, remaining there for six straight weeks. It charted for 31 weeks, including 9 at number one, 11 at number two and 26 in the top five. The LP charted for five weeks on the singles charts of NME (peak at 22) and Disc (peak at 19). Orders exceeded 750,000 by the end of 1964.

As was the case with *A Hard Day's Night,* EMI waited four months to pull an EP from its next Beatles album, *Beatles For Sale*. The EP was issued on April 6, 1965, and entered the Record Retailer EP chart on April 8 at number 13. Three weeks later, the disc hit number one for the first of five straight weeks at the top. After dropping to number two for two weeks, the EP returned to the top for one more week on June 10. After 26 straight weeks, *Beatles For Sale* dropped from the chart on October 7, only to return three weeks later for 21 more weeks. The EP spent a total of 47 weeks on the charts, including six weeks at number one, four at number two, 12 in the top five and 19 in the top ten.

The front of the EP jacket features the same photograph found on the cover to the *Beatles For Sale* LP. Tony Barrow's back liner notes state that the album was issued in December 1964, and that, in the weeks before Christmas, it became one of the world's fastest selling albums. Barrow indicates that the EP's three Lennon-McCartney compositions were each recorded with a new single in mind, and that any one of them might have become a multi-million seller as an A-side. While such talk about "No Reply" and "I'm A Loser" was pure albeit safe speculation, by the time the EP was issued, "Eight Days A Week" had been released as a single in America on February 15, 1965, and had topped the charts for two weeks and sold over a million copies. Barrow states that Chuck Berry's "Rock And Roll Music" has been a show-stopper ever since the group put it into their act on the opening night of their Christmas stage show. The remainder of the notes describe each of the four tracks. "Rock And Roll Music" is a "Lennon vocal rave" with George Martin joining John and Paul on piano. "Eight Days A Week" is noteworthy for its fade-in opening "which must have confused some of the folk who put on records for radio deejays!" "No Reply" "wastes no time in coming to a boil" and is "tailored to bring out the leathery quality of [John's] vocal delivery." "I'm A Loser" is "the one everybody has been talking about" as it "demonstrates the powerful influence which Bob Dylan's style has had on John." The May 3 Record Mirror's review of the *Beatles For Sale* EP described its contents as "the cream of the album."

Two months after releasing its *Beatles For Sale* EP, EMI issued a second EP from the album, *Beatles For Sale (No. 2)*, on June 4. As the LP had been out for half a year and was already in numerous collections, the EP had little appeal, selling in diminished numbers reminiscent of the second *A Hard Day's Night* EP. The disc has Buddy Holly's "Words Of Love" and three Lennon-McCartney songs, "I'll Follow The Sun," "Baby's In Black" and "I Don't Want To Spoil The Party."

Beatles For Sale (No. 2) entered the Record Retailer EP chart on June 10 at number 12. Four weeks later, the disc reached its peak spot of number five on July 8. After 19 straight weeks, the EP dropped from the chart on October 21, 1965, which was the first week since July 18, 1963, that the Beatles did not have at least one title on the EP chart. The disc returned to the charts on December 2 for five of the next six weeks before disappearing in early 1966. The EP spent a total of 24 weeks on the charts, including four weeks at number five and 16 in the top ten. Like its predecessor, the EP did not appear on any of the singles charts. With LP sales gaining momentum, the EP (extended play) format of two tracks (normally pulled from an album) on each side of a 45 RPM disc was heading towards irrelevancy.

The front jacket features a color portrait of the group taken by Robert Freeman. The back lists the song selections and the previous eight Beatles EPs under the heading "More enjoyable EP recordings by THE BEATLES." This marked the first time that a Beatles EP or album was issued without liner notes, a trend that would continue until the 1969 release of the album *Yellow Submarine*. The Beatles would now let the music speak for itself.

The March 20 music weeklies reported on the Beatles first single for 1965. The record, set for April 9 release, featured two Lennon-McCartney compositions. John and Paul sang "Ticket To Ride," with John taking the lead. The B-side, "Yes It Is," had a three-part harmony with John again singing lead. Disc and Record Mirror added that both songs would be featured in the Beatles upcoming film [only "Ticket To Ride" was used], while NME (cover dated March 19) wrote that "Ticket To Ride" introduced Paul instead of George on lead guitar. Disc further reported that EMI anticipated initial advance orders of over 700,000 for the new single. This would prove to be an overly optimistic forecast.

Melody Maker provided the most extensive coverage, with Ray Coleman obtaining details directly from the Beatles, when he was with them in Austria as they were filming scenes for their new movie. The songs were recorded at EMI Studios "some weeks ago" [actually in mid-February] as part of the sessions for their second film. The final selection of the tracks was made the previous week by the group and manager Brian Epstein as they flew over the Alps to Austria. Paul spoke about the A-side. "'Ticket To Ride' is quite different from anything we have done. It is pretty slow and we are all very pleased with it because we feel we have some good vocal harmonies going on with John's lead voice. I suppose it has a bit of an Arabian rhythm going on." He added that when they heard the play back, "we all thought it sounded very weird" and was "so unusual for us." Coleman wrote that the song is "about a girl who has a ticket to ride away from her boyfriend." John agreed that it was a very far out title for a Beatles song, saying: "But you see, we are very far out people." As for "Yes It Is," Lennon said it was "the slowest B-side we've put out. But it has a beat." The group had difficulty deciding which song to feature as the A-side.

Coleman gave his impressions of the new single the following week in the March 27 Melody Maker after hearing acetates of the songs played to him by the Beatles in their hotel room in Austria. "Ticket To Ride," which would be in the film (although Paul wasn't sure where at the time), is "slower and bluesier than any other Beatles A-side." It is reminiscent of "You Can't Do That," with "John's raw and real voice cutting through marvellously." Paul provides great vocal harmonies. As the song nears its end and seems to be flagging, it "roars to life with their voices going almost falsetto and the beat doubling up." The song is a "tremendously exciting Beatles performance." "Yes It Is" is a slow ballad in the style of "This Boy." Coleman praised the song: "After two plays, you are hooked by its charm and memorable tune." He indicated that John's wife Cynthia told him that "Yes It Is" was "her favourite Beatles track so far." George preferred the song over "Ticket To Ride" and thought "Yes It Is" should have been the A-side. Paul admitted he probably preferred it, too, but astutely pointed out: "You mustn't confuse what you prefer with what's the best A-side. They're two totally different things."

The front cover to the April 3 Melody Maker featured a teaser box titled "Beatles New Single." The group would star with "Ticket To Ride" on multiple television shows: Lucky Stars on Saturday, April 3; The Eamonn Andrews' Show on April 11; and Top Of The Pops on April 15. John provided comments on the song. "It's the slowest A-side we've done, I think. It's not that unusual though — I mean, it's still US. It's no more unusual than we are — does that make it unusual? We're quite pleased with the record." And so were most of the reviewers and fans.

Ray Coleman continued his praise of "Ticket To Ride" in the inside pages of the April 3 Melody Maker, calling it among the group's very best. The song has a medium tempo, with John's voice "asserting the story-line with real power" and Paul adding "some really inspired breaks" on lead guitar. The track "kicks off instrumentally before the vocals come and the unified singing makes it." At the end, the beat doubles up behind the pretty falsetto singing of "My baby don't care" during the fade. As for the lyrics: "The story, about a girl with a ticket to ride away from her man, is typically Beatles, and the words have a curious sort of logic." Coleman described "Yes It Is" as a "beautiful, slow ballad in the 'This Boy' vein but with more soul."

That same week, Derek Johnson lauded the group and its new single in the April 2 NME, observing: "The depth of sound which the Beatles create is quite fantastic, and is again in evidence with 'Ticket To Ride.'" Johnson compared the tempo to "I Feel Fine," adding that the sound "bounds along at a jaunty pace and with tremendous drive, with tambourine for added effect." John sang lead, "aided by Paul's colourful harmonies and occasional falsettos in some passages." Johnson described the song as "catchy," advising "you soon pick up on the tune" and proclaiming "they've done it again!" The flip side "Yes It Is" was a slow, melodic "rockaballad" with a "plaintive quality" featuring John's lead and harmony vocals by Paul and George.

Record Mirror indicated that "Long-awaited" and "Heavily (ridiculously heavily) ordered in advance" new Beatles single arrived just before the magazine went to press. It came "in an ordinary plain wrapper...though it might as well have had hit, hit, HIT written all over it!" The top side, "Ticket To Ride," was a "mid-tempo beater, with a distinct bluesy, almost R and B feel." John and Paul sing, with John's "distinctive and rough-edged voice" on lead. The song opens with an interesting George Harrison guitar phrase followed by "Ringo's drum powerhouse." The magazine indicated that the story is "about a girl who 'just couldn't feel free if I was around' ... so she's got a ticket to ride." [The actual words are "For she would never be free when I was around."] The backing is very effective, with vocal climaxes cleverly "linked" by guitar passages in a "tumbling cascade of notes." Ringo lays down the beat "with precision" and a "feeling of relaxed inspiration." At the end, there are "touches of falsetto work from the voices, repetitiously working over the title again" for a "delicately-contrived fade-out finish." [Actually, John and Paul sing "My baby don't care."] The magazine disagrees with George's preference for "Yes It Is," but adds: "Let's just settle for saying that it's a very good value-for-money coupling." With no time to check, the writer was uncertain of the instrument that opens the song, speculating it might be harmonica or organ. [It is a pedal-tone guitar passage played by George.] The song has a "much quieter, more subdued, treatment" with a "tiny touch of folk approach in the opening stages, but unmistakably Beatles." The voices provide a "fine, close, well-knit sound on the main passages–but with violently bluesy link-pieces." As with the A-side, "John's slightly gravelly tones dominate." The song is a "slow, deliberate, almost tortuous, number...of extra-high quality." While it may not be as commercial as "Ticket To Ride," it is "another positive statement of the boys' versatility." Record Mirror concludes: "A number one hit quite definitely. And quite definitely proof that there's no waning in the Beatle recording field. Freshness is there; originality, too."

By the time Disc reviewed the new Beatles single in its April 3 issue, its name had been expanded to Disc Weekly (as of December 5, 1964) and Don Nicholl had been replaced by Penny Valentine and her "Penny picks the new singles" weekly reviews. Penny admitted that it was a foregone conclusion that "Ticket To Ride" would be a Number One. She then proceeded with her opinions. "The song had a splendid title and a country flavour. Paul is on bass guitar and they say she doesn't care that she's going away. It has the same close sound that 'A Hard Day's Night' had, and at the end of the lines they make a very hard noise. I don't like the middle break much, and if you listen hard you'll hear the guitar riff from 'When You Walk In The Room.' An interesting record. A great performance, of course, but it needs listening to." She was much harsher on the B-side. "May I slam the flip side, "Yes It Is"? This is very naughty and dull, and they should be ashamed of themselves writing such diabolical words like 'blue,' 'you,' 'true' nonsense. Only interesting thing is George's playing." [Many Beatles fans probably thought Penny was trying to make a name for herself in her new coulmn and should be ashamed of herself for writing such nonsense.]

Record Retailer was not all that enthusiastic about the disc in its April 8 issue, stating it was neither one of their best nor one of their worst. The magazine said the song's droning guitar had a "hypnotic effect that will stay in the mind." "Yes It Is" was described as "dirge-like" and "perhaps a little drawn out." Peter Aldersly reviewed "Ticket To Ride" in the April 10 Pop Weekly, calling it "another typical Beatles performance–lots of gusto, drive and contrast" with the "unmistakable Lennon/McCartney stamp from the first chord." It was "a song which will grow on you." The April Beat Instrumental noted "Ticket To Ride" was over three minutes long, but "there's not a boring second on it." The flip side "Yes It Is" demonstrated why the Beatles and Brian had such a difficult job in selecting the A-side from the two songs.

In an interview with Ray Coleman in the March 27 Melody Maker, Paul was asked what was becoming a recurring question with each new release: "What will be your reaction if the next Beatles single, 'Ticket To Ride,' does not go straight to number one in the hit parade?" Paul said it would be "a terrible drag," sarcastically adding "then I'll really pay attention to the knockers who say the Beatles are slipping!" He admitted: "Truthfully, I'd feel very disappointed." When asked if he expected the single to reach the top immediately, Paul responded: "It's not a question of expecting, but hoping...Once you start expecting success you get blase. We'll never get to the stage of releasing rubbish because we know people will buy it. Disaster." Paul explained the group's concern. "We've always been terrified with each new release and we're the same now. We like it, but people might hate it–and that's their right. This business of singles has always been a real worry for us, and I mean this, because every time we've tried for something different, and we have done [so] this time. Not that we've got the Black Dyke Mills Band backing us! The worst attitude everybody in the chart can have is: 'The last one did okay so this one will.' All I say is: let us pray." He also admitted his frustration with the Beatle "knockers" who constantly criticize the group. "Let's face it: our knockers aren't interested in helping us or giving us advice. They're simply malicious."

Although Paul's mention of the Black Dyke Mills Band must have seemed strange at the time, he would soon show his fondness for brass bands. One year later, in 1966, the Beatles added brass instruments to Paul's "Got To Get You Into My Life." In 1967, the Beatles featured brass on several of their recordings and took on the identity of a fictional brass band, Sgt. Pepper's Lonely Hearts Club Band. And in 1968, Paul produced a Black Dyke Mills Band single for Apple Records featuring the famous brass band performing "Yellow Submarine" and one of Paul's instrumental compositions, "Thingumybob."

The teaser box for the Beatles new single on the cover to the April 3 Melody Maker questioned whether the disc would go straight to the top of the charts. John responded: "It's not at all certain that it'll be another immediate number one. We're not taking it for granted, by any means. Ask me the day before it goes into the shops when I know the final advance order figure...But let's emphasise this business of the number one thing. It's not BOUND to make it first go."

Fortunately for the Beatles, their concerns were unwarranted. Although the single entered the Britain's Top 50 chart published by the music industry trade magazine Record Retailer on March 15 at number 11, "Ticket To Ride" debuted at number one in the charts published by Melody Maker, NME and Disc. As for Record Retailer, whose charts received wider distribution in Record Mirror, the single quickly shot up the listing the following week, replacing Cliff Richard's "The Minute You're Gone" at the top. It remained there for three weeks before Roger Miller's "King Of The Road" crowned the chart at number one. The Beatles disc charted for 12 weeks, including seven in the top ten.

"Ticket To Ride" entered the Melody Maker Pop 50 chart on April 17 at number one, where it remained for five weeks. The record charted for 12 weeks, including seven in the top ten. The single debuted in the NME Top Thirty on April 16 at number one, remaining there for five weeks. It charted for nine weeks, including seven in the top ten. "Ticket To Ride" entered the Disc Top Thirty on April 17 at number one, also remaining at the top for five weeks. It charted for ten weeks, including eight in the top ten. The single also topped the BBC chart. "Ticket To Ride" had advance orders of 300,000 units and went on to sell over 500,000 copies. It received a Silver Disc award from Disc on May 1, 1965.

The April 17 Melody Maker ran the headline "Beatles Crush Knockers" after the group "roared back to number one" with "Ticket To Ride," ending a month of speculation on whether the Beatles could once again hit the top in the first week of release. The magazine reported that the Beatles "were completely knocked out." George admitted the group was "always worried with each record" and that with this one they "were even more worried." He added it was "great while it lasts, but now we'll have to start all over again and people will start predicting funny things for the next one." Ringo said he didn't expect it, adding: "Of course it makes it even more difficult for the next single. The knockers can't have a go at us just yet but I suppose their day is bound to come eventually. It's got to stop somewhere hasn't it?"

Readers of May 1 Melody Maker were able to read about that next single nearly three months before its release in a front page column titled "Ray Coleman Hears the Beatles Next No.1 Single." Coleman wrote that the group's next single "Help!" was "the sort of song John Lennon and Paul McCartney have been aiming to write for a long time" and was "the nearest they have come to doing a straight rock number." He added that "McCartney has been keen on doing a Little Richard style rocker since the Beatles started." [Although "Help!" was not really in the style of the American singer/pianist, the single's B-side "I'm Down," which would be recorded two months after "Help!" on June 14, was pure Little Richard.] Coleman described "Help!" as a "raving, pounding song featuring Lennon on lead vocal with Paul coming in on an attractive counter melody, and George Harrison singing what he describes as [Searchers lead singer] Chris Curtis falsetto parts." Coleman praised George's guitar work, calling it "dazzling." The song is the title track of the Beatles film nearing completion, which had previously been titled *Eight Arms To Hold You* before being changed to *Help!*. Harrison said he was knocked out by the record, adding: "It's probably the best single we've done." It would be released about two weeks ahead of the film's premiere in early August. Coleman indicated that the song was "a plea for help by someone who is down" with the line "Help me get my feet back on the ground" repeated several times. His verdict: "It is a great record with the Beatles in instrumental and vocal top form–and better than 'Ticket To Ride.' 'Help!' is a new Beatles sound–but still unmistakably them."

Paul told Norman Jopling in the May 15 Record Mirror that he didn't like "Ticket To Ride" that much. He liked "Help!," calling it different and the fastest record made by the group. He compared it to the middle eight in "It Won't Be Long."

Record Mirror

Largest selling colour pop weekly newspaper
No. 218 Week ending May 15, 1965
Every Thursday 6d. Registered at the G.P.O. as a newspaper

PAUL McCARTNEY — a shot taken at Twickenham during the last stages of filming "Help." By Feri Sukas.

HOW THE BEATLES SPEND AN EVENING

Norman Jopling talks to PAUL McCARTNEY

IT was a typical quiet evening at London's Savoy Hotel. Quiet that is until the Beatles turned up to see Bob Dylan. They all trooped down to the restaurant and ordered Porridge and Pea Sandwiches.

They got them. Then one of the boys spotted Owls Legs on the menu. They ordered them as a joke. It didn't take too long before the Owls Legs were actually served, piping hot, to the group.

"But we wouldn't have known if they hadn't been Owls Legs" said Paul.

An evening out for the Beatles is something of a rarity nowadays. The boys are leading almost entirely self-contained lives and the latest development of theirs to entertain themselves are film projectors.

"We've all bought 16m.m. film projectors with sound and everything," explained Paul. "And we hire loads of films—it's surprising but you can get some of the really latest top films. For instance I've got "Topkapi" and "Tom Jones". And we hire some of **Elvis's** films too . . . I like them in the same way that I like "Double Your Money."

JOHN'S HOUSE—LIKE A CINEMA

"The projectors cost a lot of money, about two hundred quid I think. But they're worthwhile to us at least, because we don't get a chance to get out and see these films. **John** is the really keen one. He has it all organised, showing two films a night now. It's just like a cinema round his place. We all sit there eyes glued to the screen. And he doesn't start showing them until late, well, after television has finished and none of us get to bed until fantastically late hours.

"We all sit bleary-eyed in front of the screen making signs with our hands on the screen—little animals and all that . . .

"So far we haven't got a copy of "Hard Day's Night". Not that it bothers me. I didn't like the film anyway. Seriously, I mean that. The original novelty of seeing yourself on screen wears off. You know, like home movies of yourself at the seaside. The good thing is that at least you can come out with anecdotes every ten seconds about what happened behind the scenes."

Paul talked about the Beatles next film "Help".

"I like this one better. It has been great filming it. But all the residents of the Bahamas hated us. Really. They're so rich there and they were so rude to us that we just didn't care. We all rented Triumph Spitfires and drove them around the island. They didn't like that either.

"But there are some good scenes from the film. There are shots of us in a disused quarry, using it as a race track. We found it when we were waiting for the technicians. We were screeching around it like mad. Well, they filmed it slyly and put it in the film. Just like that.

"There are no speeded up shots, like in "A Hard Day's Night", but there are some other visual gimmicks. Like standing on a rock in the middle of the ocean playing our instruments. And the next shot with us up to our necks in water, still playing. And one of **Ringo**, lying on his stomach on the beach swimming in the sand."

PAUL DIDN'T LIKE "TICKET"

Then Paul started to sing the Beatles next disc "Help" to us, taking the part of all the voices, and even the backing. He maintains it's much better than "Ticket To Ride".

"Can't say I liked 'Ticket' much," he stated. "But this new one is—in my opinion—good. I hope I don't sound big-headed. But I like it—it's certainly the fastest record we've made and it's very different. It's a bit like the middle eight in "It Won't Be Long" . . .

"I think that John and I are writing different sort of songs to what we were a couple of years back. I can't say whether they're better or worse but they're certainly different. And that is O.K. by us because we wouldn't want to stand still, to stagnate musically."

Somehow I can't imagine the Beatles ever doing that . . .

Readers of the weekly music magazines first read about the "Help!" single's July 23 release date in the June 5 Melody Maker. The June 11 NME and June 19 Disc added that the single's flip side would be a new song not in the film. The June 26 editions of Disc and Melody Maker revealed that the single's B-side was an up-tempo Lennon-McCartney song sung by Paul. Melody Maker also ran Mike Hennessey's report on the Beatles concerts in Paris. He was invited to the Beatles suite at the George V Hotel, where the group played him songs from the *Help!* sessions on a record player, including a "real screamer of a rock number called 'I'm Down.'" NME's Chris Hutchins filed his report of the Beatles Paris shows in the magazine's June 25 issue. He was also treated to a surprise listening session featuring some of the *Help!* tracks. Hutchins wrote that the "most riotous" song was "I'm Down," which would be the flip side of the "Help!" single. Paul sings the song, which also features John on organ. It is similar in style to [Little Richard's] "Long Tall Sally" and captures what writers John and Paul have been trying to achieve for a long time–a great rock 'n' roll composition."

Record Retailer reviewed the new single in its July 15 issue, describing "Help!" as "catchy, swinging" with "all the gimmicks that has made up their previous hits," and "I'm Down" as "an enormous rave-up." NME ran Derek Johnson's rave review of the record in its July 16 edition. Johnson wrote: "There's always the danger of running out of superlatives when one reviews a Beatles disc. Especially when it's like "Help!" (Parlophone), which is undoubtedly one of their best yet." The song bounds along at a medium-fast tempo "with a tingling rhythm backing." Johnson adds that he doesn't "know any drummer who uses the cymbals as liberally as Ringo!" The track also features "some resonant guitar chords...But as usual, it's the melody that hits you like a sledgehammer. Basically so simple, yet catchy and infectious, it registers on the very first spin." The lyric is "one of the most thoughtful that the boys have come up with." John sings lead, with Paul and George "supplying their familiar harmonies." Johnson assures readers that they will "love the inevitable falsetto trademark on the phrase 'Won't you please, please help me?'" As for "I'm Down," he writes: "I haven't yet recovered from the 'B' side–I'm still feeling limp and breathless after listening to such a fantastic wild rave-up." The song "showcases Paul's throaty shouting and screaming–it's a wonder he had any voice left after the session–plus some great Harrison guitar and the novelty of John on Hammond organ." [Johnson would have been even more impressed had he known that after singing lead on "I've Just Seen A Face" and "I'm Down" during the afternoon session of June 14, Paul came back that evening to record "Yesterday."]

George provided a detailed description of "Help!" for Ray Coleman in the July 17 Disc. "It's quite involved–a bit more involved than others we've done because it has a counter-melody going as well as the main melody. It features John singing the lead lines, with Paul and me doing counter-melody in between. There's a repeating line in each chorus." As was the case with "Ticket To Ride," "people will have to hear it a few times before they get the gist of it." Harrison said the group was really pleased with the song, adding "it's the best single we've had out for a long time." When asked by Coleman if it compared to any other Beatles track, George said it was a bit like "It Won't Be Long." George also talked about the flip side. "It's a rocker, and Paul takes the lead vocal. John is on Hammond organ. It's pretty wild... because it has Paul's wild voice." George supposed Paul did it with "his Little Richard-type voice" because "it's that sort of number." Coleman observed: "The Beatles have always been striving for more genuine rock." George added: "'Help!' is an A-side song...But John and I wanted to have 'I'm Down' as the A-side, if there wasn't a film to consider."

The next week Disc ran comments from other recording artists about the new disc. Mick Jagger thought it was great but preferred "Ticket To Ride." He advised the group "to do something different to shock everyone." Lulu also said the song was great, commenting that John's voice "sounds very earthy" and "gets better and better." Donovan liked the single, adding: "I dig the Beatles. A lot of people don't think they write from their experiences, but they do." Marianne Faithful said: "I loved this the first time I heard it at Paul's flat...Isn't that bass part lovely? I like this much better than the others." Disc also ran comments from teenagers. Richard Johnson (15): "I'm glad the Beatles have changed their sound." Patricia Johnson (16): "It's the best record they've ever made." Susan Rowe (14): "Tremendous beat to dance to and the lyrics are wonderful." Caroline Harris (14): "I love the Beatles and I think this is marvelous." Paul Willis (16): "Horrible. I'm fed up with their same old sound...this is dull." [Obviously a Beatle knocker!]

Keith Relf, lead singer for the Yardbirds, gave his opinion of "Help!" in the July 24 Melody Maker as part of the magazine's Blind Date feature in which the participants hear the latest singles without being told the artist in advance. Relf, recognizing it was the Beatles, said: "I think this is going to be a case like all the Beatles' songs, they grow on you. It's great actually. They always seem to find a new chord progression–I don't know how they do it...It doesn't strike you as immediately as the last one, but it's certainly very clever and certain to be a hit...It's very awe inspiring."

Norman Jopling and Peter Jones opened their review of the single in the July 24 Record Mirror by joking: "We've a feeling this might possibly be a massive hit." The theme song from the film is taken "at a lively pace, with John on lead vocal, supported by George and Paul" with "Falsetto pieces towards the end of the chorus and interesting bass phrases" along with "Solid cymbal work from Ringo behind it all." Later in the song, "there's a sort of hush over the proceedings before the boys build up vocally once more." The lyrics are "well-sustained." They found the record "needed a couple of spins before getting full impact" and adding "it'll get more than that from dee-jays." Their conclusion: "Must be massive Number One, of course." Jopling and Jones also praised "I'm Down," with its "Little Richard type opening," proclaiming: "Paul gets a lot of excitement going in good rock style, throatily easy. Marvellous guitar break from George. It's a raver all the way. Would be a Number One on its own."

"Help!" entered the Record Retailer chart at number five on July 29. The following week it replaced "Mr. Tambourine Man" by the Byrds at number one, where it remained for three weeks before giving way to "I Got You Babe" by Sonny & Cher. "Help!" charted for 14 weeks, including seven in the top five.

Chris Welch speculated in the July 17 Melody Maker whether the Beatles could do it again–go straight to number one with their new single, "Help!" He advised readers not to underestimate the Beatles power because "as long as John and Paul keep writing good material there is little likelihood of a Beatles recession." George told Welch that the group was "waiting to see what happens," adding: "If it doesn't go straight to the top, the knockers can have another go." But, once again, the knockers would have to wait. Melody Maker, NME and Disc each reported the Beatles new single at number one for its first four weeks on their charts. Melody Maker debuted "Help!" on July 31, charting the disc for 13 weeks, including seven in the top five. NME first charted the disc on July 30, with the record charting for ten weeks, including seven in the top five. Disc debuted the single on July 31, also charting the record for ten weeks, including seven in the top five. The magazine awarded the Beatles another silver disc for "Help!" in its July 31 issue. By that date, the record had shipped over 800,000 units. By year's end, sales exceeded 900,000 copies. Melody Maker reported in its July 31 edition that the Beatles were "delighted and surprised" with the news that they had debuted at number one for the sixth time in a row. "Help!" was the group's ninth straight single to reach the top.

PARLOPHONE

45 R.P.M.

NORTHERN SONGS NCB

7XCE 18280

R 5305

SOLD IN U.K. SUBJECT TO RESALE PRICE CONDITIONS SEE PRICE LISTS.

℗ 1965

HELP!
(from film of same name)
(Lennon – McCartney)
THE BEATLES

MADE IN GT. BRITAIN

THE PARLOPHONE CO. LTD. · ALL RIGHTS OF THE MANUFACTURER AND OF THE OWNER OF THE RECORDED WORK RESERVED · UNAUTHORISED PUBLIC PERFORMANCE BROADCASTING AND COPYING OF THIS RECORD PROHIBITED

PARLOPHONE

45 R.P.M.

NORTHERN SONGS NCB

7XCE 18281

R 5305

SOLD IN U.K. SUBJECT TO RESALE PRICE CONDITIONS SEE PRICE LISTS.

℗ 1965

I'M DOWN
(Lennon – McCartney)
THE BEATLES

MADE IN GT. BRITAIN

THE PARLOPHONE CO. LTD. · ALL RIGHTS OF THE MANUFACTURER AND OF THE OWNER OF THE RECORDED WORK RESERVED · UNAUTHORISED PUBLIC PERFORMANCE BROADCASTING AND COPYING OF THIS RECORD PROHIBITED

Melody Maker

July 31, 1965 9d weekly

pop or folk?

DONOVAN

on Newport

COLTRANE

at Antibes

ALEX WELSH

star backer

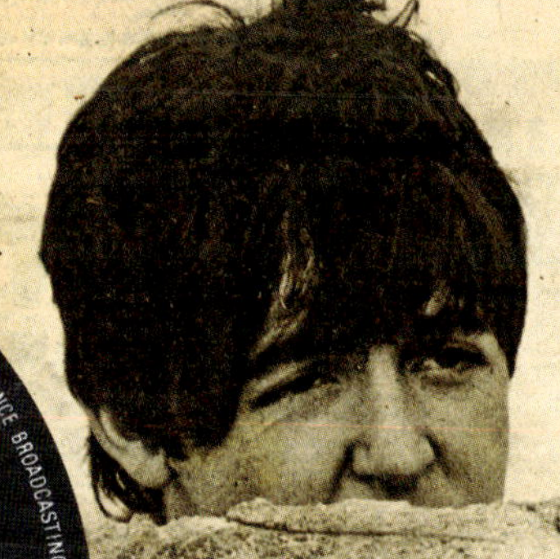

—they've done it again!

H—MM JUDGE

be the most … of the year— … of the Melody … Beat Contest at … is on August 15. … is helping to … mounting enthu- … Saturday (July 30) … ws of the contest … every day, in all of … swinging shows. … of Big L's top dee- … Brady, will compere … final which will be … a personality panel … Graham Nash of the … Hollies, glamorous dee-jay Muriel Young and Radio London's Kenny Everett.

A couple of Rolling Stones are among the many top stars who will be there to applaud the winners from among the 13 groups from all over Britain who have battled their way through to the Final.

Tickets are going fast so for a great night out send a 12s. 6d. postal order to Wimbledon Palais, London, S.W.19.

And don't forget to keep tuned in to Radio London on 299 metres for up-to-the-minute news of the contest.

'Delighted and surprised'

THE incredible Beatles have gone straight to the top of the Pop 50 with "Help!"—the sixth time they have jumped straight to number one and their ninth disc to reach the top.

Told the news, the Beatles commented: "We are delighted and surprised—we always are surprised when it happens."

Next big date for the Fabulous Four is the World Premiere of their second film—"Help!" is the title song — at the London Pavilion today (Thursday).

And it will be a Royal occasion, with Princess Margaret and Lord Snowdon as the guests of the Variety Club of Great Britain who have organised the premiere in aid of the Dockland Settlements and the Club's charity fund for children.

The Beatles will attend the premiere with their manager Brian Epstein.

Ode to the Beatles—Page 9.

PROBY REVIEWS NEW SINGLES

Prior to British fans learning any details about the Beatles second film, Beatles Book editor Johnny Dean (actually publisher Sean O'Mahony) asked readers in the October 1964 issue (No. 15): "What sort of film do you think the Beatles should make next? A western? A thriller?" Dean said he would award five pounds to the writer of the best letter. The following month Dean acknowledged that readers had thought up some "weird and wonderful plots." Anne Lindsell of Ramsgate suggested putting the boys in space, while Alyson Street of London wanted them to meet a ghost and be transported back to the time of King James I. The winner of the contest was M.E. Evans of Ebbw Vale in Wales, who cast the group in a James Bond thriller. Dean indicated that most writers wanted the next Beatles film to be in "FULL COLOUR." He added that no decision has been made about the plot of the next movie, so reader suggestions had "arrived at just the right time." John would have significant input in the script which could "only produce one result–some hilarious happenings!!!" Although readers of The Beatles Book obviously had no influence on decisions pertaining to the upcoming film, it would be in full color and incorporate many elements found in a James Bond thriller, including exotic locations, a mysterious beautiful woman who is not what she seems, exciting chases, a parody of Bond's deadly gadget-filled Austin Martin car, bits of music similar to the James Bond theme, close brushes with death, a strange and diabolical villain (Clang), and another bad guy who wants to, dare I say, rule the world.

In an interview with Alan Walsh in the October 24 Disc, Paul talked about the Beatles second big feature film set to start production in February. "This will probably be in colour and will have more of a story. We'll have to be ourselves in it, because we don't kid ourselves we can act. But it'll have a definitive plot." The October 30 NME reported that the Beatles next film would be a "comedy thriller with Ringo being hunted down by a would-be murderer!" Filming would begin on February 22 and was expected to last three months. American Mark Vahm [actually, Behm], co-credited with the story for the motion picture *Charade*, was writing the screenplay. The magazine provided an "outline of the story...revealed exclusively to the NME this week." As with their first film, *A Hard Day's Night*, the Beatles would play themselves and "be seen again on stage in front of television cameras and in the recording studio, providing ample opportunity for new songs." [Although the Beatles would be filmed in a recording studio, there would be no on-stage television appearance.] The story has the group "evading a man who mistakenly believes Ringo is in possession of 'an object' the man will do anything to get! George, John and Paul spend most of their time trying to protect Ringo."

The November 7 Disc furnished additional information from Walter Shenson, producer of the first and upcoming Beatles films. Shenson said there would be six or eight new Beatles songs, with no plans to use any previously published songs. [A bit of "She's A Woman" ended up in the film.] The color film would be a "wild comedy with the boys playing themselves, of course." The script was in development and would be completed in about two months. Shenson told more about the film in the November 14 Record Mirror. The movie would get a summer release, probably in July. Mark Behm's script would be "a strong, zany, wild comedy to really emphasise The Beatles' natural comedy abilities." The picture would have at least six new songs to be recorded during the week of February 15. The Beatles would start writing new material after their Christmas shows [ending on January 16]. Shenson added: "There will probably be no other stars in the picture...and although there will be 'a lot of pretty girls there will be no romantic interest for The Beatles." The December 11 NME ran a short article titled "Beatles to Help Pen Film Script." The group would meet with screenplay writer Mark Behm, giving them "the chance to put their own phrases into the script and change the story if parts of it doesn't suit them." Shenson would take the group and film crew to the Bahamas for location shooting before moving to Switzerland "or somewhere else there is snow." The rest would be shot at a London studio.

Laurie Henshaw interviewed Shenson about the film in the January 16, 1965 Disc. Shenson indicated that director Dick Lester was "very excited about the prospect of filming in the tropics and in the Alps," adding that the "colour of the Bahamas and the snow of the Alps will provide a wonderful background for The Beatles and the action of the film." Marc Behm had already drafted an outline script, and they had met with John and Paul to discuss "how the storyline should be developed" and how to "translate the comedy into the special Beatles brand of humour." Shenson insisted: "We are in no way attempting to do another 'Hard Day's Night,' but The Beatles will again play themselves. And there will be even more opportunities for them to show their natural acting talent as they get unwittingly involved in intrigue, and find themselves pressurised by big things from the mysterious East." Because the first film already captured fan fever, the Beatles would not be playing songs "on a stage or in a television studio before screaming fans." Instead, their songs would be "worked into the film to compliment the story-line and the action." Shenson admitted that coming up with a film title is always a problem. "But Ringo came up with such a perfect one last time–it became a catchword of 1964–we may again rely on The Beatles' spontaneity to do the trick."

Chris Hutchins wrote in the January 22 NME how the Beatles planned to spend their time off prior to recording the songs for their next film. John was heading to the Alps for his first ski trip with wife Cynthia and producer George Martin. Ringo was house hunting, while George was keeping his plans to himself. Paul would be at home writing songs for the film, telling Hutchins: "We've written some but still have to do most of them, including a title song–and that could be difficult because the film hasn't even got a title yet!" The following week, NME provided film production details from Brian Epstein. Filming would begin in the Bahamas, with the Beatles flying there on February 22. Starting on March 13, the entire film unit would be in Austria for a week to ten days. They hoped to finish the film on May 12.

The February 12 NME ran Keith Altham's report on the press reception introducing Eleanor Bron as the leading lady of the Beatles upcoming film. After viewing costume sketches of her character, she joked: "This film should be a sensation if that's all I'm wearing!" She held up the script for the movie, which was titled "Beatles II." After admitting she had yet to read it, she said: "But who cares? It's such a marvellous chance." Bron indicated that Paul was the only Beatle she had met and that the only pop record she ever bought was *Beatles For Sale*. Altham briefly chatted with Dick Lester, who revealed little about the planned filming in a small village between two mountains in Austria. "We'll go up one and down the other in glorious colour." When Altham speculated that John had been taking ski lessons for a "good reason," Lester smiled and replied: "No, that's just part of his death wish." Laurie Henshaw filed a report on the film in the February 20 Disc. After running through the production schedule, Henshaw indicated that Marc Behm had already delivered the script to Shenson. A synopsis of the film was presented mostly as a series of questions. Why were the high priests and the terrible goddess of Kaili interested in The Beatles? Why was Ringo pursued to the ends of the earth by a gang of Eastern thugs? What did they want of him–they certainly weren't fans! Two leading scientists hope to rule the world, Paul is threatened by a beetle (yes, that's the spelling) and an Eastern beauty–Eleanor Bron–saves the boys' lives time and time again. A Channel swimmer ends up in an Alpine lake–and Buckingham Palace has a busy day. When Scotland Yard advances on the sunny Bahamas after manoeuvres on Salisbury Plain, they find FOUR Ringos, but only one George, one Paul and one John. When power-hungry scientists arrive in the Alps, the boys miraculously escape their deadly weapons. Will John live to sleep in his pit again? Will Paul get back to his electric organ? Will George be reunited with his ticker-tape machine? And Ringo–will he ever play the drums again?

The February 27 Melody Maker noted that the Beatles viewed the success of their first film as a handicap in making their next film having set such a high standard. According to Ringo: "It's just like doing your first one–only worse. People will be watching us and expecting better." That week, Laurie Henshaw continued his reporting on the film for Disc. Before heading for Nassau, Lester indicated that the boys wouldn't have much time for leisure activities as they would "work until the sun goes down" with a strenuous schedule every day starting at 8:30 AM and going until about 6:00 PM. He did not anticipate fan interruptions because they had selected places that were a "bit more isolated than most." The Beatles would be staying at the Balmoral Club on Cable Beach (shown below), a "self-contained 'village' of stately Georgian houses set amid luxurious gardens, with a private island, and magnificent new swimming pool." Tony Howard, Press Officer for the film, reported from Nassau that the Beatles were greeted by thousands of local teenagers when their jet touched down at Windsor Field. After a quick press conference, the group went straight to their accommodations. Before going to bed, they went for a dip in the Atlantic Ocean. Filming would take place on New Providence Island. Location manager Peter Manley described the plot of the movie as "crazy."

DISC WEEKLY, february 27, 1965 3

beatles in the bahamas

There'll be hard days of filming for the boys

GEORGE

ON Monday, at 2 p.m. precisely, The Beatles flew off to an island paradise. The sort of place George Harrison once told me he might want to retire to "If I ever gave up music—which is highly unlikely."

by LAURIE HENSHAW

And John, Paul, George and Ringo's "magic carpet" was a Boeing 707—"with Rolls Royce engines," as "A Hard Day's Night" film producer Walter Shenson quipped just before he joined the boys on their trip to Nassau, capital city of the Bahamas, where "Beatles Two"—working title of the new all-colour Beatle film—started its shooting itinerary yesterday (Wednesday).

"We shall be in Nassau until March 10," added Mr. Shenson. "Then we come back to London for a few days before leaving for Salzburg, in Austria, on March 13, where we remain until March 22. Then it is back to London, again."

colourful

But, meanwhile, it's all sunshine for The Beatles before they are whisked into the cold climate of Austria for some of the snow sequences that promise to be just one of the highlights of a film whose locales are as colourful as the story-line—revealed in last week's DISC WEEKLY indicates.

Dick Lester, brilliant director of "A Hard Day's Night," has already been to Nassau to look over the locations for the new film.

And, just after attending an EMI recording session last week with Walter Shenson, he gave me an exclusive run-down on the setting those Beatles are now in, and on the working itinerary that will keep them busy from sunrise to sunset for the next couple of weeks.

That recording session? It took place all last week, when The Beatles recorded the numbers they had specially written for the new film.

And there's a ton of other attractions to tempt the Beatles in the Bahamas during their spare time. Sailing, skin-diving, golf, cycling, fishing—the lot! Temperature? That's about 88!

As souvenirs to bring home, they can buy colourful straw hats made by the natives, or collect some of the massive conch and turtle shells.

Deep sea fishing? Says Dick Lester: "I believe George Harrison did some last time he was there—and caught something pretty big.

"Exactly what we shall be shooting each day depends on what is being arranged. Scenes we shoot depends on the equipment that will be ready first.

"Frankly, the boys won't have much time for leisure activities. We shall work until the sun goes down, and I shou'dn't imagine they would want to stay on the beaches after that.

"After all, it's going to be a pretty strenuous day—every day. I should think the boys would have to be up by about seven a.m. They will have to go to make-up, which, as we are shooting in colour, will take a little longer.

sea food

"We want to start shooting around 8.30 a.m. and run through to about 6 p.m. There will be a break for lunch, of course, but whether this will be taken in a restaurant or brought out to us depends upon the location we are working in at the time."

And what will The Beatles' staple diet consist of? "Well, the food is sort of American," says Dick Lester. "Then there are the traditional dishes like local sea fish and local fruits. Probably, we shall have to rely on a lot of packed lunches. These things have to be flexible—so many things crop up that you can't predict."

Does Dick Lester anticipate

(Continued on next page).

THE BEATLES and the whole film unit will be staying at The Balmoral Club, one of the most attractive resort clubs in the Caribbean.

The Club, situated on the famous Cable Beach — two miles of spotless, white coral sand—and just five miles from town, is virtually a self-contained "village" of stately Georgian houses set amid luxurious gardens, with a private island, and magnificent new swimming pool. The sort of suite The Beatles will have would cost about £20 a night each just for bed and breakfast!

Says Dick Lester: "I have worked and stayed at this hotel twice now. The colonial cottages have six to eight rooms each and a central lounge.

There is a main dining room with a small orchestra, and patio overlooking the ocean where lunches are served. The swimming pool is delightful.

"It is ideal for a swim before breakfast, so if the boys want to splash about first thing in the morning, then they have plenty of opportunity to do so.

"I bathed all the time, and I am sure the boys will want to do so as well."

DICK LESTER

(Continued from previous page).

any "fan" interruptions by the wealthy tourists who flock the island? "We have chosen places that are a little bit more isolated than most," he said, "so I should think we should be able to keep to ourselves."

So, although the Bahamas are traditionally the playgrounds of the wealthy, it looks as though the fab four will be doing more work than play.

But one thing—they will at least be working in an island paradise. "To go from Britain into the sun is marvellous," adds Dick. "And that's one thing you can guarantee in the Bahamas."

Thousands turn out

NASSAU, Monday

THOUSANDS of local teenagers greeted The Beatles when their chartered plane touched down on Nassau's Windsor Field on Monday evening, cabled DISC WEEKLY's special Bahamas correspondent Etienne Dubuch.

Prior to the arrival, Nassau police officials geared themselves for what really promised to be "A Hard Day's Night."

The 70-strong film party on the plane is divided between the Royal Victoria Hotel and the Balmoral Club, seen in the accompanying photographs.

Although no special police escort is planned for The Beatles during their two weeks here, law officers were standing by "just in case."

It is understood that all the filming will be done on the 21-mile-long island of New Providence. Describing the plot of the film, location manager Peter Manley said it was "crazy."

AND THE BOYS GO FOR A MOONLIGHT DIP

THE BEATLES all took a moonlight dip in the clear emerald waters of the Atlantic shortly after arriving in Nassau on Monday after their long flight from London.

"It was a pretty tiring flight," said Tony Howard, Press Officer with producer Walter Shenson's film unit when DISC WEEKLY phoned him on Tuesday morning. "But the boys were all in good spirits, cracking jokes and taking turns to move around the plane to sit with various members of the crew unit.

"They got through a big quantity of Cokes on ice on the trip. Our first stop was Kennedy Airport, in New York. We were able to stretch our legs, but The Beatles had to be locked in the plane—there were so many fans there to welcome them.

"There were also scores of photographers and fans present when we arrived at Nassau. The Beatles held a Press conference, then went straight to the lovely Georgian house that had been reserved for them in the grounds of the Balmoral Club. They didn't even have time for a meal.

"But, before retiring for the night, they did take a dip in the sea. It is wonderfully warm here."

GEORGE HAS WRITTEN COUPLE OF SONGS

THE BEATLES were busy at the EMI recording studios last week cutting songs to be featured in their next film before leaving for location work in the Bahamas.

"We're hoping to get 12 in the can before they leave," Beatle A & R Man George Martin told me afterwards. "This will make up the film album. We want to get them done before the boys go so that they can take the results with them for the location work."

'both very good'

The bulk of the numbers for the picture have come from the prolific pens of John Lennon and Paul McCartney, whose music publishing company Northern Songs Ltd. made a very successful debut in the London Stock Exchange last week.

"George Harrison has written a couple for the film, too," said George Martin, "and they're both very good."

Linking musical segments and background for the film will probably be penned by him as before.

Nigel Hunter

The March 5 NME contained a report from the Bahamas by Brian Epstein. George Harrison's 22nd birthday was celebrated at the home of [Beatles financial advisor] Dr. Walter Strach, with whom George had previously spent a holiday on the island. The Beatles and the film crew were treated to fabulous party fare and listened to the 11 songs the Beatles had recorded the previous week at EMI Studios. Epstein said: "Six of these will be used in the film... they're easily hotter than the Bahama sunshine–and that's very hot!" Two of the songs were written by George, who had recently signed a three-year publishing contract with Northern Songs. Ringo was filmed holding a conch sea shell to his ear [in a scene that would not make the final cut of the movie]. The Beatles were filmed swimming fully clothed. The next day they were riding bicycles on a public thoroughfare [Interfield Road] and chatting away. Brian was impressed with their "improved naturalness of speech and movement." [Brian's report has the sequence of the filming incorrectly described.] Brian called the script "zany, almost to the point of surrealism, and certainly very, very different." He observed that the Beatles were enjoying the filming and were "relaxed, inventive and effervescent."

Ray Coleman ran a report from Ringo and George on the film in the March 6 Melody Maker. Ringo said the group was having fun. They were "filmed cycling round the island and it was very hot." George indicated the shooting was "very disjointed." He described a scene in which they emerge into a swimming pool in their clothes and a bit in a quarry driving sports cars. [The latter item is not in the film.] "We enjoy working here–it's all new, different, and we've got something different to tackle all the time. Who wants leisure time?" Laurie Henshaw contributed a short article on the Beatles first week of filming in the March 6 Disc, noting that while Britain was enduring the cold, the Beatles "basked in the balmy breezes of the Bahamas." The group was filmed taking a dip in the pool of the Nassau Beach Hotel with their clothes on and riding bicycles. George celebrated his 22nd birthday with a special cake baked for him by the caterer for the film unit. The next week Disc ran Henshaw's report from George, who was able to telephone Henshaw as the Beatles were enjoying their first morning off. "We've been up most days at seven. And yesterday we got up at six." Despite this, George said that the filming had been fun, adding: "We dived into the sea with our clothes on. And some of the sequences were shot through a glass-bottomed boat." George did some stunts for the movie, including leaping off the back of a car and diving through a window. The Beatles were due back in London on Thursday [March 11] and would fly to the "snowy slopes of Salzburg" on Saturday. George hoped it wasn't too cold in Austria.

BRIAN EPSTEIN reports from the BAHAMAS

All about the BEATLES

JOHN and PAUL (below) display emotion as they are "made wet" for a film shot.

LAST Thursday we celebrated George's 22nd birthday in sunny Nassau. It was a quiet affair at the home of Dr. Walter Strach, a great friend of George's, with whom he recently spent a holiday on the island.

The doctor's daughters were away in London—with all the suitable records. But we made do with the eleven titles the Beatles had recorded the previous week at EMI studios.

Six of these will be used in the film and, what can I say . . . they're easily hotter than the Bahama sunshine—and that's very hot!

Incidentally, two of the titles are written by George Harrison, and will be published by Northern Songs, with whom he signed a three-year contract just before he left London.

So George provided part of the music for his own birthday party, at which 50 members of the film unit enjoyed the tunes and the fabulous party fare provided by the generous doctor.

It is unlikely that the stars of any film could have had a warmer and more encouraging beginning than the Beatles did for their second movie.

I travelled out from town to London Airport with Paul and Ringo. John and George had arrived there a couple of minutes before us. As our car approached the back of Queens' Building, we were mildly surprised to see a packed group of fans at the top of the building.

When we turned the corner and walked on to the tarmac, there it was! An unbelievably **enormous** crowd of wonderful fans, cheering, waving and holding banners which gave us their good wishes.

A thrilled Paul and Ringo joined up with an equally amazed John and George, already acknowledging the crowd. None of us had anticipated anything like this.

The group posed for the mass of photographers, continuing to wave to the fans as long as the airline would allow them. It was the most wonderfully loyal demonstration the group could receive of their fans' affection.

I would like to thank each and every one in that crowd for giving the film the best send-off it could possibly have had!

The unexpected excitement at London Airport naturally contributed to a happy, if tiring, journey. Our unit travelling to the Bahamas numbered 78, making for a full load. Among them were Eleanor Bron, "Not So Much," actors Victor Spinetti, John Bluthal, Patrick Cargill, producer Walter Shenson and director Dick Lester both of "Hard Day's Night" fame.

ALL BEATLES' GEAR

Beatles' road managers Neil Aspinall and Malcolm Evans were there, too, of course—suitably equipped with the usual stack of photos, throat sweets, ciggies and other Beatle touring gear. With some of the group, I spent the first few hours catching up on sleep — earlier that day I'd flown from Liverpool, following the final night of Cilla's wonderful, and certainly eventful, tour—a big night for Cilla at the top of the bill for the first time in her home city!

Later on the trip the chat was animated about the making of the film. The cold, cold air of New York gusted in as we touched down to refuel and then about 11 hours after leaving England—at 7 p.m. local time, our chartered BOAC Boeing touched down here in Nassau.

We disembarked to receive a warm welcome like the weather.

We were then whisked off by the authorities to a Press conference without so much as an option as to whether the boys wanted to get a bit nearer to the waiting crowd at the airport building.

THIS IS USUALLY THE TRUE REASON WHEN YOU READ OF ARTISTS "IGNORING THEIR FANS."

Following a somewhat chaotic Press conference, we finally arrived at the bungalow where the boys were to stay in Nassau. Contrary to the usual glamorous reports of our staying in palatial and luxurious apartments, this proved to be a pleasant and comfortable place (expensive, yes), its best feature being its situation beside the sea, invisible in the darkness when we arrived but much in evidence the following morning—great, vivid, emerald sea glistening with the light of the hot, albeit sometimes humid, sunshine.

RINGO does some solo acting on a pile of shells and (below) GEORGE and PAUL do some cycling.

ON BICYCLES

THE group started shooting the morning following their arrival. Among first scenes shot were the Beatles cycling on a public throughfare and chatting away at the same time. Personally, I was greatly impressed with what seemed improved naturalness of speech and movement.

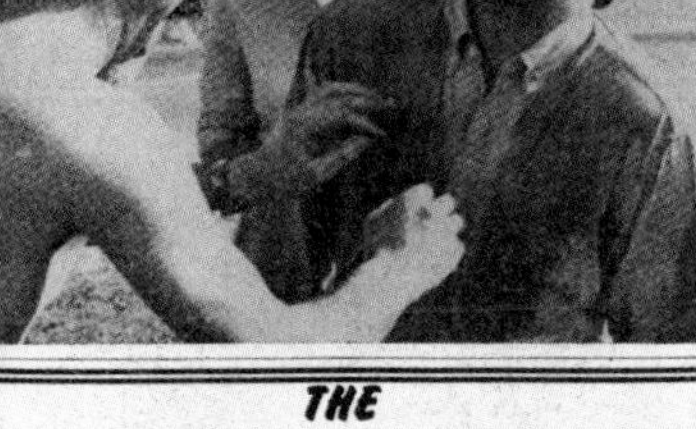

Ringo proved as good an actor as he was in "Hard Day's Night," when he was depicted sitting on a mound of conches (sea shells), holding one to his ear and beating out its music with his free arm!

Another day the four enjoyed a swim fully clothed (well, shirt, jeans and shoes). John said he'd always wanted to try this, and thought it might be even better to bathe in a lounge suit—tie and all!

The producer has asked that the story be kept on the secret list for the moment, so I can't say too much, except that the script itself is zany, almost to the point of surrealism, and certainly very, very different.

Before leaving Nassau on Friday, I took a speed boat out to a tiny island where the boys were working. I arrived just in time to get a boxed picnic lunch used on these occasions and to join up with the group for the break.

No doubt about it, I thought, they're enjoying making this film very much. Relaxed, inventive and effervescent as ever.

I left the Bahamas with no doubts that my clients will be well looked after by the gentle and brilliant director Lester, the efficient and understanding Mr. Shenson and, of course, our genial and hospitable Dr. Strach—not forgetting the people of Nassau, their sea and sun.

POST-SCRIPT

NEW YORK, Monday.—Great to see Gerry and the Pacemakers' name in big letters over Astor Cinema, bang in the middle of Times Square. United Artists report splendid reception for FERRY CROSS THE MERSEY. The powerful "Los Angeles Times" said: "The British have not only taken over the beat, they have outdone us when it comes to making a movie about it . . . pretty good entertainment, even for squares." B.E.

Last word on Beatles

SAID Brian Epstein to columnist Earl Wilson: "I think the Beatles will do even better as film entertainers than as live entertainers. And they'll make many more films . . . I think they will explode again in their next picture. Then they must eventually fit into pictures not just as Beatles but as actors."

Asked why American groups haven't made an impact in England in recent years compared to the impact the Beatles have made in America, Epstein said: "I don't know. The Americans seem to have forgotten how to do it."

Melody Maker's Ray Coleman traveled to Austria with the Beatles. Coleman contributed articles in the magazine's March 20 issue on the new single, the plane ride over the Alps and the first few days at the Obertauern ski resort. His main article, titled "Beatles in a Winter Wonderland!," described Obertauern as a sleepy village 100 miles from Salzburg, where people normally care only about skiing. The group spent their first night at the Hotel Edelweiss eating, drinking and signing autographs. The next morning, the boys were fitted in tight black trousers. They were filmed on a sleigh, with Ringo falling off. The scene nearly took four hours to film due to people getting in the way of cameras. The spectacular mountain scenes brought the movie to life. The color film's budget was £700,000 compared to the £190,000 it cost to film *A Hard Day's Night*. The group was also filmed on a horse-driven sleigh going through the snow. They lay in the snow for another bit that George said would be fitted in for a song ["Ticket To Ride"], with Harrison adding: "But God knows how." By the time the sun went down, Ringo said he was "fed up with the sight of snow." That same week Disc reported that the Beatles were "snowed under" by fans in Obertauern, 7,000 feet up in the Alps. Because they were filming in public places, it was difficult to keep people away. Due to the group's work schedule, they had little time for the resort's night life. They have been sledding and skiing, but the more difficult ski sequences have stand-ins with Beatle haircuts. The film has plenty of "off-beat comedy." The March 19 NME ran a picture of the Beatles on a sled.

The April 2 NME contained Chris Hutchins' report on his visit to Twickenham Studios where the Beatles were filming *Eight Arms To Hold You*. Based on what he saw, Hutchins thought the new film would be "even funnier than its worthy predecessor." He described a scene in which George, Paul and John drop into a hollow sacrificial alter filled with water to escape an Eastern temple. The fully clothed trio had to stay under the surface until the entire sequence was shot. When it was over, John joked: "We should get danger money." The issue contains film still pictures of the Beatles in a marching brass band and of Ringo getting the "James Bond electronic torture treatment." The April 10 Disc gave readers "more secrets of the Beatles film" courtesy of reporter Susan Shaw. The article focused on the Beatles fabulous flat shared by them in the film. The apartment contains an electric organ, played by Paul, that "rises out of the floor and is a scaled-down version of the cinema variety!" George has a patch of real grass next to his bed. The flat also has a Coke machine and a coffee bar with an espresso machine.

In an interview with Ray Coleman in the April 10 Melody Maker, John said that there was more now than making good records and selling them, adding: "I'd like to see us making better and better films. That's very difficult, and unlike pop music it allows you to grow up as a person." The magazine's April 17 issue reported on the Beatles reaction to "Ticket To Ride" entering the charts at number one. The group was at Twickenham Studios filming *Eight Arms To Hold You*, which they would complete in about a month. Readers of the April 16 NME learned that the movie's name *Eight Arms To Hold You* had been scrapped prior to John and Paul trying to write a song with that title. The film was now called *Help!*, and John and Paul had already written the title song, which the Beatles had recorded on Tuesday [April 13]. The April 24 Disc, in a story titled "Ringo is Trapped!," told readers that a Bengal tiger named Sheba was brought from the Scarborough Zoo [North Yorkshire] to Twickenham Studios for a scene showing Ringo trapped in a wine cellar with the big cat. The animal's trainer had a safari gun, while poor Ringo, at times only four feet from the tiger, had nothing.

The May 1 Disc ran an article on the film by Walter Shenson, who indicated that the Beatles had performed their own stunts, including "jumping on and off moving automobiles, crashing through windows, dropping though trapdoors, and being strung up by ropes!" Although the boys do ski in the film, experienced skiers were used for some of the long downhill shots to lower the risk of "broken legs–or worse." Shooting was on schedule. The film would be finished around May 14 with a London premiere in late July or early August. Shenson promised everyone "a feast of fun," adding: "We are playing the film for laughs, and I can confidently say you will have plenty of them!...The boys have had a real ball making this film. [We] hope you will have as much of a thrill when it is finally shown."

The following week, the May 8 Melody Maker informed its readers that the Beatles were still filming *Help!* The group was doing location work on the Salisbury Plain, hoping rain would not cause a delay in their schedule. That same week, NME ran a picture of the Beatles on the cover with the caption "Singing on the Plain." The magazine explained that the group had spent the week "playing on Salisbury Plain–miles of nothing, used mainly as a tank testing ground and artillery range!" It was for their new motion picture, *Help!*. Disc ran a picture of the Beatles being grabbed by a dozen bobbies with the caption: "It's all right–The Beatles haven't been arrested! At least, only in their new film, where they just have been chucked out of a pub the hard way–through a plate glass window!"

Alan Smith wrote about his visit to Twickenham Studios in the May 14 NME. The Beatles were filming a scene in a recording studio miming to a song called "Lose That Girl" [sic]. John sang lead, with Paul and George on the refrain. Between takes, the Beatles ran through songs such as Tom Jones' "It's Not Unusual," Ben E. King's "Amor," the jazz standard "How High The Moon," P.J. Proby's "I Apologise," the folk song "Michael Row The Boat," the traditional Irish song "Can You Wash Your Father's Shirt," the Yardbirds' "For Your Love" with John on bongos, "Rule Britannia" and Donovan's "Catch The Wind." [Four years later, the Beatles would once again run through a variety of songs at Twickenham during the filming of the *Get Back/Let It Be* project.] George told Smith: "We're very happy with this film. The director's made a great use of colour, with weird effects and that. Just look at this scene...a recording studio, but made to look way out by the lighting effects." In the May 15 Record Mirror, Paul said he liked *Help!* more than the first film. He talked of the group racing cars in a disused quarry. "We were screeching around it like mad. Well, they filmed it slyly and put it in the film. Just Like that." [Lester decided not to use the bit.] Although there were no speed-ed up shots like in *A Hard Day's Night*, there were visual gimmicks such as the group "standing on a rock in the middle of the ocean playing our instruments" [miming to "Another Girl" on a coral reef on Balmoral Island, Bahamas].

The June 19 Disc had more information on *Help!*, now set to premiere on July 29 at the London Pavilion. Laurie Henshaw reported that the film was being cut and edited, with the Beatles taking time from "a week's heavy recording schedule" for a "post-sync" session. Shenson explained that the boys were re-recording some of their lines that were not audible due to extraneous noises picked up during location shooting in Nassau and the Alps. He added that this was "normal filming procedure" and other cast members were doing the same. Shenson thought "Help!" was one of the finest songs the group had written. He also praised "The Night Before," heard during the Salisbury Plain sequence. He insisted that all involved were determined that *Help!* would not be anything like *A Hard Day's Night*. "I can tell you that *Help!* is pure entertainment, and the colour is absolutely wonderful." Shenson summed up the film in the July 31 Disc, describing it as a "comic strip vividly brought to life and packed with colour, thrills and that distinctive Beatles humour." *Help!* was a "different kind of magic....Instead of depicting a day in the life of the Beatles, we show their adventures...that take them from England to the Alps–where you'll see breathtaking scenery and wonderful skiing sequences–to the Salisbury Plain, and then on to the Bahamas. But, apart from scenery, there are plenty of thrills."

Ringo talked about the upcoming film in the July 31 Disc. "I've seen the picture–we all went to the American embassy to see it. They can go ahead and release it–I'm not ashamed of it, or anything. I hope the fans like it, really. If they liked *A Hard Day's Night* they ought to find this 100 percent better. As a picture it's much better made, although this is fantasy compared with *A Hard Day's Night* being documentary." As for his major role in *Help!*, Ringo added: "I hate being put in front on anything, And I don't want ANYBODY to think the film hangs on me. But it's all about the ring, and it would have been soft if Paul, for instance, had been chosen as the central figure–it would have been daft."

Ringo acknowledged that *Help!* could very well receive its share of negative reviews. "We're quite prepared for a knocking. We've had a hell of a lot of it lately, what with the MBE business. When you get popular, you must expect it."

Chris Hutchins' review of *Help!* in the July 30 NME opens with details of Ringo being in danger, culminating with his description of bad men attacking "with bombs big enough to explode our four heroes into the next James Bond picture." He laments that the Beatles "have to do their best with a sequence of thin lines and un-funny quips." Although there are moments when "John's great natural wit breaks through," such moments are rare. Hutchins describes all the scenes featuring Beatles songs. For "You've Got To Hide Your Love Away," John sounds "more like Bob Dylan than Bob Dylan." During "Ticket To Ride," the boys "frolic in the snow (complete with grand piano!)" in one of the best sequences in the movie. Beatles road manager Malcolm Evans is the "scene-stealer of the picture," popping "up through the icy water in swimming gear" asking directions to Dover. While Dick Lester's direction is brilliant, Shenson allows it to "outshine the other aspects of the picture." Hutchins advises those who enjoy the Beatles to go see the film for they are "rarely off the screen." His verdict: *Help!* is "100 minutes of nonsense containing much good fun," but "don't go expecting a GREAT picture because *Help!* is not that."

Editor Jack Hutton began his review of *Help!* in the July 31 Melody Maker with a quote of a young girl who had attended the July 27 press showing of the film at the Odeon, Leicester Square: "Not nearly enough of the Beatles." Hutton seemed to agree, lamenting that there was "far too much professional buffoonery from the hardened character players" (such as Roy Kinnear and Victor Spinetti) and not nearly enough chat from the Beatles. The film was at its best in scenes "where the Beatles were merely being themselves." Their humor was "better than the forced cracks from the pros which seemed strangely mistimed." Hutton found the music to be "wonderful," adding that "Help!," "You're Gonna Lose That Girl" [sic] and "The Night Before" were "among the best John and Paul have written." On the cinematic side, "Dick Lester's direction demonstrates he hasn't lost the knack [a pun on the director's previous film, *The Knack ...And How To Get It*] and the colour photography is big and beautiful." Of the Beatles, Ringo once again took the acting honors. While the film provided great entertainment, Hutton hoped that next time there would be "fewer 'aids' for the Beatles" as they did not need them.

Disc gave a more positive verdict of the film in its July 31 issue, advising theater goers to put *A Hard Day's Night* out of their minds when going to see *Help!* The picture is a "flight of fantasy loaded with gimmicks, garlanded with colour and capped with brilliant photography." Its comedy and chase scenes "sometimes seem like a hazardous merger of the Marx Brothers; 'It's A Mad, Mad, Mad, Mad World' and 'The Running, Jumping, Standing Still' films." This leads to the Beatles often seeming "to take a back-seat in the breathless, all-out rush to raise laughs from the slapstick situations." The film had "inspired moments of comedy" such as the Salisbury Plain war sequences. "That incisive Beatle humour knifes through–but too infrequently. Ringo shines as a comedy star, and John Lennon splashes around his customary vitriolic wit. Best of all are the songs–marvellous!"

In the July 31 Record Mirror, Peter Jones noted that *Help!* got "several outbreaks of warm applause" at its press showing. It is a "gigantic send up of all adventure films" with the Beatles "moving in a slightly baffled way...through it all." The songs fit naturally into the film, such as a recording session "in the bleakest parts of the Salisbury Plain." As for the camera work: "Everything is jazzed up from within the alarmingly inventive mind of director Dick Lester." Once again, Ringo displayed "a knack of capturing the attention most strongly," aided by being the central figure. There were also funny bits with Beatles road manager Mal Evans, who plays a long distance swimmer looking for the white cliffs of Dover, but showing up in the Alps and the Bahamas. Jones concludes: "Go back to the Bowery Boys, the Marx Brothers, the Three Stooges. Add colour, more originality, plus million selling music you've got some idea of it all."

The August 7 Disc printed fan reactions. Shirley Cookson, an 18-year-old shop assistant in Wittle-in-Woods, liked *Help!* more than the first film. Michael Moxham, age 18 from Preston, said: "It was silly and not as good as 'A Hard Day's Night.'" Pamela Cohn, a 13-year-old schoolgirl from Manchester, thought is was more exciting and a better story than *A Hard Day's Night*. Susan Styles, a 17-year-old clerk from Sussex, liked the music and story, also finding it better than the last film. Robert Thompson, a 15-year-old carpenter from Birmingham, didn't like it as much as the prior movie. "There were too many camera tricks. The gimmicks were overdone." Jennie Thirkill, a 16-year-old TV assembler who saw *A Hard Day's Night* seven times, thought *Help!* was "twice as good." Lynn Peters, a 15-year-old schoolgirl from Jarrow, found it foolish to criticize the film for not having a plot. "After all, what plot did the great musicals have?"

Although Reuters reported that *Help!* "won long applause from London's usually-reticent critics at a press showing," the film drew mixed reviews from London newspapers and tabloids. The Guardian provided two perspectives. In the paper's July 30 edition, Ian Wright correctly predicted that *Help!* would "attract more stringent criticism" than its predecessor, but still be "another triumph" for the Beatles and Richard Lester. The film was basically "a chase, Goonlike and zany." Although Lester's direction matches the Beatles exuberance, Wright found fault. "But this is a chrome-plated, fast-moving vehicle that Lester has provided for the Beatles–and on occasions they look too much like passengers. The director and his screenwriters, Marc Behm and Charles Wood, have crammed so much into the film that parts are bound to fail–and do." An uncredited review from August 2 acknowledged that the "cult worshipers will doubtless think [*Help!*]...is all as gear as can be," but found the film to be a "terrible mess." Lester directed "with an excess of enthusiasm and dedication to the zany" that occasionally comes off, but more often the "visual tricks flop from sheer lack of thought" as "madness is only effective if there is a method in it." The dialog is "unrelievedly bad," exploding the myth that "the Beatles only had to be themselves to be funny," and the songs "all sound exactly the same." [Really?]

The Daily Telegraph also ran two reviews. Patrick Gibbs' criticism of *Help!* was aimed primarily at Dick Lester and the screenplay. Gibbs attributed Lester's "frenetic style" to a "lack of confidence" in the script, described as a "preposterous piece into which...any old pop group might have been dropped, so little is made of the Beatles' individual qualities." He presumed the goal was a "crackpot or screwball comedy," but "the fantastic situation they develop gives few really comic opportunities" for the Beatles or supporting cast. He thought the film's "silly plot" provided more misses than hits, and that Lester's attempts to enliven the script "have the air of absolute desperation." The most enjoyable sequences were on the ski slopes, where "the camera makes abstract compositions of their antics." Gibbs admitted that the color produced "some pretty pictures of the Beatles singing," which was not frequent enough, "for it is only then that they appear at ease and are seen–and heard–to advantage." Margaret Powell described the movie as "unrealistic, unreasonable, grossly exaggerated and very, very funny." She advised movie-goers not to follow the story, which was "really irrelevant," but rather to "just sit back and watch." The film was brilliantly shot in color, using "every trick of the camera." The humor ranged "from slapstick to situation comedy to biting sarcasm." The supporting cast members were "perfect foils for the zany antics of the Four, whose musical contributions are suitably unobtrusive."

in the gracious presence of
HER ROYAL HIGHNESS THE PRINCESS MARGARET, COUNTESS OF SNOWDON
and the EARL OF SNOWDON

Sponsored by the Variety Club of Great Britain
to aid THE DOCKLAND SETTLEMENTS SCHOOL OF ADVENTURE and THE VARIETY CLUB HEART FUND

LONDON PAVILION
PICCADILLY CIRCUS
THURSDAY JULY 29th 1965
at 8·30 p.m.

Doors open at 7.30 p.m. Seats must be taken by 8.20 p.m.

TICKET ORDER FORM

ROYAL WORLD PREMIERE
in the gracious presence of
HER ROYAL HIGHNESS THE PRINCESS MARGARET, COUNTESS OF SNOWDON
and THE EARL OF SNOWDON
Sponsored by The Variety Club of Great Britain
to aid THE DOCKLAND SETTLEMENTS and THE VARIETY CLUB HEART FUND
on
THURSDAY 29th JULY 1965
at the
LONDON PAVILION
PICCADILLY CIRCUS

Donald Zec of the Daily Mirror swore he wanted to laugh "like the girl who giggled gushingly and remorselessly behind my right ear," but his "sides remained unsplit." He was not "rolling in the aisle." Zec added that *Help!*, "for all its strenuous nitwittery and relentless tomfoolery, just did not come across" to him despite it being a zany romp full of "gadgets, gimmicks, daft tricks and cockeyed camera angles." He lamented that John, George, Paul and Ringo are not another Harpo, Groucho, Zeppo and Chico. "Half Marx is the most I can award them for this energetic flogging of a limp if not lifeless horse." Although the film had a promising opening, it then faltered. During its chase scenes, "the film leaned heavily on the likeable vacant grin of John Lennon, the smooth charm of Paul, the long-haired good looks of George and the darkly villainous looks of the Long-Nosed One." This was "not enough to carry a movie" in Zec's view. With the exception of the title number, the tunes were "pleasantly forgettable." He did find some good moments, noting: "First-rate photography and revved-up direction make this picture look good and move fast." He praised Leo McKern, Victor Spinetti and Roy Kinnear as "seasoned performers who can grab laughs from the most tenuous comic situations." Zec supposed that "millions will declare themselves well and truly satisfied," but he was "perplexed, at the whole bemused affair." The Sunday Mirror was also unimpressed. "Brilliant at times but too 'way out' to capture the natural magic of the Beatles' first film. The whacky camera-work and zany comedy, if used in moderation, could have resulted in something to scream about."

Writing in the Evening Standard, Alexander Walker gives the Beatles their due for not making another film exactly like *A Hard Day's Night*, instead taking a risk with a totally different type of movie. Even if *Help!* does not have "the same anarchic impact as that breakthrough pop musical, it is still a wonderfully unpredictable vehicle for this overly-familiar quartet." The film is a "screwball fantasy...jig-saw of jokes, an Eastmancolourful comedy you could call Helpsapoppin" complete with "tongue-in-cheek take-offs on James Bond." Richard Lester "plays all kind of gags with the camera–phoney intermissions, spoof captions, subtitles of lunatic import, and trick photography" including Paul shrinking to the size of a toe. Lester's "inventiveness breaks up the numbers [songs] into an eye-jerking battery of rainbow colours and lens focuses that at one point make the keys of a guitar as big as the pillars of Stonehenge." While *Help!* does not settle the question of how far the Beatles "can push their talents in a new direction and still be the Beatles," as long as they have a team as clever as Lester and Shenson, "they will be with us a long time yet."

Clive Barnes, writing for the Free Press-London Express Service, called the film "Marvelous!," adding: "Any lucky fools might have made a good first film. But to make a good second film–that's the test the Beatles triumphantly, effortlessly, nonchalantly, and above all cheerfully survive with 'Help!'" Barnes praised Richard Lester for providing a "dazzling film that leaves no one time to think, let alone ponder." While Lester does "outrageously corny things with cameras and colours," the film has "pace and brilliance" and a "zap and panache that leaves you gasping but happy." Barnes provides credit to the script and direction, but notes that "the basic talent of the boys remain," adding that they are "the closest thing to the Marx Brothers since the Marx Brothers," with their "slightly bewildered, wholly skeptical charm...flavoured with an anarchic craziness that is easy on the mind." The film's music, composed by Lennon, McCartney, Harrison, Peter Ilyich Tchaikovsky, Ludwig Von Beethoven and Gioacchino Rossini, "sounds super."

Cecil Wilson of the Daily Mail said: "It's the Beatles who need help. Where the first film was a highly personalized piece of surrealism woven around their special talents, the second one reduces them to robots in a great beanfeast of gimmickry and gadgetry. The gags, despite their Marxian craziness, lack the buildup, the comic momentum, the sustained invention of a Marx Brothers film." Kenneth Tynan of The Observer described *Help!* as "a brilliant, unboring but ferociously ephemeral movie" and "a shiny, forgettable toy: an ideal playwith." Tynan observed that the Beatles were neither "natural actors" nor "exuberant extroverts." They were "dry and laconic, as benefits the flat and skeptical Liverpool accent." Realizing their style, Lester "capitalizes on their wary, guarded detachment" by "confining the Beatles to deadpan comments and never asking them to react to events with anything approaching emotion." Tynan's favorite sequence is the one with Ringo trapped by a Bengal tiger who can be tamed by the choral passage of Beethoven's Ninth Symphony. He thought that the musical numbers were "superbly shot," with the title song being "the most haunting Beatle composition to date." In the August 1 edition of The People, Ernest Betts wrote that *Help!* wasn't "so much a film," but rather was "more of an accident, with every colour from marmalade to ice-cream pink." Betts observed: "Wherever the Beatles go in this film there's panic and pandemonium, varied by some good numbers put over with their usual professional flair." He noted Richard Lester's brilliant talent for slapstick comedy, having "revived the gimmicks of the earliest Hollywood clowns and adding a few of his own." Betts added that the photography "makes you gasp" and called the film a "huge success." Surprisingly, The Times did not review *Help!*.

The Acton Gazette in Ealing, London wrote that *Help!* "discards the semi-documentary style of the first venture and gives the Beatles a chance to prove the theory that 'all Liverpudlians are born comedians; they have to be to live in the place.'" The film is "one long crazy chase" proving "the Beatles have the potential to outlive the current Beatles craze."

Unnamed London reporters for the Liverpool Echo and the Liverpool Daily Post attended the July 27 press showing of *Help!* at the Odeon Theatre in Leicester Square. The Echo reporter described the film as "a riot of a comedy, in dazzling colour and on a Cinemascope screen that does justice to the image of the Liverpool quartet." The movie was "packed with comic situations, and just the kind of off-beat humour which the Beatles are famed for." The highlights of the film were the splendid song sequences, with every number a "chart-topper in its own right." The photography was superb, with Lester using "every conceivable angle shot to capture the boys in the most comic poses, whether singing as they ski on Alpine slopes, or on a Bahamas beach." The Echo reporter observed that throughout the movie, the "highly critical audience found plenty to laugh at and the production as such claimed much applause for photographic technique" His conclusion: "From all points of view, action, music, and purely as photography, 'Help!' is a riot." The Daily Post reporter wrote that from the opening of the title tune, "one could sense the appreciation of the audience," adding: "Time and again the audience–the type not usually warmed to laughter early in the morning–laughed their appreciation at the boys' antics, particularly the droll humour which they appear to ad lib into the official script." An elegant young lady captured the general verdict of those attending: "This shows the Beatles aren't on the way out. While they can write music like that they'll always be at the top." A young woman from Marseilles added: "This is far better than their first film. They've brought sunshine to your dull summer climate."

The London film critic of the Liverpool Daily Post, Raymond Anker, wrote that the Beatles had done it again [made a winner of a film] with help from director Richard Lester, the screenwriters and the actors. Lester, with Beatles films in two distinct styles, had "established the Beatle persona as something worth savouring with or without tune." The screenplay allowed the Beatles "to indulge in iconoclastic fun without making them look like projections of a public relations item." The cast shared in the "surrealist idiocy." Anker summed it up: "The visual and verbal jokes sparkle for the most part. The colour is good. And only occasionally does the camera work seem more frenetic than the action."

A few days later, Felix Barker provided a more critical review in the Liverpool Echo, writing that although the film was "still pretty good," Shenson and Lester should have "made a far better film" given that they had "the world's most successful pop group," a large budget, exotic locations and a strong supporting cast. The movie was a "wild farce which consists not so much of a story as a string of running, jumping, and never standing-still gags." Barker praised the scene of the boys recording "I Need You" on the Salisbury Plain surround by seven Army tanks for protection. But while Lester achieved his magic by indulging in quick cuts, in-and-out focusing, back lighting and "every nazzy trick he can devise," this was done "at the almost total sacrifice of the actors and the Beatles."

John Stratten, in the July 31 Manchester Evening News & Chronicle, wrote that *Help!* defies "orthodox criticism" and "is like no other film that ever was." If anything, "it's an overlong Goon Show, in which everything's off-key, off-balance and off-beat" with a plot that "might have served the Marx Brothers well enough." Richard Lester, knowing that the Beatles weren't the brothers Marx, left the "more complicated slapstick to more experienced clowns like Leo McKern, Victor Spinetti, Roy Kinnear, and Eleanor Bron," leaving the boys "to be just their lively, uninhibited selves." Stratten praises the camerawork as "always exciting and occasionally quite lovely," with the sound being as good as he has "heard in a musical film." The means that the Beatles "come across loud and clear," whether recording on Salisbury Plain, ski slopes or in their "gadget-infested super-flat." Stratten supposes that "is the real object of the exercise."

The Daily Mail in Hull, East Yorkshire County advised readers: "Fasten your safety belts. It's the new-look, globetrotting Beatles doing a jet-age Marx Brothers." The "high-powered Merseysiders hop from the snow-capped Swiss Alps to the sweltering Bahamas" in a "series of chaotic sequences, packed with action and laughs, and some highly-novel touches." *Help!* had "plenty of dry Liverpool humour" and was a "worthy follow-up" to *A Hard Day's Night*. The headline to Tony Crofts' review of *Help!* in the Western Daily Press in Bristol, Avon describes the movie as a "zany Beatle romp." Crofts writes that the film does not bother about realism. After describing parts of the plot, he concludes: "The whole thing is a glorious send-up of the public's ideas of the Beatles, its attitude to them, authority, the police, the Army, science and the brain-drain, and the obvious enjoyment they derive from their prosperous present situation, these four simple, unspoilt, Rolls-Royce-driving lads."

Three newspapers in Newcastle upon Tyne in the north of England reviewed the film. Fred Billany had only words of praise for *Help!* in the July 27 Evening Chronicle. "The Beatles have scored another bullseye with their second film...It is a rip-roaring lark in which Paul, Ringo, John and George show themselves as splendid clowns and brilliant harmonists. The seven new songs are among the best they have ever done." Although the Beatles dominate the story, they do not overshadow the excellent performances of the supporting cast. Billany added that the film was "certain to break box-office records" and that the "famous Liverpool quartet have never been better." Michael Beale expressed mixed feelings about the movie in the paper's July 30 edition. Although he admitted that *Help!* was the "zaniest piece of screen comedy you are likely to see for some time," the film had the "flimsiest plot" where "everything happens" often "without any rhyme or reason." Sometimes the film was "hilariously funny" and "exceptionally clever," but "at other times it drags." Dick Lester "uses all sorts of gimmicks, switching colors mid-scene...using silent screen jokes with captions." Beale was "certain that the Beatles do a deliberate and perfect send-up of themselves as a pop group." They burst into musical numbers "in the most unlikely places–the Austrian Alps...where a piano suddenly appears... and on Stonehenge where they made a recording behind barbed wire and guarded by a ring of tanks." Although jokes "follow one another in a fast and furious manner," towards the end "there is some rather tedious repetition, and flatly directed melees." The newspaper's August 3 Cinema column thought that *Help!* was "really Dick Lester's film," adding that he is "the outstanding director of crazy comedy, and does he go crazy in this film!" The movie was "often brilliant in its mad, mad way, and the Beatles, although not great actors fit into the pattern of things very well." The film's gags were "neat and topical." The writer implies that the movie would have been very funny even without the Beatles.

Lynn Fenton wrote in the July 31 edition of The Journal that *Help!* did not meet expectations, based on *A Hard Day's Night*, that "there would be a big leap forward, away from the pop group" to the Beatles becoming a "first-class comedy team." The movie was a "zany piece of film fun with very little rhyme or reason, exceptionally clever in parts, but with...long stretches of boredom." Fenton did not hold the Beatles responsible as they are "just their natural selves, doing whatever is required of them." The film failed by trying to be in two worlds: the Beatles as a pop group "cleverly bashing out their musical numbers" and that of zany comedy "in the Marx Brothers sphere." Fenton concluded: "The two do not mix."

In the August 1 Sunday Sun, Simon Stanford wrote that after *A Hard Day's Night*, he thought the boys "could become English Marx Brothers." While he still held that judgment, he regretted to report the Beatles had not "advanced their progress very far" with *Help!*. Many scenes would have been just as funny with other actors. It wasn't the Beatles fault that "they do not emerge as side-splitting comedians." They are "overshadowed by the situations which the writers have thought up, and by Dick Lester's gimmicky screen presentation." As for the good, there are "imaginative comedy sequences" that give the Beatles a chance to display "their high-spirited humour." He thought there were too many musical numbers and was looking forward to seeing the Beatles as "straight comedians in their own right" in the group's next movie," adding that "as the English successors to Groucho, Harpo and Chico they do not earn full 'Marx.'"

Brimingham newspapers also covered the film. Nicolas Cottis observed in the July 28 Birmingham Post that "Britain in the eyes of the world today means Beatles." And with their latest film, the Beatles weren't exporting "British commonsense, British pragmatism [or] British political maturity." It was "British nonsense, the vein of humourous anarchy which has given us the Great Panjandrum, the Jabberwock, the Goons and now Ringo." Cottis, a self-admitted old Goon addict, had wished for a "higher standard of lunacy from *Help!*," finding that 90 minutes was "a long time in which to sustain a flight of fancy, and the screenwriters...occasionally overstrain themselves in keeping theirs aloft." He concludes that the "best laughs are visual rather than textual." The Sunday Mercury opined that *Help!* "is not as good as their first film by half." The movie was "decidedly too clever," with Richard Lester using far too many "fancy-angle shots" that left the reviewer's head spinning. While *Help!* was far from a bad picture and gave the reviewer one of his "most enjoyable trips to the cinema this year," he was disappointed that "so much of the spontaneity of the original [movie] has been lost." With *A Hard Day's Night* being a "break-through" in cinema, it was foolish to be disappointed that *Help!* "doesn't fully measure up to something that was, after all, unrepeatable."

The August 6 Middlesex County Times and West Middlesex Gazette thought that *Help!* started "most promisingly," but ran short of ideas in its later stages. It described the "Ticket To Ride" performance sequence as "exhilarating," adding that it "combines musical drive and catchy melody with pretty visual composition" shot on white snow. Despite the film going downhill after the Alpine scenes, its "verve and ingenuity" made *Help!* a "picture to visit."

In the August 7 Disc, Ray Coleman gave Paul an opportunity to answer the film's critics in an article titled: "No! The Beatles Have Not Lost The Knack!" Paul noted many people made a big mistake "in believing that all they read in certain newspapers is correct." He thought that some writers "went along with pre-conceived ideas about the film and wanted some sort of headline like 'BEATLES FLOP.'" When they saw the movie, they "couldn't honestly say that, because it isn't a flop." McCartney added: "They had to get something to justify their ideas, and so they found little things to niggle about." In that week's Melody Maker, George stated: "We're a bit baffled that some of the critics should knock 'Help!.' I must confess that when we first saw the completed film we were knocked out. But obviously some people were not. Let's face it–the whole thing is just a fast moving comic strip." Ringo added: "Some of the critics seemed to be going out of their way to knock it–or us." Paul pointed out that *A Hard Day's Night* was "so much better than they all expected," so it was hopeless for *Help!* to live up to it.

The August 14 Melody Maker compiled an opinion poll of British fans regarding the two Beatles films. Of the 91 people interviewed, 57 were "quite definite" that *Help!* was a better movie than *A Hard Day's Night*, with only 32 favoring the first feature film. This led to the assessment that: "The critics were wrong!" The August 20 NME reported that *Help!* was "smashing cinema records all over Britain!"

Despite the film's box office success, John remained skeptical about the Beatles acting abilities. When a reporter asked him in the September 11 Record Mirror, "Can we look forward to more Beatle movies?," Lennon replied: "There will be more but I don't know if you can look forward to them." By the time Ray Coleman interviewed John for the October 2 Disc, Lennon had gone sour on the film, telling Coleman: "We went wrong with the picture somehow." He then compared the movie to "Eight Days A Week," adding: "A lot of people liked the film, and a lot of people liked the record. But neither was what we really wanted–we knew they weren't really US. We weren't ashamed of the film. But close friends knew that the picture and 'Eight Days A Week' as a record weren't our best. They were both a bit manufactured." It was the loss of control that seemed to upset Lennon, causing him to have second thoughts about the Beatles planned third movie. "The film [*Help!*] won't harm us, but we weren't in full control. We're not sure what comes next in the way of a film–it isn't definite that the next will be 'Talent For Loving.' Nothing's certain about it."

Fans first learned about the recording sessions for the Beatles new film and album in two February 27 articles. In Disc, George Martin said that he hoped to get 12 songs “in the can before they leave…so that they can take the results with them for the location work.” George Harrison had written two songs, with Martin indicating that “they’re both very good.” Melody Maker’s Ray Coleman attended the group’s February 18 session. John summed up the new tracks: “They haven’t been tailored to the film or anything. They’re just songs. If they fit the story and the sequences, some of them will be in it. It’s up to the film bosses. Not us. We’ve just concentrated this week on making records. There are a couple of obvious songs for the film, at least we think so, but nothing’s been decided. We haven’t written anything with the film in mind. If you do that, it restricts the story line.” John noted that Paul had “been doing quite a bit of lead guitar work this week. Gear. I reckon he’s moving in.” He added that the group was still searching for the ideal sound. “I don’t know if we’ll ever find it. We still haven’t made the sort of sound we want to, and we don’t even know what we’re after.” Coleman described the recording of two songs [“If You’ve Got Trouble” and “Tell Me What You See”].

By the time the Beatles were in Paris for a pair of June 20 shows, they had completed the songs for their next LP. The group brought acetates of the new recordings with them and played some of the songs for journalists covering the European tour. Mike Hennessey reported in the June 26 Melody Maker that “these tunes are some of the best John and Paul have ever done.” He called out Ringo’s country and western number [“Act Naturally”] as “his best ever,” but thought that the “most fantastic song” was Paul’s solo ballad, “Yesterday.” The song was “completely different from anything the Beatles have ever done” and had a string quartet. He observed: “It has number one engraved on every bar and it’s a pity it won’t be released in Britain as a single.” Chris Hutchins praised the same two songs in the June 25 NME, whose cover ran the headline: “Beatles Sensation: PAUL goes solo.” The short cover blurb indicated that Paul had recorded a song without John, George and Ringo, using a string quartet for the backing. Paul also played guitar on the track, which would be on the Beatles next LP due out the first week of August. The song would not be issued as a single, “so the problem of Paul being presented as a solo artist in his own right does not arise.” Inside the magazine, Hutchins said the song “sounds like something out of the eighteenth century; and Paul drags his voice in a somewhat Dylan-ish manner.” He agreed with John’s assessment that the old country and western song sung by Ringo was the best he had ever done, adding: “Watch out for this track yourselves!” [Capitol later issued both songs on a single.]

The July 9 NME and July 10 Melody Maker and Record Mirror each provided details about the songs on the Beatles upcoming *Help!* LP. All four weekly music magazines reviewed the new disc in their July 24 (July 23 for NME) editions.

NME's Derek Johnson guaranteed that the album is "the ideal cure for the depressions!" Johnson described it as a "gay infectious romp which doesn't let up in pace or sparkle from start to finish–with the exception of one slow track." *Help!* would surely top the LP chart within a week of its release. He observed: "It's typical Beatles material, and offers very few surprises. But then who wants surprises from the Beatles?"

Johnson did not describe "Help!" as he had already reviewed the song the previous week. Paul handles the lyrics on "The Night Before" while "John and George repetitively chant the title phrase." The track is a "mid-tempo pounder" whose "insistent beat is given added depth" by John on electric piano. John sings the plaintive lyric of "You've Got To Hide Your Love Away" in "hushed tones, but projects rather more forcefully in the catchy chorus." The song has "an intriguing guitar riff, and tambourine punctuates the rhythm." The flutes lend a "wistful quality to the scoring." George's "I Need You" features a double-tracked Harrison lead vocal "with John and Paul chanting lustily." George provides a "spirited effervescent vocal, despite the doleful heart-searching nature of the lyric." The track has a "great sound...with a throbbing up-tempo beat and supporting handclaps." Paul solos on "Another Girl" with John and George adding "familiar ear-catching harmonies." The peppy bouncer "swings along with an irresistible beat, thanks to Ringo practically knocking himself out!" John sings lead on "You're Going To Lose That Girl" and "colours his interpretation with frequent falsettos." Paul and George "answer back at the end of each phrase, employing some fascinating ear-catching counter-harmonies." The medium-pace song is a "very good track." Johnson did not see any need to write anything about the Side One closer, "Ticket To Ride" [which was the group's previous hit single].

While the first side is devoted to songs from the movie, Side Two has non-film songs recorded specifically for the LP. "Act Naturally," written by Morrison-Russell, is Ringo's sole lead vocal, "a perfect novelty vehicle for him....set to a cheerful jog-trotting pace, with Paul harmonizing, and a guitar interlude from George." John's "It's Only Love" has a "pleasant, whistleable melody, and a tambourine to maintain the steady shuffle beat." "You Like Me Too Much" is

George's "second party piece." The song is a "bounding vibrant finger-clicker, with Paul warbling in the background." Its honky-tonk keyboards are provided by John on electric piano, along with Paul and George Martin on standard piano. "Tell Me What You See" has an appealing John and Paul duet, with Paul adding "some clanking piano." The track has "delightful Harrison guitar work [actually John], added tambourine, and the faintest trace of a Latin rhythm." The song's strong melody makes this "another good 'un." Paul's "I've Just Seen A Face" is an "up-tempo shuffler, with a sort of chugging, railroad rhythm, which gives a suggestion of c-and-w." The song has a "resonant guitar interlude." Paul's sorrowful ballad "Yesterday" is the only slow song on the album. Paul accompanies himself on guitar backed by a string quartet. Paul's "rendition is sincere and meaningful, and in total contrast from his frenzied screaming on the flip of the group's new single ['I'm Down']." The old Larry Williams specialty "Dizzy Miss Lizzy" [issued on Specialty Records In the U.S.] closes the LP. "John semi-shouts this raving rocker, aided by strident raucous twangs from George, and Ringo almost going berserk!" Johnson concludes that the album is "a must for every collector," adding that *Help!* "maintains the Beatles' usual high standard–and although apart from 'Yesterday' it's largely the mixture as before, it's a mixture renowned for its tonic properties."

Record Mirror wrote that the new Beatles album "could easily be titled 'The Many Moods Of The Beatles'" as the disc's 14 tracks include "ballads, rock and roll, folk, country and western and a helping of straight pop." The magazine admonishes those unacquainted with the album's opening track "Help!": "If anyone isn't familiar with it by now they'd better have a good reason why not." Paul's lead vocal on "The Night Before" is described as "slightly rusty." The medium-fast number has George and John singing on the chorus and "a short bluesy guitar break." John is in a "very folksy mood" for "You've Got To Hide Your Love Away," a sad, slow number with strumming guitars and tambourine throughout. The flutes at the end of the song "add to the sombre effect." George makes a rare vocal appearance on "I Need You," but fails to impress the magazine: "The cha cha rhythm carries the song along, but it is not outstanding." Paul's voice is mellower on "Another Girl," which has "some good guitar phrases and an insistent beat combined with the guitars to keep the pace going," making it "good for Mod dances." John sings lead on "You're Going To Lose That Girl" with Paul and George "repeating phrases in the background." The mid-tempo number has a short guitar break over the chorus and ever present bongos from Ringo. The Side One closer, "Ticket To Ride," still sounds "great as ever."

Ringo sings lead on "Act Naturally," a country style song penned by Morrison and Russell "about a lad who's going to make it big in the movies by just acting himself." John's "It's Only Love" is another "slow weepie" with "wistful guitar from George adding to the melodrama." John's "almost in tears and you can almost imagine the wet hankies clutched in female paws as they listen to this." George's "You Like Me Too Much" opens with "barrelhouse piano" and "develops into a bright, gentle beater with John on electric piano and Paul and George Martin on Steinways." Its chorus is "faster and aided by a tambourine." "Tell Me What You See" is a medium tempo "softish number" with a vocal duet from John and Paul and two short piano breaks from Paul. "I've Just Seen A Face" is "very fast with prominent drums" and a slight country western flavor. Paul's vocal has "snatches of scat-type singing." Paul sings and plays guitar on "Yesterday," a "slow sombre and painful song" with a string quartet that lends a "mournful quality as Paul tells how he lost his love the day before and is very, very hurt and alone." It is the favorite track of the reviewer, who adds: "Hankies out again, girls." The album's closer, Larry Williams' "Dizzy Miss Lizzy," is described as "Rockarama!" The track opens with a "screaming guitar and crashing drums [that] lead into John's raucous voice" belting out the lyrics. The song's guitar break "involves occasional vocal encouragement from John who gets even wilder as the song progresses."

Disc called the Beatles fifth LP their best yet. As for the ten new Lennon-McCartney songs, the magazine wrote: "The Beatles balladers' gift for melody and lyrics show no sings of flagging. These new ones are quite brilliant, and do not fall into any monotonous rut of similarity." Disc did not comment of the title track "Help!" apparently believing that its readers were quite familiar with the Beatles current hit single. "The Night Before," starring Paul vocally backed by George and John, is a "sad ditty about a girl who changes her mind, and the bloke wishes things could go back to the night before it all finished." Disc adds that George solos well and John plays electric piano. John's "You've Got To Hide Your Love Away" is "an excellent folky kick somewhat a-la Jackie DeShannon" with Ringo belting a tambourine. In addition, "some flutes come in." George takes the lead on his composition "I Need You" backed by John and Paul. The medium tempo track is a "good simple, melodic piece" with "some cha cha cha-type drumming from Ringo." "Another Girl" is a "medium bouncer" with Paul on lead vocal backed by John and George. Paul also plays the guitar solo. "You're Going To Lose That Girl," with John on the vocal lead backed by Paul and George, has a "Latin-tinged beat, and more nice George guitar work." As for "Ticket To Ride," the song "needs no more introduction now than 'Help' except to remind you that John is leading vocally, backed by Paul, who also takes the guitar break."

"Act Naturally" is Ringo's big vocal moment. It is a non-Beatle song "in Country and Western humorous vein, and tells how the chap singing became the biggest fool in movie stardom merely by acting naturally." Paul sings back up, and George adds "some good guitar fill-ins." "It's Only Love" is a "vocal showpiece for John," with "some well-organized double tracking." George's second composition, "You Like Me Too Much," has him on vocal lead backed by Paul. It is about "a girl liking a boy so much that he won't leave her." The track's most interesting instrumental feature is John on electric piano. Ringo [actually John] plays tambourine. "Tell Me What You See" has John on lead vocal backed by Paul, who plays electric piano. The medium tempo track has "some exotic percussion flavouring." Paul sings solo on "I've Just Seen A Face," which has "some more tasty Harrison guitar." The song has "a deceptive introduction resembling South American harp music, and then unexpectedly breaks into a swinging up-tempo." "Yesterday" is a "vocal vehicle for Paul," who also plays guitar. "Dizzy Miss Lizzy," another non-Beatles song, is a "suitable climax to a magnificent set" with John taking "the vocal spotlight over a powerfully rocking beat laid down by Ringo." The July 31 Disc added that the *Help!* LP "proves beyond doubt that the boys are losing none of their touch for either writing songs or singing."

Chris Welch described *Help!* as brilliant in his Melody Maker review, adding that the group had "written a whole new crop of unique, memorable songs, performed with the Beatles' painless soul" and observing that they "don't sound as if it hurts to sing with feeling." The title track "Help!" is a "microcosm of their style–plenty of chords, unexpected twists and wry lyrics." "The Night Before" features Paul with John "comping" on electric piano. "You've Got To Hide Your Love Away" is "a tribute to Bob Dylan" with flutes and tambourine and one of the album's best. Welch wonders: "Was Dylan on the session?" "I Need You" features George on lead vocal and has "an almost Searchers feel." "Another Girl" features Paul with "some great backing harmonies." John's "You're Going To Lose That Girl" is a "tremendous song" that "proves the Beatles are still involved in their music." While Welch thought that the "Ticket To Ride" single sounded a bit slow, he states that on the album track "you can hear the bass line better and the rhythm makes more sense." [Perhaps Welch heard the stereo LP for his review.] Ringo sings "Act Naturally," one of the tracks not written by Lennon-McCartney. It is the "only number that sounds as though it comes from a film." John sings solo on "It's Only Love." "You Like Me Too Much" is "another knock-out track," sung by George backed by John on electric piano, and George Martin and Paul on piano. "Tell Me What You See" also has electric piano. It ends with a "traumatic 'oh' from all Beatles present." "I've Just Seen A Face" is "an oddity sung at high speeds by Paul, with some folky 12-string from our George." Welch writes that "Yesterday" is "unbelievable" and the best track on the album. It is sung by Paul and played by a string quartet. He predicts that the song will become "a giant standard." He finds that "Dizzy Miss Lizzy" is strangely "a bit of a let down after 'Yesterday.'" The track is "just straight rock n' roll and sounds a bit unconvincing." Welch concludes his review on a positive note: "There's something of the medieval minstrels in the Beatles. One imagines them performing beneath some bird's window. They communicate." In the August 7 edition of Melody Maker, Ringo spoke fondly of the new album: "It's far and away the best we've made, has a lot of variety."

The *Help!* LP had advance orders of 250,000 units. It debuted in Record Retailer on August 12 at number one, where it remained for nine weeks before dropping behind *The Sound Of Music* soundtrack, charting for 37 weeks, including 25 in the top five. It also debuted at number one in Melody Maker and NME, holding down the top spot for 15 weeks during its 28-week run in Melody Maker and for 11 weeks during its 26-week run in NME, where it also spent four weeks on the singles chart, peaking at 23. Disc charted the album on its singles chart for five weeks, with a peak at 17.

In the October 22 NME, Paul talked to Chris Hutchins about "Yesterday." That week Matt Monro's recording of the song was number 11 on the magazine's singles chart. [It would peak at number six.] Paul told Hutchins: "I'm always pleased when somebody has a hit with one of our songs–it's almost as good as us doing it. One or two people thought we should have put 'Yesterday' out as the title track of an EP, but of course, it's too late now. So good luck to Matty!"

But in the music business, it's never too late if a record company believes there will be demand for a disc. Seven months after the release of the *Help!* album, EMI issued its *Yesterday* EP on March 4, 1966. Allen Evans provided the following review in the March 28 NME: "title this EP 'Yesterday,' with Paul singing it so wistfully. They add Act Naturally (Ringo), You Like Me Too Much, and It's Only Love–all winners!" With George and John each singing lead on one of the Side Two tracks, the EP gave each Beatle a vocal spotlight. While all songs were winners, gone were the days when an EP containing no new material could enter the singles chart and earn a silver disc with sales in excess of 250,000 units. The *Yesterday* EP entered the Record Retailer EP chart on March 10 at number seven. Two weeks later it replaced *The Beatles' Million Sellers* at the top of the EP chart, where it remained for eight straight weeks. The disc charted for 13 weeks. As will be seen in the following chapter, Capitol's "Yesterday" single sold significantly more copies than the EP.

Billboard HOT 10[0]

For Week…

★ STAR performer—Sides registering greatest proportionate upward progress this week.

Record Indu[stry] … of certifica[tion] …

This Week	1 Wk. Ago	2 Wks. Ago	3 Wks. Ago	TITLE Artist, Label & Number	Weeks On Chart
1	1	2	5	I FEEL FINE — Beatles, Capitol 5327	5
2	2	1	4	COME SEE ABOUT ME — Supremes, Motown 1068	8
3	3	3	1	MR. LONELY — Bobby Vinton, Epic 9730	10
4	4	14	29	SHE'S A WOMAN — Beatles, Capitol 5327	5
5	11	30	49	LOVE POTION NUMBER NINE — Searchers, Kapp Winner's Circle 27	6
6	6	7	14	GOIN' OUT OF MY HEAD — Little Anthony & the Imperials, DCP 1119	9
7	5	4	2	SHE'S NOT THERE — Zombies, Parrot 9695	12
8	12	24	30	AMEN — Impressions, ABC-Paramount 10602	7
9	9	12	21	THE JERK — Larks, Money 106	8
10	14	17	26	THE WEDDING — Julie Rogers, Mercury 72332	7
11	7	5	3	RINGO — Lorne Greene, RCA Victor 8444	10
12	41	87	—	DOWNTOWN — Petula Clark, Warner Bros. 5494	3
13	13	16	17	SHA LA LA — Manfred Mann, Ascot 2165	8
14	34	60	77	YOU'VE LOST THAT LOVIN' FEELIN' — Righteous Brothers, Philles 124	4
15	23	39	44	KEEP SEARCHIN' — Del Shannon, Amy 915	7
16	21	25	28	MY LOVE FORGIVE ME (Amore, Scusami) — Robert Goulet, Columbia 43131	11
17	19	19	24	ANY WAY YOU WANT IT — Dave Clark Five, Epic 9739	8
18	24	28	36	WILLOW WEEP FOR ME — Chad & Jeremy, World Artists 1034	8
19	27	34	40	HOW SWEET IT IS (To Be Loved by You) — Marvin Gaye, Tamla 54107	7
20	10	6	6	TIME IS ON MY SIDE — Rolling Stones, London 9708	12
21	17	13	13	I'M INTO SOMETHING GOOD — Herman's Hermits, MGM 13280	12
22	8	8	10	DANCE, DANCE, DANCE — Beach Boys, Capitol 5306	9
23	28	33	58	LEADER OF THE L…	
24	25	26	27	OH N…	
25	32	35			
26	26				
33	37	48	53	DEAR HEART — Jack Jones, Kapp 635	6
34	35	40	43	ONE MORE TIME — Ray Charles Singers, Command 4057	8
35	31	31	33	SHE UNDERSTANDS ME — Johnny Tillotson, MGM 13284	10
36	38	32	23	WALKING IN THE RAIN — Ronettes, Philles 123	11
37	40	45	55	WALK AWAY — Matt Monro, Liberty 55745	6
38	39	41	51	WILD ONE — Martha & the Vandellas, Gordy 7036	5
39	43	46	54	DO-WACKA-DO — Roger Miller, Smash 1947	6
40	59	75	—	HOLD WHAT YOU'VE GOT — Joe Tex, Dial 4001	3
41	51	63	81	I'LL BE THERE — Gerry & the Pacemakers, Laurie 3279	4
42	45	50	74	SMILE — Betty Everett & Jerry Butler, Vee Jay 633	5
43	46	56	56	MY LOVE (Roses Are Red) — "You Know Who" Group, 4 Corners 113	6
44	18	10	7	YOU REALLY GOT ME — Kinks, Reprise 0306	15
45	55	65	89	PROMISED LAND — Chuck Berry, Chess 1916	4
46	48	51	59	WHAT NOW — Gene Chandler, Constellation 141	5
47	57	64	70	YOU'RE NOBODY TILL SOMEBODY LOVES YOU — Dean Martin, Reprise 0333	4
48	49	55	67	BOOM BOOM — Animals, MGM 13298	5
49	52	58	69	HAWAII TATTOO — Waikikis, Kapp Winner's Circle 30	5
50	60	73	90	THE NAME GAME — Shirley Ellis, Congress 230	4
51	53	53	57	THE 81 — Candy & the Kisses, Cameo 336	7
52	54	54	65	(There's) ALWAYS SOMETHING THERE TO REMIND ME — Sandie Shaw, Reprise 0320	6
53	47	47	47	SINCE I DON'T HAVE YOU — Chuck Jackson, Wand 169	8
54	69	—	—	ALL DAY AND ALL OF THE NIGHT — Kinks, Reprise 0334	2
55	63	78	—	SEVEN LETTERS — Ben E. King, Atco 6328	3
56	58	59	63	I'M GONNA LOVE YOU TOO — Hullabaloos, Roulette 4587	6
57	83	—	—	GIVE HIM A GREAT BIG KISS — Shangri-Las, Red …	
			85	MAKIN' WHOOPE[E] — Ray Ch…	
				…IN' PI…	
67					
68					
69					
70					
71					
72					
73					
74					
75					
76					

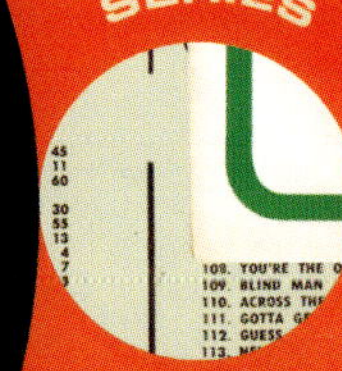

Beatles For Sale in America in 1965

The second year of Beatlemania in America wasn't quite as explosive as Year One, but was still quite remarkable. The January 2, 1965 Billboard Hot 100 had the Beatles "I Feel Fine" at number one for its second of three weeks at the top. The single's flip side, "She's A Woman," was at number four. "I Feel Fine" had debuted at number 22 on December 5, 1964, working its way to the number one slot on December 26, replacing the Supremes' "Come See About Me." The new Beatles single spent a total of seven weeks in the top five during its eleven weeks on the charts. Billboard charted "She's A Woman" for nine weeks with a peak at number four.

Cash Box and Record World charted "I Feel Fine" for 12 weeks, with Cash Box reporting the song at number one for four weeks, while Record World had it at the top for two weeks. The magazines each charted the flip side for ten weeks, with Cash Box showing a peak at eight and Record World at seven. The single had advance orders of 750,000 and was certified gold by the RIAA on December 31, 1964, signifying sales of one million units.

The January 2 Billboard Hot 100 reflected how the Beatles had opened the floodgates for the British invasion. Half of the songs in the top twenty were by artists from the U.K., including the Searchers' "Love Potion Number Nine" (#5, originally recorded by the Clovers), the Zombies' "She's Not There" (#7), Julie Rogers' "The Wedding" (#10), Petula Clark's "Downtown" (#12), Manfred Mann's "Sha La La" (#13, originally recorded by the Shirelles), the Dave Clark Five's "Any Way You Want It" (#17), Chad & Jeremy's "Willow Weep For Me" (#18, an American standard from the 1930s) and the Rolling Stones' "Time Is On My Side" (#20, based on the recording by New Orleans R&B singer Irma Thomas). Other songs in the top twenty included the Supremes' "Come See About Me" (#2), Bobby Vinton's "Mr. Lonely" (#3), Little Anthony & the Imperials' "Goin' Out Of My Head" (#6), the Impressions' "Amen" (#8), the Larks' "The Jerk" (#9), Lorne Greene's "Ringo" (#11, a western song with no relation to the Beatles drummer), the Righteous Brothers "You've Lost That Lovin' Feelin'" (#14), Del Shannon's "Keep Searchin'" (#15), Robert Goulet's "My Love Forgive Me" (#16) and Marvin Gaye's "How Sweet It Is (To Be Loved By You)" (#19).

The following week the January 9 Billboard Top LP's chart had the latest Beatles album, *Beatles '65*, at number one in just its second week on the charts (having debuted at 98). The group also held down the sixth and seventh spots with the soundtrack LP for *A Hard Day's Night* and the double-disc documentary *The Beatles' Story*. Other Beatles albums on the chart included *Something New* (#13), *Meet The Beatles!* (#69 in its 50th week), *The Beatles' Second Album* (#70 in its 38th week), *Songs, Pictures And Stories Of The Fabulous Beatles* (#138) and *Introducing The Beatles* (#146 in its 49th week). The non-Beatles albums in the top ten were the soundtrack to the Elvis Presley film *Roustabout* (#2), the Supremes' *Where Did Our Love Go* (#3), the soundtrack to *Mary Poppins* (#4), *The Beach Boys Concert* (#5), The Rolling Stones' *12 x 5* (#8), the soundtrack to *My Fair Lady* (#9) and Barbra Streisand's *People* (#10).

Americans began hearing "I Feel Fine" and "She's A Woman" in November 1964, with some radio stations broadcasting the new Beatles single significantly ahead of its November 23 release. Los Angeles' KRLA began airing the songs on an hourly basis after disc jockey Dave Hull obtained a copy of the record on Friday, November 6, from an employee at the Capitol Records L.A. pressing plant. On November 10, KFWB in Los Angeles purchased a copy of the single from a record store that had accidentally been sent a 25-count box of the disc, and became the second station to play the songs. That evening, KFWB disc jockey Sam Riddle played the record on his Ninth St. West local TV show. It was dubbed off the TV by the program director of San Bernardino's KFXM, giving that station the songs. With the record no longer being exclusive, KRLA provided dubs of the songs to stations in Fresno and Phoenix. KRLA received calls from stations in Florida, New York, St. Louis, Denver and Cleveland offering cash (up to $1,000) for copies of the songs. Pittsburgh's KQV obtained a copy of the single on November 11. The songs were then played on KQV and sister station WABC in New York. The latter station made the new single the cornerstone of its "Beatles Week" promotion, with both songs containing multiple voiceovers by DJ Dan Ingram such as "You heard it first on W-A-Beatle-C" and "First and exclusive on WABC!" On November 13, Capitol sent the single to stations by air mail.

Cash Box's Radio Active Chart indicated that as of November 25, 66% of its reporting stations had added "I Feel Fine" to their play lists. A week later, this had grown to 96%. Stations were also playing the B-side, "She's A Woman," with 33% adding the song to their play lists by November 25, with the number growing to 78% the following week.

I FEEL FINE

(John Lennon-Paul McCartney)

Maclen Music, Inc.
BMI-2:20
5327
(45-X45085)
Recorded in England

THE BEATLES

MFD. BY CAPITOL RECORDS, INC., U.S.A. • T.M. Capitol MARCA REG.

SHE'S A WOMAN

(John Lennon-Paul McCartney)

Maclen Music, Inc.
BMI-2:57
5327
(45-X45086)
Recorded in England

THE BEATLES

MFD. BY CAPITOL RECORDS, INC., U.S.A. • T.M. Capitol MARCA REG.

New for Christmas!

THE GREATEST PROFIT PACKAGE IN HISTORY

You're going to get a rush like you've never known before on these! Don't be caught short this year! Order your FULL requirements now!

Backed with special window streamers and eye-catching counter-holders! On-the-air promotion on more than 100 top 40 major stations. STBO 2222

CAPITOL FULL DIMENSIONAL STEREO

THE BEATLES' STORY

A NARRATIVE AND MUSICAL BIOGRAPHY OF BEATLEMANIA ON 2 LONG-PLAY RECORDS

includes
SELECTIONS FROM THEIR HIT RECORDS
INTERVIEWS WITH THE BEATLES AND THEIR FANS
MANY NEW PHOTOS
THEIR WHOLE STORY ON RECORD . . . FROM BEGINNING TO FABULOUS FAME!

HIGH FIDELITY

NEW SINGLE!
Their next Number One! 5327

THE BEATLES
I FEEL FINE
SHE'S A WOMAN

PLUS THESE CONTINUING BEST-SELLING ALBUMS

ST 2047 ST 2080 ST 2108

THE BIG 5 FOR CHRISTMAS THIS YEAR!

The music trade magazines reviewed the new Beatles single in their November 28 issues. Billboard noted that the "Boys will re-enter the chart quickly with both sides," calling the record a "gift to Capitol on the group's first anniversary with the label." Cash Box confidently predicted that "England's wonder quartet" would "delight their American fans with both sides of their latest [disc]." "I Feel Fine" was "imbued with a colorful, almost blues-based approach," but was the Beatles "styling all-the-way." "She's A Woman" also borrowed from the "blues idiom." The magazine concluded: "Looks to be a two-for-the-money issue." Record World observed: "Skeptics have been wondering how long it will last. The answer is: as long as The Beatles know what to do with their talent." "I Feel Fine" showcased the group's "inimitable style," while "She's A Woman" featured a "new and much bluesier beat." Record World predicted that "I Feel Fine" would "take off," but "She's A Woman" would also get much attention.

As detailed above, the trade magazines' forecasts for the new Beatles single were spot on. "I Feel Fine" had an infectious guitar riff and exhilarating drumming (both borrowed from Bobby Parker's "Watch Your Step") and tight backing vocals behind John's lead. "She's A Woman" also excited fans with Paul's powerful blues vocal over a stripped down beat carried out on guitar, bass and drums, with piano filling in the cracks in the background.

Unlike Beatles fans in the United Kingdom who had several music weeklies to keep them informed on the group's upcoming releases, Americans in 1965 were, for the most part, left in the dark until hearing the latest Beatles songs on the radio. In the States, nationally distributed rock 'n' roll magazines would not appear until later with Crawdaddy! (1966), Rolling Stone (1967) and Creem (1969). Those who took the initiative could sometimes learn about upcoming Beatles releases by thumbing through the music industry trade magazines at local record stores.

The November 28 Billboard reported that Capitol would be releasing the album *Beatles '65* the day after Christmas (actually December 28). The LP, "produced" by Capitol's Dave Dexter, would feature seven new Lennon-McCartney tunes. Dexter indicated that the LP would not be identical to the group's British album as the Capitol disc would contain the group's latest single, "I Feel Fine" and "She's A Woman." Dexter added that the Beatles were immune to weakening sales because they were the "first moptops" and had "captured the 'hearts' of teen-agers."

The Billboard article is interesting for several reasons. Although releasing a record shortly after Christmas was unconventional, Capitol had done the same the previous year with the Beatles single "I Want To Hold Your Hand." In addition, Dexter was taking credit for producing the album even though all he was doing was selecting the songs to place on the disc. Word was also getting out that Capitol's Beatles albums differed from the British releases.

Some radio stations, including New York's WABC, obtained copies of the British LP *Beatles For Sale* and began playing tracks from the album in early December. The station's December 1 album cuts play list included 10 tracks from the LP. Looking back, it is surprising that the list included "Mr. Moonlight," which later became one of the few Beatles songs often maligned by critics and fans, and did not include the two songs that Capitol would later issue as a single from the disc, "Eight Days A Week" and "I Don't Want To Spoil The Party." The December 12 Cash Box reported that "some American jockeys, proclaiming 'exclusive,' were playing the British album or tapes of the album despite the fact that most of the songs had not been cleared by BMI for stateside airing." Although playing the non-cleared songs infringed on BMI licenses and made stations liable for penalties, BMI decided not to go after the stations. Cash Box speculated that this might cause Capitol to push up the release date of *Beatles '65*. That same week Billboard reported that WABC, Pittsburgh's KQV and Atlanta's WQXI were playing tracks from the British LP.

As indicated by its December 8 playlist, WABC continued playing cuts from *Beatles For Sale*. By this time, WABC also had obtained a copy of *Beatles '65*, as evidenced by its broadcast of "I'll Be Back," which was not on *Beatles For Sale*, but was on the Capitol disc. (The song first appeared on the U.K. version of the *A Hard Day's Night* LP, but had yet to be issued in America.) WABC continued playing songs from these Beatles albums through March 1965.

Cash Box reported in its December 19 issue that the album *Beatles '65* was getting an advance rush release "due to demand created by 'wildcat' airplay on U.S. stations" of the British disc. Although Capitol didn't begin taking orders until December 9, advance orders exceeded 750,000 units. Capitol A&R Vice-President Voyle Gilmore expected sales to pass the million mark within a few days of the album hitting the stores. By subcontracting with Columbia, RCA and Decca to supplement its Scranton and L.A. pressing plants, Capitol was able to release *Beatles '65* on December 15.

By the time *Beatles '65* hit the stores, Americans in some cities had been hearing songs from *Beatles For Sale* for two weeks. In addition, many U.S. fans had seen the Beatles perform two of the British album's tracks on television over two months earlier.

On October 7, 1964, the Beatles headlined a special British edition of the American pop music variety show, Shindig! The show was in its first season, having debuted on the ABC television network on Wednesday, September 16. The program featuring the Beatles was taped at Granville Studio (a converted theater built in 1898) in Walham Green, London with members of the Beatles Fan Club in attendance. Billy Shepherd reported on the October 3 taping of the show in the November 1964 edition of The Beatles Book (No. 16). Prior to its start, while the engineers were checking the sound balancing, John strummed his acoustic guitar and sang a bit of "The House Of The Rising Sun," startling those in attendance when he roared out the word "down" at the top of his voice towards the end of the second verse. Shepherd called it a "good, brash show, with the Beatles turning in a marvelous act." Other performers included Scottish singer Karl Denver ("Wimoweh" and "Old Folks At Home"), Liverpool pop/jazz singer Lyn Cornell ("Fever"), Tommy Quickly ("Stagger Lee"), Sandie Shaw ("(There's) Always Something There To Remind Me"), the instrumental band Sounds Incorporated ("Whale Out On The Drums") and P.J. Proby ("You'll Never Walk Alone" and "Hold Me"). Although TV Guide indicated that Cilla Black would be performing the Lennon-McCartney tune "It's For You," she was not on the show. Tommy Quickly, Sounds Incorporated and Cilla Black were managed by Brian Epstein.

The Beatles opened the program with Paul singing Little Richard's arrangement of "Kansas City," which the Beatles would soon record at EMI Studios on October 18, 1964. The song, once an integral part of their stage show, had been previously performed for the BBC in July 1963 and May 1964. When it was over, host Jim O'Neill informed the audience that the Beatles would "be back later with some songs they've never sung on television before, including one which John Lennon and Paul McCartney have just written and has never been heard anywhere until tonight." The Beatles returned with "I'm A Loser," which, at the time, was a leading candidate to be the group's next single. Despite the song's somewhat somber lyrics, John smiled and sang his way through the number, playing acoustic guitar and harmonica, which was on a neck holder. The Beatles third and final performance had Ringo singing "Boys."

YEAH, YEAH, WE'VE GOT IT

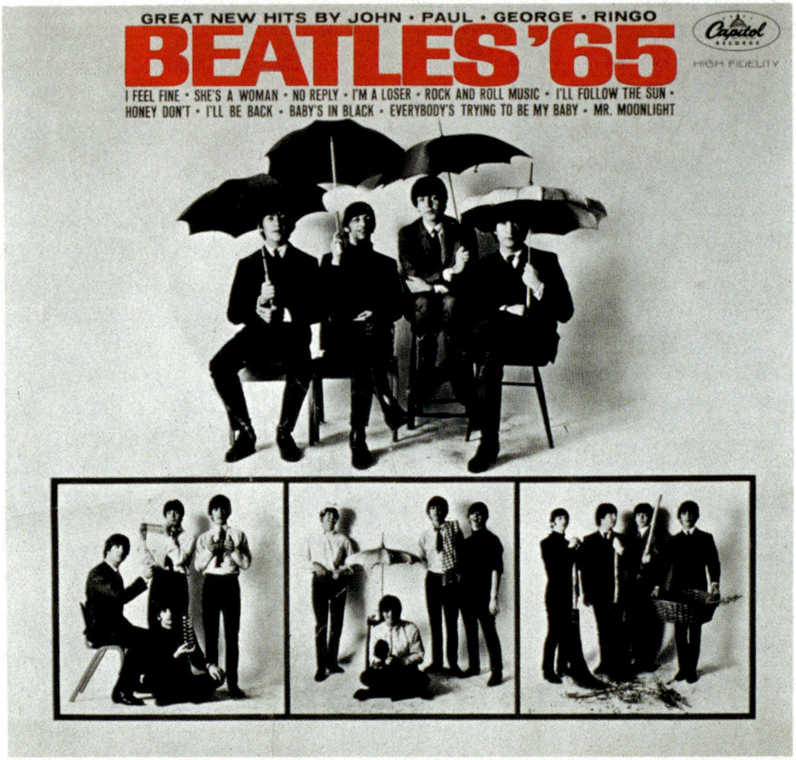

GREAT NEW HITS BY JOHN • PAUL • GEORGE • RINGO

BEATLES '65

Capitol RECORDS

HIGH FIDELITY

I FEEL FINE • SHE'S A WOMAN • NO REPLY • I'M A LOSER • ROCK AND ROLL MUSIC • I'LL FOLLOW THE SUN • HONEY DON'T • I'LL BE BACK • BABY'S IN BLACK • EVERYBODY'S TRYING TO BE MY BABY • MR. MOONLIGHT

AND WE HAVE THE GIFT-OF-THE-YEAR, TOO

BOTH ON

The Capitol album *Beatles '65* was compiled by Dave Dexter, who effectively made the Capitol disc a sort-of *Beatles For Sale*, Part One. The changes were brought on by Capitol's well-founded belief that hit singles make hit albums (thus necessitating the inclusion of "I Feel Fine" and "She's A Woman") and its economic decision to limit its albums to the U.S. standard of 11 or 12 tracks instead of the British norm of 14. (In the U.K., song publishing royalties were computed on a per disc basis, with the publishers receiving their proportionate share of the total royalty paid per disc, whereas in the U.S., royalties were on a per song basis, meaning each additional song was an added cost.)

In programming *Beatles '65*, Dexter placed the first six (of seven) songs from Side One of the British LP on Side One of the Capitol disc in the same order: "No Reply," "I'm A Loser" (first heard on Shindig!), "Baby's In Black," "Rock And Roll Music," "I'll Follow The Sun" and "Mr. Moonlight." Side Two has both sides of the latest single, two Carl Perkins songs and "I'll Be Back" (a leftover in Capitol's Beatles inventory) in the following order: "Honey Don't," "I'll Be Back," "She's A Woman," "I Feel Fine" and "Everybody's Trying To Be My Baby." *Beatles '65* is an enjoyable listening experience, giving fans most of the first side of *Beatles For Sale* plus both sides of the group's current hit single.

Beatles '65 entered the Billboard Top LP's chart at number 98 on January 2, 1965. The next week the album soared to number one, replacing Elvis Presley's *Roustabout* soundtrack LP at the top. This was the biggest single-week LP chart advance in the magazine's history. *Beatles '65* stayed at number one for nine weeks before falling to three behind the soundtracks to *Mary Poppins* and the latest James Bond film, *Goldfinger*. The Beatles LP spent 71 weeks on the 150-position chart, including 16 in the top ten. The December 26, 1964 Cash Box debuted *Beatles '65* at number 48 in its Top 100 Albums Monaural chart and at 22 in its Top 50 Stereo chart. On January 2, 1965, it topped both the Monaural and Stereo charts. The next week Cash Box switched back to a single album chart. The magazine charted *Beatles '65* for 37 weeks, including eight at the top. Record World reported the LP for 35 weeks, with seven at number one. *Beatles '65* was certified gold by the RIAA on December 31, 1964. In 1996, Capitol submitted sales records for several of its Beatles albums to the RIAA, which certified sales of three million for *Beatles '65* on January 10, 1997.

The music trade magazines reviewed the album in their December 26 issues. Billboard stated that the "Beatles should have no difficulty in continuing in their outrageously successful money-making ways with this fifth album outing featuring the famous foursome reading a bevy of their recent vintage single hits and other favorites." The magazine mentioned both sides of the current hit single and "I'm A Loser." Billboard predicted that the "Package should sell straight through the holiday season into the new year." Cash Box noted that: "1964 proved to be the year of the Beatles! No flash-in-the-pan act, John, Paul, George and Ringo are now part of history." The review referred to their current smash single and a "wild version" of Chuck Berry's "Rock And Roll Music." Cash Box correctly predicted that *Beatles '65* was "destined for the No. 1 spot in the U.S."

Capitol went all out in creating point of purchase counter displays to promote the Beatles new LP. The company's unique *Beatles '65* carousel display (shown next page) put a new spin on the Capitol album catalog. Heat from two light bulbs (as shown in its instructions) rotated a lampshade to illuminate all five Beatles album covers as they passed through the front window of the display. Consumers were instructed to see, hear, love and, of course, buy the Capitol blockbuster albums. Capitol also created a 20" x 20" cardboard display with an enlargement of the album cover. The bottom three boxed photos and the umbrellas projected outward for a three-dimensional effect.

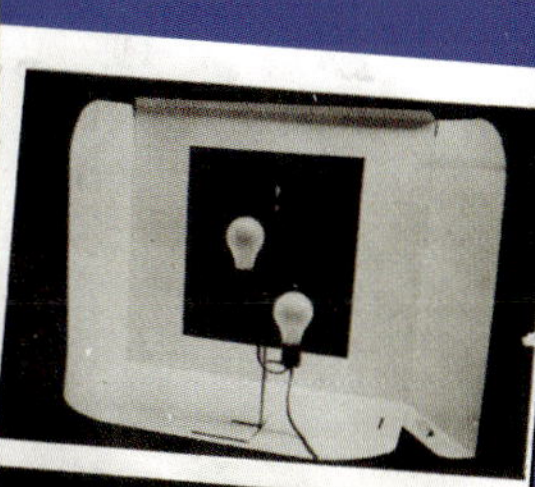

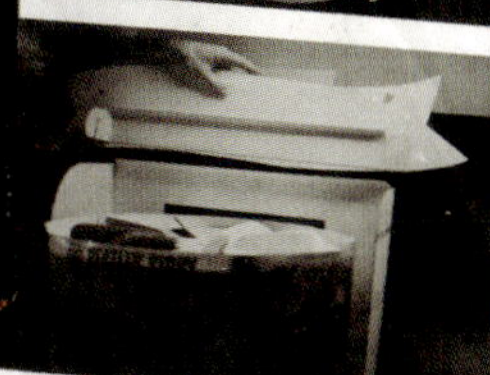

FOLD BACK LUGS AND INSERT INTO SLOTS PROVIDED AT THE TOP OF EACH SIDE OF THE BASE UNIT.

4. COMPLETE CAPITOL RECORDS BEATLES HEAT CYLINDER DISPLAY.

Capitol planned on issuing a disc featuring four tracks from *Beatles '65* on February 1; however, it was rush-released a week or so earlier as part of Capitol's short-lived series of super singles under the label's "4-By" moniker. (The other discs were *4-By The Beach Boys*, issued in September 1964, and *4-By Buck Owens*, released in June 1965. A fourth 4-By disc set for August 1965 was canceled.) The idea was to place four songs by a single artist, principally in the teen-age field, on a 45-RPM disc to be merchandised and sold as a single rather than an EP. The inspiration behind the "4-By" series was the success of Capitol's first Beatles EP, *Four By The Beatles*, which sold like a mildly successful single when released in May 1964, peaking at 92 in Billboard, 86 in Cash Box and 97 in Record World.

The *4-By The Beatles* disc, which featured "Honey Don't" and "I'm A Loser" on one side and "Mr. Moonlight" and "Everybody's Trying To Be My Baby" on the other, was marketed by Capitol as "The Best of Beatles '65!" (although "I'm A Loser" was the only song written by John Lennon and Paul McCartney included on the EP). The disc was issued in a hard cardboard full-color jacket featuring the primary photo from *Beatles '65* on both sides. Capitol ran full-page ads for the record in Cash Box and Record World, but for reasons unknown skipped Billboard.

The disc entered the Billboard Hot 100 on February 27, 1965, at number 81 and peaked at 68 during its fifth and final week on the charts. Cash Box charted the record for four weeks, also with a peak of 68. Record World charted the EP for five weeks, with a peak of 67. The record was deleted from the Capitol catalog on December 31, 1965, less than a year after its release.

Cash Box reviewed the disc in its January 30 issue, alerting readers that "The English sensations" were "back on the wax scene with a 'Four By...' session that the label markets at a singles price...on what looks like a 4-tune monster." The magazine listed and described the songs as: "Honey Don't" (a "driving rock-a-rhythmic blueser"), "I'm A Loser" (a "heavy, steady beat weeper"), "Mr. Moonlight" (a "tantalizing toe-tapper romantic" tune) and "Everybody's Trying To Be My Baby" (an "all-dance delight"). Cash Box concluded that "Each one of these rock-a-billy-slanted [tunes] can come thru in a big way." The January 30 Record World kept it short and sweet, listing the four tunes by the quartet and asking, "'Nuff said?" (possibly in a nod to Stan Lee's catch phrase frequently appearing in Marvel Comics).

ANOTHER GREAT BEATLES 4-BY IN HARDBACK COVER!

1. Honey Don't 2. I'm a Loser b/w 1. Mr. Moonlight 2. Everybody's Trying to be My Baby

THE BEST OF "BEATLES '65"! R-5365

Capitol's habit of turning one British Beatles album into two American Beatles albums also gave the label the opportunity to issue twice as many "new" singles as those released in England. The reconfiguration of Parlophone's *Beatles For Sale* is a classic example of Capitol's two-for-one marketing strategy. In compiling *Beatles '65*, Capitol used only eight of the fourteen songs from *Beatles For Sale*, leaving six songs to form the foundation of its next Beatles album. Of the songs initially withheld from the American market, "Eight Days A Week" and "I Don't Want To Spoil The Party" appeared on a 45 issued between the worldwide releases of "I Feel Fine" and the next U.K. single.

The decision to withhold "Eight Days A Week" from *Beatles '65* for release as a single was a wise one. Released on February 15, the song entered the Billboard Hot 100 at number 53 on February 20. Three weeks later, on March 13, the song replaced the Temptations' "My Girl" at the number one spot, which it held for two weeks before being replaced by the Supremes' "Stop! In The Name Of Love." In all, "Eight Days A Week" charted for ten weeks. Cash Box also charted the song for ten weeks, with three weeks at number one. Record World charted the song for 11 weeks, including three weeks at the top. Cash Box indicated that as of February 10, 60% of its reporting stations had added the song to their play lists. A week later, this had grown to 90%. The disc was certified gold on September 15, 1965.

Billboard charted the flip side, "I Don't Want To Spoil The Party," for six weeks with a peak of 39. Cash Box charted the song for two weeks, showing at peak of 83. Record World reported the song for five weeks, with a peak of 62.

The music trades reviewed the new Beatles single in their February 13 issues. Billboard called "Eight Days A Week" a "hand-clapping swinger and a winning follow-up to 'I Feel Fine.'" "I Don't Want To Spoil The Party" was described as a "sad folk-country-flavored tale with a good dance beat." Cash Box stated that the "famous four Liverpool lads should have no difficulty in continuing in their outrageously successful ways with this latest Capitol entry tabbed 'Eight Days A Week.'" The tune was touted as a "hard-driving, rollicking pledge of romantic devotion with a contagious repeating rockin' riff." Cash Box called the flip side a "funky, country-bluesish teen-angled tear-jerker" that also merited a close look. Record World had little to say about the songs, instead commenting on the group: "It's phenomenal. Hit after hit. More happy sounds from the Britishers who recently announced their second summer tour of the States."

TWO BRAND NEW BEATLES SONGS

EIGHT DAYS A WEEK
(John Lennon-Paul McCartney)
Capitol
RECORDS
Maclen Music, Inc.
BMI-2:43
5371
(45-X45147)
Recorded in England
THE BEATLES
MFD. BY CAPITOL RECORDS, INC., U.S.A. • T.M. Capitol MARCA REG.

AVAILABLE ONLY ON THIS CAPITOL SINGLE!

THE BEATLES
EIGHT DAYS A WEEK
I DON'T WANT TO SPOIL THE PARTY

(John Lennon-Paul McCartney)

Capitol 5371

In late March 1965, a new Capitol LP titled *The Early Beatles* began appearing in stores with little fanfare. The back cover's liner notes told the tale: "Early birds all over the United States—millions of them—got the bug for the Beatles in the first weeks of 1964. The eleven great songs in this album were among those that launched the Beatles. They appeared then on another label. They appear now for the first time on Capitol—added, with pride and pleasure, to the fine Capitol treasury of Beatles recordings which, together, constitute an unprecedented phenomenon of entertainment history." That other label was Vee-Jay Records, a Chicago-based R&B and gospel label, that ended up with the Beatles in early 1963 after several other companies, including Capitol, turned down the rights to issue the group's records in the U.S. The songs had appeared on Vee-Jay singles and the album *Introducing The Beatles*, which pulled its tracks from the Beatles first U.K. album, *Please Please Me*. Under the terms of a settlement with Capitol, Vee-Jay's rights to the Beatles terminated on October 15, 1964. Capitol released its album on March 22, 1965. By coincidence, this was exactly two years after the release of the group's first British LP on March 22, 1963.

The Early Beatles first appeared in the Billboard Top LP's listing on April 24 at number 132. It slowly worked its way up to 43, its top position, on June 12, during its 35 weeks on the chart. Cash Box reported the LP for 16 weeks with a peak at 24. The album peaked at 29 in Record World during its 14-week run. Even though the LP's chart performance was substandard for a Beatles record, it sold over one million copies as certified by the RIAA on January 10, 1997.

Cash Box provided the following assessment in its April 3 issue: "Before establishing their reputation or ties to Capitol, the Beatles came out with an LP on Vee-Jay, the selections from which have been repackaged in the new album, 'The Early Beatles.' The fabulous foursome should find plenty of replays packed into this package, though, since it contains such smashes as their 'Love Me Do,' 'Please Please Me' and 'Do You Want To Know A Secret.' The sound still has the old Beatle drawing power, and loads of teens who missed the tunes on the first go round will turn out for it now." That same week Record World observed that Capitol was "rounding up all the Beatle product for its catalog" and noted the cover's "soulful portrait." Billboard ran its review in its April 10 issue: "This package contains the first songs and recordings that started the unprecedented phenomenon known as the Beatles. Although these selections have been on the market before, this reassembling into one LP will undoubtedly prove a bonanza."

THE EARLY BEATLES

JOHN LENNON, PAUL McCARTNEY, GEORGE HARRISON and RINGO STARR

T-2309 (T-X-1-2309) 1

1. LOVE ME DO (BMI-2:19) (John Lennon-Paul McCartney)
2. TWIST AND SHOUT (BMI-2:32) (Bert Russell-Phil Medley)
3. ANNA (Go To Him) (BMI-2:56) (Arthur Alexander)
4. CHAINS (BMI-2:21) (Gerry Goffin-Carole King)
5. BOYS (BMI-2:24) (Dixon-Farrell)
6. ASK ME WHY (ASCAP-2:24) (John Lennon-Paul McCartney)

MFD. BY CAPITOL RECORDS, INC. U.S.A. T.M. Capitol • MARCA REG. • U.S. PAT. NO. 2,631,859

THE EARLY BEATLES

JOHN LENNON, PAUL McCARTNEY, GEORGE HARRISON and RINGO STARR

T-2309 (T-X-2-2309) 2

1. PLEASE PLEASE ME (ASCAP-2:00) (John Lennon-Paul McCartney)
2. P. S. I LOVE YOU (BMI-2:02) (John Lennon-Paul McCartney)
3. BABY IT'S YOU (ASCAP-2:36) (Davis-Williams-Bacharach)
4. A TASTE OF HONEY (ASCAP-2:02) (Ric Marlow)
5. DO YOU WANT TO KNOW A SECRET (BMI-1:55) (John Lennon-Paul McCartney)

MFD. BY CAPITOL RECORDS, INC. U.S.A. T.M. Capitol • MARCA REG. • U.S. PAT. NO. 2,631,859

File Under: The Beatles T 2309

The Early BEATLES

ELEVEN OF THEIR 1964 AMERICAN HIT RECORDINGS NOW ON CAPITOL

LOVE ME DO · TWIST AND SHOUT · ANNA · CHAINS · BOYS · ASK ME WHY · PLEASE PLEASE ME · P.S. I LOVE YOU · BABY IT'S YOU · DO YOU WANT TO KNOW A SECRET · A TASTE OF HONEY ·

T 2309

HIGH FIDELITY RECORDING

ALSO AVAILABLE IN STEREO

The Early BEATLES

great hits by John, George, Paul and Ringo, newly released on Capitol Records

Early birds all over the United States — millions of them — got the bug for the Beatles in the first weeks of 1964. The eleven great songs in this album were among those that launched the Beatles. They appeared then on another record label. They appear now for the first time on Capitol — added, with pride and pleasure, to the fine Capitol treasury of Beatles recordings which, together, constitute an unprecedented phenomenon of entertainment history.

side one

LOVE ME DO 2:19 BMI
TWIST AND SHOUT 2:32 BMI
ANNA 2:56 BMI
CHAINS 2:21 BMI
BOYS 2:24 BMI
ASK ME WHY 2:24 ASCAP

side two

PLEASE PLEASE ME 2:00 ASCAP
P.S. I LOVE YOU 2:02 BMI
BABY IT'S YOU 2:36 ASCAP
A TASTE OF HONEY 2:02 ASCAP
DO YOU WANT TO KNOW A SECRET 1:55 BMI
Produced by GEORGE MARTIN

MORE GREAT ALBUMS FOR YOUR BEATLES COLLECTION:

SOMETHING NEW THE BEATLES

THE BEATLES' SECOND ALBUM

THE BEATLES' STORY

MEET THE BEATLES!

BEATLES '65

THIS MONOPHONIC MICROGROOVE RECORDING IS PLAYABLE ON MONOPHONIC AND STEREO PHONOGRAPHS. IT CANNOT BECOME OBSOLETE. IT WILL CONTINUE TO BE A SOURCE OF OUTSTANDING SOUND REPRODUCTION, PROVIDING THE FINEST MONOPHONIC PERFORMANCE FROM ANY PHONOGRAPH.

TICKET TO RIDE
(John Lennon-Paul McCartney)
From the United Artists Release "Eight Arms To Hold You"
Capitol
RECORDS
Maclen
Music, Inc.
BMI-3:02
5407
(45-X45219)
Recorded
in England
THE BEATLES
MFD BY CAPITOL RECORDS INC. U.S.A. • T.M. Capitol MARCA REG.
YES IT IS
(John Lennon-Paul McCartney)
From the United Artists Release "Eight Arms To Hold You"
Capitol
RECORDS
Maclen
Music, Inc.
BMI-2:40
5407
(45-X45220)
Recorded
in England
THE BEATLES
MFD. BY CAPITOL RECORDS, INC., U.S.A. • T.M. Capitol MARCA REG.
THEY NEVER MISS
Capitol
RECORDS
NEITHER WILL JODY MILLER!
THE BEATLES
TICKET TO RIDE b/w
Yes It Is 5407
Just released in the U.S. and Britain. Both sides are from their forthcoming United Artists movie, Eight Arms To Hold You.
THE BEACH BOYS
HELP ME, RHONDA b/w
Kiss Me, Baby 5395
This could be their biggest single yet! It's the top song in their great new album, The Beach Boys Today DT 2269
JODY MILLER
QUEEN OF THE HOUSE
b/w The Greatest Actor
5402 The smash hit answer to Roger Miller's King Of The Road

"Ticket To Ride" b/w "Yes It Is" was the first Beatles single issued in 1965 for worldwide release. Capitol released the record on April 19, ten days after the British date. At that time, the working title for the Beatles second film was *Eight Arms To Hold You*. Capitol jumped the gun, adding "From The United Artists Release 'Eight Arms To Hold You'" to the labels of both sides of the disc. This was a double error for the B-side because "Yes It Is" did not appear the film.

"Ticket To Ride" entered the Billboard Hot 100 at number 59 on April 24. Two weeks later it rode to number three, where it remained for another week before moving up to the top on May 22, passing "Mrs. Brown You've Got A Lovely Daughter" by Herman's Hermits and "Count Me In" by Gary Lewis and the Playboys. A week later it was replaced by the Beach Boys' "Help Me, Rhonda." Of the song's 11 weeks on the charts, five were spent in the top five. Cash Box charted "Ticket To Ride" for 12 weeks, with one week at number one following three weeks in the second spot. Record World also charted the song at number one for one week during its 11 weeks on the charts. Cash Box indicated that as of April 7, 55% of its reporting stations had added "Ticket To Ride" to their play lists. A week later, this had grown to 95%. Although Capitol VP Voyle Gilmore indicated that "Ticket To Ride" was an apparent cinch for a gold record with nearly 750,000 units initially shipped, it was never certified gold by the RIAA.

The single's flip side, "Yes It Is," received sufficient air play to be reported separately by Billboard, appearing for four weeks in The Hot 100, peaking at number 46. Record World listed the song for four weeks, with a peak of 65. "Yes It Is" failed to make the Cash Box Top 100, but did reach the equivalent of number 107 on the Looking Ahead chart.

"Ticket To Ride" was reviewed in the April 10 trade magazines. Billboard focused on the mag's Hot 100, noting: "Just as 'Eight Days a Week' drops on the charts, up comes a slow hard driver to replace it!" "Yes It Is" was called a "well done teen ballad." Cash Box gave record stores and distributors a heads up: "The Beatles are back again and their outrageously successful reputation should be further enhanced on the basis of this power-packed newie." "Ticket To Ride" was described as a "throbbingly bittersweet, rhythmic weeper about a fella whose romance is headed for the rocks," while "Yes It Is" was a "tender, shufflin' feelingfully-essayed tale of devotion." Record World was rather blasé: "Here's another. Tunes are from the up-coming Beatles film and will ride far" (meaning up the charts).

IS HERE!

And sales will be just like "Meet the Beatles" all over again!

FOUR NEW SONGS–NEVER AVAILABLE BEFORE!
FOUR MORE NEW SONGS–NEVER AVAILABLE IN AMERICA!
THREE BEATLES CLASSICS!

New Songs:
You Like Me Too Much • Tell Me What You See
Bad Boy • Dizzy Miss Lizzie

New U. S. A.:
Kansas City • Words of Love
Every Little Thing • What You're Doing

Classics:
Eight Days a Week • Yes It Is
I Don't Want to Spoil the Party

Here's the end of your "no-traffic" blues. But don't be timid!
Make your first, second, third and fourth orders Beatles-$ize!

CALL YOUR CRDC REP–AND RIGHT NOW!

Capitol RECORDS (S) T 2358

In early May 1965, Dave Dexter began programming his *Beatles For Sale*, Part Two album. Although Capitol had issued *Beatles '65* in mid-December 1964 and an album containing songs previously issued by Vee-Jay Records, *The Early Beatles*, on March 22, 1965, Capitol believed it needed new Beatles product to maintain consumer interest. As the soundtrack album for the second Beatles film, *Help!*, was not scheduled for release until mid-August, the summer of 1965 looked bleak unless Capitol could hastily assemble and issue a new Beatles album.

Capitol's inventory of Beatles songs previously unreleased in America consisted of four tracks from Parlophone's *Beatles For Sale*, namely "Kansas City," "Words Of Love," "Every Little Thing" and "What You're Doing" (described as "New U.S.A." in the company's two-page trade advertisement shown previous page). Also available were both sides of the Capitol single "Eight Days A Week" and "I Don't Want To Spoil The Party," which had originally appeared on *Beatles For Sale*. As the group's then-current single, "Ticket To Ride," was to be featured in the upcoming film and appear on the soundtrack LP, Capitol decided against placing the song on its new album. However, the single's flip side, "Yes It Is," could be included as the song was not selected for the movie. These three songs were described in Capitol's ad as "Classics." This left Capitol four selections short of having an 11-song album. Discussions with George Martin revealed that there were two completed songs from the movie recording sessions that would not be used in the film, namely "You Like Me Too Much" and "Tell Me What You See." To help Capitol complete its album, the Beatles, who at the time were filming the Buckingham Palace scenes for *Help!* at Cliveden House in Berkshire, made a special trip to EMI Studios on the evening of May 10 to record the remaining two songs needed for the album. As time was of the essence, the group decided to play it safe with two Larry Williams rockers, "Bad Boy" and "Dizzy, Miss Lizzy" (mistitled "Dizzy Miss Lizzie" by Capitol) that had been part of the band's stage show during their formative years. After recording was completed, mono and stereo mixes were made, and tapes of the songs were sent the next day by air freight to Capitol. This gave Capitol "Four New Songs — Never Available Before!" In the May 29 Billboard, George Martin explained: "It's a long time since America had a Beatles LP. Certain numbers issued here have been left off the LPs there and with these two tracks we now have enough odd ones to make a complete LP."

In an article appearing in the June 5, 1965 Billboard, Brown Meggs, then Capitol's merchandising vice-president, stated that *Beatles VI* was created expressly for the American market and was being rush released "to stimulate dealer traffic." In its trade magazine ad, Capitol boldly proclaimed that "BEATLES VI IS HERE! And sales will be just like 'Meet the Beatles' all over again!" Retailers were told: "Here's the end of your 'no-traffic' blues. But don't be timid! Make your first, second, third and fourth orders Beatles-$ize!" Capitol was confident that sales would be brisk and initially pressed 500,000 units. The company began taking orders on June 8 and hit the half-million mark in just five days. The LP's release was set for June 14, although it may have taken a bit longer for the records to appear in stores.

Beatles VI is another of Capitol's "specially created for the American market" albums mixing tracks previously issued on British albums, singles and recordings making their world debut. Copying George Martin's tradition of opening an LP with a rocker, Capitol chose the powerful and exuberant "Kansas City" (the Little Richard version) as the lead tune. This is followed by the fade-in opening of "Eight Days A Week," the hit single anchoring the album. George is then featured on "You Like Me Too Much." The program continues with John's wild vocals on the Larry Williams' rocker "Bad Boy" and the previously released B-side "I Don't Want To Spoil The Party." The side closes with the gentle fade out humming on the group's beautiful harmony showcase performance of Buddy Holly's "Words Of Love."

Side Two kicks off with Ringo's drum intro to "What You're Doing." The song's excellent drumming, rollicking piano and effective pacing make for a strong opener. After the slow and somewhat somber "Yes It Is," John's passionate lead vocals on the roller coaster rocker "Dizzy Miss Lizzie" provide much needed relief. The album closes with "Tell Me What You See" and "Every Little Thing," two songs with upbeat love themes in sharp contrast to the lyrics of the side's first two tracks. The latter song's timpani drums and memorable ending provide an effective closing statement.

As was the case with *Beatles '65*, some radio stations were able to play tracks from *Beatles VI* well in advance of its release. In the June 9 KRLA Beat, the station bragged it had scored another world-wide first with its broadcast of the "exciting new Beatles album, 'BEATLES VI!'" The article told of how disc jockeys Dave Hull and Von Filkins entered the studio in the middle of Dick Biondi's "nightly nine-to-midnight riot act," placed the album on the turntable and insisted it be played next. KRLA listeners became the first radio audience anywhere to hear the new album. Although the station implied that the Beatles were responsible for setting up this exclusive for the KRLA deejays ("John, Paul, George and Ringo seem to have gone out of their way to provide any possible favors"), Dave Hull later revealed (in an interview with the author of this book) that he obtained advance copies of Beatles records from an employee at Capitol's Los Angeles pressing plant. KRLA Beat called the album one of their finest and noted that it provided a "good cross-section of the unique musical abilities which have made the Beatles the most popular entertainers in history." The article mentioned that two of the songs, "Dizzy Miss Lizzy" and "Bad Boy," were recorded especially for the album. They supposedly had been previously heard in some European countries in live versions from a Beatles concert in Hamburg. (An album of the 1962 Beatles Hamburg performance at the Star-Club would be issued in 1977; however, it did not contain either song.) Playlists from New York's WABC indicate that the station began broadcasting tracks from the album in late May and continued doing so throughout June.

Beatles VI sneaked into Billboard's list of the top 150 albums at number 149 on June 26. The following week it moved up over 100 places to number 48 before reaching the top on July 10 by replacing the soundtrack to *Mary Poppins* and holding off *Herman's Hermits On Tour*. *Beatles VI* spent six weeks at number one before being sandwiched at number two behind the Rolling Stones' *Out Of Our Heads* and ahead of the Beach Boys' *Summer Days (And Summer Nights!!)*. *Beatles VI* remained on the Billboard Hot LP's chart for 41 weeks. The LP also topped the Cash Box LP chart for six weeks during its 31-week run. Record World charted the album for 32 weeks, including five weeks at the top.

Record World reviewed the album in its June 12 issue, commenting: "Change of pace from song to song and, of course, fans won't be able to grab fast enough." As an added service, Capitol had identified the lead singer(s) in the liner notes, which would "take the guesswork out of it for the young-uns."

The other trades reviewed *Beatles VI* the following week. The June 19 Billboard observed: "Obvious from the album title, this is the Liverpool group's sixth LP and one to rapidly hit the top of the charts." [It was actually the Beatles sixth **Capitol** LP.] Billboard noted the disc was timed to coincide with the group's summer U.S. tour and contained the smash hit "Eight Days A Week" and well done revivals of Buddy Holly's "Words Of Love" and Larry Williams' "Bad Boy." Cash Box stated that: "The grand-daddies of the Liverpool Sound, the Beatles have an unprecedented solid gold chain of hit LP's and singles and seem certain to add another link with their latest Capitol album. For their millions of fans throughout the world, the Mop Tops wail with a powerful assortment of rock tunes coming mostly from the combined pen of the Lennon-McCartney team." The magazine listed their latest chart topper, "Eight Days A Week," as a featured track and erroneously stated that "Bad Boy" and "Dizzy Miss Lizzie" were from their new movie, *Help!*. Cash Box ended with: "This one is definite." That same week Cash Box reported that *Beatles VI* qualified for gold (sales of one million dollars) the day of its release. In 1997, the RIAA certified sales of one million units.

THE PERFECT GIFT FOR THE JUNE GRAD!

BEATLES VI IS HERE!

NEW IMPROVED FULL DIMENSIONAL STEREO

BEATLES VI

THE WORLD'S MOST POPULAR FOURSOME! JOHN · PAUL · GEORGE · RINGO

YOU LIKE ME TOO MUCH · TELL ME WHAT YOU SEE · BAD BOY · DIZZY MISS LIZZIE · EIGHT DAYS A WEEK · YES IT IS
WORDS OF LOVE · KANSAS CITY · I DON'T WANT TO SPOIL THE PARTY · EVERY LITTLE THING · WHAT YOU'RE DOING

RECORDED IN ENGLAND

Capitol RECORDS

(S) T-2358

1 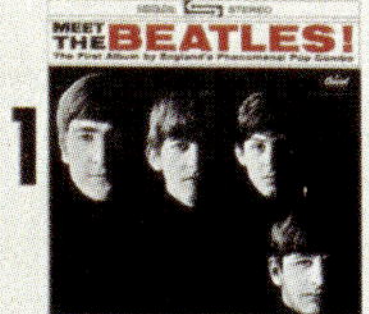

(S) T-2047

2 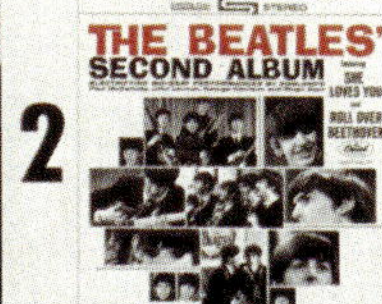

(S) T-2080

3 

(S) 2108

4 

(S) T-2228

5 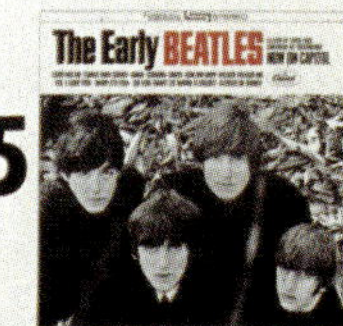

(S) T-2309

The title song from the Beatles second film, *Help!*, was scheduled for release as a Capitol single on July 19, although it may have been delayed by a week. Prior to the disc's release, Capitol reached a gentlemen's agreement with four Los Angeles radio stations to end the practice airing "exclusives" of Beatles songs ahead of their airplay dates. The disc duplicated the British pairing of "Help!" and "I'm Down." The Capitol single entered the Billboard Hot 100 at number 41 on August 7. Three weeks later, the song moved up to the second spot between Sonny & Cher's number one smash "I Got You Babe" and the Beach Boys' "California Girls." The next week, September 4, it topped the charts ahead of Bob Dylan's "Like A Rolling Stone." After three weeks, "Help!" gave way to Barry McGuire's "Eve Of Destruction" and dropped to number five. During its 13 weeks on the charts, the song spent six in the top ten. Cash Box charted the single for 14 weeks, including three weeks at number one. Record World reported the single for 13 weeks, with one week at the top. Cash Box indicated that as of July 21, 42% of its reporting stations had added the song to their play lists. A week later, this had grown to 92%. "Help!" was certified gold by the RIAA on September 2, 1965. The single's terrific but overlooked B-side, "I'm Down," spent seven weeks Bubbling Under The Hot 100, but could not break on through to the other side, peaking at 101. Cash Box reported the song at 126 and Record World at 106.

The music trades reviewed the single in their July 24 issues. Billboard noted that the group's "new film title tune is a wild rouser with an excited beat aimed at the top of the pop chart." The flip side was mentioned by name only. Once again, Record World chose to comment on the group rather than the songs: "In a world so beset with uncertainty, isn't it a pleasure to be able to fall back on a new Beatles record and say with confidence, 'This will be number one'? Yes, it is. Yes, it will be." Cash Box observed: "The fabulous foursome are sure of generating instantaneous sales acceptance with this new release," the "tag tune" to their new flick. "Help!" was described as "hard-driving, rollicking ode about a poor lad who loses some of his independence after he becomes involved with a new girl." Although the magazine missed what the song was really about, at least it provided a description. "I'm Down" was called "a raunchy, blues-drenched rocker with an infectious repeating danceable riff." KRLA Beat reviewed the single in its August 14 issue. "Help!" showed the group's "unique ability to cut a record which is unmistakably Beatles and yet 'different' from their previous sounds." The Beatles "opened up a brand new bag," using much stronger backing vocals behind John's lead. "I'm Down" was depicted as a "hard-rocker, as wild if not wilder than anything else they ever recorded."

HELP!
(John Lennon-Paul McCartney)
From the motion picture "HELP!"
(A United Artists release)

Capitol RECORDS

Maclen Music, Inc.
BMI-2:16
5476
(45-X45292)
Recorded in England

THE BEATLES

MFD. BY CAPITOL RECORDS, INC., U.S.A. • T.M. Capitol MARCA REG.

HELP! IS HERE FROM THE BEATLES!

THE BEATLES
HELP!/I'M DOWN

I'M DOWN
(John Lennon-Paul McCartney)

Capitol RECORDS

Maclen Music, Inc.
BMI-2:30
5476
(45-X45293)
Recorded in England

THE BEATLES

MFD. BY CAPITOL ... MARCA REG.

You know what it is – from the soundtrack of the picture of the same name. There's nothing like Help! when you need it! Get it!

5476 Capitol RECORDS

Although *Help!* would not arrive in U.S. theaters until mid-August 1965, word of a second Beatles movie started within two months of the first film's American debut. The September 26, 1964 Record World reported: "The Beatles' second feature motion picture following their triumph with 'A Hard Day's Night,' will probably be a Western, according to UA's George Martin, who will again arrange the soundtrack for United Artists. Filming is expected to begin in February, possibly in color." Three months later, British journalist Chris Hutchins wrote about the movie in his London column in the December 26 Billboard. Based on information received from producer Walter Shenson, Hutchins reported that "production of the Beatles next UA film was set to begin on February 22, with filming in the Bahamas." He added: "The remainder of the film would be shot in London, although some sequences may be shot in Switzerland. The Beatles would be meeting with American Mark Behm to help him with the script." Record World reported in its January 30, 1965 issue that Walter Shenson shall "commence pre-recording of six new songs by John Lennon and Paul McCartney for the second Beatles movie on Feb. 16 at E.M.I. studios." George Martin would be in charge of musical arrangements. Billboard added new details about the film in its February 13 issue. Location shooting in the Bahamas would begin on February 22 and run for nearly three weeks. The group would then fly to Austria for ten more days of filming before returning to London to finish shooting the movie. The Beatles would start their third film in October 1965. The next week, Billboard indicated that the movie would be released worldwide in mid-summer.

Los Angeles radio station KRLA began publishing a weekly 4-page newsletter, KRLA Beat, in early October 1964. By its February 25, 1965 issue, KRLA Beat changed its appearance and content with the hiring of professional photographers and writers, including former Beatles press officer Derek Taylor. The magazine reported that Taylor and KRLA disc jockey Dave Hull were heading to the Bahamas to interview the Beatles as they film their second movie. In the March 10 edition, Taylor wrote that the group recorded some great new songs the week before they came to the Bahamas. He observed that the Beatles were "far more mature and ready for filming than they were in 'A Hard Day's Night.'" John told him: "We were doing the unknown then. Now we've all our mistakes to learn from." The following week, Taylor assured readers that the color film "should be marvelous" and "full of action." It had a wild scene where "Paul is shrunken to thumb-size" and "Ringo is nearly murdered for his precious ring." There would be scenes in the Bahamas, the Alps and London. Taylor predicted that the movie would be "one of the huge events of the cinema in 1965."

In This Issue:
ROLLING STONES
RIGHTEOUS BROS.
BEAU BRUMMELS

KRLA BEAT

RINGO
Before & After

February 25, 1965 Los Angeles, California Ten Cents

BEATLE-BALL AT KRLA!

DEREK TAYLOR, BEATLE ASSOCIATE

Derek Taylor and An Unidentified Frie

Hull, Taylor To Visit Beatles During Filming

KRLA explodes another Beatle bombshell!

And all of you have a chance to get in on the excitement.

Dave Hull, the world's biggest Beatle booster, and Derek Taylor, the Beatles' press agent and liaison man before coming to KRLA, are flying to Nassau for a series of exclusive interviews with John, Paul, George and Ringo as they film their latest movie.

Fun For You

Here's where you come in.

Through Dave and Derek, you can ask the questions! Just jot them down on a postcard and mail them to BEATLE QUESTIONS, KRLA, PASADENA. But hurry – there isn't much time left.

Here are some that have already been submitted:

What does Ringo think of married life? What does Maureen think of John, George and Paul? What's it like to be married to a Beatle? What do the other Beatles think of her? What is their reaction to Ringo's marriage? Do they think it will hurt the Beatles' popularity? Does Maureen want Ringo to stay with the group?

Lots of Questions

What special activities do they plan during their next visit to Los Angeles? How long will they be here? With John and Ringo married, are Paul and George thinking about giving up their bachelor life? What is the truth about the latest report that Paul may be altar-bound? Who is the man trying to break up the Beatles, and for what purpose?

Keep your ears glued to KRLA for the FIRST and ONLY answers to such questions – by the Beatles themselves.

Beatles' August T To Include L.A. Sh

We can't give you any official word yet, but negotiations are almost completed to bring the Beatles back to Los Angeles for another live concert spectacular.

Word of a final agreement is expected to be announced any day now . . . and KRLA and the Beat will be first to announce it, naturally!

They are expected to do two concerts this time, so that a lot of people who missed out on their first performance will have a chance to see them in person.

The boys have expressed a preference for Los Angeles, and they have reserved two open dates on the schedule for their American tour this summer – Aug. 29 and 30.

Revealing his plans for the Beatles for the rest of 1965, Brian Epstein indicates they will make the third of their three-picture commitment for United Artists this year.

The Beatles are starting their second film this week. They have flown to the Bahamas for

location shooti take almost the they fly to Aust for about ten turning to Lon the picture.

They will b pean tour in J concert in Pa combined with the Eurovisio French capita will follow i drid, Milan a city to be na

Then com American fa awaiting. Th don for the and the foll spot for the

The four L selected ni certs, inclu Others are lanta, San Minneapoli go, Detroit

They are tour Aug. 1 will probab the two sho

STIRS LOTS OF TALK

KRLA DJs On New Sho

The big story everyone is talking about is the "big switch" at KRLA.

It brought a promotion for Hullabalooer Dave Hull, and it brought KRLA one of the best and best-known disc jockeys in the entire world – the one and only Dick Biondi.

At the request of thousands of his fans the scuzzy one stepped into the afternoon "traffic" slot from 3-6 p.m. Daffy Dick is messing up people's minds in Dave's old period of nine-to-midnight.

While Dave had the greatest time of his life during his nightly parties on KRLA, he likes to "mix" with his listeners in public appearances and of course he wasn't able to do that with a night-time show.

But look out for him now!

The old up unexp gathering treat him used to b

Everyo formation Like . . . really hu (We're s answer t but the a

KRLA BEAT

March 17, 1965 Los Angeles, California Ten Cents

BEATLE MOVIE A BLAST!

Derek Taylor's Report

The Beatles are fine. They feel fine, they look fine, act brilliantly, sing better than ever. On and off-set they have the air of assured young men who have it made. They may not ever claim to be the greatest act showbiz has ever known, but they certainly look it and certainly are. I hadn't seen them for three months and of course, they hadn't changed too much. But the feature which struck me most was that they looked more mature. They have more assurance than ever; they are no longer boys.

As Peter Evans, Britain's most important entertainment columnist wrote in the London Daily Express: "They are man-talking adults beneath those little-boy haircuts."

Evans came away from meeting them in the Bahamas, soured. He wrote a biting attack on their off-stage attitude to the press and described them as "rude and arro-

Turn to Page 2

VISITORS TO MOVIE LOCATION TELL OF BEATLEMANIA ANTICS

By Dave Hull

If I wasn't a complete raving, total Beatlemaniac before, then I certainly am now!

What an experience! After spending four days with them in the Bahamas while they filmed portions of the second movie, I feel as wrung out as a piece of laundry.

There is so much to tell I'm sure neither Derek Taylor nor I will be able to do much more than scratch the surface during this edition of the Beat. But we'll continue it from week to week until you have the whole story . . . the whole book is more like it, because anyone could write a book after spending a few days with those guys.

They are so full of life and mischief that they're perpetual motion machines. They really wear a person down – even the old Hullabalooer himself.

Different Atmosphere

My previous associations with the Beatles had mostly been in situations where there were crowds all about or near-impossible schedules to meet so that we were unable to really sit down and talk for more than a few minutes at a time.

But this trip was completely different. Although they are working about 12 hours a day on the movie, there is a much more relaxed and casual atmosphere.

After inviting Derek and me to visit them, they were great hosts. Completely friendly, relaxed and outgoing.

To our surprise, Derek and I found that anyone going to the Bahamas where they're shooting the film is allowed to see the Beatles. This includes visiting them on the set!

Friendly to Visitors

Tourists were constantly snapping pictures of them, and the Beatles actually seemed quite happy about it. They even took the time and trouble

—Turn to Page 4

KRLA TOP TEN

1. STOP IN THE NAME OF LOVE
2. EIGHT DAYS A WEEK/I DON'T WANT TO SPOIL THE PARTY
3. MY GIRL
4. THIS DIAMOND RING
5. THE BOY FROM N. Y. CITY
6. RED ROSES FOR A BLUE LADY
7. HURT SO BAD
8. DOWNTOWN
9. FERRY ACROSS THE MERSEY
10. GO NOW

(Complete Listing Page 4)

Here they are! The Beatles in the Bahamas on location for their new film. You will see this picture later in other publications, but this week it is a world-wide exclusive for the KRLA Beat . . . a gift from the Beatles to KRLA's Derek Taylor and Dave Hull. Other exclusive pictures of the Fab Four on page 3.

In the March 24 KRLA Beat, Hull wrote that the group was "strongly considering '8 Days a Week' as the title" of their new film. George told Hull and Taylor that he had suggested "Who Fell Into My Porridge?" That same issue reported that George Martin was in London listening to tapes of the group's recent recording session during which "George and Ringo danced to a playback of another soon-to-be Beatle hit." The March 31 edition, under the headline "Beatle Title Chosen!," indicated that the boys "finally hit upon a title" for their film: "Eight Arms To Hold You." Hull speculated that the movie would have a song with the same title, which would also probably be the title of record album accompanying the film. Hull added that the "'Eight Arms' applies to John, Paul, George and Ringo," and that the "giant idol to which Ringo is to be sacrificed also has eight arms." [The idol actually had ten arms.] In an interview in the Bahamas with Derek Taylor, Ringo explained why he had red paint all over his suit and provided a summary of the film's plot–"basically a chase film and it's about a ring."

Record World reported in its March 27 issue that "the new UA motion picture will be called '8 Arms To Hold You,' a title invented by the four singers themselves." The following week, Billboard indicated in its April 3 issue that both sides of the next Beatles single, "Ticket To Ride" and "Yes It Is," would be featured in the Beatles second film, "Eight Arms To Hold You," which would premiere on both sides of the Atlantic in early August.

In the April 7 KRLA Beat, George told Derek Taylor that he enjoyed making films and was getting tired of touring. "And when the film's finished you get more satisfaction from it. You feel as though you've done something worthwhile, more so than a tour." In response to Dave Hull's questions about how the new movie compared to the last one, George said: "The only thing, really, that's the same as 'A Hard Day's Night' is the fact that we are still playing ourselves. But I mean, this has got a story line to it whereas 'A Hard Day's Night' didn't, really. It was more or less like a documentary." In contrast to the spontaneity in the first film, George indicated that "so far we seem to be sticking to the script." He added that the group had recorded 11 songs in one week before leaving England, with about seven to appear in the movie. The following week, KRLA Beat ran its interview with John, who said that the group had written 14 songs, but that only seven would be in the film. John refused to provide any titles, explaining that they don't disclose titles in advance because someone "might write songs with the same title and confuse the market."

John provided a concise summary of the film's plot. "[Ringo] comes in possession of this ring, and whoever wears it has to be sacrificed..., and we're trying to save him and get this ring off his finger. [There are] other people trying to get it off for various reasons. It's very complicated. Basically what it is is to stop him from getting sacrificed." John also indicated that the group was sticking to the script, at least "until there's an opportunity of...going away from it." John told Dave Hull that he had spent his last holiday in St. Moritz, Switzerland, skiing. He thought that he and Cynthia became above average skiers by having a private instructor. [This would help in the film's skiing scenes.]

KRLA Beat published its interviews with Paul in the April 21 issue. Derek asked Paul how many people from the last film were in the new one besides the Beatles. Paul indicated that all the actors were different except for Victor Spinetti, who was the TV producer in the first film and one of the baddies in the new one. Dick Lester and Walter Shenson were back [in their roles as director and producer, respectively]. When Derek asked if George Martin was cooperating with the score and background music, Paul indicated that nobody had gotten around to it yet because the group had just completed the songs, and Martin would "have to write the score around the numbers." Paul confirmed that there were no new songs ready in December, and that he and John had each written a few on holiday and "a lot together." Paul said that if he got stuck on a song, he knew John could finish it for him. Even with songs Paul wrote by himself, he might tell John: "I need a middle eight for this one." When Derek mentioned he saw photographer Bob Freeman in the Bahamas, Paul said that Freeman had done the cover to the group's latest British album, but in America they changed the cover. Derek explained that the British disc had another title and two more songs than the American album, causing Paul to say: "That's it, you see. Better value. Buy Britain, folks, buy Britain!"

The May 5 KRLA Beat reported that the Beatles no longer liked the title *Eight Arms To Hold You*, which had been selected for their new movie. The film was now being "edited, dubbed and prepared for release." The issue recapped the plot of the film and stated that the movie "starts with a song penned by Paul McCartney." [The opening song would actually be written by John.] Chris Hutchins reported in his London column in the May 1 Billboard that "Help!" was the title of the Beatles second film and next single. Soon after director Dick Lester suggested the title, John and Paul "penned a song around it and the Beatles rushed into EMI's studios...to wax [record] the tune."

Tony Howard, who was in charge of publicity for the film, provided inside stories of its production in the June 2 and 9 issues of KRLA Beat. In advance of filming in the Bahamas, the huge ten-armed statue of the goddess Kaili that loomed above the high walls surrounding Twickenham Film Studios was dismantled by crane. Reports from those witnessing the procedure led to a rumor that the Beatles second film had been canceled. However, the idol was merely being taken apart so it could be transported to and reassembled in the Bahamas. Parts of Kaili's dismembered body were stowed away throughout the passenger section of the BOAC Boeing 707 chartered by Walter Shenson to transport the cast, unit and film equipment to Nassau. Assisted by the chief of the Bahamas Tourist Board, Shenson's location manager found accommodations for the 70-strong film cast and crew [erroneously typed "700-odd" in KRLA Beat]. Despite the constant presence of curious tourists, over 40 sequences were filmed in the Bahamas. Howard wrote of the multiple skindivers handling air tanks and pressure bombs "to stage the dramatic rising out of the water" off Paradise Island of the 40-foot tall Kaili. [The complex scene did not make the cut as the statue is shown atop a non-moving platform in shallow water.] The Goodyear blimp also made an appearance. After completing filming in the Bahamas, the actors and crew headed back to London for a brief stay before departing for the Austrian Alps.

Things were quite different in the Alps. While the crew had plodded through ankle-deep sand in the Bahamas, they were now working in knee-deep snow. There was also danger as an avalanche had swept a bus full of students to their deaths a week before the film's unit arrived. The Beatles and other actors had to perform physical acts such as falling from runaway sleighs, ski jumps and sprints across ice rinks. The group did a musical number atop a mountain around a grand piano hauled up there by eight men during a freezing gale. Although the nightlife in Obertauern was virtually non-existent due to the high altitude wearing people out, there was one memorable evening when the crew was celebrating the birthday of assistant director Clive Reed at Marietta Hotel. Perhaps tired of the waltzes being played by the Austrian band, the Beatles took over and, joined by Dick Lester on piano, "gave a two-hour impromptu concert that nearly took the roof off." After returning to London, filming resumed at Twickenham. Tony Howard described a scene in which British comedian Frankie Howard played an eccentric drama coach, sure to be one of the film's comedy highlights. [The scene did not make the cut.] A near "full-scale military maneuver" was shot over four days on Salisbury Plains with the cooperation of the war office, which supplied troops, tanks and other equipment.

Producer Shenson called *Help!* a holiday picture. "It was made in two totally contrasting holiday resorts. We traveled from calypso to yodel with a lot of yeah-yeah thrown in besides. It will be released in August both in England and the States–holiday time for most people–and we hope the movie itself will be something of a holiday for everyone who sees it." Director Lester described the film as an adventure comedy. "The boys will play themselves again but in a completely fictional situation, unlike 'A Hard Day's Night' which could be described best as cinema journalism."

The August 7 Cash Box reported that *Help!* would open in 250 top domestic locations on August 11. The film would open in theaters in other areas throughout August and be in over a thousand U.S. and Canadian cities by Labor Day [September 6]. The movie preview for American journalists was held in the projection room at Samuel Goldwyn Studios in Los Angeles on or about August 5. Barbara Gius, who attended the press screening, opened her review in the August 7 Ventura County Star [Ventura, California] by asking if the Beatles were slipping [though there was no indication they were]. Gius responded that their motion picture *Help!* might be "the comeback their many fans are looking for." She contrasted the new film with *A Hard Day's Night* by stating that *Help!* has "more of a plot, a larger cast, and is filmed in brilliant color." Its thrilling action is "superbly photographed" though the plot is "definitely farfetched." While the "quick wit of the Beatles is generously expressed," in contrast to their first film, "there is no ad-libbing to speak of." She provided examples of humorous scenes such as John's ribbing of Scotland Yard about the recent Great Train Robbery and the boys performing "I Need You" while surrounded by an army battalion. Although the film lacked deep drama, *Help!* would prove to be entertaining even for "not-so-Beatle fans."

United Press International reported that the Beatles "made a poor showing Monday [August 9] at the opening of their new movie, 'Help!,' when less than 50 faithful fans lined up in advance at the Beacon Theater on Broadway [New York City]...for free tickets to be the first to see a preview of the film by the long-haired foursome." The article claimed that the girls in line "chatted about their idols–Soupy Sales, the Rolling Stones, Herman's Hermits and the Dave Clark Five." It should be noted that the lack of pandemonium was most likely due to a lack of publicity as tickets were distributed through fan clubs. While the Beatles would start their 1965 North American tour in New York City's Shea Stadium on August 15, *Help!* would not appear in the city's theaters until its August 23 special premiere showings.

As with *A Hard Day's Night*, fans could purchase special advance tickets for the Beatles second film. In San Francisco, the New Esquire, Empire Theatre and Geneva Drive-In began selling tickets on August 5 for the movie's August 11 premiere. Stanley Eichelbaum began his review in the San Francisco Examiner with: "Four cheers for the Beatles and one loud, long hurrah for the pleasure they inflict in their new movie." Eichelbaum describes the film as "agreeably batty and good humored," adding that he had a better time at *Help!* than at *A Hard Day's Night*. The new movie is a "more expensively organized production, superbly enhanced by David Watkins' inventive color photography," with Richard Lester directing "with even more original cinematic playfulness than before, under far more relaxed circumstances, with a great deal more assurance from the Beatles." The result is "an uncannily sophisticated, tongue-in-cheek exercise in slapstick goonery and hyperbolic satire." He thought adults might appreciate the film more than children, who would relish the sight gags and Mersey sounds, but might "miss a large measure of the far-out, antic humor" of the movie's "wantonly madcap screenplay." While *Help!* is not as impromptu as its predecessor and lacks "screaming hordes of Beatlemaniacs scampering semi-documentary through London on the heels of the millionaire crooners," the Beatles "play themselves and the mood is still wild and wacky...with wit and non-sequitur wisecracks."

The film jumps from London to the Austrian Alps to the Bahamas with "breath-taking agility...in a lunatic pastiche of a suspense melodrama" where "the emphasis is strictly on fun, farce and op-art fantasy, with a nod to the Marx Brothers and a wink to James Bond." It pokes fun at "cloak-and-dagger thrillers, science-fiction, Scotland Yard, military might, Queen Elizabeth, Goodyear blimps, Far Eastern restaurants, winter sports and, most of all, the Beatles themselves," who "perform with ingratiating and good-natured zest, their campy clowning and strange, Liverpudlian accents, being particularly suited to the cockeyed and abstract spirit of Lester's film." Eichelbaum enjoyed the London pub scene where an escaped Bengal tiger is tamed by Beethoven's "Ode To Joy" from his Ninth Symphony. He was less enthusiastic about the Beatles music, writing that "their songs and bleating vocal style have a monotony that only youngsters will appreciate," but noting that "the musical numbers are marvelously rescued by Watkins' fresh and ingenious photography." Overall, the movie's "scenery is unusually handsome, especially the snowy Austrian ski slopes, where no madness is too much for director Lester or his high-spirited stars." Eichelbaum concludes that *Help!* is a "riotous film, full of absurd whimsy and splendid droll hoopla."

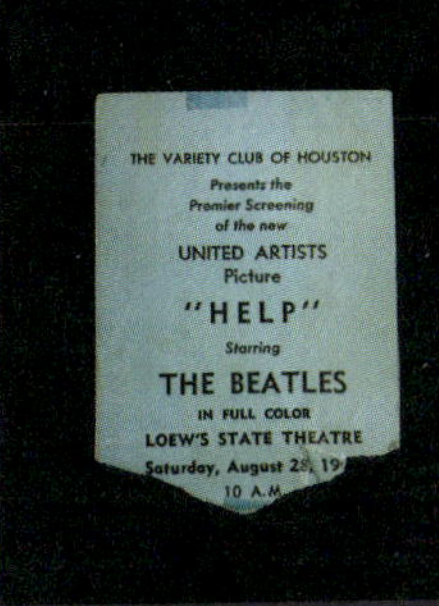

"HELP! I'm kidnapped!"

"HELP! I'm lost on a tropic island!"

"HELP! I'm surrounded by women!"

"HELP! keep our city clean!"

STOP WORRYING!

HELP!

IS ON THE WAY!

The Colorful Adventures of

THE BEATLES

are more Colorful than ever...in COLOR!

HELP YOURSELF TO SEVEN GREAT NEW BEATLE HITS!

ALSO STARRING LEO McKERN

ELEANOR BRON VICTOR SPINETTI ROY KINNEAR

PRODUCED BY WALTER SHENSON SCREENPLAY BY MARC BEHM AND CHARLES WOOD STORY BY MARC BEHM DIRECTED BY RICHARD LESTER

EASTMANCOLOR A WALTER SHENSON-SUBAFILMS PRODUCTION A UNITED ARTISTS RELEASE

STOP WORRYING!

YOU CAN BEAT THE CROWDS!

GET YOUR TICKETS IN ADVANCE FOR Special Gala Premiere Performances

RUN FOR

HELP!

BE THE FIRST TO SEE

The Colorful Adventures of

THE BEATLES

...more Colorful than ever...in COLOR!

FIRST COME... FIRST SERVED! TICKETS GO ON SALE These Special Tickets will guarantee you a seat. A Souvenir Tag will be presented to each ticket buyer

ALSO STARRING LEO McKERN

ELEANOR BRON VICTOR SPINETTI ROY KINNEAR

HELP YOURSELF TO SEVEN GREAT NEW BEATLE HITS!

PRODUCED BY WALTER SHENSON SCREENPLAY BY MARC BEHM AND CHARLES WOOD STORY BY MARC BEHM DIRECTED BY RICHARD LESTER

EASTMANCOLOR A WALTER SHENSON-SUBAFILMS PRODUCTION A UNITED ARTISTS RELEASE

Help! had its exclusive Chicago debut at the Woods theater on Wednesday, August 11, followed by a general release on Friday, September 24. The Cliff Robertson film *Masquerade* was a co-feature on many screens. After admitting that her words wouldn't have any effect on the Beatles youthful fans, Mae Tinee wrote in the August 12 Chicago Tribune that "the Beatles' second film lacks the appeal of 'A Hard Day's Night,' at least for adults." The film is a "way-out-there spoof of science-fiction movies, with a dash of James Bond–a comedy crowded with slapstick, much of it wildly contrived." Tinee found it problematic that the boys are "too busy being chased to have an opportunity to display their brand of kooky humor." She believed that the film was at its best "when the Beatles take over the screen, apparently happy at looking as idiotic as possible." Tinee admitted that "they handle gags neatly" and "have a quality which makes you forget their utterly atrocious appearance." She thought the plot was thin. While she found the Beatles adventures on skis and in an Indian restaurant to be "mildly funny," the script "reaches too hard and the results are more frantic and less appealing than their previous screen adventures." She praised the performances of Leo McKern as a crazy cultist and Victor Spinetti and Roy Kinnear as inept scientists. Tinee concluded: "There are many songs, all of which will undoubtedly appeal to the younger generation, who will find the film good, clean fun."

The movie opened in four Cleveland area theaters on August 11, including the Mapletown (ticket shown on the preceding page) in Maple Heights, Ohio. In the August 11 Plain Dealer, W. Ward March stated that *Help!* was "wilder than" *A Hard Day's Night*. He compared the film to the slapstick comedies of Mark Sennett's Keystone Studios: "The plot gallops with the speed of a Sennett two-reeler and a good deal of the time is just as funny." His bottom line: "Even those who may not care for John, Paul, Ringo and George will find their new film really entertaining."

The Democrat and Chronicle of Rochester, New York reviewed *Help!* on August 12, calling the film a "little nothing" movie with "a little of this and a little of that and a strenuous day's night for our musical heroes." The newspaper added that the Pink Panther cartoons shown in theaters provide "an idea of what the Beatles film is about–in and out of one blasting dynamite trap after another." The movie contains "wild nonsense" and is "spattered with good-natured gags and tricks." It is "fun at first but wears thin when the scriptwriters run out of bright ideas for attempts upon the life of [Ringo]." The "young screamers" at the earlier shows approved of "Help!" and the other new songs.

The Morning Union of Springfield, Massachusetts reported in its August 13 edition that the local Parkway Drive-In "put a real feather in its cap" with its booking of the new Beatles film *Help!* on August 11, the first date the film was shown in the United States. The movie is "so ridiculous with everything being done for laughs that one just doesn't know what to make of it right away." The paper noted that the "zany antics of the Beatles are highly reminiscent of the old Marx Brothers comedies that are now justly considered classics." After describing the "plot(?)," the paper praised director Richard Lester for making a "top-notch comedy." It noted that the Beatles singing would please teenagers and that the background music, which utilizes parts of old Beatles hits and the classics (such as the *1812 Overture*), is "very well done and fits into the madcap mood of the film," moving it "along its merry old way." The Morning Union concluded that "it would be wise to take in the film and learn to laugh again." Those wishing to see the movie at Springfield's Fox Theater instead of a drive-in had to wait a week until August 18.

Although most residents of New York City would not see *Help!* until August 25 or thereafter, some fans in other parts of the state got to see the motion picture a week earlier. In Glens Falls, the Rialto Theatre began its screening of the movie on August 18. The following day, The Post-Star ran Marilyn Nason's review titled: "New Beatles Film Is Kooky but Fun." Nason wrote that every locale "becomes a veritable stage for the clowning, kooky quartet of 'singers.'" After dismissing the story line as not being worth much, she provides the following advice: "If you want to enjoy this movie forget the plot and just concentrate on watching the Beatles to see what makes them tick and what has made them the mass hysteria among teen-agers." In Buffalo, *Help!* debuted at Shea's Buffalo. The Buffalo Evening News opened its review with a comparison to the first film, noting: "'Help!'...is naturally far more expensive and ambitious than the hasty, low-budgeted first, 'A Hard Day's Night,' which fetched scads of dollars, pounds and pence, francs and rupees. As usually happens, the spend-thrift second issue falls far shy of the wild free rapture of the first...The lack of anything resembling a story allowed slapstick rampant and seemed a genius stroke of originality. This time the jolly four are stuck with a plot." After describing the story line and some of the more memorable scenes, the paper continued with its criticism: "When things get dull as they often do, the Beatles oblige with seven rock 'n' roll items which require an expert to tell apart and all sound like the work of seven early Elvises." During the songs, director Richard Lester "conspires with the camera to photograph the Beatles from every possible angle in every possible light and color."

Help! had a special 8:00 PM preview screening on Thursday, August 19, at the Olympia Theater in Miami. WQAM disc jockeys served as emcees for the event, which included performances by the Invaders, the Calientes and the Stops. The film opened the following day in theaters and drive-ins throughout Miami and Florida. George Bourke's review in the August 20 Miami Herald stated that there were "no dull moments...nor many sane ones" in *Help!*, with director Richard Lester abandoning "all reason in telling this combination spoof of secret agents and the Far East sacrificial victim formats." Lester crams a lot into the movie "by the use of inventive photographic montages in color and an almost complete absence of footage-wasting transition shots." Bourke's summary of the film refers to Marx Brothers style chases through the English countryside and the Alps, with a tumultuous finale in Nassau. He observes that "Part of the picture's zany charm stems from the casual and unassuming manner in which the boys run through their rapid paces." Although some of the comedy will not register with American audiences, *Help!* is a "highly gimmicked production" that "should enlarge the prospective audience far beyond the limits of the Beatles own following."

In the Miami News, Herb Kelly shared his experience attending the local opening of *Help!* at the Olympia, observing that each new scene was "greeted with piercing shrieks." Although the new Beatles movie, like *A Hard Day's Night*, is aimed at juveniles, it is "pretty good fare for square adults too." Once again, "the boys remind you of the Marx Brothers with their gags and sight comedy that seem to be done on the spur of the moment." The movie has "plenty of singing and music" that has little to do with the plot, "but rock 'n' roll is what you expect" from the Beatles. Some of the color film's "scenic shots are breath-taking, particularly those in the Alps." As for the story, it "is impossible but it's up the Beatles' alley." Kelly concludes: "Color, natural scenery and crazy action make 'Help!' a better picture and if the children will just shush for awhile grownups will enjoy it too."

Thomas Sander's review in the August 20 Orlando Star states that the film "needs all the help it can get," being a "curiously unamusing blend of way-out nonsense, self-consciously cute dialogue, and helter-skelter action that doesn't quite jell." On the whole, it is "confusingly overdone and just not funny." Sander claims that the "sparse opening-night audience of teenagers watched this foolishness in almost utter silence." He said that he liked the Beatles, but believed that they "over-reached" themselves. He wished them better luck with their third film.

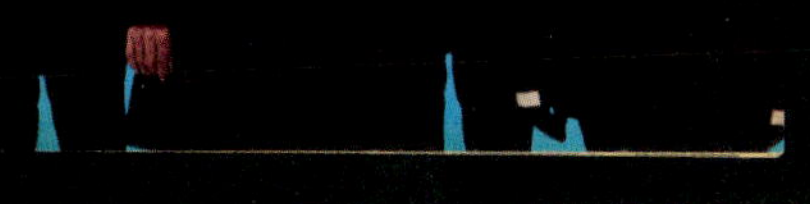

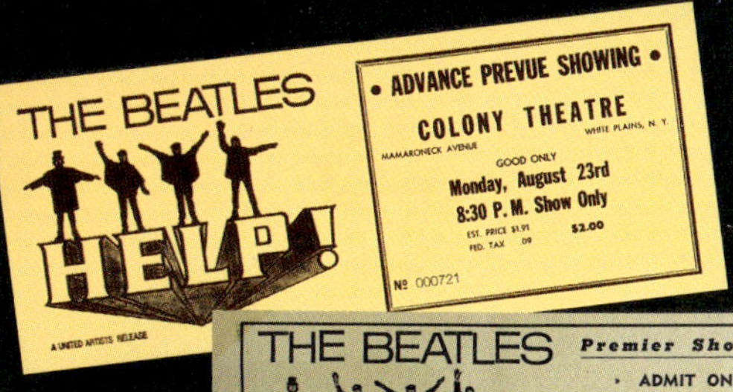

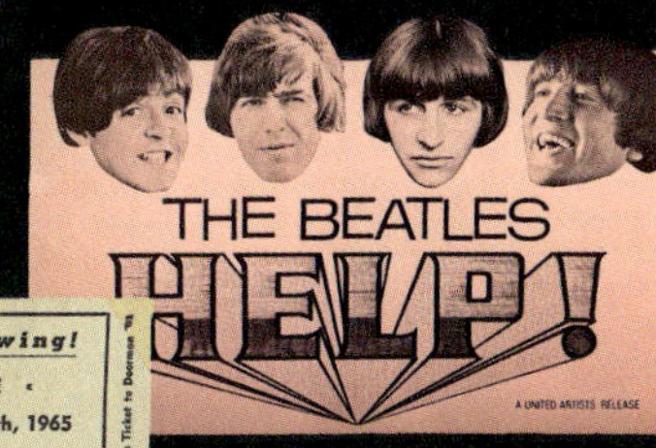

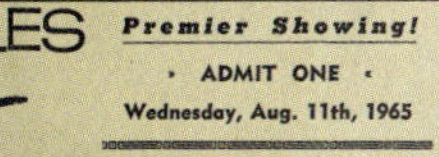

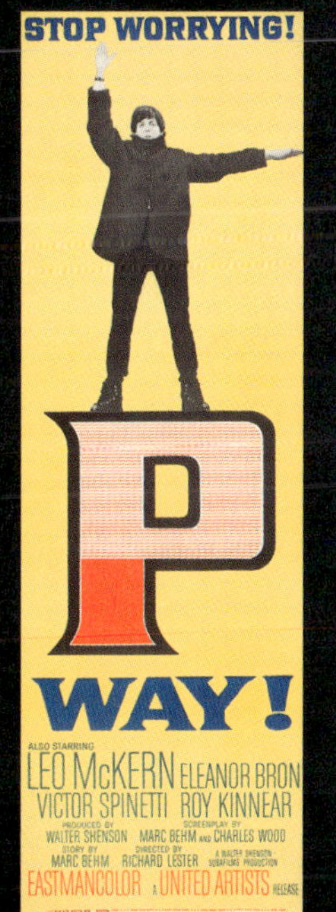

HELP Yourself To Seven Great New Beatle Hits!

STOP WORRYING! HELP! IS ON THE WAY!

The Colorful Adventures of

THE BEATLES

are more Colorful than ever...in COLOR!

ALSO STARRING LEO McKERN

EASTMANCOLOR

A WALTER SHENSON-SUBAFILMS PRODUCTION

A UNITED ARTISTS RELEASE

Help! opened in Kansas City, Missouri on August 18 at the Uptown and Avenue theaters. Giles Fowler's review in The Kansas City Star was titled "Merry Chase in Fantasyland Has Beatles Howling 'Help!'" Fowler writes that unlike *A Hard Day's Night*, "which had the Beatles romping through a madcap but semi-believable 36 hours in their lives," *Help!* "hasn't a whit of realism" and "takes the form of a hard week's nightmare, involving the quartet in a hilarious, mad-hatter flight from a gang of Oriental cutthroats." Fowler adds that almost everything about *Help!* is "bigger, gaudier, crazier, faster and more excessive than anything in the earlier film." Only the Beatles "remain the same–impudent, impetuous, quizzical and refreshing." Fowler notes that "their antics suggest those of the Marx Brothers," with Ringo being the best comedian of the group. The band's seven musical numbers "have the same irrepressible energy." Under Richard Lester's direction, the four stars "should win over even the keenest of Beatlephobes."

New Yorkers could attend preview showings of *Help!* on August 23 before the film's official run started in theaters in and around the city on August 25 (see poster, next page). Kate Cameron reviewed the film in the August 24 Daily News. Cameron wrote that "the boys never have a dull moment in their latest screen effort," adding: "The action is fast, the gags funny and the color exceptionally good." While *A Hard Day's Night* was "designed as adult entertainment," *Help!* is "for the kiddies," having much more slapstick "to tickle the young" and "a touch of fantasy to appeal to their imagination." Although the Beatles new movie "hasn't the subtlely of the first," *Help!* "is, nevertheless, a very funny film." In the August 24 New York Times, Bosley Crowther called the Beatles "royal rock 'n' rollers" and labeled the film as "90 crowded minutes of good, clean insanity." This time, the Beatles "go for the utterly absurd," and consequently, "preposterousness is rampant and boundless." Perhaps there is a "vague intent to lampoon the crazy characteristics of mystery comic strips." The Beatles music is "dished out to an infectious beat." Unlike *A Hard Day's Night*, there is no respite "from the frantic pace and mood," it is "wham, wham, wham all the way." "The boys themselves are exuberant and uninhibited in their own genial way. They just become awfully redundant and—dare I say it?—dull."

In the August 24 Newsday (Long Island), Joseph Gelmis was impressed with the "total professionalism" of the Beatles: "They are talented, disciplined and completely poised. They never lose their equilibrium...They are cool when the world is falling apart around them." He describes *Help!* as a "ridiculous chase" and adds: "It is all one frantic put on, or hip joke. Nothing sacred, nothing serious, and they carry it off, as well as the Marx Brothers or Laurel and Hardy did most of the time." While there are some stale moments, "there is enough to make the film fun." He praises Lester as a "master of the sight gag" and screenwriter Marc Behm as a "purveyor of way-out comedy." His verdict: "A good show, Beatles." The August 25 Asbury Park Press (New Jersey) told its readers: "Yes, the Beatles are back on film once more and the more one sees of them, the more one realizes the magnitude of the Marx Brothers influence upon a whole new generation of comedians...It is not that the foursome has patterned itself after the comedy stars of another era, but that the style and feeling which they project is essentially the same." The paper notes "the plot isn't much but it's the madcap improvisations and offhand approach to comedy that make 'HELP" the delightful 90-minute it is."

In the August 26 Boston Globe, Michael Steinberg found parts of the film very funny, adding: "There are some good gags, an agreeable sense of the pleasures of non-sequitur, and especially the near-surrealist montage that accompanies the seven songs in the picture is very charming." The Beatles "have a certain style...But it's all sex, really. Visual symbols are uninhibitedly explicit." His verdict: "There is a lot of humor and fantasy mixed in with the noise and rubbish, though whether you can survive a room full of hysterical little girls is...another matter."

Philip K. Scheuer had praise for *Help!* in the September 1 Los Angeles Times. The Beatles second film was "in astonishing color" and "even funnier and more Marx-like" than *A Hard Day's Night*. He acknowledges that critics have said that the new film is not as wistful or poetic as the Beatles first movie; however, he does not care. *Help!* is a "nutty film and sometimes an inspired one, semi-improvised like its predecessor....The whole thing is shot as informally as a home movie, with the camera and sound track jumping when the boys are not, and the wise person will not try to analyze it, let alone rationalize it. The point is that it made me laugh." As for the plot, it is "James Bondish." He sees the high priest Clang, played by Leo McKern, as a takeoff on Gert Frobe's portrayal of Auric Goldfinger in the latest Bond film. Victor Spinetti plays a scientist who sees Ringo's ring as a chance to rule the world. There is little effort to bridge events other than through the film's subtitles, some of which are "hilariously redundant." The boys' musical performances are "as rocking as they are brassy." He has praise for the cinematography: "The color camera, like a whirling dervish, catches the Beatles in focus and out of focus, shoots into the sun and out of the sun, with filters achieving some of the most startling (i.e., blue Alps) and often enchanting effects." Scheuer concludes: "The Beatles are strange young men, but also likeable. They aren't really actors but in all this razz-matazz, who's to notice?"

Andrew Sarris, who had praised *A Hard Day's Night*, expressed his disappointment of *Help!* in the September 9 Village Voice. While "Director Richard Lester clearly has the knack as well as 'The Knack,' and the Beatles look and sound as if they will endure a while longer," it was a mistake "to throw the Beatles into a parody of old Maria Montez movies and the current vogue for James Bond" because "parodies don't work" and "the Beatles bear no resemblance to the Marx Brothers." The Beatles "are not funny in the classical ha-ha sense" as they don't move or talk funny. Sarris reasons that "the Marx Brothers tried to be mad in a sane world whereas the Beatles try to be sane in a mad world."

The September 3 Time was not overly enthusiastic in its assessment of the film: "**Help!** is the Beatles' all-out try at carving a new career as a screen team before their long love affair with the squealers dies out. As such, it is a failure, for as actors they are still nothing but Beatles, without enough characterization–or even caricaturization–to play anything but sight gags." The magazine was impressed with the movie's production, recognizing its "carefully calculated camera work and cutting, plus a story line made out of finely wrought jack-in-the-boxes." After describing the storyline, Time adds that "the color camera dances in and out of focus, zooms up and away, tilts with the music, splashes light like liquid, and cuts so fast from this to that that the effect is almost subliminal." The magazine concludes: "*Help!*, in short, is a Beatle production rather than a Beatle movie. It must have cost, as the British say, a packet. It will certainly make, as the Americans say, a bundle."

Newsweek's review of the film in its August 30 edition consisted of a long series of short descriptive phrases that pretty much summed it all up: "The Beatles are loose again in **HELP!** Ringo has a ring. Whole plot. Sacred ring he can't get off his finger. Fiendish Orientals in pursuit, bent on sacrifice. Beautiful, fiendish Oriental priestess, bent on Beatles: 'I am not what I seem.' Goldfinger gadgets: flame-thrower umbrella, tack-thrower jalopy, paint-thrower bagpipes. Shrunken Paul dressed in Wrigley Spearmint wrapper: Tiny Alice's beau? Eyeglasses in soup. Fake fakir on spike bed. Fiendish British scientists in pursuit of Ringo's ring. Armed with deadly laser. No, not laser. Relativity condenser! Even deadlier. Poker in Buckingham Palace. Essence of orchid juice. No logic, none needed. Beatles skiing, Beatles curling, Beatles at Stonehenge, Beatles on bicycles in the Bahamas, Beatles vs. tanks and bazookas, Beatles sing seven songs, count them; 3,651 laughs vs. 3,650 laughs in 'A Hard Day's Night,' but this one much longer. Leo McKern superb, Beatles Beatles–great clowns in a great clown show. HELP!"

In North America, the soundtrack album for the Beatles first film, *A Hard Day's Night*, was released well in advance of the motion picture. By the time that movie began appearing in theaters, many viewing the film had been hearing the Beatles new recordings for five to six weeks. This time around, *Help!* was in theaters and drive-ins in some markets before the release of its soundtrack LP. Thus, many fans seeing the film during its early screenings were hearing five new Beatles songs for the first time having yet to purchase or hear the Capitol soundtrack album.

The Beatles film contract with United Artists ("UA") was for one movie with an option for two more. While the agreement gave UA the rights to the American soundtrack LP and split publishing for the first film, apparently these rights for the remaining two films were not specified in the contract. Although the February 20 Billboard reported that UA confirmed Capitol had the U.S. album rights for the Beatles next film, the May 22 Cash Box indicated that the matter was still unresolved. It appears that the labels reached a deal under which Capitol got the second movie soundtrack and UA the third. This enabled Capitol to issue an official soundtrack LP for *Help!*, giving Capitol the exclusive rights to the film's recordings. UA got co-publishing for the Beatles songs in the second film, *Help!*, but not the third.

For its album featuring songs from the Beatles second film, Parlophone repeated its practice of issuing an LP with songs from the film on Side One and additional new recordings by the group on Side Two. Capitol, on the other hand, chose to issue an album featuring the seven Beatles songs from the movie mixed with "Exclusive Instrumental Music From the Picture's Soundtrack." The label's decision to issue an original motion picture soundtrack LP was influenced by the strong sales performance of the United Artists soundtrack album for *A Hard Day's Night* and the overall strong performance of soundtrack albums such as *Mary Poppins*, *Goldfinger* and *The Sound Of Music*.

For its *Help!* album, Capitol prepared a colorful gatefold cover, which described the package as a "very special movie soundtrack souvenir album." Beatles fans quickly found out that Capitol had something else special for them—a list price of $4.98 for mono and $5.98 for stereo albums, a full dollar more than other rock albums of the day. The practice of charging a premium for gatefold original Broadway cast albums was common in the fifties and sixties, but unheard of for rock LPs. But this was the Beatles, and Capitol reasoned that Beatle fans would be willing to pay an extra dollar for the soundtrack album. The label was so confident in its marketing strategy and pricing structure that it ordered an initial pressing of one million units, which was reported by Billboard in its August 14, 1965 issue as the "largest single order in the history of the business." The album was released on August 13. Capitol's strategy paid off as few fans were deterred by the high list price for the single LP, with the label receiving advance orders of one million units. By Saturday, August 14, 750,000 copies of the record had been distributed to stores. The *Help!* LP was certified gold by the RIAA on August 23, 1965. In 1997, the RIAA certified sales of three million units.

AIRPLAY BEGINS: AUGUST 9!
NATIONAL RELEASE: AUGUST 13!

While George Martin served as musical director for the Beatles first film, he and movie director Richard Lester did not get along too well. This led to Lester hiring Ken Thorne, who had provided the incidental music for Lester's 1962 film *It's Trad, Dad* to come up with the soundtrack music supplementing the Beatles recordings for *Help!* Thorne's score consisted of a mix of Thorne originals, classical music, James Bond-style themes and orchestrated Beatles tunes, often with an Indian flavor (see pages 262-263). It was during the filming of *Help!* that George Harrison had his first encounter with Indian music and the sitar. On the Beatles next album, *Rubber Soul*, Harrison played sitar on "Norwegian Wood," making him the first musician to play the Indian instrument on a released rock song.

Side One of the Capitol *Help!* album opens with an uncredited 15-second variation of the "James Bond Theme" pulled from the film's Harrods truck "chase scene." The orchestrated opening adds sitar to the guitar-dominated tune. The attention-grabbing James Bond-style opening is followed immediately by the Beatles recording of "Help!" Capitol's decision to use Ken Thorne's variation of the "James Bond Theme" as the introduction to its *Help!* soundtrack album leading directly into the title song has caused many Americans to link the songs together forever in their minds.

The program continues with the Beatles recording of "The Night Before" with Paul on lead vocals, followed by the album's first full instrumental track, "From Me To You Fantasy," which bears little resemblance to the group's third British single. Then its back to the Beatles with John's "You've Got To Hide Your Love Away" and "I Need You" by George Harrison. Side One closes with another mixed-bag instrumental from the mind of Ken Thorne titled "In The Tyrol." Due to its incorporation of a classical piece, the track is subtitled "Introducing Wagner's Overture To Act III of 'Lohengrin' Beatles Style."

Side Two opens with Paul singing lead on "Another Girl." This leads into another track with "another" in its title, "Another Hard Day's Night." The instrumental recording is a medley of music from the Beatles first movie performed on Indian instruments, featuring the title track and bits of the melody lines from "Can't Buy Me Love" and "I Should Have Known Better." The program then shifts back to the Beatles with the group's single, "Ticket To Ride." Next up is a track combining Ken Thorne's "The Bitter End," a slow and dreamy instrumental containing many of the suspense elements present in John Barry's James Bond scores, which segues into a jazz-flavored, barely recognizable version of Lennon and McCartney's "You Can't Do That." The final Beatles recording on the disc is John's "You're Gonna Lose That Girl" (as titled on the Capitol LP). The album closes with "The Chase," another Ken Thorne selection dominated by Indian instruments. The fast-paced selection (which is not heard in the film) is a raga containing many of the elements that would later turn up on George's Indian music selections such as "Love You To" and "Within You Without You."

Help! entered the Billboard Hot LP's chart on August 28, 1965, at number 148. After jumping up to 61 the following week, it replaced the Rolling Stones' *Out Of Our Heads* as the number one album on September 11, holding off *Look At Us* by Sonny & Cher. That week the album's title song "Help!" was in its second of three weeks atop the singles chart. After nine weeks at the top, the *Help!* album was replaced by the soundtrack to *The Sound Of Music*. Billboard charted the *Help!* LP for 44 weeks, including 15 weeks in the top ten. Cash Box charted the album at number one for ten straight weeks during its 32 weeks on the charts. Record World charted the album for 35 weeks, including eight weeks at number one. Some U.S. radio stations obtained copies of the Parlophone *Help!* LP. During August, WABC played "I've Just Seen A Face" and "Act Naturally" in addition to the Beatles songs on the Capitol *Help!* album.

THE
E
L
P
H

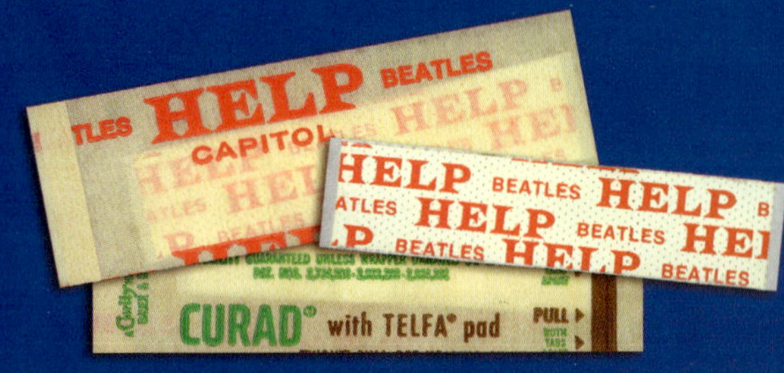
HELP BEATLES
CAPITOL
HELP BEATLES HELP
HELP BEATLES
CURAD® with TELFA® pad

Capitol
RECORDS
ORIGINAL MOTION PICTURE SOUNDTRACK
THE
BEATLES
HELP!

HELP IS HERE!
NEW IMPROVED FULL DIMENSIONAL STEREO
ORIGINAL MOTION PICTURE SOUNDTRACK
THE
BEATLES
Capitol
HELP!
HELP! · THE NIGHT BEFORE · YOU'VE GOT TO HIDE YOUR LOVE AWAY · I NEED YOU
ANOTHER GIRL · TICKET TO RIDE · YOU'RE GONNA LOSE THAT GIRL
And Exclusive Instrumental Music From the Picture's Soundtrack
GET IT!

Record World reviewed the *Help!* soundtrack LP in its August 14 issue, describing it as a "non-stop entry" and stating: "Singles 'Help!' and 'Ticket To Ride' are here along with other songs and George Martin instrumentals teens and their parents will like." [The score was actually the work of Ken Thorne.] The other trades ran reviews the following week. Billboard called the hot soundtrack a No. 1 chart contender. It predicted that the picture was destined to top the successful previous film, *A Hard Day's Night*, and that the LP would go right along with it. Ken Thorne's film score was called exceptional. Cash Box gave the following forecast: "The Beatles boom coupled with a recent surge in soundtrack sales make for a record breaking potential to be expected on this newie from the newly released 'Help!'" It went on to say that "the English foursome comes up in high style" with "Ticket To Ride," "Help!" and "other fine vocal and instrumental rollickers." The album was a "Great sounding set with excellent sales to be expected."

Capitol ordered one million customized band-aids from Curad to plug the LP. The September 11 Billboard reported that the band-aids were a "much sought-after commodity," with a Boston dealer creating a band-aid window display and a Detroit youngster nicking himself to get a "help aid." Capitol also distributed 18" x 5" band-aid shaped bumper stickers. The most elaborate *Help!* promo item was a 17¼" x 17½" x 16¾" cardboard battery-operated motion display box. The motor opens and shuts the box's lid. As the top opens, four paper hands rise up out of the box. Each has a white cuff with an orange letter that together spell "HELP." Ringo's hand is adorned with a large red ring. The inside of the lid has the same color picture as album's back cover. "THE BEATLES" appears above the photo in orange with the HELP! logo below. The outside of the box is orange. The front side has an enlargement of the stereo cover to the album and the messages "HELP IS HERE!" and "GET IT!" Capitol distributed 2,000 of the displays free to dealers.

Capitol's decision to program its *Help!* album only with songs from the film (which appeared on Side 1 of the British *Help!* LP) meant that it would have an inventory of four unissued Beatles tracks from Side 2 of the Parlophone disc. (Three of the seven songs on Side 2, namely "You Like Me Too Much," "Tell Me What You See" and "Dizzy Miss Lizzie," were included on *Beatles VI* ahead of their release on the British *Help!* album.) Capitol's initial plan was to place the four leftover songs on an EP, with "Act Naturally" and "It's Only Love" on Side 1 and "I've Just Seen A Face" and "Yesterday" on Side 2. Capitol prepared an acetate for the EP, which was mastered by engineer Billy Smith on August 6, 1965. The disc, which was to be part of the "4-By" series, was assigned catalog number R-5498.

Prior to announcing the record's release, Capitol decided to issue a single instead. The company most likely realized that the added costs for two additional songs and a cardboard cover for an EP sold for the price of a single did not make economic sense. Consumers in America normally bought singles, not EPs. In addition, Capitol learned that the Beatles would be performing two of the four songs on the season premiere of The Ed Sullivan Show on September 12.

The Beatles arrived in New York City on Friday, August 13, 1965, for their second tour of North America. The following day the group headed to CBS-TV's Studio 50 to tape their performance for The Ed Sullivan Show. After rehearsals from 11:00 AM through 2:00 PM, a dress rehearsal was held at 2:30. The show, set for broadcast on September 12, was taped that evening at 8:30 before an audience of over 700 lucky fans. The group performed "I Feel Fine," "I'm Down" and "Act Naturally" in their first segment. This was later followed by "Ticket To Ride" (shown next page), "Yesterday" (Paul solo on acoustic guitar backed by pre-recorded strings) and "Help!" These same six songs were performed by the Beatles on August 1 for the British TV show Blackpool Night Out. The Beatles began their North American tour with an historic concert at Shea Stadium on August 15, which was filmed for a television special.

After learning that the Beatles would perform "Act Naturally" and "Yesterday" on The Ed Sullivan Show, Capitol decided to issue those two songs as its next Beatles single with the same 5498 catalog number as the aborted EP. The decision to drop the EP and hold "I've Just Seen A Face" and "It's Only Love" for future release had a significant impact on the Capitol version of *Rubber Soul*, which would add the two tracks, giving the LP a cohesive folk-rock sound.

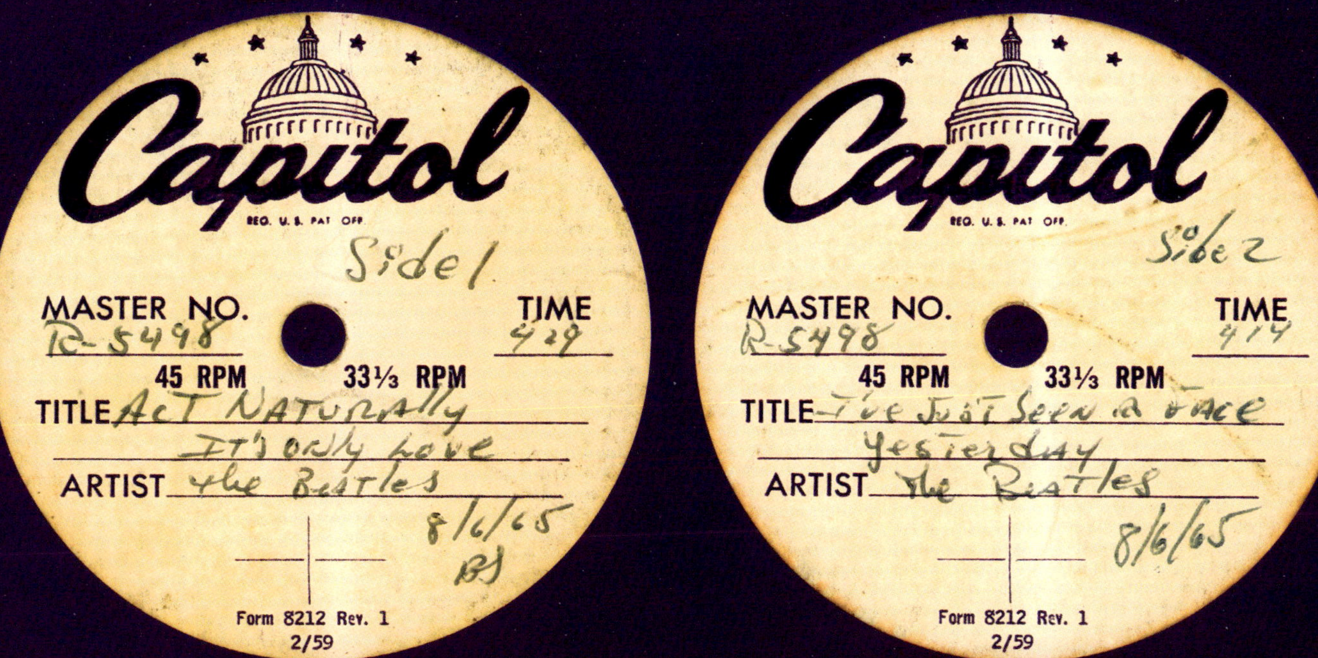

Capitol
REG. U.S. PAT. OFF.
Side 1
MASTER NO.
R-5498
TIME
4:29
45 RPM
33⅓ RPM
TITLE Act Naturally
It's only love
ARTIST The Beatles
8/6/65
BJ
Form 8212 Rev. 1
2/59

Capitol
REG. U.S. PAT. OFF.
Side 2
MASTER NO.
R-5498
TIME
4:14
45 RPM
33⅓ RPM
TITLE I've Just Seen a Face
Yesterday
ARTIST The Beatles
8/6/65
Form 8212 Rev. 1
2/59

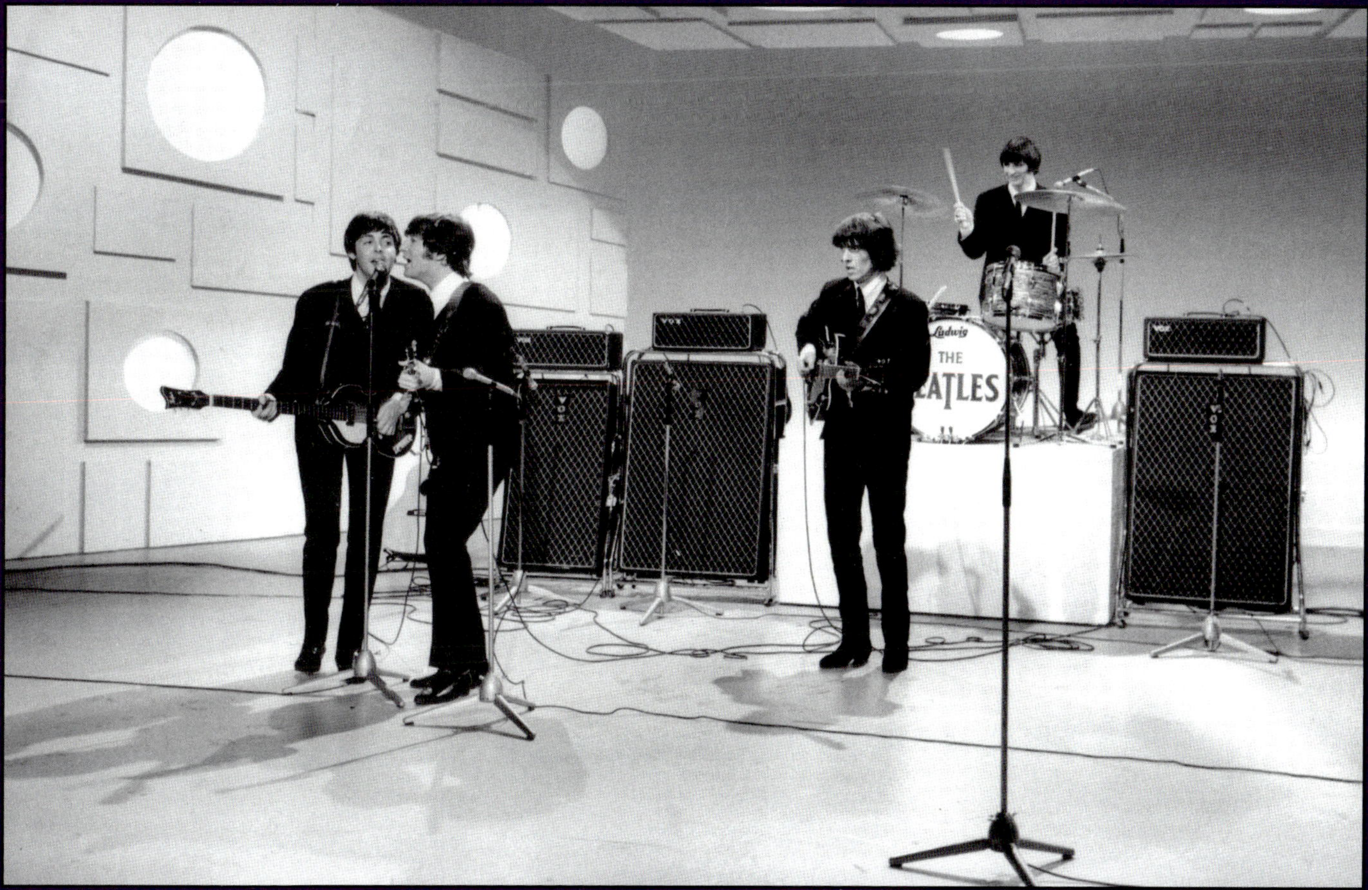
Ludwig
THE
EATLES

PREMIERE U.S.A.!

RINGO STARR SINGS SOLO!
PAUL McCARTNEY SINGS SOLO!

Watch both numbers performed
in person by Ringo and Paul on the Ed Sullivan Show, September 12.

Stock up — and see!

THE BEATLES

ACT NATURALLY • YESTERDAY 5498

5498

In late August, Capitol announced that "Act Naturally" would be the next Beatles single. The company heralded the U.S.A. premiere of "Act Naturally" and "Yesterday" in the September 11 music trades. Both sides were marketed as solo vocal performances—one by Ringo and one by Paul. Capitol shrewdly scheduled the single's release for September 13, the day after the group's performance of both songs on the September 12 Ed Sullivan Show. While "Yesterday" was clearly the superior song, Capitol initially designated "Act Naturally" as the A-side. At the time, Ringo was the most popular Beatle in America and had gained added attention due to his central role in *Help!*

"Yesterday" hit number one in its third of eleven weeks in the Billboard Hot 100 on October 9, replacing the McCoys' "Hang On Sloopy." It remained at the top for four weeks before falling to number three behind the Rolling Stones' "Get Off Of My Cloud" and the Toys' "A Lover's Concerto." Cash Box charted "Yesterday" for 13 weeks, including three at the top, while Record World listed the song for 12 weeks, with two weeks at number one. Ringo's "Act Naturally" charted for seven weeks in all three charts, peaking at number 47 in Billboard, 28 in Cash Box and 21 in Record World. Cash Box indicated that as of September 8, 46% of its reporting stations had added "Yesterday" to their play lists. A week later, this had grown to 96%. Stations were also playing "Act Naturally," with 34% adding the song by September 8, with the number growing to 70% the next week. "Yesterday" was certified gold on October 20, 1965.

The music magazines reviewed the single in their September 11 issues. Billboard commented on both sides, with "Yesterday" drawing the most praise: "Paul goes it alone on a Dylan-styled piece of material. Backed by strings he displays a rich, warm ballad style. Good sound." "Act Naturally" was described as "interesting change-of-pace material, folk-flavored with tongue-in-cheek humor featuring solos by Ringo and Paul." Cash Box noted that although "Help!" was still at number one, either side of the potent follow-up single was capable of reaching the top. "Act Naturally" had Ringo on Buck Owens' country & western hit, "soloing the twangy tale of show biz success in a feelingfull, sincere country style." "Yesterday" featured Paul singing a "plaintive, slow-moving heart-breaking romantic lament with an interesting neo-classical backing." Readers were told to "Eye 'em both." Record World saw "Yesterday" as a strong contender to top the charts and described the song as "an offbeat Beatles number...that has Paul soloing against the group augmented by a string quartet under George Martin's guidance."

On October 11, 1965, Capitol simultaneously issued six Beatles singles as part of its Star Line oldies series. The titles included four discs duplicating the four Beatles 45s issued by Vee-Jay Records and its Tollie subsidiary during the first four months of 1964: "Twist And Shout" b/w "There's A Place;" "Love Me Do" b/w "P.S. I Love You;" "Please Please Me" b/w "From Me To You;" and "Do You Want To Know A Secret" b/w "Thank You Girl." The remaining two singles were unique Capitol creations: "Roll Over Beethoven" b/w "Misery" and "Boys" b/w "Kansas City." Three of the songs, "From Me To You," "There's A Place" and "Misery," were making their Capitol debut. At the time of their release, "Yesterday" was topping the Billboard Hot 100; however, that did not stop Capitol from promoting "Boys," with Ringo on lead vocals, as its next Beatles single despite the song being issued on the group's debut British album in March 1963, Vee-Jay's *Introducing The Beatles* in January 1964 and Capitol's *The Early Beatles* in March 1965.

The music trades reviewed "Boys" in their October 23 issues. Cash Box treated the disc as if it was a major new release: "The Fab Four are back again and this-time-out, hot off their two-sided 'Yesterday'/'Act Naturally' smash they offer 'Boys.'" The song was described as a "rollicking, fast-moving blues-tinged rocker with an infectious years-back rock 'n' roll flavor." As for the flip side, "the lads turn in a high-spirited rendition of 'Kansas City.'" Billboard, in a Top 20 Pop Spotlight review, recognized that the disc offered nothing new: "Finally released by popular demand from an early LP, this swinging rocker should prove a rapid chart winner." The magazine listed "Kansas City" as the flip side. Record World matter-of- factly stated "Beatles pull a full-blown rock and roll song from an album for 'Boys.'" Billboard charted "Boys" for one week at number 102, while Record World ignored the disc. Cash Box charted "Boys" for three weeks with a peak of 73 and "Kansas City" for one week at 75. Many radio stations initially gave both sides some spins, with Cash Box reporting that as of October 13, 50% of its reporting stations had added "Boys" and 42% had added "Kansas City." The following week this had grown to 82% for "Boys" and 62% for "Kansas City."

The single quickly disappeared from the airwaves when Beatles manager Brian Epstein visited the U.S. to voice his objections to Capitol, complaining that the songs were not current enough. The October 30 Cash Box reported that Capitol had withdrawn the disc because its performances were "no longer representative of the Beatles as they perform today." The Beatles Star Line singles were officially deleted from the Capitol catalog on December 31, 1965.

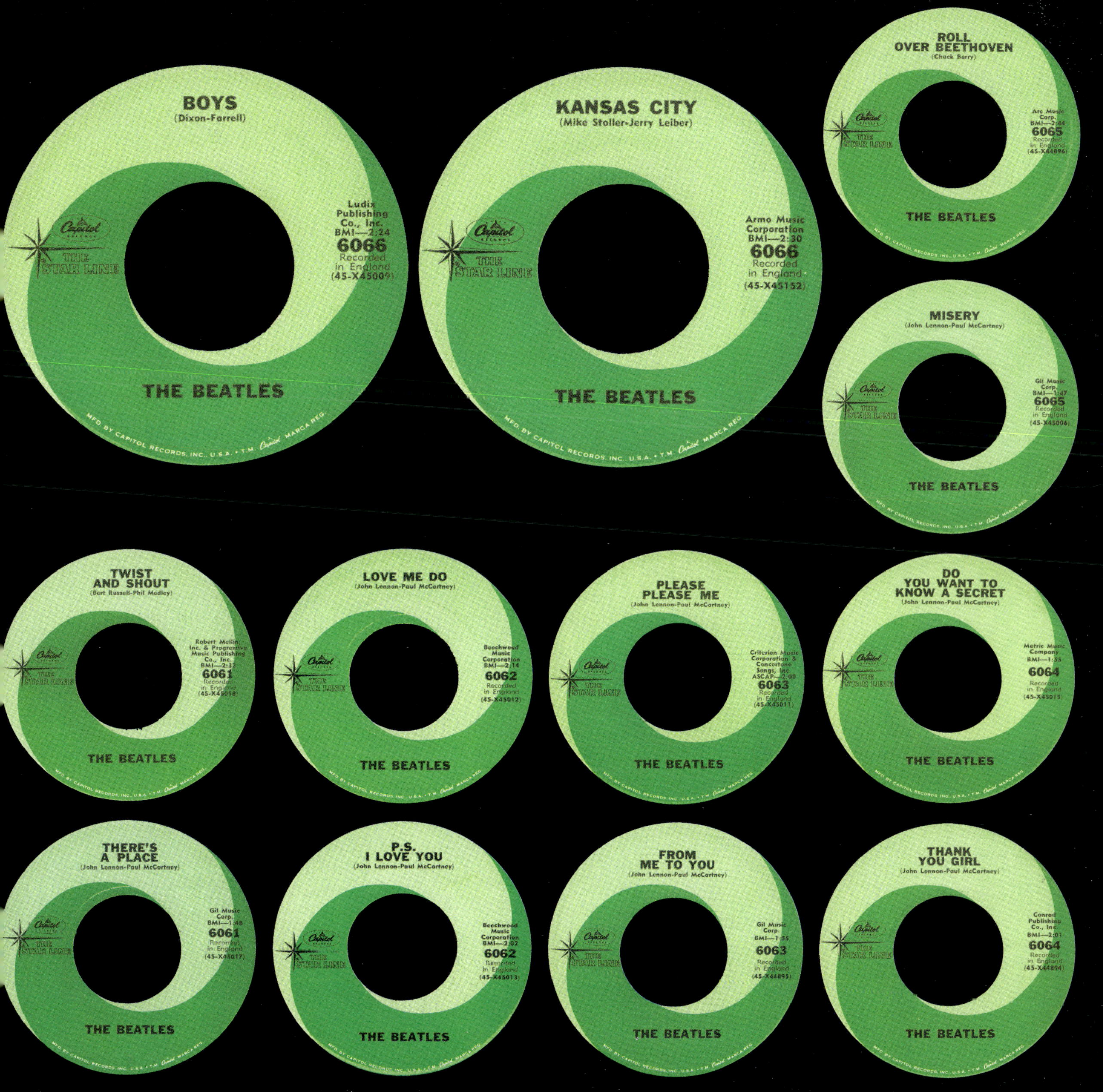
BOYS
(Dixon-Farrell)
Ludix Publishing Co., Inc. BMI—2:24
6066
Recorded in England
(45-X45009)
THE BEATLES
KANSAS CITY
(Mike Stoller-Jerry Leiber)
Armo Music Corporation BMI—2:30
6066
Recorded in England
(45-X45152)
THE BEATLES
ROLL OVER BEETHOVEN
(Chuck Berry)
6065
THE BEATLES
MISERY
(John Lennon-Paul McCartney)
6065
THE BEATLES
TWIST AND SHOUT
6061
THE BEATLES
LOVE ME DO
(John Lennon-Paul McCartney)
6062
THE BEATLES
PLEASE PLEASE ME
(John Lennon-Paul McCartney)
6063
THE BEATLES
DO YOU WANT TO KNOW A SECRET
(John Lennon-Paul McCartney)
6064
THE BEATLES
THERE'S A PLACE
(John Lennon-Paul McCartney)
6061
THE BEATLES
P.S. I LOVE YOU
(John Lennon-Paul McCartney)
6062
THE BEATLES
FROM ME TO YOU
(John Lennon-Paul McCartney)
6063
THE BEATLES
THANK YOU GIRL
(John Lennon-Paul McCartney)
6064
THE BEATLES
THE STAR LINE
MFD. BY CAPITOL RECORDS, INC., U.S.A. • T.M. Capitol MARCA REG.

Capitol prepared its 1965 Christmas catalog booklet in November, prior to receiving the art work or music for the Beatles upcoming *Rubber Soul* LP. Santa was shown on its cover providing "HELP!" for shoppers with gift problems. And with its release of multiple Beatles albums and singles, Capitol made sure there was plenty of Beatles for sale.

Although the Beatles had won Grammy Awards the previous year for Best New Artist and Best Performance By A Vocal Group for "A Hard Day's Night," they were shut out at the 8th annual Grammy Awards ceremony for outstanding performances of 1965 despite garnering ten nominations. As expected, it was a very good year for Frank Sinatra, who was honored with a Lifetime Achievement Award. Roger Miller was the king of the night, winning six awards on the strength of his "King Of The Road" single. The Beatles *Help!* LP lost out to Sinatra's *September Of My Years* for Album Of The Year. The other nominees were *My World* by Eddy Arnold, *My Name Is Barbra* by Barbra Streisand and the soundtrack to *The Sound Of Music*. The Beatles album was bested by *The Sandpiper* for Best Original Score. The "Help!" single lost out to the Statler Brothers' "Flowers On The Wall" for Best Contemporary Rock & Roll Group Vocal Performance and to "We Dig Mancini" by the Anita Kerr Quartet for Best Vocal Performance. [Ouch!] "Yesterday" had six nominations, but failed to win in any of its categories. Song Of The Year went to "The Shadow Of Your Smile," written by Paul Francis Webster & Johnny Mandel. Herb Alpert & the Tijuana Brass won Record Of The Year for "A Taste Of Honey." (The year before, "I Want To Hold Your Hand" lost to "The Girl From Ipanema.") Best Contemporary Rock & Roll Single went to Roger Miller's "King Of The Road." The string quartet backing in "Yesterday" earned the song a nomination for Best Arrangement Accompanying A Vocalist Or Instrumentalist, but it lost to Sinatra's "It Was A Very Good Year." Paul McCartney was passed over for Best Male Vocal Performance by Frank Sinatra for "It Was A Very Good Year" and for Best Contemporary Rock & Roll Vocal Performance by Roger Miller for "King Of The Road."

Capitol's decision to release "Yesterday" as a single gave the song added attention. Although it failed to win any Grammy Awards, it would later be inducted into the Grammy Hall of Fame in 1977. "Yesterday" was voted Best Song of the 20th Century by a group of music experts assembled by BBC Radio 2 in 1999. The following year it was voted the No. 1 pop song of all time by MTV and Rolling Stone. There are over 2,200 cover versions of the song. According to Broadcast Music Incorporated (BMI), "Yesterday" was performed over seven million times in its first 35 years.

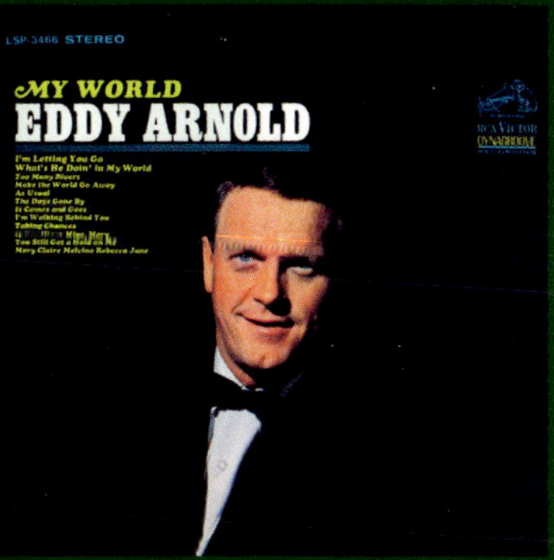

GIFT PROBLEMS?
HERE'S "HELP!"

...AND 197 OTHER PERFECT GIFT IDEAS FROM CAPITOL AND ANGEL RECORDS!

Capitol RECORDS

Angel

ORIGINAL MOTION PICTURE SOUNDTRACK

THE BEATLES

HELP!

Beatles For Sale in Canada

by Piers Hemmingsen

Canadian fans most often heard about new Beatles recordings from their local radio stations. And Canadian stations got their Beatles news from The Sizzle Sheet, a weekly newsletter authored by Capitol of Canada's Paul White. In the October 9, 1964 edition, White addressed questions regarding an "ALLEGED new Beatle disc on Capitol" titled "I'll Be Back." He assured stations that Capitol did not have any new Beatles single and explained that "I'll Be Back" was on the English release of *A Hard Day's Night*, but not on the United Artists soundtrack LP. He noted that many U.S. stations had acquired the British LP from the U.K. and were playing the song "like crazy." He added that some Canadian stations were doing the same. Although the song was not available in Canada, he was sure it would be soon.

The November 13 Sizzle Sheet told of a new Beatles disc, "I Feel Fine" b/w "She's A Woman," set for November 23 release. White noted: "Everyone it seems has been waiting for a new one from the most fabulous group of them all... and both sides will hit No.1 across the Nation." This prediction was not far off. R.P.M., the Canadian music industry magazine, debuted "She's A Woman" at number 18 in its December 7 issue before switching the listing for the disc to "I Feel Fine," which topped the R.P.M. Top 40 on December 28. Toronto's CHUM listed "I Feel Fine/She's A Woman" at number one for five weeks. The single sold 112,217 copies. [Canadian sales figures in this chapter are through 1967.]

The November 13 Sizzle Sheet also announced a Beatles album for late December "with some great new songs- like- KANSAS CITY- and songs from the team of Lennon-McCartney, Buddy Holly and Chuck Berry! WOW!" White obtained his information from the U.K., jumping the gun as Capitol did not include "Kansas City" or Holly's "Words Of Love" on the LP, holding them for later release. The next week, White wrote that "I'll Be Back" would be on the album. The December 11 Sizzle Sheet disclosed the LP's name, *Beatles '65*, and contents. The mono LP was rush released on December 14, initially packaged in U.S. covers. CHUM charted the LP at No. 1 for eight weeks. It sold 151,152 copies.

From the Desk of Paul White

Dateline: Week Ending December 11/64 NO.. 113

* *

BEATLEMANIA STRIKES AGAIN - AGAIN!

We just looked at issue No.63 of the "Sizzle" (December 13,1963) and find the whole first page was devoted to news about the new disease- Beatlemania! Under the heading "Beatlemania Taking Over" we told you that the first Beatle LP was selling like crazy and that "She Loves You" was an out and out hit . . . now in this issue of "Sizzle", we are happy to report 'Beatlemania Strikes Again!'

"I Feel Fine" and "She's A Woman" have established The Beatles as No.1 in the nation again - and interest in the 'Beatles '65' package is running high. This new one (T 2228 - mono and stereo) is to be RUSH released on Monday (14th). It's a gas, real fab, the gear, featuring these songs . . .

Side 1
No Reply
I'm A Loser
Baby's In Black
Rock and Roll Music
I'll Follow The Sun
Mr. Moonlight

Side 2
Honey Don't
I'll Be Back
She's A Woman
I Feel Fine
Everybody's Trying To Be My Baby

And also on its way - the two-record set "The Beatles Story" - a deluxe package packed with interviews with John, Paul, Ringo and George, with their fans, their recording manager Brian Epstein (did I leave anyone out!!) — a real bonanza for their fans!

...

GARRY FERRIER'S SMASH HIT!

"RINGO DEER" is a sizzling hit in Toronto, Montreal and Ottawa - and when we say this - it's because it's selling with gusto! On our official best selling list that goes to distributors and branches, Garry's disc jumped tremendously!!

...

=OTHER CANADIANS ON THE MOVE=

THE ESQUIRES with "So Many Other Boys" continue to move at a fast pace - and JACK LONDON AND THE SPARROWS are off to a great start with "If You Don't Want My Love". Jack appeared with Dave Johnson on CHUM'S "Liverpool School" Wednesday night and was such a success that when he was leaving the station he found hundreds of teenagers waiting and screaming for him. Jack eventually had to climb out onto the roof of CHUM and make his escape! Mail has been pouring into this office for Jack - nearly 1,000 this week!! The disc hit the CHUM chart at No.44 this week. Jack and The Sparrows appear on "Hi Time" (CFTO-TV-Toronto) December 12th.

-OVER-

ZZLE SHEET

UT HOT Capitol SINGLES

ober 9,1964 NO:..104 From the Desk of Paul White

* *

. . . . Once again the "Sizzle" reports news on radio nterest seems to be with Hamilton stations. at CHML, FRANK ation's FM librarian and TONY LUCIANI takes over. Tony has t 'ML for over 15 years, and has been with the station for record for loyalty . . . we'd like to hear from some of you on M POULTON, formerly with CKLC-Kingston has moved in to take n. We wish both men every success in their new positions.

the station has a new face this week . . . he's GARY CALBERT BN-Ohio . . . a big Canadian 'hello' to you Gary - welcome et.

CKFM (that's CFRB in stereo). This week BILL BALLANTINE reet address as Programme Director . . .

IL, PD of CHEX-Peterborough who brings us up to date des the regulars, Del Crary, Vern Rombough, "Sunshine" s a new face - or CHEX-MATE as Don so aptly describes now swinging out every night with 'music for young mming changes lately and come up with a winning

that he too has moved. Chuck, formerly with O in Chatham. Welcome to Ontario, Chuck!

egina, who gave us some hot news about the reaction on his morning show. . . the two Campbeltown Loch" and the RUSS MORGAN LP

. . . Nice hearing from you Johnny - why not make it a habit?

ROBINSON of C-FUN-Vancouver report great reaction to Dave Clark's new ODY KNOWS" and Nancy Wilson's "I WANNA BE WITH YOU" . . .by the way folks, received new label copy on that one this week and the title has been changed to "I Want To Be With You" . . . okay?

THOSE ELUSIVE BEATLE SINGLES!

Boy, what a week . . . I think every station in the country has been asking about the ALLEGED new Beatle disc on Capitol . . . we now have the names of at least three different sides. To start with, and for the book to show we haven't been holding anything back from you, let me say we DO NOT have a new Beatle single on release and we haven't seen one scheduled for at least the next three weeks! The one everybody seems to think we have is called "I'LL BE BACK" . . . well, we'll tell all we know. The song is contained on the ENGLISH release of the "Hard Days Night" album - as you are all aware it was omitted from the United Artists sound track album and therefore we gather Capitol has the rights to the disc. Many American stations have acquired copies from the UK and are playing it like crazy . . we note that some Canadian stations have done this too. For instance, it's listed on the CKCK REGINA chart this week! So here's just another case of everyone wanting to play a record that is not even available for sale in this country - we are sure it will be soon though. As for the other reports . . . they are all UNCONFIRMED - but you'll hear from us as soon as the position changes.

....over...

The December 11 Sizzle Sheet also promoted the two-record set *The Beatles' Story* as a "deluxe package packed with interviews with John, Paul, Ringo and George, with their fans" and "a real bonanza for their fans!" The album, released only in mono on December 21 in U.S. manufactured covers, sold 10,798 copies.

In the February 12, 1965 Sizzle Sheet, White urged stations to "celebrate Ringo's wedding with new single," adding: "Ringo assures himself of always having a hairdresser handy by marrying his girlfriend of 18 months and Capitol wishes the happy couple on their way with the release of a new disc: EIGHT DAYS A WEEK (an appropriate title!!!) and I DON'T WANT TO SPOIL THE PARTY." The single was issued on February 18. R.P.M., which had charted the *Beatles '65* album track "No Reply" for two weeks in January with a peak at number 28, reported "Eight Days A Week" for three weeks, including two weeks at number one. CHUM charted the single as "Eight Days A Week/Spoil The Party" for 11 weeks, including four weeks at number one. "Eight Days A Week" sold 103,561 copies.

The March 26 Sizzle Sheet provided details about a new Beatles single: "Two new songs from the Beatles latest movie 'Eight Arms To Hold You' is now in the works and just as soon as our production department have it pressed it will be on its way to you. The titles . . . . 'Ticket To Ride' and 'Yes It Is'!!!!!" In the April 2 Sizzle Sheet, Paul White discussed a new Beatles album being advertised in the U.S. trade magazines, *The Early Beatles*: "All tunes contained in this LP are included in the Canadian-Capitol 'Twist And Shout' package–Therefore no release of this in Canada...'Nuff said?" He added that "Ticket To Ride" would be released by April 12. The following week he announced that the single was now available and that the Beatles would be back in Toronto for two shows on August 17. "Ticket To Ride" charted for six weeks on the R.P.M. Play Sheet, finally working its way to the top on May 24. CHUM charted "Ticket To Ride/ Yes It Is" for 14 weeks, including three weeks at number one. "Ticket To Ride" sold 81,536 copies.

The May 28 Sizzle Sheet contained the exciting news of a new Beatles LP. "SOUND THE TRUMPETS-- BLOW THOSE HORNS-- a new Beatles package is due for release on June 14- featuring a whole bunch of goodies for their fans." White then provided the album's name, *Beatles VI*, and a list of the songs, along with the vocalist(s) and songwriter information for each track. CHUM charted *Beatles VI* at number one for six weeks. The LP sold 63,774 copies.

THE SIZZLE SHEET

FAST TALK ABOUT HOT 

RECORDS

Dateline: Week Ending May 28th, 1965 No:136 From the Desk of Paul White

* *

NEW BEATLES ALBUM !!!

SOUND THE TRUMPETS — BLOW THOSE HORNS — a new Beatles package is due for release on June 14 - featuring a whole bunch of goodies for their fans. You may want to give your listeners the line up of each song on the LP - which is called "BEATLES VI" by the way...

SELECTION	SUNG BY
Eight Days a Week	John, Paul & George
Kansas City	Paul
Words of Love	John & Paul
Yes It Is	John, Paul & George (solo by John)
Don't Want To Spoil The Party	John & Paul
What You're Doing	Paul
Every Little Thing	John & Paul
You Like Me Too Much	George
Tell Me What You See	John & Paul
Bad Boy	John
Dizzy Miss Lizzie	John

The songs written by the song writing team of Lennon-McCartney are "What You're Doing", "Yes It Is", "Tell Me What", "Every Little Thing", "Spoil The Party" and "Eight Days A Week". "Bad Boy" and "Dizzy Miss Lizzie" are by Larry Williams and "Words of Love" is from the pen of Buddy Holly.

CANADIAN ARTISTS HAVE HITS!

THE BIG TOWN BOYS first Capitol outing is so good we are still trying to decide which is the "A" side. "I LOVE HER SO" looked like it before release but the flip "I WONDER" has had great reaction from stations after their initial auditions.

ROBBIE LANE also debuts with Capitol with "WHERE HAS LOVE GONE" - a strong side. This artist did well with his last release and is a talent to watch!

THE SPARROWS come on strong with their first outing for Capitol . . . here again it's a wait and see situation with their sides as both are excellent . . . "HARD TIMES WITH THE LAW" and "MEET ME AFTER FOUR".

AND NEXT WEEK . . . .

WES DAKUS and BARRY ALLEN have new releases chartbound - in fact we're predicting Wes' Side will be the instrumental hit of the year!

THE STACCATOS have had split reaction with "SMALL TOWN GIRL" and "IF THIS IS LOVE" - the uptempo side "LOVE" looms big in the East.

OVER-

STARS - SUCH ...
ST. THOMAS AND CFGM RICHMOND ...

SPARROWS INVADE LINDSAY . . .

LAST SATURDAY WAS "JACK LONDON DAY" IN LINDSAY SPONSORED BY CKLY - UNDER THE DIRECTION OF TEX BAGSHAW. THE DAY ALSO WOUND UP THEIR VERY SUCCESSFUL "CANADIAN STARLINE" CONTEST. BOB GODFREY DID A HALF-HOUR INTERVIEW WITH JACK . . . AND THE RESULT . . . 157 PHONE CALLS IN A HOUR FROM TEENS WANTING TO JOIN THE JACK LONDON & SPARROW FAN CLUB AND REQUESTING MORE AIRPLAY ON THEIR RECORDS. TO QUOTE TEX "COULD BE THE BIGGEST THING SINCE QUAKER DISCOVERED OATS" . . .

NEW BEATLE LP ? ? ? ?

SOME OF YOU HAVE BEEN WONDERING ABOUT THE NEW BEATLE ALBUM ADVERTISED IN THE TRADE PAPERS "EARLY BEATLES" . . . ALL TUNES CONTAINED IN THIS LP ARE INCLUDED IN THE CANADIAN-CAPITOL "TWIST AND SHOUT" PACKAGE — THEREFORE NO RELEASE ON THIS IN CANADA . . . , NUFF SAID? INCIDENTALLY, THE BEATLES NEW SINGLE WILL BE AVAILABLE BY APRIL 12TH....

YOUNG SWINGERS Selection OF THE MONTH

Happy Birthday to the Beatles!

THEY'RE VI ALBUMS OLD ■ John, Paul, George and Ringo are four of the most famous people in the world—there's never been anything like them before and it's doubtful that there will ever be. Help them celebrate their sixth album (appropriately called BEATLES VI) with these smashing songs:

NEW SONGS
You Like Me Too Much • Tell Me What You See • Dizzy Miss Lizzie • Bad Boy

NEW IN CANADA
Kansas City • Words of Love • Every Little Thing • What You're Doing

BEATLE CLASSICS
I Don't Want to Spoil the Party • Eight Days a Week • Yes It Is

HAPPY BIRTHDAY DEAR BEATLES, HAPPY BIRTHDAY TO YOU! (and your album BEATLES VI).
F2358, $4.20; SF2358, $5.20.

YOUNG SWINGERS ALTERNATE

Peter & Gordon

This phenomenal pair of English lads hasn't stopped climbing since they started and small wonder. Their sound is driving, excitingly different and has everyone caught up in its enthusiasm. It's all quite smashing... hear, hear for yourself.
I Go To Pieces; Sleepless Nights; Tears Don't Stop; If You Wish; All Shook Up; Whatcha Gonna Do 'Bout It; Good Morning Blues; Someone Ain't Right; A Mess Of Blues; I Still Love You; I Don't Care What They Say.
Mono Only (F2324, $4.20)

5

The Capitol Record Club of Canada's Keynotes magazine (shown above) promoted the LP *Beatles VI* with a birthday salute to the Beatles for being "VI ALBUMS OLD." This was the group's sixth Capitol of Canada LP not counting *The Beatles' Story*. Capitol's art department added a birthday cake. The original picture (shown on page 213) has the group cutting a Christmas cake.

The July 16 Sizzle Sheet announced that a new Beatles single with "Help" and "I'm Down" was being rushed to stations. White predicted "these two tremendous sides by The Beatles will soon be No. 1 in North America." The single, issued on July 26, was listed on the R.P.M. Play Sheet for five weeks, hitting the top in its last week on August 31. CHUM charted "Help!/I'm Down" for 13 weeks, including three at number one. "Help!" sold 148,661 copies, including over 50,000 in its first two weeks. The July 22 Sizzle Sheet informed stations: "IT'S OFFICIAL . . . The Beatles second movie soundtrack 'HELP' will be on Capitol...set for release around August 9." The Beatles dominated the front page of the August 6 Sizzle Sheet with news of the group's upcoming concerts at the Maple Leaf Gardens in Toronto, the premiere of the *Help!* film, and the movie's soundtrack album, which was packaged in a "double jacket job filled with fabulous colour pictures of the boys- plus great new songs too!" White announced that the album had advance orders of 50,000, adding: "Who said they [the Beatles] were dying out???? In Canada, we have sold close to 3 million albums and singles- not bad eh!!" CHUM charted the *Help!* LP at number one for seven weeks. It was released in mono and stereo, and went on to sell 106,001 copies. The Toronto concerts were a big success, with the afternoon show being professionally recorded, complete with the opening acts and press conference.

Help! opened in Toronto on Thursday, August 12, at a dozen theaters. Frank Morris reviewed the film the next day in The Globe and Mail, describing it as a "bizarre collection of gags" and "an exercise in the cinema of the absurd" where anything goes. Morris noted that some of the humor was "over the heads of most of the youngsters, although they howled at some of the more outrageous slapstick." He observed that a few Beatles fans dutifully screamed at the first appearance of their idols, but reduced their response to fitful yelps "when it became obvious that their zeal wasn't contagious." The film is "often heavy-footed and foolish, sometimes brilliantly funny in a stream-of-consciousness vein." The Beatles "move nimbly" and "never overplay their parts." Barrie Hale's review in the August 12 Toronto Telegram is titled "Oh My, 007! Beatles Call Bond To Help." The film has "sort of a plot" and a "lot of mechanical gimmicks, beautiful color and The Boys just strolling through it." As for the weapons the Beatles must face, Hale writes: "Trouble is, most of them have been done so much better in the Bond movies, where they are so funny because they are so deadly in earnest. Here, they are manipulated by villains who...[are] a lovable, bumbling lot." The film is not as amusing as *A Hard Day's Night*, but does have its strong moments, particularly the music sequences with "The Boys themselves performing it, or cavorting as Beautiful People to it, or both." Hale concludes that *Help!*, despite its defects, is "an ingratiating movie, and one you might find yourself returning to more than once." David Cobb knocked the film in the August 19 Toronto Star. "The boys are a likeable bunch–with Lester's help they come across far better than any of the other groups hustled onto the screen–but the picture is sad proof that no matter how jazzy the direction or sharp the camerawork, nothing can conceal desperation...the film being really a collection of sight gags and dialogue that tries strenuously to be off-beat in the Beatle idiom, and hopelessly fails."

The movie also premiered in Vancouver on August 12. The next day, Lorne Parton reviewed the film in The Province, stating that although the Beatles showed a "fine flair for the necessary madness" in their films, there needed to be "more method in their madness–and a lot of work, practice and restraint before the hirsute four can be classified as first rank comedians." The movie was a "surrealistic spoof" with a silly story line, "but no sillier than those plotlines on which the Marx Brothers and Abbott and Costello hung their comedies." His verdict: "On the whole, the movie is a bit long and drags near the end, and if you can't stand the Beatle music, forget it." Les Wedman had a more positive view in the August 16 Vancouver Sun, writing: "This film [*Help!*] is crazier than the first; every bit as funny–though the biting satire has been replaced by a series of sight and sound gags that range from slapstick to slick sophistication...They have a slight and often silly plot to work with, but the amazing point is it does work." Wedman notes that something in print cannot come close to describing the "howling start" to *Help!* and the "rib-tickling and daffy ideas and situations that follow." His advice was "seeing is believing, and seeing Help! will help."

The movie was released throughout most of the rest of Canada a week later on August 19. The film received a few excellent reviews in the Montreal press. In the August 20 Montreal Star, Sydney Johnson wrote: "'Help!' is a first-class slapstick farce in which a thin story line is an excuse for a constant stream of fast-moving hilarious comic gags interspersed every few minutes by a selection from the repertoire of the famous quartet." Although the film was "not in the same class as its distinguished predecessor," Johnson advised: "Don't let that put you off if you like the Beatles and slapstick comedy of the kind made famous by the Marx Brothers, the Ritz Brothers, Crosby and Hope, and Martin and Lewis, because it is excellent entertainment."

In the August 21 Gazette, Jack Baker wrote: "**HELP** is one of the most welcome cinematic surprises of the year. The Marx Brothers in their finest hour were never more hilarious than the madcap quartet of John, Paul, George and Ringo." While the movie doesn't have the immediacy of its predecessor, *Help!* has "an originality, a pace and a cleverness that the first came nowhere near achieving." Baker adds: "Help! is a brilliant satire on everything from the British Empire to the Keystone Cops to James Bond. And speaking of Bond, Help is to A Hard Day's Night what From Russia With Love was to Dr. No–bigger, better and more imaginative." Baker raved about the film's "amazingly creative photography by David Watin and its brilliant colors" and noted that the music composed by John, Paul and George is "apropos in every instance." His advice: "Even if you can't stand the Beatles or their music, go to the film with your ears stuffed with cotton batting. The colors, photography and ingenious devices will insure [sic] [ensure] that you enjoy yourself."

The August 20 Edmonton Journal provided two points of view, first from staff journalist Barry Westgate. After noting that *A Hard Day's Night* was "an hysterical movie, filled with the symbolism of The Beatles' electric popularity" that was "expected from the leading purveyors of teenage mass hysteria," he found *Help!* to be "almost sedate by comparison." Nonetheless, he described the second film as a "gay romp...with the ingredients of song and slapstick knit to hit hard at the younger audiences...the ones that will still scream insanely and be satisfied with that." While the Beatles "will never...be more than token actors," *Help!* is "far and away a better production than the first." The song sequences are "first rate–filled with exuberance and enjoyment" and "marked highlights" that "fit, unattached, into a story that has nothing to do with reality, is almost a comic strip of Beatles personality." *Help!* "lives through their songs and somehow emerges...as a fluffy glittery adventure into an intriguing world." Westgate misheard the lyrics of one of the musical numbers, titling the song as "She's Got A Ticket To Write." The newspaper gave teenager Lydia Dotto a ticket to write about the film. She indicated that hundreds of Edmonton Beatlemaniacs, herself included, lined the street for two blocks to see the premiere. Once inside, screaming was at a high pitch even before the appearance of "the famous four idols." When they did appear, "the reception was ear-shattering, reminiscent of *A Hard Day's Night*." Those in attendance liked *Help!* "as much, if not more, than the first one." There could be multiple reasons for this. *Help!* had more of a plot then its predecessor, living up to its billing as a "riotously funny chase-comedy." It was funnier, "featuring more of The Beatles' zany wit." And simply, "it was The Beatles–in color yet!"

The September 3 Sizzle Sheet announced a new Beatles single: “Watch out! The Beatles are invading again! This time they are hitting the C & W trail with Ringo singing ‘ACT NATURALLY’- The same song that took Buck Owens to the top of the charts. The Ringo fans will go wild over this one! The flip ‘YESTERDAY’ features Paul backed by a string quartet. Both sides will be sung by The Beatles on the September 12 Ed Sullivan Show and predictions are that this will be an instant monster! Official airplay September 7 . . . Your copies are on the way!” Stores began selling the record the day after The Ed Sullivan Show appearance. Incredible as it may seem, Capitol in the U.S. and Canada initially marketed “Act Naturally” as the A-side of the new single, failing to recognize the brilliance of “Yesterday.” CHUM charted the single for 11 weeks, with the record being listed as “Act Naturally/Yesterday” on the CHUM Hit Parade through October 11, the first of two weeks at number one. Subsequent charts during the single’s 11 total weeks on the survey listed the disc as “Yesterday/Act Naturally.” R.P.M. charted the disc solely as “Yesterday” during its surprisingly short five weeks on the R.P.M. Play Sheet, with the song unexpectedly stalling at number four. This seems odd as several top-tier Canadian stations charted “Yesterday” at number one, including Montreal’s CFCF, Ottawa’s CFRA, London’s CFPL, Winnipeg’s CKRC and Vancouver’s CFUN. The single sold 119,555 copies. As was the case with “Eight Days A Week” and “Ticket To Ride,” the initial 5,000 copies of the record were shipped inside picture sleeves imported from the U.S.

The October 22, 1965 Sizzle Sheet referred to a single with “Boys” and “Kansas City” as being “the new giant.” White wrote: “The Beatles have done it again! The re-issue of two of their best numbers as a single has started another massive sales pile-up. Both sides are on the trade charts and look destined for the Top-10.” R.P.M. charted “Boys” for two weeks, with a peak at 32. The single sold 12,241 copies, with its sales significantly hampered when Beatles manager Brian Epstein insisted that Capitol cease promotion of the disc because it did not represent the group’s current sound. The record was one of four Beatles Star Line singles issued on October 18 with green swirl labels. The others in the series were “Twist And Shout” b/w “There’s A Place” (1,724 copies sold), “Love Me Do” b/w “P.S. I Love You” (1,420 copies sold) and “Please Please Me” b/w “From Me To You” (1,606 copies sold). None a giant.

The Sizzle Sheets detailed above are historic documents that give a time capsule picture of how Capitol of Canada informed radio stations that the company had Beatles for sale. The next release would be a real giant–*Rubber Soul*.

1965: Another Year of Change and Turbulence

by Al Sussman

On October 2, 1964, President Lyndon B. Johnson ("LBJ") gave a speech in the State Dining Room of the White House in which he proclaimed that 1965 would be International Cooperation Year in the United States of America, adding that its observance would be "commemorated around the world by the members of the United Nations." He stressed that "international cooperation is simply not an idea or an ideal" but "a fact of life" and "a clear necessity to our survival" for the "greater the nation the greater is its need to work cooperatively with other people, with other countries, other nations."

Although the lofty goals set by LBJ in his speech would face severe headwinds, the youth of America was ready to continue its contribution to international cooperation by remaining fascinated with the Beatles and other British acts gaining popularity in the States. On October 7, those tuning in to the fourth episode of ABC-TV's new rock 'n' roll showcase, Shindig, saw the Beatles perform a new John Lennon composition that was different from anything the group had yet released, a Bob Dylan-influenced tune called "I'm A Loser." The group had begun taking its first musical steps away from the sound that most fans had grown to expect.

As 1964 neared its end, the year was already being remembered as a time that brought significant change, including the U.S.'s growing commitment to South Vietnam in its battle with the Viet Cong guerrilla force supported by the communist government of North Vietnam, which would continue to escalate in 1965, and the passage of the most comprehensive civil rights legislation since Reconstruction. Climaxing a tumultuous year in that struggle, the movement's acknowledged leader, Rev. Dr. Martin Luther King, Jr., was presented on December 10 with the Nobel Peace Prize for "his non-violent struggle for civil rights for the Afro-American population" at the annual ceremony in Oslo, Norway. King told The New York Times that he was "deeply gratified" and "glad people of other nations are concerned with our problems here." But the early months of 1965 would starkly show how much struggle lay ahead.

LIFE
DEEPER INTO
THE VIETNAM WAR
A Marine is evacuated
during patrol action
against the Vietcong
JULY 2 · 1965 · 35¢
®

Despite his campaign pledge not to increase the American commitment to the war in Vietnam, by the beginning of December 1964, President Johnson and his military advisors had begun planning the aerial bombing of North Vietnam. But there were already a sizable number of U.S. troops on the ground so, on December 24, Bob Hope gave his first Vietnam-era Christmas Eve show at Bien Hoo Air Base in South Vietnam. When the 89th Congress began its session on January 4, 1965, a future President, Michigan Republican Congressman Gerald Ford, was selected as minority leader of the House of Representatives. That evening, Johnson gave his State of the Union address in prime time and, with a landslide electoral mandate in hand, announced his plans for his Great Society programs.

On January 27, 1965, National Security Advisor McGeorge Buddy and Defense Secretary Robert McNamara presented Johnson with what came to be known as the "Fork In The Road" memorandum. It recommended major escalation of the war in Vietnam, rather than pursue a peaceful solution. As Viet Cong raids intensified, President Johnson gave the order on February 7, 1965, to evacuate American dependents from South Vietnam. Newsweek magazine reported on evacuees heading for the ramp leading up to Pan American Jet Clipper Defiance for the journey from Saigon to Hawaii. Although unnoticed at the time, this was the exact same Boeing 707 jet that had brought the Beatles from London to America one year earlier on February 7, 1964.

By mid-February, the United States had begun its operation of sustained bombing of North Vietnam, code-named Rolling Thunder. On February 17, the Defense Department announced that 37 Americans had been killed that week in Vietnam. That same day, Sen. Frank Church (D-Idaho) became the first member of Congress to begin open debate on the Senate floor over the war.

For many of the world's leaders, World War II was still a fresh memory. On January 24, the man who had led England through its darkest days of that war, Sir Winston Churchill, died at the age of 90, two weeks after suffering a major stroke. The former prime minister's state funeral procession on January 30 drew an estimated one million people to the streets of London. It was attended by the largest number of world figures since President Kennedy's funeral 14 months before. 350 million viewed the ceremonies on television, including 45 million in the United States.

Newsweek

FEBRUARY 1, 1965

35c

Churchill

1874 - 1965

On February 21, Malcolm X, a controversial civil rights advocate, was assassinated at New York's Audubon Ballroom. Previously a spokesman for the Nation of Islam, his extremist views brought about an acrimonious separation from the organization. He converted to Sunni Islam and founded his own Islamic organization. By this time, he had received multiple death threats. Three members of the Nation of Islam were convicted of his murder. His funeral was televised live and was attended by several civil rights leaders, many of whom strongly disagreed with his black separatist views.

Earlier that month, Malcolm X had made an appearance in support of voting rights while in Selma, Alabama, where Dr. King was organizing a series of demonstrations that were mostly peaceful but had led to a series of mass arrests. On February 18, Alabama state troopers and local police broke up a march in nearby Marion. During the ensuing fracas, a state trooper shot a 26-year-old church deacon, Jimmie Lee Jackson, who died a week later in a Selma hospital.

Jackson's death led to a scheduled march on March 7 from Selma to the Alabama state capital in Montgomery. After the 550 marchers crossed the Edmund Pettus Bridge (shown next page), they were violently attacked by 200 Alabama state troopers with clubs and tear gas when they refused to disperse. Student Nonviolent Coordinating Committee leader John Lewis, who would later serve in the U.S. House of Representatives for over 30 years, was among the most seriously injured. Two days later, a second attempted march, this time led by Dr. King, was again stopped by state police. On March 15, President Johnson addressed a joint session of Congress in reaction to the events in Selma, invoking the civil rights anthem "We Shall Overcome," and calling for federal voting rights legislation that would be passed that summer as the Voting Rights Act of 1965. Two days later, Federal District Judge Frank M. Johnson, Jr. issued an injunction barring Alabama state and county authorities from interfering with the march along U.S. Highway 60 to Montgomery. On March 20, LBJ federalized the Alabama National Guard and authorized U.S. Army troops to protect the marchers. The next day, a multi-denomination group of religious leaders, including Dr. King, led the demonstrators across the Edmund Pettus Bridge. By March 25, the march had swelled to 25,000 participants when it reached the steps of the State Capitol Building, where Dr. King gave his historic "How Long, Not Long" address. But the march had a tragic aftermath as Viola Luizzo, a 39-year-old white mother of five from Detroit, was shot to death while she transported a marcher back to Selma. Four Ku Klux Klan members were arrested the next day.

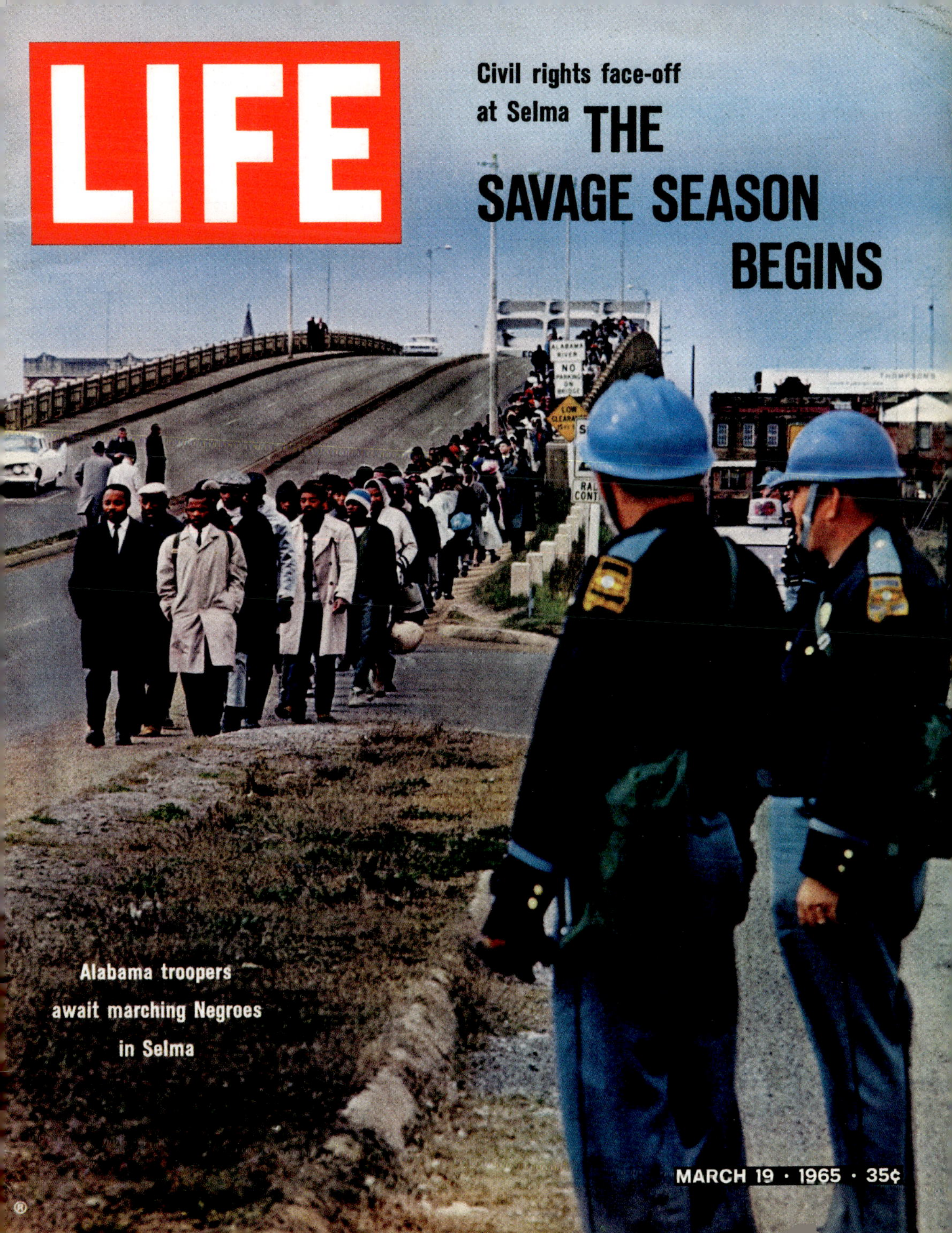

Alabama troopers await marching Negroes in Selma

The Soviet Union took the early lead in the space race by placing the first artificial satellite into orbit with Sputnik 1, launched on October 4, 1957, and putting the first man in space, Yuri Gagarin, in Vostok 1 on April 12, 1961. After the National Aeronautics and Space Administration ("NASA") completed America's first manned space program, Project Mercury, in May 1963, the Soviet Union continued its lead with a pair of additional achievements, conducting the longest solo orbital flight with Valery Bykovsky in Vostok 5 for just under five days from June 14-19, 1963, and sending the first woman into space, Valentina Tereshkova, in Vostok 6 on June 16, 1963. Soviet cosmonauts continued to grab headlines in the country's new Voskhod capsules. Voskhod 1 carried three cosmonauts into space for a 24-hour mission launched on October 12, 1964. Shortly before NASA sent its first manned Gemini capsule into orbit, the Soviets once again stole the thunder with its Voskhod 2 mission launched on March 18, 1965, with Pavel Belyayev and Alexei Leonov on board. Just over 90 minutes after liftoff, Leonov left the spacecraft through an inflatable airlock and became the first human to step into the vacuum of space. His 12 minute, nine second space walk captured headlines across the world. Leonov's great difficulty in squeezing back into the spacecraft was kept secret, as was the Voskhod capsule's problems on re-entry into the earth atmosphere that led to a landing 800 miles from its intended target. The U.S.S.R. waited more than two years before launching another crewed mission, the ill-fated Soyuz 1.

Although overshadowed by Voskhod 2 and Alexei Leonov's space walk, NASA's first manned mission with its new spacecraft, Gemini III, was a big success for the publicized start of a program that would put America ahead of the U.S.S.R. in the space race. On March 23, 1965, Virgil "Gus" Grissom, who was the U.S.'s second man in space, and rookie astronaut John Young completed a three-orbit mission to test the capsule's systems, maneuverability and re-entry flight path. The crew changed the size and shape of their orbit by firing thrusters. Young smuggled a corned beef sandwich on board, with each astronaut taking a few bites, leading to a reprimand. Gemini III splashed down 45 miles from its targeted landing spot in the Atlantic Ocean. The next morning, Ranger 9, which had been launched by NASA on March 21, neared the moon and took 5,814 pictures in the 20 minutes before its planned crash into the lunar surface. It was the last of NASA's series of unmanned lunar probes to check out potential landing sites for Apollo missions to the moon. As for the vehicle that would take astronauts to lunar orbit, scientists at NASA's Huntsville, Alabama space flight center performed the initial test of the first stage of the three-stage Saturn V rocket on April 16.

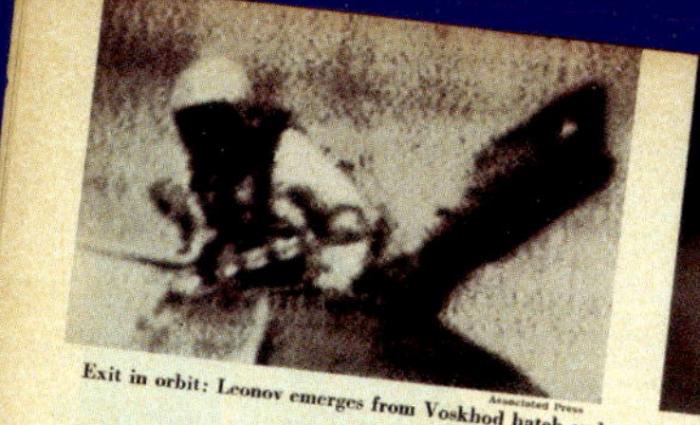

Exit in orbit: Leonov emerges from Voskhod hatch and, support-pack on back, clings cautiously to the ship . . .

Associated Press

CBS News

TAKE A GIANT STEP—INTO SPACE

Frost hung in the cloudy morning skies as the two cosmonauts clambered aboard the Voskhod (Sunrise) II spaceship at the Baikonur cosmodrome in Kazakhstan, U.S.S.R., one day last week. Both wore bulky white pressure suits, but one had a twin-bottled pack on his back. Less than two hours later, the Voskhod hatch opened again, and 30-year-old Aleksei Leonov took earthman's

ards of the bends. He slipped into a separate escape chamber, opened it up to the vacuum of space, and climbed out in his partially pressurized suit without difficulty. Belyayev was still on the other side of the chamber's air lock. He and his companion lived in two different worlds for those minutes, breathing different airs at different pressures.

As he left the Voskhod II via the hatch at the beginning of the second orbit, Leonov was above southwest Russia—in perfect line-of-sight so that a TV camera inside the cabin could relay pictures to ground stations. The

his helmet face plate. Some viewers could make out the Cyrillic initials for U.S.S.R. lettered across the visored white helmet.

Reassured, Leonov released his hold, and, connected to his ship only by the cable, drifted away. He floated horizontally, then vertically, then did slow somersaults as the TV camera and a motion-picture camera mounted on a boom outside the ship recorded his movements. At one point he disappeared from the camera's field of vision. Then, eerily, loops of his cable reappeared on screen, followed by the space walker a moment later. As Voskhod arched over the Arctic Ocean he gently hauled himself in, re-entered the ship, and closed

short minutes, he had

LIFE

The Astronauts' Own Story

GEMINI'S JOURNEY

by Gus Grissom and John Young

Frogmen escort Young as he awaits pickup in raft near capsule. Marker dye stains water.

APRIL 2 · 1965 · 35¢

®

Newsweek

MARCH 29, 1965 35¢

VOSKHOD VERSUS GEMINI

The Space Race Now

Back on Earth, protests against the war in Vietnam were beginning to percolate on American college campuses. The Faculty Committee to Stop the War in Viet Nam held a "teach-in" at the University of Michigan on the night of March 24 and would hold 26 more such events at universities over the next three weeks. On April 7, President Johnson gave an address titled "Peace Without Conquest" at Johns Hopkins University in which he explained the reasons for the escalation of the U.S.'s involvement in the war. However, the speech proved to be counterproductive and, in the opinion of some, began the erosion of LBJ's credibility. On April 17, Students for a Democratic Society ("SDS") carried out a major anti-war demonstration in Washington, including picketing in front of the White House. That same day, a group of students at the University of Wisconsin presented McGeorge Bundy with a petition of support for the war signed by 6,000 students and faculty. Meanwhile, at month's end, 14,000 U.S. troops invaded the Dominican Republic on LBJ's orders to protect American citizens from an ongoing civil war against the Dominican government and prevent "another Cuba," a second communist takeover of a Latin American nation. Like the escalating protests against the war in Vietnam, 40 male students at UC-Berkeley met on May 5 in front of the local draft board office and burned their draft cards as part of a larger protest against the U.S. invasion of the Dominican Republic.

In April, Time magazine ran two memorable cover stories in back-to-back issues. The April 2 edition focused on "The Computer in Society." After noting that man's exploration of space would be impossible without computers, the story commented that the biggest changes caused by these machines were taking place on earth. "Just out of its teens, the computer is beginning to affect the very fabric of society, kindling both wonder and widespread apprehension. Is the computer a friend or enemy of man?...Will it ever learn to think for itself?" Britain's Sir Leon Bagrit predicted that the computer would bring "the greatest change in the whole history of mankind." Professor Thomas Whisler of the University of Chicago's Graduate School of Business noted that "it will change everybody's life, and all change requires some effort and some cost to people." The article concluded that "the computer is not so much a challenge to man as a challenge for him; a triumph of technology to be developed, subdued and put to constantly increasing use." Charles Schulz's Peanuts characters graced the cover of the April 9 issue. The story observed: "Religion, psychiatry, education–indeed all the complexities of the modern world–seem more amusing than menacing when they are seen through the clear, uncompromising eyes of the comic-strip kids from Peanuts."

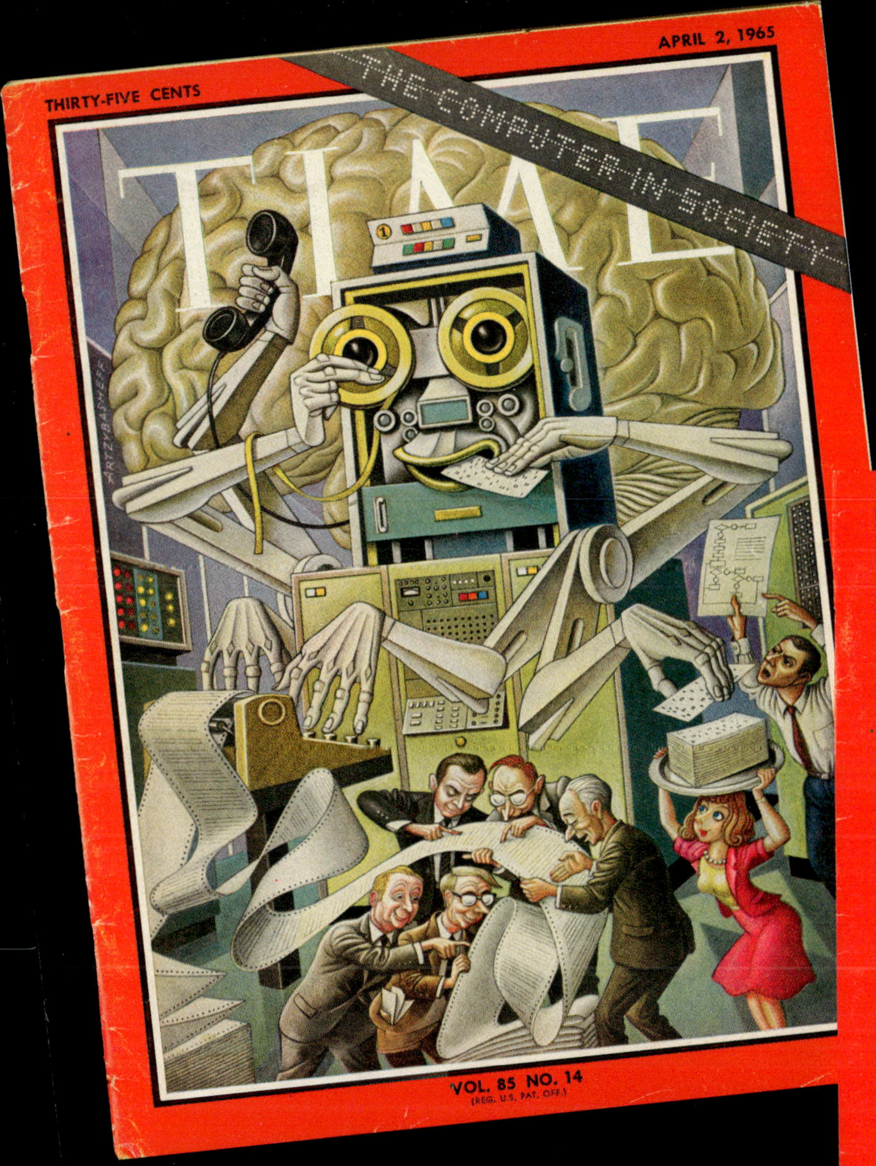

THIRTY-FIVE CENTS

APRIL 2, 1965

TIME

THE COMPUTER IN SOCIETY

ARTZYBASHEFF

VOL. 85 NO. 14

(REG. U.S. PAT. OFF.)

The long battle to enact federal health insurance for seniors 65 or older and people with disabilities neared its end when the House of Representatives voted to approve Medicare 313-115 on April 7. A highly amended version of the bill passed the Senate 68-21 on July 9. The reconciled bill passed 70-24 in the Senate on July 28 and was signed into law two days later at the Harry S. Truman Presidential Library in Independence, Missouri. Truman and his wife Bess were the first recipients of Medicare cards. May 18 saw the launch of one of LBJ's Great Society programs, Project Head Start, which would provide summertime education to more than 500,000 preschool-age children from underprivileged families. The voting rights bill introduced by LBJ during the Selma march crisis faced much the same opposition from southern Democrats that the Civil Rights Act had faced in 1964 before being signed into law by LBJ on August 6 in a ceremony attended by Dr. King, John Lewis, Rosa Parks and other civil rights leaders. Four days later, LBJ signed the Housing and Urban Development Act of 1965, which expanded funding for federal housing programs. By September 9, he had signed legislation creating the Department of Housing and Urban Development (HUD).

As the academic year came to an end in May, protests against the war in Vietnam continued to ramp up. On May 22, 30,000 attended a huge "teach-in" at Berkeley. On June 8, a State Department spokesman told a press conference that Gen. William Westmoreland, commander of U.S. forces in South Vietnam, had been given authorization by LBJ to commit American ground troops to combat duty in support of South Vietnamese forces. Although the White House issued a denial the next day, the decision had been made. On June 16, Defense Secretary McNamara announced that another 22,000 American troops would be sent to South Vietnam, raising the U.S. troop strength to 72,000, while conceding that the war was not going well. Anti-war demonstrators distributed leaflets in and around the Pentagon.

On Thursday morning, June 3, the second crewed Gemini mission, Gemini IV, lifted off from Cape Kennedy with a two-man crew of James McDivitt and Edward White II. That afternoon, on the mission's third orbit, White, tethered to the spacecraft and holding a maneuvering gun, left the capsule and went on a 20-minute space walk, the U.S.'s first. Four days and 62 orbits later, Gemini IV made a successful reentry and safe splashdown despite the shutdown of its onboard computer. On June 26, NASA announced the selection of six "scientist-astronauts" for future crewed space missions, one of whom, Harrison Schmitt, would become one of 12 Americans to walk on the moon.

LIFE
16 PAGES OF
FANTASTIC COLOR
The Space Walk

120 miles up,
Astronaut White floats
over Lower California
JUNE 18 · 1965 · 35¢

JUNE 21, 1965 35c
Newsweek

On July 4, Dr. King delivered a holiday sermon, "The American Dream," at the Ebenezer Baptist Church in Atlanta following up his 1963 "I Have A Dream" speech from the March on Washington. King admitted that "the dream has been shattered, and I have had my nightmarish experiences, but I tell you this morning once more that I haven't lost the faith. I still have a dream..." At the cradle of democracy, Independence Hall in Philadelphia, the first Annual Reminder was held as a group of gay activists picketed in front of the building in what is considered to be the first LGBT demonstration in the U.S.

On July 14, Mariner 4 completed the first fly-by of Mars, sending back 22 photographs and scientific data. That same day, the U.S. Ambassador to the United Nations, Adlai Stevenson, died of a heart attack in London at the age of 65. Stevenson, who had previously run unsuccessfully for President, distinguished himself during the Cuban missile crisis by effectively confronting Soviet representative Valerian Zorin at the U.N. Following Stevenson's death, President Johnson appointed Supreme Court Justice Arthur Goldberg to succeed Stevenson at the U.N. and nominated Abe Fortas to take Goldberg's place on the Court. On July 27, LBJ signed the Federal Cigarette Labeling and Advertising Act into law, which mandated that all cigarette packs have a warning label reading "Caution: Cigarette smoking may be hazardous to your heath." The next day, Johnson announced that 50,000 troops would be sent to South Vietnam, upping the troop commitment to 125,000 and fully committing the U.S. to a land war. On August 3, members of the 3rd Marine Division entered the South Vietnamese village of Cam Ne, which had been fortified with traps and mines by the Viet Cong. After taking some sporadic sniper fire, the Marines set fire to 150 huts and bulldozed other homes, ignoring the pleas of the village's inhabitants, mainly old men and women. CBS News filmed part of the attack, including a Marine setting one hut on fire and the pleas of villagers being ignored. Correspondent Morley Safer's report aired on The CBS Evening News with Walter Cronkite on August 5, infuriating LBJ and shocking Americans. In the impoverished Watts neighborhood of Los Angeles, a simple drunk driving incident on August 11 involving a black motorist and California Highway Patrolmen escalated into a disturbance that brought in Los Angeles police, leading to a full-scale riot lasting six days and involving 35,000 people. Nearly 14,000 members of the California Army National Guard were brought in to restore order. The uprising caused over 40 million dollars in property damage and led to 34 deaths and 3,438 arrests.

THIRTY-FIVE CENTS
AUGUST 20, 1965
THE LOS ANGELES RIOT
TIME
THE WEEKLY NEWSMAGAZINE

Newsweek
Adlai Stevenson
1900—1965
JULY 26, 1965 35c
Mariner
to
Mars

Newsweek
AUGUST 30, 1965 35c
THE RIOTS IN COLOR
Los Angeles: Why?

Meanwhile, in the United Kingdom, Sir Alec Douglas-Home was replaced by Edward Heath on July 28 as head of the Conservative Party, then the Opposition Party to the then ruling Labour Party led by Prime Minister Harold Wilson. These two political leaders would be name checked a year later by George Harrison in the Beatles song "Taxman." August 6 marked the 20th anniversary of the U.S.'s dropping of the first atomic bomb on Hiroshima, Japan leading to the end of World War II. A crowd of 30,000 gathered at the city's Peace Memorial Park to see Mayor Shinzo Hamai add 469 names to the list of the thousands of identified victims of the bombing.

On August 20, the U.S. Manned Space Flight Center announced a four-month schedule to begin work on the concept of an "orbital workshop," a precursor to the first U.S. space station, with the plan of converting a used Saturn V rocket stage into a shelter suitable for extended habitation and use. The next day, Gemini V lifted off from Cape Kennedy's Pad 19 with a crew of Mercury veteran Gordon "Gordo" Cooper and first-time pilot Charles "Pete" Conrad. Thanks to new fuel cells that generated enough electricity for longer missions, Gemini V doubled the elapsed time of Gemini IV. Conrad described the mission as "eight days in a garbage can," referring to the cramped quarters of the Gemini capsule. While the actual elapsed time of the mission was 65 minutes short of eight days, Gemini V remained in space for the amount of time necessary to complete a mission to and from the moon. Although a scheduled rendezvous with a pod ejected from the capsule had to be canceled due to issues with the fuel cells, the crew performed a phantom rendezvous with a given point in space.

On October 3, President Johnson signed the Immigration and Nationality Act of 1965 on Liberty Island in New York Harbor, next to the Statue of Liberty. The act ended quotas based on ethnicity, replacing the National Origins Formula, which had been the basis of U.S. immigration policy since the 1920s. The next day, LBJ met with Pope Paul VI, who became the first leader of the Roman Catholic Church to visit America. This was a little over a year and a half after he became the first pontiff to travel outside Italy in centuries and the first to travel in an airplane when he visited the Holy Land in early January 1964. In a whirlwind one-day visit to New York, Pope Paul VI gave Mass before a huge crowd at Yankee Stadium and addressed the United Nations. In his speech, the pontiff made an impassioned plea for peace, "No more war, war never again. Peace, it is peace that must guide the destinies of people and of all mankind."

On October 15, an order by the Federal Communications Commission took effect that mandated radio stations in markets with a population of over 100,000 that used their FM broadcast signal to simulcast programming from its AM station had to provide original programming for the FM station for at least half of the broadcast day. This would bring various music formats to the FM dial — jazz, folk, classical music and, during 1966, a more relaxed and eclectic presentation of rock music. Music broadcast on FM was in stereo and sounded better than the often-tinny AM signals. FM stations offered an alternative to the screaming DJs on Top 40 radio. Over the next two years, FM rock formats would debut in a number of major markets while music formats on AM began a gradual decline.

The year also brought forth the announcement of plans for a massive family entertainment attraction in Florida and the debut of an iconic sports stadium in Houston, Texas. On November 15, Walt Disney and Florida Gov. Haydon Burns appeared at a press conference in Orlando to unveil plans for a $100 million family attraction on 27,000 acres of land in Orange County that would be called Disney World. Gov. Burns called it "the most significant day in the history of Florida." Disney envisioned that Disney World would be made up of two communities, the City of Yesterday (which would become the Magic Kingdom) and the City of Tomorrow (which would become EPCOT). Previously, on April 9, for better or worse, a new era dawned with the opening of what was officially named the Harris County Domed Stadium but would soon be known as the Astrodome. It would be the new home of Houston's major league baseball team that had changed its name from the Colt .45s to the Astros in recognition of NASA's Manned Spacecraft Center located in the city. LBJ and Lady Bird Johnson, along with 47,876 fans, attended an exhibition night game in which the Astros beat the Yankees, 2-1. During day games, players had trouble seeing fly balls against the glare caused by the sun shining through the roof's 4,596 skylight panels made of translucent Lucite. That issue was quickly solved by spraying 700 gallons of off-white paint over the panels, which then killed the stadium grass. This would lead to the installation the following year of Monsanto's artificial turf playing surface, which became known as AstroTurf.

On November 30, attorney/auto safety advocate Ralph Nader published his book *Unsafe At Any Speed*, which quickly became a bestseller. Nader's book targeted the auto industry for resisting safety features, such as seat belts, to keep manufacturing costs down. The book's first chapter was a brutal critique of the Chevrolet Corvair.

On November 27, the largest anti-Vietnam war protest at that time took place with 35,000 demonstrators attending the March on Washington for Peace in Vietnam. Undeterred by growing anti-war sentiment, Secretary of Defense McNamara recommended that U.S. troops in Vietnam be expanded from 125,000 to 400,000 during 1966.

One of the year's most memorable events took place on November 9. New York's WABC, with its 50,000-watt AM signal, had the biggest audience of any Top 40 station in the nation. Disc jockey Dan Ingram was doing his very popular late afternoon drive-time show when suddenly the lights in the studio began to dim. Shortly after he went to the 5:25 PM news break, the lights went out and the signal went silent. It was the start of the Great Northeast Blackout. It began at about 5:17 PM with an improperly set circuit breaker at a power station in Queenston, Ontario. A minor power surge caused the breaker to trip. By 5:28, power was out in much of Ontario and Quebec and most of the U.S. Northeast except for a few pockets that were on a different electrical grid. Almost 30 million people were affected by the blackout, which lasted for 13 hours. In New York City, with thousands of people stuck in skyscraper elevators and subway cars, the citizenry rose to the occasion and performed heroically. In the ensuing months, the question one heard over and over was: "Where were you when the lights went out?" Legend has it that the answer for many would come nine months later with a sudden spurt of babies being born throughout the Northeast.

One of the bright-spots of 1965 took place on the night of September 9 at Dodger Stadium in Chavez Ravine when the great Los Angeles Dodgers pitcher Sandy Koufax threw just the eighth perfect game in baseball history and his fourth no-hitter in four seasons, beating the Chicago Cubs, 1-0. Koufax struck out 14 Cubs batters, including the last six. The Dodgers went on to win the World Series, beating the Minnesota Twins in seven games, with Koufax winning two.

The day before the 1964-65 New York World's Fair closed on October 17, a time capsule was buried under the Flushing, New York fairgrounds. It contained 117,000 microfilmed pages of information covering the years since the 1939-40 Fair on the same grounds, along with a number of objects symbolizing the era of the 1964-65 Fair, including credit cards, a bikini, contact lenses, birth control pills, tranquilizers, a plastic heart valve, a pack of filter cigarettes, an electric toothbrush, photographs of celebrities and recordings by Thelonious Monk, Joan Baez and the Beatles.

Newsweek
NOVEMBER 1, 1965 35c
THE DEMONSTRATORS
Who? Why? How Many?
VIETNAM NOW!
STOP THE
NOW
Newsweek
NOVEMBER 22, 1965 35c
THE BIG
BLACKOUT
LIFE
5:28 P.M., NOV. 9th
THE LIGHTS
WENT
OUT
In view looking east
from Times Square
during blackout, moon
reflects in windows of
Union Carbide
Building
NOVEMBER 19 · 1965 · 35¢
Newsweek
OCTOBER 11, 1965 35c
DOWN
TO THE
WIRE
Koufax of the Dodgers

A Ticket To Ride To Rock 'n' Roll's Summit

by Al Sussman

1964, which saw seismic changes in popular music and pop culture, climaxed with the last two U.S. number one singles of the year belonging to the Supremes (their third straight number one single) and the Beatles (their sixth American chart-topper of the year). The Supremes' "Come See About Me" and the Beatles "I Feel Fine" served as perfect appetizers for the musical delights of the greatest year in the history of rock 'n' roll. There, I said it... The musical delights of 1965 are pretty much unparalleled. The British Invasion hitting its first peak. An American rock renaissance that produced two new musical forms — punk/garage rock and folk-rock. R&B/soul music in the midst of its golden era. And, thanks to the musical democracy of Top 40 radio, listeners got a daily dose of classic songs in diverse musical styles. And the pivot point for all of this was the Beatles, indisputably the biggest pop act in the world by the end of 1964. They would never again be as universally popular as they were in 1965 and, as their music rapidly evolved, their influence would be felt in many of the year's musical success stories, and vice versa.

The last weeks of 1964 were marred by the death of one of pop/soul's most influential figures. Sam Cooke had been a consistent hitmaker since his move from gospel's Soul Stirrers into the pop scene in 1957. By 1964, Cooke had spread his musical wings from uptown soul to sophisticated supper club pop and was in the midst of forming his own record label. But all that came to a sudden end on December 11 when Cooke was shot and killed at a motel in south central Los Angeles in an incident that has never quite been believably explained. As so often happens following an artist's death, Sam's first posthumous single was a double-sided hit, with the dance floor hit "Shake" reaching the U.S. Top 10 early in 1965 and the gospel-tinged "A Change Is Gonna Come" just missing the Top 30. The latter would soon become an anthem of the civil rights movement. Cooke was a favorite of the British bands. The first half of 1965 saw the Rolling Stones release covers of "Little Red Rooster" (though the Stones' number one U.K. single was based more on the original Howlin' Wolf recording) and "Good Times," the Animals' cover "Bring It On Home To Me" (#7 U.K.; #32 U.S.) and Herman's Hermits have success with their version of Cooke's "Wonderful World" (#7 U.K.; #4 U.S.).

By the final weeks of 1964, the first wave of the British Invasion had moved from the jaunty pop of the Liverpool/Manchester bands to blues-based groups like the Rolling Stones and the Animals to bands with their own unique sound. The Zombies' sound was exemplified by Rod Argent's keyboard work and Colin Blunstone's breathy vocals on their first hit singles, "She's Not There" (a #12 U.K. hit in the summer of 1964 that reached the second spot in the Billboard Hot 100 in December) and "Tell Her No" (stalling at #42 in the U.K. but a #6 U.S. hit). In contrast, the Kinks' "You Really Got Me" (#1 U.K. and #7 U.S. in the summer of 1964) and its follow-up single "All Day And All Of The Night" (#2 U.K. and #7 U.S.) came roaring out of the speakers courtesy of lead guitarist Dave Davies and producer Shel Talmy. The band's first 1965 single, "Tired Of Waiting For You" (#1 U.K.; #6 U.S.), was a change of style. The Kinks' sound would mature with nearly every single that year, mainly due to the rapid development of the group's primary writer and lead singer, Ray Davies. By the fall of 1965, Ray's songs had taken on a more melodic tone, with a bent toward social commentary. "A Well-Respected Man" reached #13 when issued as a U.S. single.

Shel Talmy also produced the early singles by another band from the London suburbs, the Who, a wild, high-energy resident band of London's mods. The Who didn't make nearly as much of an initial American impression as the Kinks or the other British bands despite having U.S. TV exposure on Shindig, ABC-TV's prime-time rock 'n' roll showcase, and three Top 10 U.K. singles during 1965, topped by the number two success of their mod anthem "My Generation." The band would have to wait until 1967 to enter the Top 30 in America. Similarly, the Hollies, yet to catch on in America, scored big in the U.K. with the chart-topping "I'm Alive" and "Look Through Any Window" (#4).

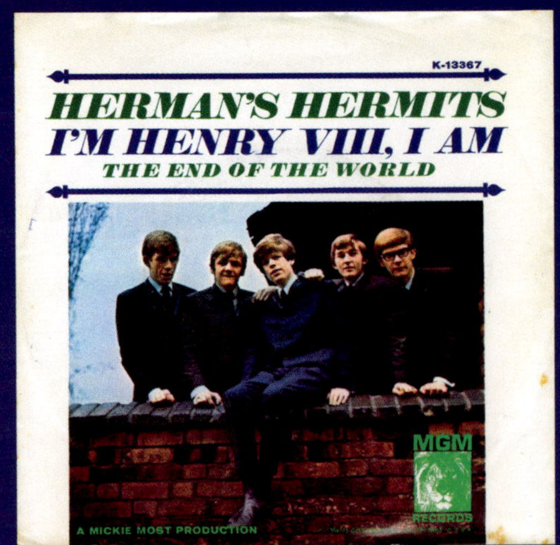

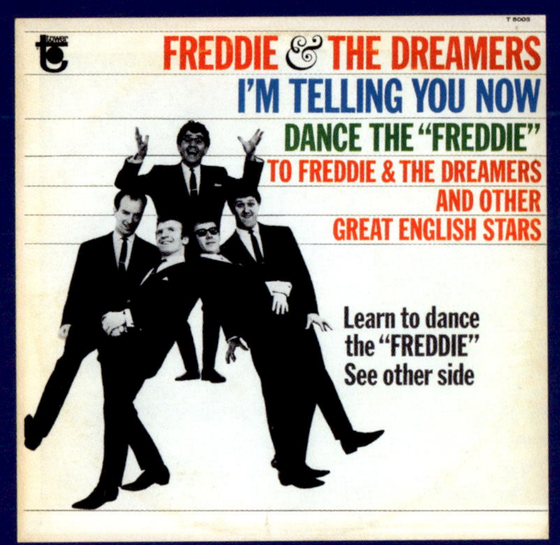

The Dave Clark 5, the first of the British bands to invade America following the Beatles trailblazing visit, were working on their seventh single of 1964 to reach at least the U.S. Top 20 (including four Top 10s) with the bombastic "Any Way You Want It." In the summer of 1965, the DC5 would rack up two more Top 10 singles with their cover of Chris Kenner's "I Like It Like That" (#7 U.S.) and "Catch Us If You Can" (#5 U.K.; #4 U.S.), the hit single from their lone feature-length film, before gaining their only U.S. number one single at year's end with a cover of "Over And Over."

Manchester-based Herman's Hermits, with their cuddly teen idol lead singer Peter Noone, had six U.S. Top 10 singles in 1965, including the #2 "Can't You Hear My Heartbeat" and the chart-toppers "Mrs. Brown, You've Got A Lovely Daughter" and the British music hall comedy nugget "I'm Henry VIII, I Am." None of these three songs were issued as singles in Great Britain. A cover of the Rays' "Silhouettes" was a Top Five hit in both markets. Another Manchester band, Freddie & the Dreamers, had just missed topping the U.K. charts in the fall of 1963 with "I'm Telling You Now" and "You Were Made For Me" because of a couple of tunes called "She Loves You" and "I Want To Hold Your Hand." Capitol's Dave Dexter turned down "She Loves You" but had the label release both Freddie & the Dreamers singles in the fall of 1963 and early 1964 to total indifference. But when re-issued on Capitol's Tower subsidiary label in 1965, "I'm Telling You Now" topped the charts and "You Were Made For Me" scored at 21. As Dexter and Capitol had given up on the group in 1964, its subsequent American releases were on another label, Mercury Records. "I Understand" stalled at 36, while "Do The Freddie," based on lead singer Freddie Garrity's arm-waving dance, hit #18. Wayne Fontana & the Mindbenders scored a U.S. number one (#2 U.K.) with "The Game Of Love."

The Yardbirds were a blues-based group that succeeded the Rolling Stones as the resident band at the Crawdaddy Club in Richmond, Surrey (now part of London). Led by guitarist Eric "Slowhand" Clapton and singer Keith Relf, they developed a strong English following before scoring international hits with "For Your Love" (#3 U.K.; #6 U.S.) and "Heart Full Of Soul" (#2 U.K.; #9 U.S.), both written by Graham Gouldman. Clapton left the band after "For Your Love" because he wanted to just play the blues. He was replaced by Jeff Beck, who would lead the Yardbirds to their creative peak in 1966. As for the Stones, they didn't gain a Top 10 single in the U.S. until the end of November 1964 with "Time Is On My Side" and didn't really gain an American foothold until Mick Jagger and Keith Richards began to click as songwriters in the spring of 1965 with "The Last Time." Then, during an American tour that spring, Keith literally dreamed up the immortal lick that became the fuzz box-driven hook for "(I Can't Get No) Satisfaction," in many quarters the biggest hit record of the year (though not according to Billboard). The Stones' fourth American LP, *Out Of Our Heads*, topped the charts, and "Get Off Of My Cloud" became their second straight number one single in November. By then, the Stones were second only (but a very distant second) to the Beatles in world popularity.

As the British Invasion's first wave grew during 1964, the American pop landscape was defended by America's most popular groups, the 4 Seasons and the Beach Boys. In December, the boys from New Jersey had their sixth Top 20 single of the year with "Big Man In Town." After reaching #12 early in 1965 with "Bye Bye Baby (Baby Goodbye)," the 4 Seasons had to wait until fall for their next major hit, "Let's Hang On," which reached #3 in mid-December, plus their unique cover of Bob Dylan's "Don't Think Twice" under the nom de record of "The Wonder Who?".

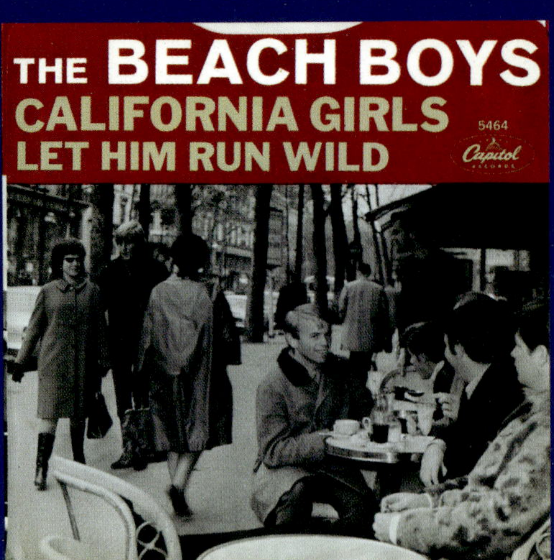

In late 1964, the Beach Boys notched their fourth Top 10 single of the year with "Dance, Dance, Dance." They nudged the Beatles "Ticket To Ride" from the number one spot in May with "Help Me, Rhonda," while *The Beach Boys Today!* was a fixture in the Top Five of the album charts. In early September, the group's "California Girls" was at #3 behind the Beatles "Help!" and Dylan's "Like A Rolling Stone," while *Summer Days (And Summer Nights!!)* was the number two album. Although their first single of 1965, a cover of Bobby Freeman's "Do You Wanna Dance," stalled at #12, its B-side, the achingly-beautiful "Please Let Me Wonder," was a great example of the introspective love songs Brian Wilson was composing, hinting at the brilliance to come the following year with *Pet Sounds*.

In Memphis, Stax Records entered into a distribution agreement with Atlantic Records. Stax had occasional R&B/pop hits going back to the early sixties, but its golden era began late in the spring of 1965 when Otis Redding's "I've Been Loving You Too Long" just missed the pop Top 20 and peaked at number two on the R&B chart. That fall, Otis' original version of his composition "Respect" reached #35 on The Hot 100 and #4 R&B. (In 1967, Aretha Franklin would top the Billboard Hot 100 with her arrangement of "Respect" issued on Atlantic Records.) Atlantic R&B stars like Wilson Pickett and Don Covay began recording at the Stax studios, backed up by members of the Stax house band, Booker T & the MGs, with their outstanding guitarist Steve Cropper. A session that May produced Pickett and Cropper's "In The Midnight Hour," which topped the R&B chart and just missed the pop Top 20 in August but, as with Otis, launched Pickett's career as a hit artist. Covay, whose 1964 song "Mercy, Mercy" peaked at #35 and was covered by the Rolling Stones, had a #44 hit in 1965 with "Seesaw" (later a #14 hit for Aretha in 1968).

The Motown hit assembly line was operating at peak efficiency. After racking up three number one singles in the second half of 1964, the Supremes notched three more during 1965, "Stop! In The Name Of Love," "Back In My Arms Again" and "I Hear A Symphony." The group's other single, "Nothing But Heartaches," stalled at 11 amid the intense competition. The Four Tops got their first number one, "I Can't Help Myself," in June and reached the Top Five with "It's The Same Old Song" in August. While the songwriting/production team of Brian Holland, Lamont Dozier and Eddie Holland ("H-D-H") was having spectacular success with the Supremes and Four Tops, the composing/producing heart and soul of Motown continued to be William "Smokey" Robinson. During 1965, Smokey produced and co-wrote two Top 10 singles for Marvin Gaye, "I'll Be Doggone" and "Ain't That Peculiar." He produced and co-wrote four Top 20 singles for the Temptations, including their first number one, "My Girl," plus a classic B-side, "Don't Look Back." And, with his own group, the Miracles, Smokey co-wrote and produced two of Motown's greatest recordings, "Ooo Baby Baby" and "The Tracks Of My Tears." Both singles stalled at number 16 on the classic-crowded Hot 100. The Miracles' "My Girl Is Gone" charted at 14. H-D-H got Martha & the Vandellas another big hit with "Nowhere To Run," which peaked at eight. Motown founder Barry Gordy co-produced Jr. Walker & the All Stars' "Shotgun" (#4 pop; #1 R&B).

In the aftermath of the Beatles historic February 1964 appearances on The Ed Sullivan Show and the subsequent British Invasion, young males (and some females) began growing their hair, making music and forming bands in garages and recreation rooms all across America. Many of those bands emerged in local music scenes and the best (or luckiest) developed national followings.

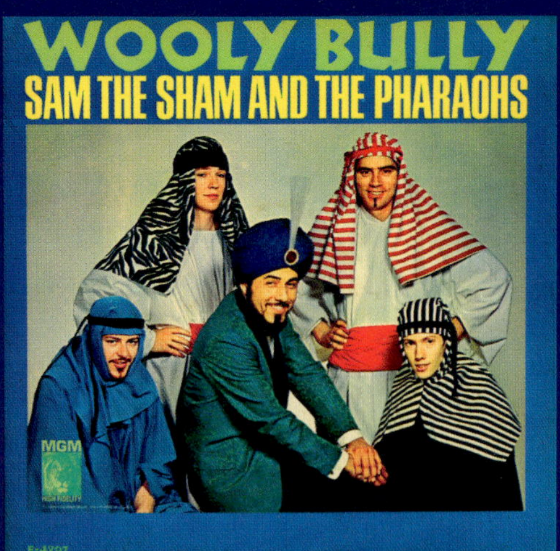

In San Francisco, where a major pop culture scene was just beginning to develop, the Beau Brummels adopted a name and a look and a sound that gave the impression they were English. Produced by local disc jockey Sylvester Stewart (the black future music revolutionary Sly Stone), the band had Top 20 hits with "Laugh Laugh" and "Just A Little" in the early months of 1965. They "appeared" on an episode of The Flintstones as the Beau Brummelstones.

Out of Texas came the Sir Douglas Quintet, a band that, again, took a name and cultivated a look that gave the impression they were English. But their sound was a blend of blues and Tex-Mex. The group was led by the growling vocals of Doug Sahm and the organ work of Augie Meyers. The Quintet had a top 15 hit in the spring with "She's About A Mover." Also out of Texas was a band fronted by Domingo Samudio, who called himself Sam the Sham. With his group, the Pharaohs, Sam spent two weeks in June at number two with "Wooly Bully." The dance party staple spent so many weeks (18) on Billboard's Hot 100 that, at year's end, the magazine proclaimed "Wooly Bully" the number one record of 1965 based on its points system. As Sam sang: "Watch it now, watch it!"

Another "band" that took on an exotic image was the Strangeloves, who, according to their press release and album liner notes, were Australian sheep farmers Giles, Miles and Niles Strange. In reality, the Strangeloves were three Jewish writer/producers from Brooklyn, Bob Feldman, Jerry Goldstein and Richard Gottehrer, who had written and produced the Angels' smash number one single "My Boyfriend's Back" in 1963. Their own fictionalized group got to number 11 in the summer of 1965 with the Bo Diddley-esque "I Want Candy" (recorded by Bow Wow Wow in 1982).

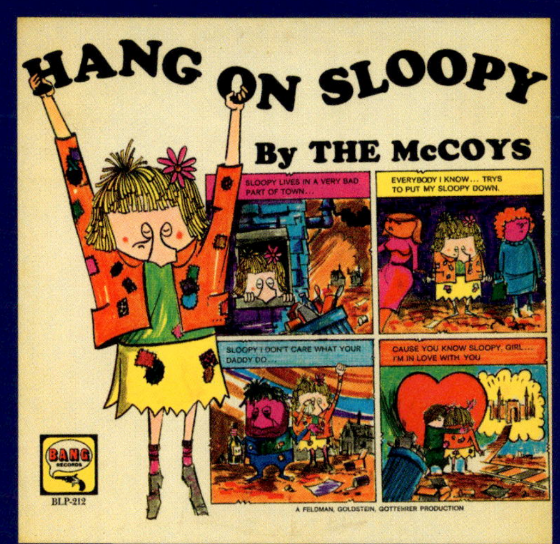

Soon after "I Want Candy," Feldman, Goldstein and Gottehrer produced a cover of the Vibrations' 1964 Top 30 hit "My Girl Sloopy" for an actual young band from Union City, Ohio, whom they dubbed the McCoys. The band was led by guitarist/singer Richard Zehringer, who would become a classic rocker in the 1970s as Rick Derringer. The single, titled "Hang On Sloopy," spent the first week of October at number one before being nudged from the top by a little ditty called "Yesterday." The McCoys' next single, a rocked-up cover of the Peggy Lee hit "Fever," reached #7 at year's end. Gottehrer would later produce early albums by Blondie, Marshall Crenshaw, and the Go-Gos in the 1970s and 1980s.

There were even celebrity garage bands that emerged out of Los Angeles/Hollywood. Dino, Desi & Billy were Dino Martin (son of Dean Martin), Desi Arnaz, Jr. (son of Lucy and Desi, Sr.) and their childhood friend Billy Hinsche. They got an audition with Reprise Records, musical home of Dean, Sr., and his Rat Pack colleague Frank Sinatra, and were quickly signed. Their first record and biggest hit, "I'm A Fool," peaked at number 17. Fellow celebrity-connected band Gary Lewis and the Playboys had the son of comedian Jerry Lewis as its lead singer. The group went from playing a recurring gig at Disneyland in 1964 to a recording contract with Liberty Records to a January 1965 slot on The Ed Sullivan Show to a number one single with "This Diamond Ring" a month later. Although producer Snuff Garrett gave into Lewis' demands that his band play on the record, Garrett had members of the famed "Wrecking Crew" of L.A. session players, including drummer Hal Blaine, bassist Joe Osborn and keyboard player Leon Russell, provide overdubs. Three more hit singles followed in 1965 alone, with "Count Me In" and "Save Your Heart For Me" reaching number two, and "Everybody Loves A Clown," written by Garrett, Lewis and Russell, hitting number four.

Some 3,000 miles away, in the tri-state area of New York/New Jersey/Connecticut, seeming armies of cover bands served their musical apprenticeships. Bruce Springsteen, Southside Johnny Lyon and members of the E Street Band and the Asbury Jukes came out of that scene. On Long Island, the Vagrants, with their pre-Mountain singer and lead guitarist Leslie West, developed a following at The Action House. In New Jersey, the Rascals began their Hall of Fame career early in 1965 in a Garfield dive called the Choo Choo Club, then scored a summertime gig at a chic club in the Hamptons called The Barge, where they were introduced to promoter Sid Bernstein. At the Beatles historic concert at Shea Stadium on August 15, Bernstein, who promoted the show, managed to get a "THE RASCALS ARE COMING!" message on the Shea scoreboard, much to the annoyance of Brian Epstein. But that stunt got the Rascals a recording contract with Atlantic. Their first single, "I Ain't Gonna Eat Out My Heart Anymore," debuted on the Hot 100 the last week of 1965. Three weeks earlier, a band from Bergenfield, New Jersey, the Knickerbockers, debuted on the Hot 100 with "Lies," a scorching rocker with a very John Lennon-esque lead vocal from lead singer Buddy Randell. "Lies" would peak at number 20 in the first weeks of 1966 but would do much better on the New York area radio stations.

The other main component of the American response to the British Invasion was the introduction of a new musical genre that directly stemmed from the influence of the Beatles. Early in 1964, three professional folkies — Jim McGuinn, David Crosby and Gene Clark — began playing together at L.A.'s Troubadour folk club largely because of McGuinn's acoustic versions of Beatles songs. Soon, their three-part harmonies covering Beatles songs and Bob Dylan-style contemporary folk took on a rock flavor, especially after adding drummer Michael Clarke and a new set of instruments influenced by those played by the Beatles in *A Hard Day's Night*. McGuinn purchased the same electric 12-string guitar frequently used by George on the songs in the film, a Rickenbacker model 360-12. Experienced bluegrass musician Chris Hillman joined the group as bassist. By the end of 1964, the group's name had morphed from the Jet Set to the Beefeaters to the Byrds, and they had signed a recording contract with Columbia Records.

A few months earlier, the group's manager, Jim Dickson, got them an acetate of a yet-to-be-recorded Bob Dylan song called "Mr. Tambourine Man." By the beginning of 1965, the Byrds had given the song a harder-edged 4/4 arrangement and had received the endorsement of Dylan, then considered the young king of the new folk movement.

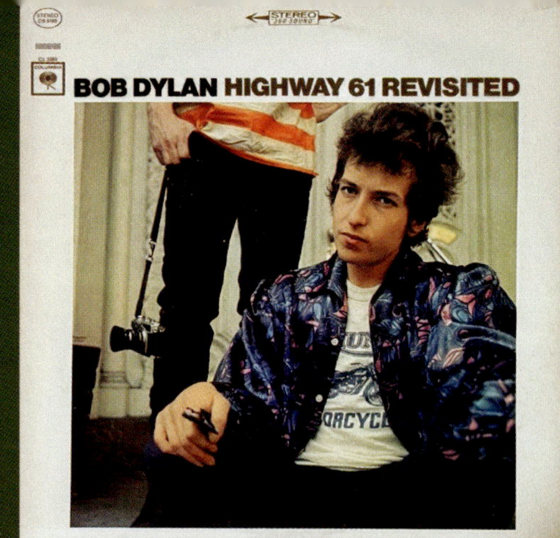

On January 20, in their first session for Columbia, the Byrds recorded "Mr. Tambourine Man" with McGuinn, Crosby and Clark's soaring harmonies over McGuinn's 12-string and backing by members of the "Wrecking Crew," though that wouldn't become public knowledge for some time. Following a very successful early spring engagement at Ciro's Le Disc nightclub on Hollywood's Sunset Strip, "Mr. Tambourine Man" was released as a single on April 12, marking the birth of folk-rock. The record caught fire nationally in early June and knocked the Four Tops' "I Can't Help Myself" from number one in the last week of the month before the Tops regained the top spot the following week.

Meanwhile, the composer of the song that launched folk-rock had been moving ever closer to taking on rock values. In January 1965, Dylan recorded his fifth album–his first to include backing with electric instruments. The half-electric, half-acoustic *Bringing It All Back Home* was released in late March and was one of Dylan's finest collections of songs, including "Mr. Tambourine Man." After an acoustic tour of England in the spring that was chronicled in D.A. Pennebaker's film *Don't Look Back*, Dylan recorded his first all-electric LP, *Highway 61 Revisited*, and played in person with electric backing for the first time at the Newport Folk Festival on July 25, just after the release of the song that would turn Dylan from folk icon into a pop star, the six-minute "Like A Rolling Stone." The song would spend two weeks in September at number two behind "Help!," on its way to being recognized as one of rock's all-time great records. *Highway 61 Revisited* was released at the end of August and, spurred by the success of "Like A Rolling Stone," peaked at number three on Billboard's album chart in November behind the soundtrack from *Help!* and the Ramsey Lewis Trio's jazz album *The In Crowd*. Dylan's album reached number four on the U.K. album chart.

Throughout the summer and fall, the charts were awash with electric covers of Dylan songs and records with folk roots but rock presentation, such as the Byrds' debut album, which was dominated by Dylan covers and folk staples. Their followup single, Dylan's "All I Really Want To Do," was rush-released in mid-June to compete with a version of the song by the female half of the team of Sonny & Cher. Sonny was former Phil Spector go-fer/session man Salvatore Bono, while Cher was former Spector session vocalist Cheryl Sarkisian (who also released the 1964 single "Ringo, I Love You" as Bonnie Jo Mason). As a duo, they portrayed a bohemian couple looked down on by the adult world but they had each other. This pose was exemplified by "I Got You Babe," which featured Spector-esque production mixed with Byrds-like jangly guitars, all produced by Bono. Cher's solo take on Dylan's "All I Really Want To Do" had similar production. Both singles entered Billboard's Hot 100 in mid-July. A month later, "I Got You Babe" spent three weeks at number one. Cher's "All I Really Want To Do" outperformed the Byrds' version, reaching 15. Sonny's solo single "Laugh At Me" charted at ten, while the duo's "Baby Don't Go" made it to number eight.

Barry McGuire had recently left the traditional folk ensemble the New Christy Minstrels. His first solo single was a protest song about the state of the world. Written by P.F. Sloan and produced by Lou Adler in full folk-rock style, "Eve Of Destruction" hit the Billboard Hot 100 in mid-August and, by late September, knocked "Help!" from the top of the charts. A Los Angeles surf music band changed its name from the Crossfires to the Turtles and got a number eight hit with their version of Dylan's "It Ain't Me Babe." Another band from L.A., the Association, released a cover of Dylan's "One Too Many Mornings." Both bands would soon have many hits. San Francisco's We Five charted at number three with its arrangement of "You Were On My Mind," originally recorded by Ian & Sylvia, a Canadian folk duo.

Of the several bands formed in San Francisco and its environs, most had roots in folk and blues. Jefferson Airplane made its debut in August at the Matrix, a club owned by charter group member Marty Balin, and by November had a recording deal with RCA Victor. For the Airplane's debut at the Matrix, the opening act was a band dubbed the Great Society, whose lead singer, Grace Slick, would be singing lead with the Airplane within two years. A group called the Warlocks formed in early 1965 out of the remnants of a jug band and a folk group in Palo Alto. As the band's lineup solidified, they adopted the name Grateful Dead and debuted under that name in early December in San Jose.

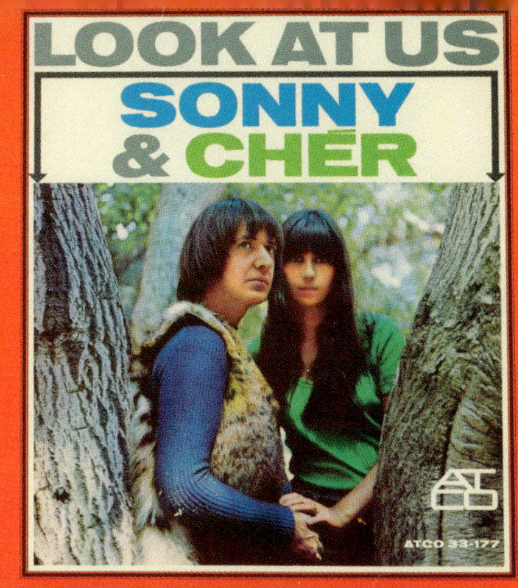

Across the country, the Lovin' Spoonful formed in early 1965 out of the Greenwich Village folk scene but were also heavily influenced by the Beatles and by Dylan's move toward rock. Indeed, the group's co-founder and principal songwriter, John Sebastian, had played on sessions for Dylan's *Bringing It All Buck Home* album. In June, the Spoonful recorded Sebastian's song "Do You Believe In Magic," which became a folk-rock anthem and reached the U.S. Top 10 in the first week in October, the same week in which "Yesterday" reached number one.

The next week, sessions began for the Beatles final single and album of 1965. Even as they reached unparalleled levels of popularity around the world, the group was absorbing the influence of much of what was happening on the pop scene in America and Britain. They had struck up friendships with Dylan in 1964 and with the Byrds in the spring of 1965. They had become friendly rivals of the Stones and other British bands. Combined with the growing maturation of their writing and musicianship, the influence of their musical contemporaries had been showing in much of their work going back to the fall of 1964 and would soon result in the Beatles next musical step forward, *Rubber Soul*.

If you turned on a Top 40 radio station at any time in 1965, you were treated to a wide-ranging, very high-quality cornucopia of sounds from all manner of pop genres. It was "musical democracy" that gave us delight after delight. There was folk singer Glenn Yarbrough's theme from the Steve McQueen film "Baby, The Rain Must Fall" and Wrecking Crew guitarist Glen Campbell's folk-rock take on Buffy Sainte-Marie's antiwar song "The Universal Soldier." There was R&B singer Barbara Lewis' "Baby I'm Yours" and actor/singer Mel Carter's "Hold Me, Thrill Me, Kiss Me," both summertime slow dance favorites. British singer Petula Clark topped the charts with "Downtown" and hit #3 with "I Know A Place." The Righteous Brothers had two huge hits that remain on radio playlists, the chart-topping "You've Lost That Lovin' Feelin'" and #4 "Unchained Melody." Girl groups were still around, from the Shangri-Las' "Give Him A Great Big Kiss" to the Toys' adaptation of a Bach minuet, "A Lover's Concerto." Shirley Ellis taught us "The Name Game," the Gentrys urged us to "Keep On Dancing" and Jewel Akens told us about "The Birds And The Bees," while Fontella Bass pleaded "Rescue Me" and Len Barry counted "1-2-3." Roger Miller, "King Of The Road," told us "England Swings." James Brown scored with "I Got You (I Feel Good)," as did Elvis Presley with "Crying In The Chapel." The Impressions made an impression with "Amen" and the jazz-oriented Ramsey Lewis Trio was part of "The 'In' Crowd." An Australian folk group, the Seekers, had hits with "I'll Never Find Another You" and "A World Of Our Own." Jackie DeShannon reached number seven with "What The World Needs Now Is Love," a song sadly as relevant in the 21st century as it was in the summer of Vietnam and Watts. And a young music business veteran named Herb Alpert reached the Top 10 at the end of November with a trumpet-led instrumental version of "A Taste Of Honey" that launched a sound that, to many, was as much a part of the soundtrack of the sixties as the Beatles.

1965 was such a landmark year for rock 'n' roll that even Time ran a cover story on what it called "The Sound of the Sixties" in its May 21 issue. The magazine declared: "Rock 'n' roll still does not exactly have the good housekeeping seal of approval. But even parents now say: 'Well, some of it's okay...' Some of it, in fact, is very good, far better than the adenoidal lamentations of a few years ago. Some of it is still awful, as might be expected in an industry that grinds out 300 new records each week. But for the first time rock 'n' roll can boast a host of singers who can actually sing. The music, once limited to four chords, is now more sophisticated, replete with counter-rhythms, advanced harmonies, and multi-voiced choirs...Conductor Leonard Bernstein likes the Beatles and does not hesitate to admit it: 'They are very intelligent, and they have made songs which are really worthwhile. Love Me Do is really stirring and very reminiscent of Hindu music.'" The weekly news magazine concluded: "Above all, rock 'n' roll today is lively, youthful, aggressive, often funny, seldom heartsick. The lyrics, showing the influence of folk music, are fresher and more intelligible. Coming the other way, the folk types are beginning to feel the beat." And as Sonny & Cher would sing two years later: "And the beat goes on."

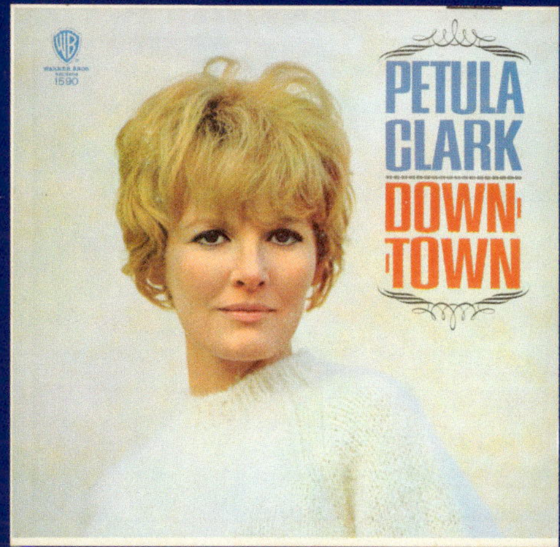

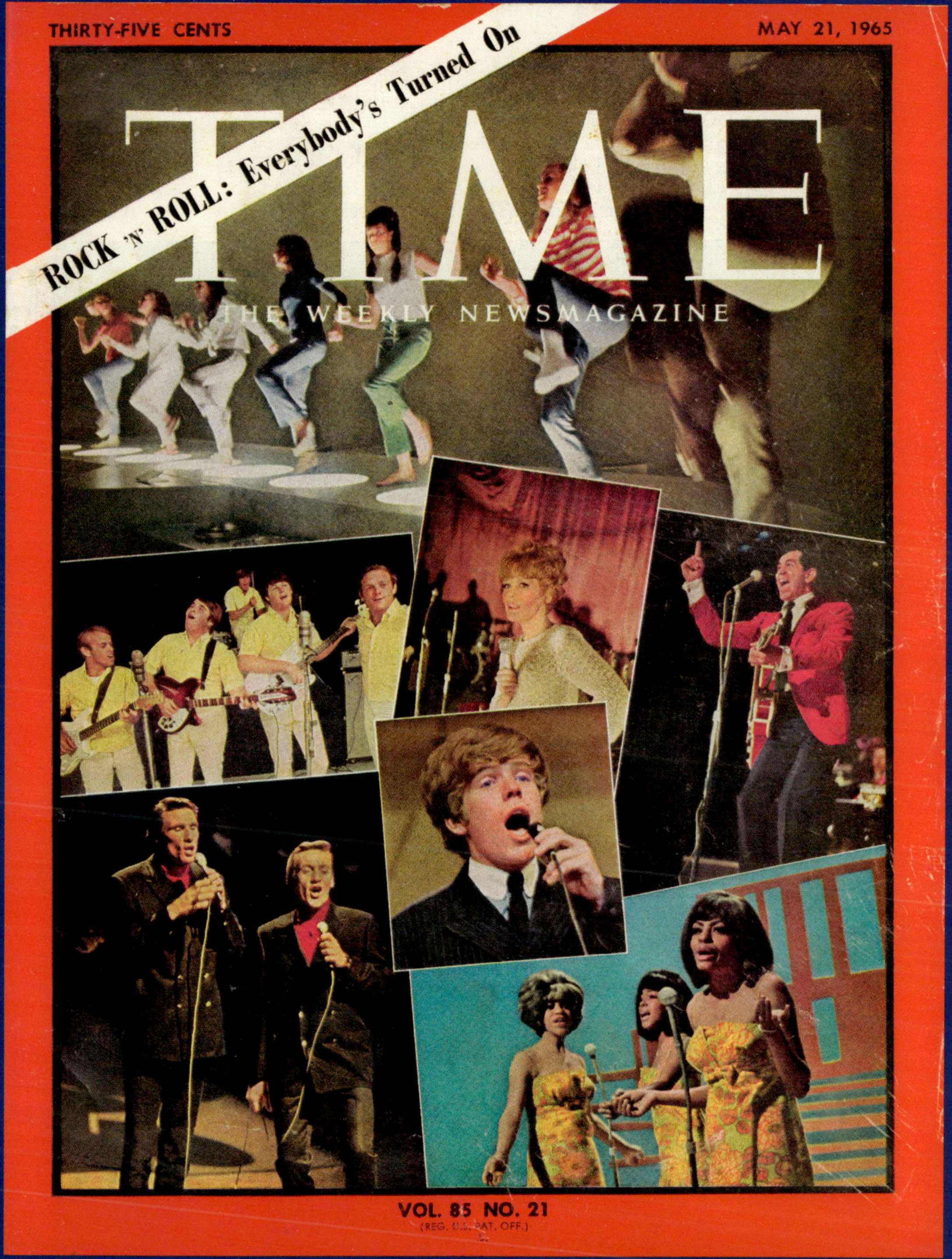

THIRTY-FIVE CENTS

MAY 21, 1965

ROCK 'N' ROLL: Everybody's Turned On

TIME

THE WEEKLY NEWSMAGAZINE

VOL. 85 NO. 21

(REG. U.S. PAT. OFF.)

There's More Here Than Meets The Eye: 1965 in Film

by Bruce Spizer

For many moviegoers in 1965, it seemed like the year of comedies, chases, intrigue and musicals. And all of that was packaged quite neatly into the Beatles 1965 movie *Help!* But as Ringo astutely observes in that film: "There's more here than meets the eye." And so it was for motion pictures in 1965.

A review of the films released in December 1964 shows that Hollywood thought Americans were looking for laughs during the holiday season and into the new year. *Kisses For My President* is the first film distributed by a major studio to feature a woman President of the United States. When Leslie McCloud, played by Polly Bergen, is elected the first female President, her husband Thad McCloud, played by Fred MacMurray, quickly becomes disillusioned by her being too busy for him and their two children, as well as his inability to find a meaningful role as the President's husband. Thad later exposes a corrupt Senator who, in addition to being his wife's political rival, is backing a Latin American dictator for financial reasons. When Leslie learns she is pregnant, she resigns the presidency to be with her family. Thad jokes that while it took 40 million women to put her into office, he, a single man, removed her from office. The fact that MacMurray received top billing over Bergen playing the President should have alerted viewers that the comedy would take a condescending view of a female President. *The Disorderly Orderly* is a comedy vehicle for Jerry Lewis, who plays an inept hospital orderly dreaming about becoming a doctor. While Lewis' film was family entertainment, the season also brought forth a pair of sex comedies: *Kiss Me, Stupid*, starring Dean Martin and Kim Novak; and *Sex And The Single Girl*, with Tony Curtis, Natalie Wood, Henry Fonda, Lauren Bacall and Mel Ferrer. The former was considered vulgar, while the latter was a commercial success. *The Pleasure Seekers,* a musical romantic comedy, follows three young women seeking love in Madrid, Spain. Ann-Margret plays an actress/flamenco dancer and sings four songs. *Get Yourself A College Girl* is little more than a beach party juke box musical set on campus.

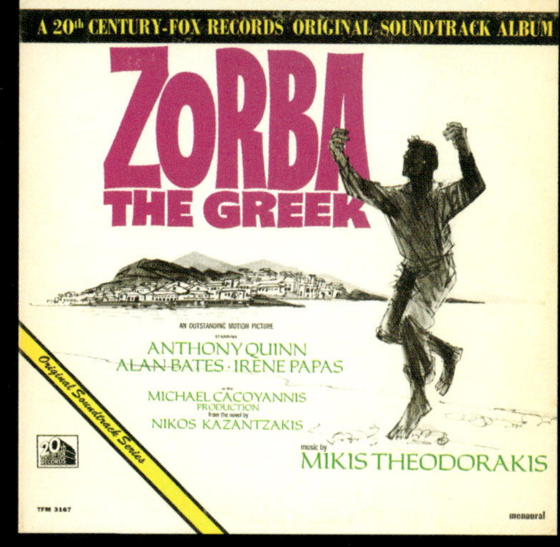

But it was not all laughs that Christmas. *Hush...Hush, Sweet Charlotte* is a psychological thriller starring Bette Davis, Olivia de Havilland, Joseph Cotten, Agnes Moorehead and Mary Astor. Davis plays Charlotte, a middle-aged Southern belle spinster who was a suspect in the gruesome murder of her lover decades ago. She is living in the family estate and takes strong exception to the government's plan to evict her from her home to make way for an interstate highway through Louisiana. Characters come to a violent end before the murder of Charlotte's lover is finally revealed. The film was nominated for seven Academy Awards. Davis won a Laurel Award for Top Female Dramatic Performance and Moorehead won a Golden Globe for Best Supporting Actress–Motion Picture. *The Night Walker* is a psychological horror film with Robert Taylor and Barbara Stanwyck, whose character, Irene, is haunted by dreams and strange occurrences after her controlling inventor husband dies in a laboratory explosion. It's promotional poster asks: "Are you afraid of the things that can come out of your dreams...Lust. Murder. Secret Desires.?."

Zorba The Greek was the most successful of the late 1964 movies, remaining in theaters well into the new year and grossing over $9,000,000. The drama, written, produced, directed and edited by Greek filmmaker Michael Cacoyannis, was shot in black and white on the Greek island of Crete. It stars Anthony Quinn as Zorba, supported by Alan Bates as Basil, Lila Kedrova and Irene Papas, with a score by Mikis Theodorakis (whose composition "The Honeymoon Song" was performed by the Beatles and is on *Live At The BBC*). The film was nominated for seven Academy Awards, winning three. The movie's iconic ending has Zorba and Basil joyfully dancing the sirtaki on the shore of a deserted beach.

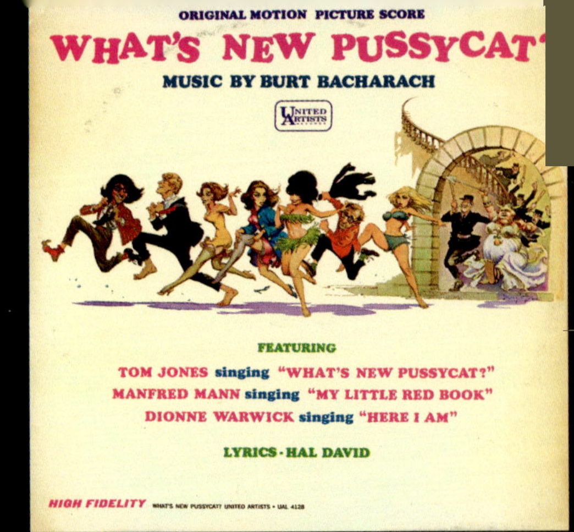

The success of 1963's *It's A Mad, Mad, Mad, Mad World* paved the way for a pair of big-production epic comedies hitting the screens in 1965. Both involve early 1900s races to Paris and sport a cast of zany international characters. *Those Magnificent Men In Their Flying Machines* is a British film co-written and directed by Ken Annakin. It covers a fictional 1910 air race from London to Paris. The film's subtitle "*or How I Flew From London To Paris In 25 Hours And 11 Minutes*" forecasts the difficulty of the task, made even worse by some participants cheating and sabotaging their opponents' planes to increase their chances of winning the £10,000 award (equivalent to over $1,700,000 in 2024). The film features magnificent flying scenes with reproductions of aeroplanes from the era and a catchy theme song ("They go up, Tiddley up, up/They go down, Tiddley down, down"). The 138-minute film grossed $31,000,000. *The Great Race* is loosely based on a real 1908 car race of drivers heading west around the world from New York to Paris. Director Blake Edwards incorporated traditional slapstick and other sight gags from the silent film era, including a four minute, 20 second pie fight in which 4,000 pies were thrown. The film stars Jack Lemmon, Tony Curtis, Natalie Wood and Peter Falk and is scored by Henry Mancini. The 160-minute movie grossed over $25,000,000.

What's New Pussycat? is a screwball comedy directed by Clive Donner. The script was written by Woody Allen, who also stars in the film with Peter Sellers, Peter O'Toole, Romy Schneider, Capucine, Paula Prentiss and Ursula Andress. The story revolves around O'Toole's womanizer character, who finds it hard to be true to his fiancée as he is constantly pursued by other woman. Tom Jones' recording of the Bacharach-David title song charted at number three.

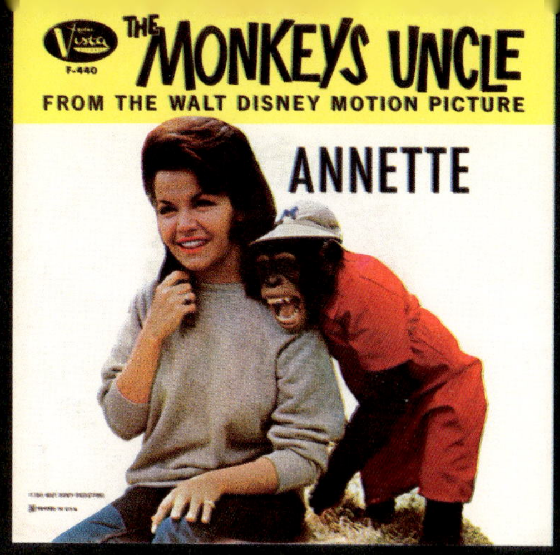

Help! was not the only Richard Lester-directed movie released in 1965. *The Knack ...And How To Get It* is a British sex comedy starring Rita Tushingham, Ray Brooks, Michael Crawford and Donal Donnelly. Crawford plays a London schoolteacher, Dolin, who notices that his tenant, Tolen, has the knack of seducing women. Colin meets a shy woman, Nancy, at a scrapyard when he purchases an old wrought iron double bed. A lot of brilliantly filmed crazy things happen along the way, many involving the bed, but in the end, Colin and Nancy get together despite Tolen sexually assaulting Nancy in public. The screenplay was written by Charles Wood, who would be brought in to assist Marc Behm with the script for *Help!* The black and white movie was scored by John Barry. As director of *The Knack*, Lester was awarded the Palme d'Or (Golden Palm) for Best Feature Film at the 1965 Cannes Film Festival.

Other 1965 sex comedies include *A Very Special Favor* with Rock Hudson and Leslie Caron, *Marriage On The Rocks* starring Frank Sinatra, Deborah Kerr, Dean Martin and Cesar Romero, and the dark comedy *How To Murder Your Wife* in which a cartoonist, played by Jack Lemmon, plots to murder his Italian wife, played by Virna Lisi.

Jerry Lewis co-wrote, produced, directed and played seven parts in *The Family Jewels*. His son's band, Gary Lewis & the Playboys, perform "Little Miss Go-Go" and "This Diamond Ring." He also co-stars with Tony Curtis in the comedy *Boeing Boeing,* which involves Curtis juggling three stewardesses. *The Monkey's Uncle* has a genius college student, played by Tommy Kirk, adopting a monkey and working on an invention. His girlfriend is played by Annette Funicello.

The success of *Goldfinger* led to United Artists re-releasing the first two Bond films as a double feature. Copycat and parody movies also appeared. *Licensed To Kill* is a British film starring Tom Adams as secret agent Charles Vine of Her Majesty's Secret Service. His mission is to protect a Swedish scientist who invented an anti-gravity device. Producer Joseph E. Levine purchased the American and worldwide rights, made some edits, changed the title to *The Second Best Secret Agent In The Whole Wide World* and arranged for Sammy Davis, Jr. to sing the title song. The French-Italian co-production *James Tont Operazione U.N.O.* stole even more from the James Bond franchise. James Tont, agent 007½, battles the villainous Goldsinger in a story that is basically a rewrite of *Goldfinger.* The film *Dr. Goldfoot And The Bikini Machine* was distributed by American Pictures International ("API"), the same company that churned out beach party movies and low budget horror films. The motion picture stars Vincent Price as Dr. Goldfoot. Frankie Avalon thwarts the villain's plan of having bikini-clad robots seduce and rob rich men. The Supremes perform the title song.

Harry Saltzman, co-producer of the James Bond films, produced a gritty spy thriller, *The Ipcress File,* that is the opposite of Flemming's 007 despite utilizing the same editor (Peter Hunt), set designer (Ken Adam) and composer (John Barry) used on the Bond movies. It stars Michael Caine as Harry Palmer, a working class former British Army sergeant who works for the Ministry of Defense. The film is a story of espionage and betrayal set in less-than-glamorous London locations. When the Beatles, their friends and Walter Shenson saw the film on April 1, John kept singing "Goldfinger" to the movie's theme tune (both composed by John Barry). Paul was completely knocked out by the film.

Brian Epstein hoped to duplicate or at least come close to the success of *A Hard Day's Night* with a film by one of his other acts, Gerry & the Pacemakers. *Ferry Cross The Mersey* is the fictional account of a group of art students in a Liverpool beat band that make it big. In addition to the title song, the group performs "It's Gonna Be Alright" and seven others tunes. Cilla Black and the Fourmost also perform. The Dave Clark 5's *Catch Us If You Can* (titled *Having A Wild Weekend* in America) was released in the U.S. shortly after *Help!* in mid-August. The film, directed by John Boorman who went on to direct *Deliverance* in 1972, bears no resemblance to either Beatles movie. It revolves primarily around Dave Clark, who plays a stuntman who runs off with an actress known as the Butcher Girl while filming a meat commercial. The band's music is heard in the film, but they are never shown performing any songs.

Beach party movies remained in vogue with API's *Beach Blanket Bingo* and *How To Stuff A Wild Bikini*. Both films have the frequent pairing of Frankie Avalon and Annette Funicello plus Harvey Lembeck as biker gang leader Eric Von Zipper, though Avalon's appearance is minimal in the latter movie, which features Mickey Rooney, Buster Keaton and the Kingsmen performing the title song. The API beach party gang take a winter vacation in *Ski Party,* which has James Brown performing "I Got You (I Feel Good)." Paramount's *The Girls On The Beach* features the Beach Boys and Lesley Gore. Elvis gets into the beach party action in Fort Lauderdale, Florida as a night club singer in *Girl Happy*, which co-stars Shelley Fabares. In *Tickle Me*, Elvis is a rodeo bull rider who can sing, while in *Harum Scarum* he plays the role of an actor who goes to the Middle East to promote his film and gets involved in a plot to assassinate a king.

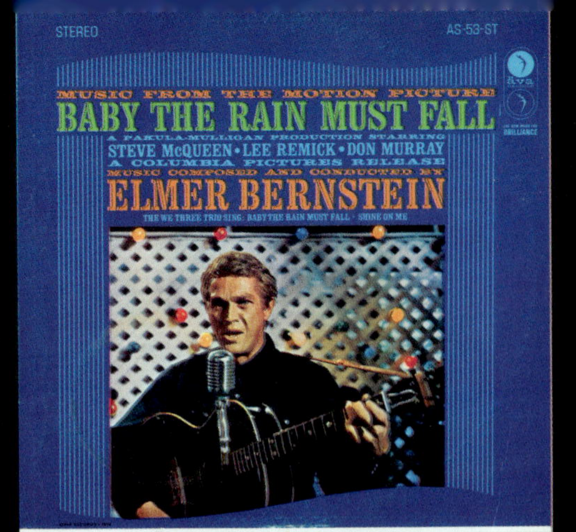

The year also had its share of dramas. *The Yellow Rolls-Royce*, set in the 1930s, features three stories, each revolving around different owners of the same 1931 Rolls-Royce Phantom II. The segments involve a British nobleman who sells the vehicle after he discovers his wife having sex with her lover in the car, an American gangster who purchases the Rolls in Italy while vacationing with his fiancée, and an American widow who buys the car in Italy for a drive to Yugoslavia shortly before it is invaded by Nazi Germany. The film stars Rex Harrison, Ingrid Bergman, Shirley MacLaine, Omar Sharif and George C. Scott. Steve McQueen plays a troubled rockabilly singer/guitarist in *Baby The Rain Must Fall*. Lee Remick plays his wife, who stays with him despite his violent tendencies and run-ins with the law. McQueen is shown performing the title song and other tunes, although he is lip-syncing to Billy Strange's vocals. His band includes Glen Campbell on guitar and Hal Blaine on drums. Glenn Yarbrough's version of the title song was a number 12 hit.

Shenandoah is a Civil War drama starring James Stewart as a widowed farmer living in Virginia with six sons, a daughter and daughter-in-law. He is focused on his own family life, remaining neutral and avoiding the war until his 16-year-old son, Boy, is taken prisoner by Union soldiers. A series of tragic events follow when he goes looking for Boy accompanied by family members, but in the end he is reunited with Boy. The movie marked the film debuts of Rosemary Forsyth and Katharine Ross. Later in the year, Forsyth co-starred with Charlton Heston in the medieval drama *The War Lord*, set in 11th Century Normandy. Frank Sinatra leads a POW train escape in the World War II drama *Von Ryan's Express*. In *The Hill*, Sean Connery plays a former British sergeant major serving time in a brutal British Army prison during WW II.

The Agony And The Ecstasy is a historical drama starring Charlton Heston as Michelangelo and Rex Harrison as Pope Julius II. The film focuses on their conflict during the artist's laborious painting of the Vatican's Sistine Chapel ceiling.

With Bonanza drawing top ratings on TV, it is not surprising that Westerns remained popular in theaters. Jane Fonda plays the title role in the Western comedy *Cat Ballou*. Nat King Cole and Stubby Kaye play traveling musicians who sing "The Ballad Of Cat Ballou" and other musical interludes to tell her story. The film opens with Cat, a captured female outlaw, in jail about to be hung for her crimes before flashing back to show how she got there. Lee Marvin won an Academy Award for Best Actor for his dual portrayal of a drunken gunfighter and an evil gunslinger. In *The Sons Of Katie Elder*, the four sons of Katie Elder reunite for their mother's funeral and take revenge on a gunsmith who falsely claims he won the deed to the Elder family farm in a card game the night their father was murdered. The film stars John Wayne and Dean Martin. The spaghetti Western *A Pistol For Ringo* has nothing to do with the Beatles drummer.

Theaters in 1965 were literally filled with *The Sound Of Music*, the year's top-grossing film with receipts later reaching $72,000,000. The screen adaptation of the 1959 Broadway show, scored by Richard Rodgers and Oscar Hammerstein II with book by Howard Lindsay and Russel Crouse, stars Julie Andrews and Christopher Plummer. Nominated for ten Academy Awards, the movie won five, including Best Picture and Best Director for Robert Wise. Andrews won a Golden Globe. The soundtrack LP stayed in the U.S. top ten for 109 weeks and topped the British charts for 70 weeks.

The Frank Look at the Beatles and Bond

by Frank Daniels

By the time Rave magazine issue No. 1 hit U.K. newsstands in February 1964, the Beatles and James Bond, British secret agent 007, were iconic symbols in Great Britain. A year later, as the Beatles started work on their second film, *Help!*, the English public had welcomed them as an important part of British culture. Whether they liked it or not, everywhere the Beatles went, they were seen as representatives of Great Britain. Although the popularity of MI-6 agent James Bond had preceded the popularity of the Beatles in both the U.K. and the U.S., as the Beatles readied their first color movie, they were keenly aware of the public comparisons between themselves and James Bond.

In the 1964 film *Goldfinger*, James Bond pokes fun at the Beatles – indicating that the people of his (slightly older) generation simply do not go for the Fabs' style of rock and roll. Bond notices that his Champagne has lost its chill, adding, "My dear girl, there are some things that just aren't done, such as drinking Dom Perignon '53 above a temperature of 38 degrees Fahrenheit. That's as bad as listening to the Beatles without earmuffs." Shortly after mocking the Fab Four, Bond is knocked unconscious by Goldfinger's muscular servant, Oddjob, and awakes to find his companion for the night dead, painted from head to toe in gold paint.

Particularly as portrayed by Scottish actor Sean Connery, Bond typified the suave, debonair image of Britain as a world cultural leader. Meanwhile, the Beatles appealed to the teen scene. They were well-dressed, witty and distinctive. James Bond defended the world from terrorism, while the Beatles offered people the "fab" life that they imagined for themselves.

Early in the first James Bond film, *Dr. No*, we hear the secret agent admire the courageous card-playing of Sylvia Trench. They are at Le Cercle, a gambling room in Les Ambassadeurs, a famous upscale club in London. The scene wasn't filmed at Le Cercle. The production team recreated the club's interior at Pinewood Studios near London. By contrast, the Beatles actually filmed two scenes for *A Hard Day's Night* at Les Ambassadeurs, including the gambling scene in Le Cercle.

When we first meet Bond, we see Sean Connery from different angles, mostly focusing on his hands. The first time we see a clear shot of his face, Ms. Trench has introduced herself as "Trench, Sylvia Trench." Quite naturally, Sean Connery introduces himself, famously, as "Bond, James Bond." As he speaks his name, "The James Bond Theme" begins to play. In *A Hard Day's Night*, Paul's fictional grandfather plays in a loose parody of the scene from *Dr. No*. Wilfrid Brambell's first line as we focus on his face at the baccarat table is "soufflé," possibly a mix-up for "shuffle." Later (twice), he utters "bingo" instead of "banco," but like Bond, he charms the ladies, including a blonde-haired buxom woman who joins him at the table. He tells her, "I bet you're a great swimmer." In real life she was actress Margaret Nolan, who would soon be cast as Bond's masseuse, Dink, in *Goldfinger*, and appear as the gold-painted lady in the film's opening credits and promotional material and on the soundtrack album cover.

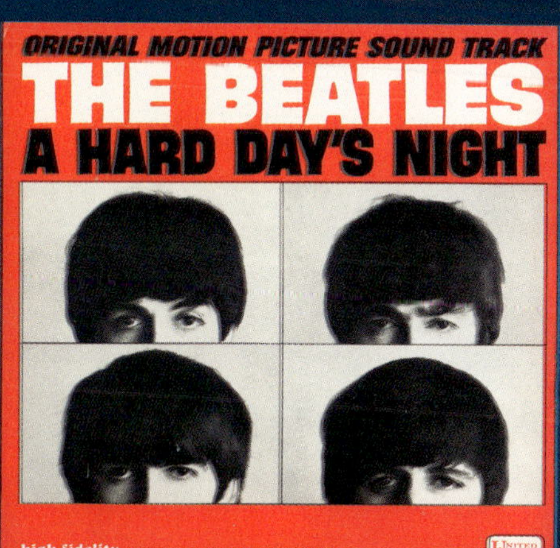

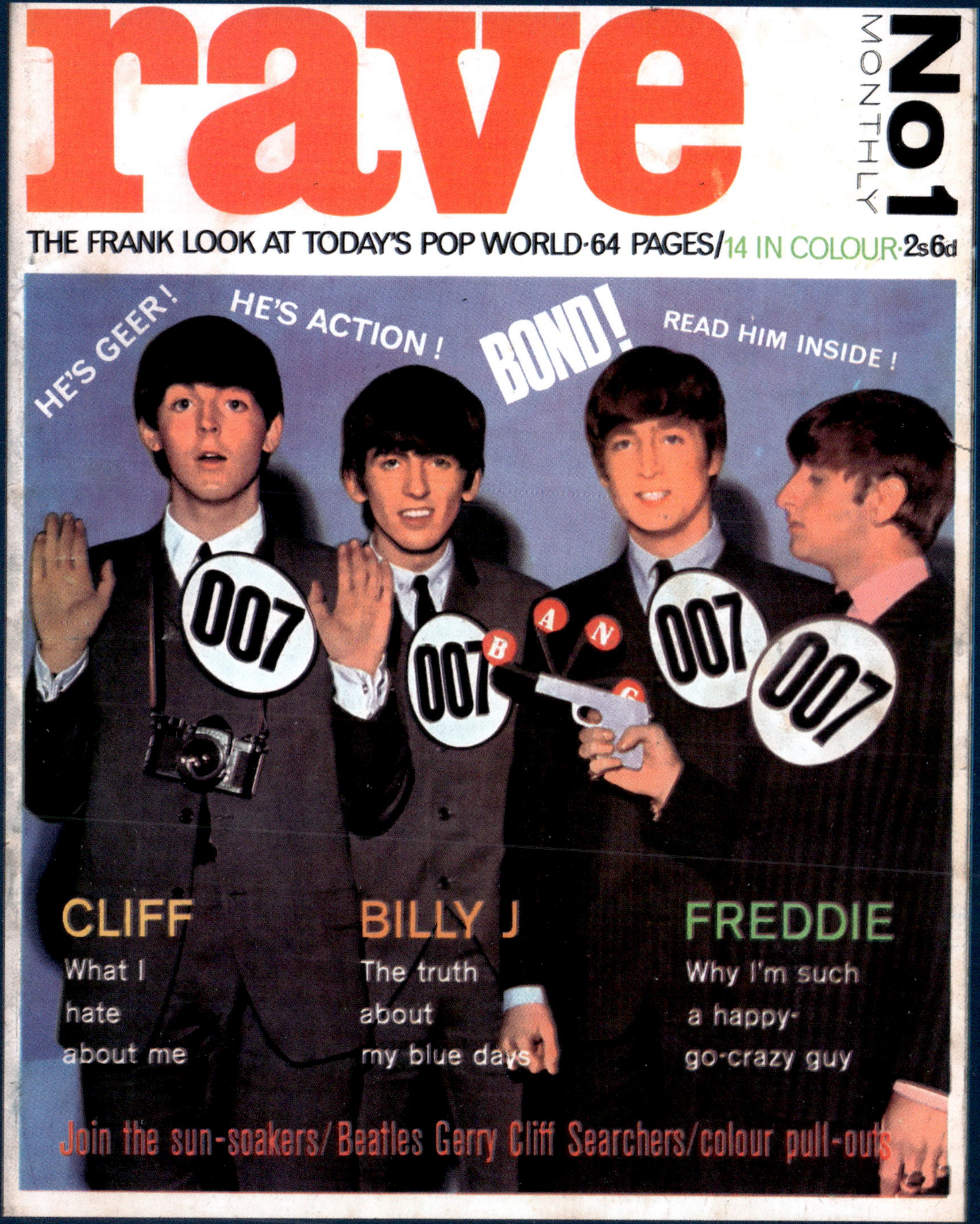

rave

MONTHLY No 1

THE FRANK LOOK AT TODAY'S POP WORLD·64 PAGES/14 IN COLOUR·2s6d

HE'S GEER! HE'S ACTION! BOND! READ HIM INSIDE!

007 007 007 007

B A N G

CLIFF
What I hate about me

BILLY J
The truth about my blue days

FREDDIE
Why I'm such a happy-go-crazy guy

Join the sun-soakers/Beatles Gerry Cliff Searchers/colour pull-outs

It is now well-known how John Lennon searched for a name for his group that would be reminiscent of Buddy Holly's Crickets. Basically, Lennon borrowed the Crickets name, eventually turning it into the Beatles.

In a 1964 interview with Jim Steck for the album *Hear The Beatles Tell All*, Lennon said: "Well, I remembered the other day when somebody mentioned the Crickets at a press conference. I'd forgotten all about that. I was looking for a name like the Crickets that meant two things, and from Crickets I got to Beetles. I changed the B-e-e because it didn't mean two things on its own–B, double-e-t-l-e-s didn't mean two things. So, I changed the 'a,' uh, the 'e' to the 'a,' and it meant two things, then...I mean, it didn't have to mean two things, but it said... It was beat and beetles, and when you said it, people thought of crawly things, and when you read it, it was beat music."

Author Ian Fleming experienced a similar but not identical issue with names when the time came to name his famous MI-6 agent.

Ian Fleming: "When I wrote the first one, in 1953, I wanted Bond to be an extremely dull, uninteresting man to whom things happened; I wanted him to be the blunt instrument. One of the bibles of my youth was *Birds Of The West Indies*, by James Bond, a well-known ornithologist, and when I was casting about for a name for my protagonist I thought, 'My God, that's the dullest name I've ever heard,' so I appropriated it. Now the dullest name in the world has become an exciting one. Mrs. Bond once wrote me a letter thanking me for using it." ("The Talk of the Town: Bond's Creator," Geoffrey T. Hellman, The New Yorker, April 14, 1962)

Although Ian Fleming's novels picked up steam quickly in Great Britain so that after a couple of novels they were very popular, that is not what happened in the United States. American reviewers had difficulty interpreting some of the elements of British language and culture. In addition, Fleming's American publisher, MacMillan, did not seem to do much to promote his books. The first American editions of Fleming's novels sold slowly, with *Casino Royale* initially selling only 4,000 copies. *Live And Let Die* fared slightly better with initial sales of 5,000 copies. *Moonraker* and *Diamonds Are Forever* continued the trend of low sales.

At first, Fleming's fifth Bond novel, *From Russia With Love*, had no more appeal in the United States than his previous offerings. In Great Britain, there was considerable negative reaction to Fleming's popularity among those who believed that his writing was of low quality and appealed to the readers' prurient interests.

In an article titled "Sex, Snobbery and Sadism" published in the April 5, 1958 New Statesman, Paul Johnson wrote about the sixth Bond novel, *Dr. No*: "I have just finished what is, without doubt, the nastiest book I have ever read. It is a new novel entitled *Dr. No* and the author is Mr. Ian Fleming....By the time I was a third of the way through, I had to suppress a strong impulse to throw the thing away, and only continued reading because I realised that here was a social phenomenon of some importance."

He continued: "There are three basic ingredients in *Dr. No*, all unhealthy, all thoroughly English: the sadism of a schoolboy bully, the mechanical, two-dimensional sex-longings of a frustrated adolescent, and the crude, snob-cravings of a suburban adult. Mr Fleming has no literary skill, the construction of the book is chaotic, and entire incidents and situations are inserted, and then forgotten, in a haphazard manner....This novel is badly written to the point of incoherence and none of the 500,000 people who, I am told, are expected to buy it, could conceivably be giving Cape [the book's publisher] 13s. 6d, to savour its literary merits."

CORAL
The "CHIRPING" CRICKETS

FIELD GUIDE OF BIRDS
OF THE WEST INDIES
JAMES BOND

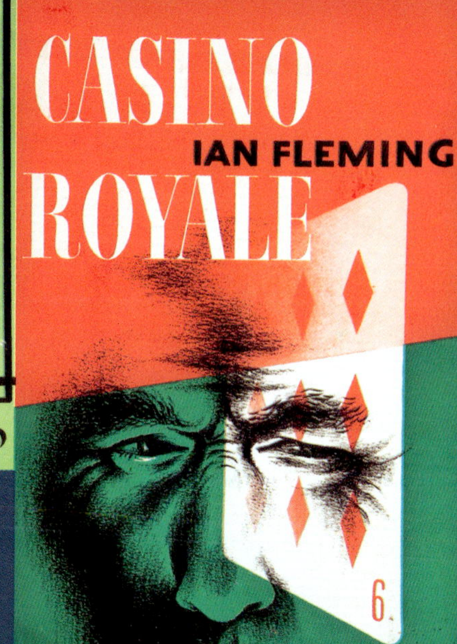
CASINO
IAN FLEMING
ROYALE
6.

IAN FLEMING
Dr. NO

Ian
Fleming
LIVE AND LET DIE
by the author of
"Casino Royale"
A Cock Robin Thriller

FROM
RUSSIA,
WITH LOVE
FLEMING

Ruthless criticism such as this did nothing to hold back James Bond's popularity among British citizens. With every new release, the character became more popular, and by 1960, he had established himself as part of British culture. Readers who worked for the National Health Service or British Railways were secretly wishing they had the exciting life of an international spy. Americans, however, had little interest in Bond until 1961.

Four years after its original publication date, President John F. Kennedy told Life magazine in its March 17, 1961 issue that *From Russia With Love* was one of his ten favorite books. Suddenly, and for the first time, Ian Fleming was the number one crime fiction author in the United States. And so it was that Fleming's fifth canonical novel about James Bond was the one that caused the character to rise to fame in the United States. Similarly, it was the Beatles fifth EMI single, "I Want to Hold Your Hand," that first propelled the group's popularity in the United States, just as they had experienced nothing but "flops" prior to that time in America.

Shortly after Life magazine reported JFK's interest in James Bond, Canadian producer Harry Saltzman got together with American producer Albert Broccoli to purchase the film rights for what would become the lucrative James Bond film series. Their company, EON Productions, stood for "Everything Or Nothing." As they formed the company in 1961, they reasoned that if their debut James Bond film was unsuccessful, then they would both be bankrupt.

Saltzman and Broccoli decided to produce *Dr. No* as their first Bond film, after which they would use much of the same crew to make a non-Bond film. The legend that appears in several places on-line states that either Broccoli or an interviewer suggested to Saltzman that they produce a movie about the Beatles, but Saltzman decisively opted to work with legendary comedian, Bob Hope, instead. The resulting movie, *Call Me Bwana*, gave EON a flop to go with the success of *Dr. No*. Some commentators speculate that turning down *A Hard Day's Night* was quite possibly a larger error than Decca Records declining to sign the Beatles in early 1962. But is that really what happened?

A famous coincidence has the first Bond movie, *Dr. No*, and the first EMI Beatles single, "Love Me Do," being released on the same day–October 5, 1962. However, the producers were arranging to work on *Call Me Bwana* back in August 1962, when Pete Best was still drumming for the Beatles. By late September, Saltzman and Broccoli had signed Bob Hope to star in the film. It is highly unlikely that Saltzman had ever heard of the Beatles in summer 1962, and even less likely that somebody would have suggested to him that a band that had never had a hit record, that never played a concert in the London area, and that was in the process of changing their drummer was worthy of starring in a movie.

We know that United Artists approached Brian Epstein in October 1963 about making the movie that became *A Hard Day's Night*, but that was over a year after Broccoli and Saltzman started working on *Call Me Bwana*. Even if somehow Broccoli and Saltzman had made a movie about the Beatles instead of a Bob Hope comedy, it would not have been the famous film that we all know.

By the time the Beatles released *Help!*, there had been 13 James Bond novels, but only four had been adapted into movies. Like every Beatles album, all of the Bond movies were enormously popular, and like the Beatles, the film exploits of James Bond were released through United Artists.

Although British newspapers once again focused on comparisons to the Marx Brothers in their reviews of the second Beatles movie, London's Evening Standard described the film as a "screwball fantasy" complete with "tongue-in-cheek take-offs on James Bond." The American press was more prone to connect Britain's current cultural icons to each other. The San Francisco Examiner wrote that the emphasis of *Help!* was "strictly on fun, farce and op-art fantasy, with a nod to the Marx Brothers and a wink to James Bond." The Chicago Tribune called the film a "spoof of science fiction movies, with a dash of James Bond." The Los Angeles Times described the plot as "James Bondish." Newsweek referenced the movie's "Goldfinger gadgets: flame-thrower umbrella, tack-thrower jalopy, paint-thrower bagpipes."

And, indeed, *Help!* is packed with James Bondish elements and parodies. As with Bond movies, *Help!* was filmed in exotic locations–the Austrian Alps and the Bahamas. It has a mysterious woman, fights in close quarters, deadly gadgets such as the "fiendish thingie" that nearly takes out Ringo and George, and a mad scientist who wants to rule the world. There are also numerous references to iconic moments in Bond's most recent film, *Goldfinger*. Bond's Aston Martin DB-5 releases a thick smoke screen and sprays oil to hamper those in pursuit, while Clang's commandeered Harrods truck drops carpet tacks onto the street. Oddjob tosses his deadly bowler hat with a steel rim to kill those posing a threat to Goldfinger, while one of Clang's gang tosses his head scarf at a cook to no effect before knocking him out with a frying pan. Goldfinger's industrial laser burns through a gold table as it moves towards a captured Bond to slice him in two. In *Help!*, the mad scientist's laser burns through the floor heading towards the Beatles before blowing a fuse. Clang's flame-thrower umbrella is a deadly device that MI-6's Q Branch would be proud of.

Ken Thorne, who served as the musical director for *Help!*, indicated that his instructions for the soundtrack were to use his own arrangements of classical music and Beatles songs. Thus, we hear multiple arrangements of "A Hard Day's Night," plus bits of "She's A Woman," "From Me To You," "You Can't Do That" and "I'm Happy Just To Dance With You." Thorne also must have been directed to incorporate elements of the James Bond soundtracks into his score. During an early segment in the film where Clang and his associates are in a Harrods truck attempting to follow the Beatles, the 40-second background incidental music cue sounds very much like "The James Bond Theme," but it is not a note-for-note copy. In particular, the details of the guitar line are clearly different from Vic Flick's famous guitar riff heard in *Dr. No* and subsequent Bond films.

Other music cues in *Help!* are reminiscent of Bond scores, but once again are different. Thorne took care to remind the viewers of James Bond, but make sufficient alterations to avoid copyright infringement. Capitol opened its *Help!* soundtrack album with an uncredited 15-second cue of Thorne's pseudo James Bond theme.

Vic Flick also played guitar on the George Martin recording of "Ringo's Theme" appearing in *A Hard Day's Night* and on the United Artists soundtrack album. He later played on Paul's *Thrillington* album.

Recent commentators on the character of James Bond are extremely unkind toward him. Brogan Morris wrote in 2015: "Sean Connery always made for one of the harsher Bonds–his original just seemed really into the job, drinking, bonking and killing not simply because he was paid to do it, but because he wanted to." He adds that in *Dr. No*, it's "the apparent glee with which Connery's Bond toys with Professor Dent, before he puts him out of his misery, that chills the blood here." (whatculture.com)

Debates have sprung up as to whether Bond is a psychopath, or a sociopath, or whether he exhibits some other sort of dangerous pathology. Psychology professor Kenneth Dutton says: "James Bond is probably one of the most nails-down functional psychopaths that there is. I mean, James Bond is ruthless. He is fearless. He's extremely focused...He's, of course, absolutely without conscience and remorse." (BigThink, 2014)

These harsh judgments fail to place Bond within his correct historical context. In the late 1950s and early 1960s, the world was engaging in the beginnings of the Cold War. The Cuban Missile Crisis (October 1962) brought everyone to the brink of global thermonuclear war, and Great Britain, which was able and willing to strike the Soviet Union with nuclear weapons, was right in the middle of it. A month later, Great Britain indicated publicly their intent to test more nuclear weapons, and the Soviet Union condemned them for it. At the drop of the proverbial hat, someone might bark out an order, and a nuclear bomb would hit your city less than an hour later – killing millions.

The villains in the Bond novels were international terrorists, interested in financing their evil worldwide schemes, often of war. Some of these plans involve the use of nuclear weapons as in *Moonraker* and *Thunderball*. Dr. No wants to turn the Cold War against the U.S. and its allies. Goldfinger tries to steal the American gold reserve. While there are a couple of cases that seem to be beneath the involvement of James Bond (*The Spy Who Loved Me* comes to mind), most of the time he's dealing with the sort of sinister characters that the world population believes are actually trying to kill them. Who is protecting them against nuclear war? Against secret criminal enterprises? Against deadly viral outbreaks? Why...the only one who succeeds at those things is James Bond!

Yes, Bond kills his enemies, but he didn't smuggle a nuke into Moscow or instigate a "Revolution" against Chairman Mao. He was never a psychopath; rather, he was a protector. He defended the world from secret threats just like the comic book hero Captain America had done.

Bond was a cool, high-society gentleman and an expert gambler. Women wanted to date James Bond; men wanted to be him. It is no surprise, then, that there are times when members of the Beatles did things that showed an admiration of the MI-6 agent.

Both Paul and George once owned Aston Martin DB-5 automobiles, which each of them ordered in 1964. While neither came with an ejector seat, Paul had a Philips Automignon in-car 45 RPM record player installed into his DB-5. For considerably less money, George purchased and wore a T-shirt with an 007 logo.

In Ian Flemming's *Goldfinger* book, Goldfinger tells Bond: "Once is happenstance. Twice is coincidence. The third time it's enemy action." There are numerous strange coincidences involving the Beatles and Bond, though none are worthy of enemy action.

On December 6, 1962, Sean Connery flew with his bride, Diane Cilento, to the famous "rock" of Gibraltar. There they got married at the registry office and stayed in the Rock Hotel. Over six years later, on March 20, 1969, John Lennon and Yoko Ono likewise flew to Gibraltar ("near Spain"), got married at the registry office, and stayed at the Rock Hotel – shortly before they "drove from Paris to the Amsterdam Hilton."

The Beatles received their New Musical Express Poll-Winners Award on April 26, 1964, from actor Roger Moore. In 1973, Moore would star as James Bond for the first time in *Live And Let Die*. George Martin scored the film, whose title song was written and recorded by Paul McCartney with his band, Wings.

In *A Hard Day's Night*, Richard Vernon played a brief part early in the film. Appearing as "Man on Train," he snobbishly suggests that the Beatles needed to defer to him because he "fought the war for your sort." Later that year, Vernon portrayed Colonel Smithers, an executive with the Bank of England who explains to Bond how important gold is to the economy of smugglers. In an attempt to show up Bond with snob appeal, Smithers passes him what he labels as a "rather disappointing brandy." Bond dryly replies: "I'd say it was a 30-year-old Fine, indifferently blended, sir...With an overdose of bon bois." M coldly reminds Bond that Colonel Smithers is giving the lecture.

Phil Collins was an extra in *A Hard Day's Night*. He was also an extra in *Chitty Chitty Bang Bang*, a 1968 movie based on a 1964 children's novel by Ian Fleming.

Although *A Hard Day's Night* had limited American screenings as early as August 1, 1964, its official release date was August 12, 1964. That was the same day that Ian Fleming died.

On February 16, 1965, filming began in Paris for the fourth James Bond film, *Thunderball*. One week later, the Beatles began shooting their second movie, *Help!,* in the Bahamas on February 23. Filming continued there through March 10. Less than two weeks after the Beatles left the Bahamas, it was Bond's turn. Sean Connery was before the cameras in the Bahamas starting on March 22. Location shooting ran through July 9.

On August 15, 1965, a young Barbara Bach was in the crowd with her sister, Marjorie, at the enormous Beatles concert at Shea Stadium. Barbara actually preferred the Stones to the Beatles, but she wanted to share the experience with her sister. Elsewhere in that same crowd was future guitar hero Joe Walsh. Bach went on to costar in *The Spy Who Loved Me* opposite Roger Moore's James Bond in 1977. She met Ringo Starr on the set of *Caveman* in 1980 and married him the following year, creating a direct link between James Bond and the Beatles. Much later, Joe Walsh married Marjorie Bach, so he and Ringo are brothers-in-law.

In 1966, as Sean Connery was preparing to film *You Only Live Twice*, which would be his fifth Bond film, word got out that the actor strongly desired to leave the series. He was worried about being typecast, and by this time, he was not very interested in the character. Charles K. Feldman, the owner of the movie rights to *Casino Royale*, decided to produce the movie as a big-budget parody – a farce. Commenting on what was happening in real life, David Niven portrays the "real" or "original" James Bond, while other actors also label themselves as James Bond. One of the Bond substitutes is Evelyn Tremble, who is played by Peter Sellers, a man with several associations with the Beatles. In the opening scene, which takes place in a public French urinal (!), we see graffiti in the background reading "les Beatles" ("the Beatles" in French).

In the Beatles TV cartoon from 1967 based on "Penny Lane," the Beatles meet up with James Blond, a dapper secret agent that was obviously based on Bond.

In March 1997, Her Majesty Queen Elizabeth II, who was a pretty nice girl, conferred upon Beatle Paul McCartney the title of Knight Bachelor. Three years later, she conferred the same honor on Sean Connery. The fictional character James Bond, is a Knight Commander of the Order of Saint Michael and Saint George.

Like the Beatles themselves, James Bond was often imitated but never equaled. They remain always a snapshot of British culture and ambassadors to the world. I only wonder what would have happened had John told Maureen Cleave: "The Beatles are more popular than James Bond right now." We might still be debating it.

The Beatles' Story According to Capitol Records

Capitol Records recorded the Beatles August 23, 1964 concert at the Hollywood Bowl with the intent of issuing an album of the performance for the 1964 holiday season. When George Martin and the Beatles blocked the live album's release, the label had to come up with something else to follow its *Something New* LP.

Its replacement took the form of a documentary double-LP on the Beatles phenomenal success. Stereo acetates were cut on September 8, 1964, with mono acetates mastered from a stereo fold-down mix on September 17. Apparently, Capitol prepared the album without any input from the Beatles, Brian Epstein, George Martin or EMI. It was produced by Gary Usher and Roger Christian, with "special material written by John Babcock, in association with Al Wiman and Roger Christian of radio station KFWB, Hollywood, California." In addition to narration and interviews, the LP contains snippets of songs by the Beatles and by the Hollyridge Strings, an orchestra led by Stu Phillips. The album was specifically created for the American market and initially issued only in the U.S. and Canada.

Capitol prepared a 4-page leaflet promoting its documentary LP *The Beatles' Story* to retailers (see page 178). Its front page had an image of the LP cover and proclaimed: "Presenting The Big Money-Maker For Christmas 1964..." Inside, Capitol explained why it would be a big-money item. "Just the jacket we've sent you, alone, should convince you that this is an album that no teenager will be able to pass up. And what about the millions of adults who'll be buying gifts for teenagers! Your orders for stock will be filled beginning about November 23! Then you, too, will be able to hear the hysterical fans, hear the Beatles' answers to some extraordinarily perceptive questions, and hear excerpts from practically all of the Beatles' hits."

At a time when the list price was $3.98 for mono records and $4.98 for stereo discs, Capitol priced its Beatles double album at a double price of $7.98 for mono and $9.98 for stereo. While this price was quite an eye-opener, Capitol was confident that Beatles fans would be willing to pay the then-record price for the album.

The Beatles' Story entered the Billboard Top LP's chart on December 12 at number 97. On January 2, 1965, the album reached its peak position of number seven, where it remained for four weeks. Billboard charted the record for 17 weeks. Cash Box charted the album at number seven, whereas Record World showed the record peaking at 13. Although not a million seller, the album was certified gold, signifying sales in excess of one million dollars, in its first week. This was a very respectable showing considering the album was little more than an elaborately packaged documentary record.

The front cover, designed by George Osaki and Rod Dyer, features jagged-edged torn black and white photos of each Beatle placed above a curved British Union Jack flag. The album's title appears at the top. The text below describes the album's contents. The back cover boldly proclaims: "It's like spending a very special evening in the company of the Beatles themselves!" But for many purchasers of *The Beatles' Story*, it was not the evening they had hoped for. With a running time of less than 50 minutes spread over four sides, the album made for a very short evening. And even more disappointing was the lack of complete performances by the Beatles. The lower left corner contains a picture of the group at its February 7, 1964 Kennedy Airport press conference. To its right is a picture of the Beatles at the Washington Coliseum on February 11.

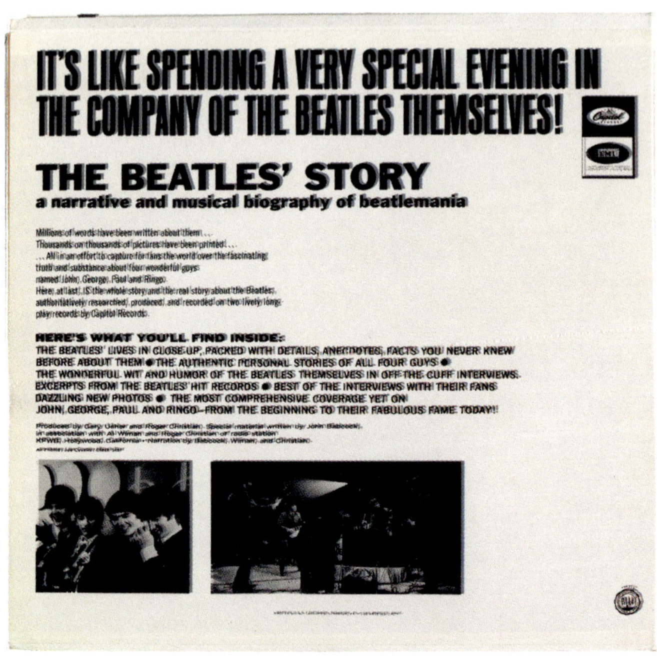

File Under: Beatles TBO 2222

THE BEATLES' STORY

A NARRATIVE AND MUSICAL BIOGRAPHY OF BEATLEMANIA ON 2 LONG-PLAY RECORDS

includes
SELECTIONS FROM THEIR HIT RECORDS
INTERVIEWS WITH THE BEATLES AND THEIR FANS
MANY NEW PHOTOS
THEIR WHOLE STORY ON RECORD . . . FROM BEGINNING TO FABULOUS FAME!

HIGH FIDELITY

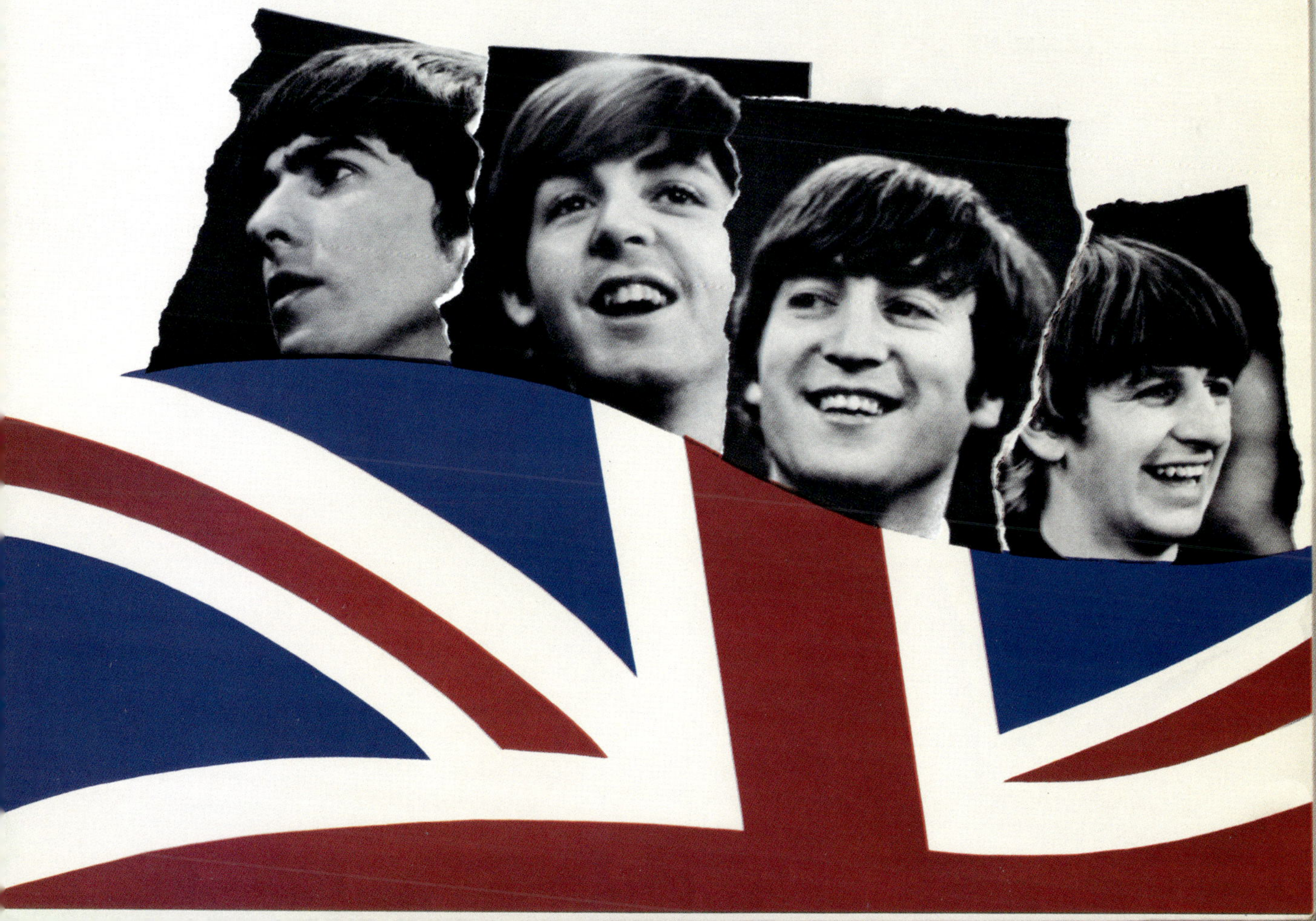

The open inside left panel has a torn-at-the-top photo of the Beatles at the Washington Coliseum. The right panel has ten Beatles pictures, with the album's selections listed to the right. The top photo shows Paul, George and John performing on The Ed Sullivan Show. Below left shows John, Paul and George gathered around a single mic singing "This Boy" at the Washington Coliseum.

The Beatles' Story opens with an instrumental version of "I Want To Hold Your Hand" by the Hollyridge Strings. And then the screaming begins. The frantic disc jockey tells the listener what it is like to be **On Stage With The Beatles**: "And here they are, the Beatles! This is the sound of Beatlemania! I don't know that this sound can be explained! The Beatles are now on stage! The entire audience has jumped to its feet! Flash bulbs are going off in every direction! I'm standing on stage about fifty feet away from the Beatles and hear the screams, shouts, yells, cheers! Listen to the crowd! This is something like I've never seen before!"

This is followed by a dramatic sounding John Babcock, backed by the Hollyridge Strings' rendition of "Can't Buy Me Love," explaining **How Beatlemania Began**: "It started in Liverpool, England. A sound, a feeling, an emotion. It started in Liverpool, England, and swept up the youth of the world. And while adults speaking in many foreign languages looked on in awe, four young boys from a poor British seaport slum town, their hairstyle a harmless defiance of convention, their musical style brash, earned renown which they never dreamed of and perhaps never really wanted ... a quartet of musical rebellion, who make no effort to charm, but strangely enough by that very act charm their most severe critics, and like Pied Pipers, their fans are legion, but their cultist reactions a phenomena."

Next there is a dose of **Beatlemania In Action**, with a hysterical crying fan trying to explain her emotions. Babcock explains that "Beatlemania is in fact a temporary state of mind which can only be accurately described by the one who's under its influence." After being told, "There are many reasons for Beatlemania," the listener is, at last, treated to the real thing, a minute or so of the Beatles recording of "I Want To Hold Your Hand." Things then get serious again for the story of the **Man Behind The Beatles—Brian Epstein**.

The exciting opening of the Beatles rocker "Slow Down" leads into Roger Christian telling tales of and reading quotes from **John Lennon**, backed by the Hollyridge Strings playing "P.S. I Love You." Al Wiman then talks about John's book and even lets John say a few words himself. The listener is treated to the opening of the Beatles recording of "This Boy," which quickly fades to the philosophical question: "But what if there had been no Cavern Club, no Brian Epstein, no George Martin, no Capitol Records, no lady luck to smile down on those four lads from Liverpool? George Harrison very simply puts it this way, 'I don't know, I know if we weren't making a lot of money, and popular, then we'd just be poor unpopular Beatles.'"

Side One closes with an interview of the group regarding **Who's A Millionaire?**. After denying that he or any of the Beatles or even Brain Epstein is a millionaire, John is asked where all the money goes. He replies, "Well a lot of it goes to Her Majesty," to which George adds, "She's a millionaire!" Roger Christian then assures the listener: "She too is a Beatle fan, and as long as we have Beatle fans, I guess we'll always have Beatlemania."

The second side opens with a snippet of John singing "You Can't Do That" leading into a track called **Beatles Will Be Beatles** that gives a reasonably accurate and interesting history of the group that closes with a bit of melodramatic fluff: "Lady luck would be Beatle number five. And with the brilliant guiding hand of young Brian Epstein as their manager, the Beatles would soon lift off the Liverpool launch pad with enough force to put the entire music world into orbit." Next is a bit of the Beatles recording of "If I Fell," which is touted as "the sound that rocked the world." The listener is told that worldwide record sales have exceeded the 30 million mark.

Credit is then given to the **Man Behind The Music—George Martin**, in a brief section discussing Martin's classical background and role as the group's producer. With the Hollyridge Strings' performance of "She Loves You" playing in the background, Capitol then gives credit to itself: "While the formula for Beatlemania was being sampled on the continent, America's first exposure to the Beatles came in short bursts from small record companies unable to marshal the promotional kickoff needed to properly introduce the young singers to America. That's when Capitol Records decided to take over distribution, and planned a full-scale coast-to-coast master plan, and the Beatles then had the winning combination to meet America." The above is Capitol's spin on how the Beatles ended up on Vee-Jay, Swan and Capitol, and conveniently ignores Capitol's initial refusal to issue the Beatles records.

The guitar solo from "And I Love Her" leads into the closing track on side two, which is a biography on **George Harrison**. He is described as an interesting combination of beat and blasé who takes his music seriously. His fans are treated to bits of information, George answering a question or two and the sounds of the Hollyridge Strings playing "From Me To You."

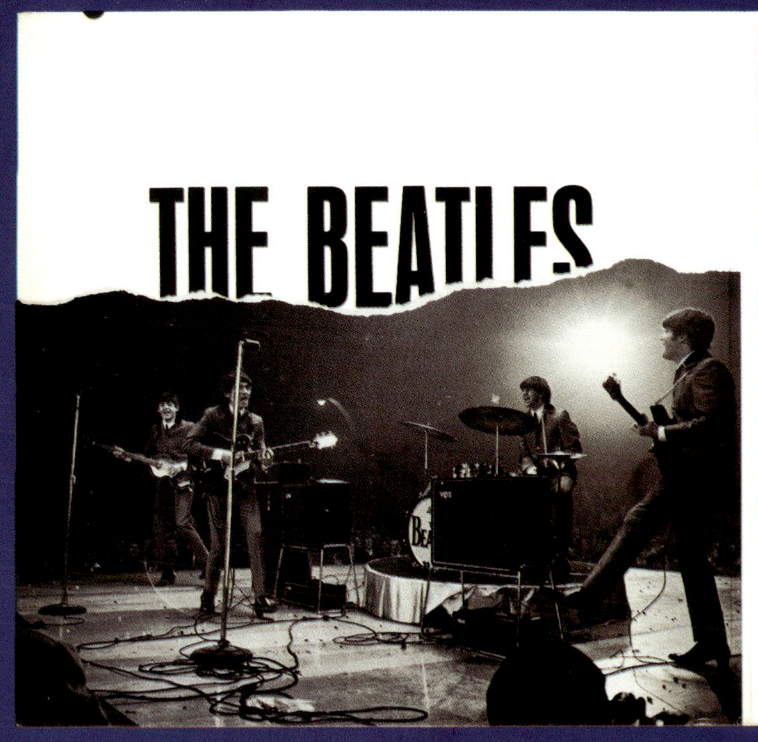

Side Three opens with an edit of the Beatles performing the title song to **A Hard Day's Night—Their First Movie**. The narrators give a brief history of the film and its critical acclaim. John even gets to say a few words about his lack of acting ability. All this and the Hollyridge Strings performing "Love Me Do." The first verse and a half of the Beatles recording of "And I Love Her" fades into the story on **Paul McCartney**, who is described as the "baby face Beatle." This is followed by a discussion on **Sneaky Haircuts And More About Paul**, to the accompaniment of the Hollyridge Strings' "All My Loving."

The fourth and final side of *The Beatles' Story* opens with a 40-second snippet of the Beatles performing "Twist And Shout" taken from Capitol's aborted *The Beatles Live At The Hollywood Bowl* album. This tantalizing sound bite from the LP Beatles fans would have preferred leads into **The Beatles Look At Life**. Despite its lofty title, this track is little more than the Beatles view of life according to John Babcock. **"Victims" Of Beatlemania** contains the ramblings of parents upset with their children's idol worship of the group. The side then rebounds with a **Beatle Medley** consisting of "Things We Said Today," "I'm Happy Just To Dance With You," "Little Child," "Long Tall Sally" and "She Loves You," all thankfully performed by the Beatles rather than the Hollyridge Strings.

The track featuring **Ringo Starr** gets off to a rousing start with Ringo singing "Boys." Behind the sounds of the Hollyridge Strings, the narrators tell the story of Ringo's childhood and his transformation from scruffy drummer to Beatle. The last track is **Liverpool And All The World!** Backed by the Hollyridge Strings, John Babcock tries to put it all into perspective, bringing the story back to where it began: "Liverpool, a poor but proud British seaport...has lifted her head. Instead of the somber rattle of poverty echoing faintly from her old cobblestone streets, sounds which mixed with the fading ships' horns and pulsating organ-like police sirens, there is now a sound of hope. It started less than a decade ago in the cellars of Liverpool's beat generation dives. It was the sound of a new music. And it's lifted the spirits and hopes of a whole city while entertaining the world.... And none of the Beatles get to spend as much time in their Liverpool homes as they would wish, but, wherever the Beatles are, Liverpool is with them in spirit. And it works the other way around, too. This is the biography of Beatlemania!" The album ends the way it starts—the sound of "I Want To Hold Your Hand" performed by the Hollyridge Strings. Although flawed, *The Beatles' Story* is a well-produced documentary that transports the listener to a time when four young men captured the attention of the world.

happy holidays
FROM THE
BEATLES
MEET THE BEATLES!
THE BEATLES' SECOND ALBUM
BEATLES '65
THE BEATLES' STORY
EXCLUSIVELY ON
Capitol RECORDS

STEREO
THE BEATLES' STORY
A NARRATIVE AND MUSICAL BIOGRAPHY OF BEATLEMANIA ON 2 LONG PLAY RECORDS
includes
SELECTIONS FROM THEIR HIT RECORDS
INTERVIEWS WITH THE BEATLES AND THEIR FANS
MANY NEW PHOTOS
THEIR WHOLE STORY ON RECORD . . . FROM BEGINNING TO FABULOUS FAME!
IT'S NEW
IT'S FABULOUS
. . . AND WE HAVE IT NOW
THE PERFECT GIFT
For Yourself, For A Friend
Don't Wait . . . Buy It Today!
THE BEATLES' STORY on Capitol Records

TEAR OUT THIS HANDY ORDER FORM, SLIP IT INTO ENVELOPE, AND MAIL TO YOUR CRDC ORDERING POINT . . .
Quantity

Presenting The Big Money-Maker For Christmas 1964 . . .

Why Is This The Big Money Item For Christmas 1964?
How Will This Gift Set Be Promoted?
Just the jacket we've sent you, alone, should convince you this is an album set no teen-ager will be able to pass up. And what about the millions of adults who'll be buying gifts for teen-agers!
Your orders for stock will be filled beginning about November 23! Then you, too, will be able to hear the hysterical fans, hear the Beatles' answers to some extraordinarily perceptive questions, and hear excerpts from practically all of the Beatles' hits.
You'll use the window streamer we've included
You'll use the handy counter-holder (holds 15 sets) we've included
You'll benefit from on-the-air promotions we've slated with major Top 40 stations
You'll find your CRDC rep has merchandising tools and co-op money available

THE BEATLES

I FEEL FINE

SHE'S A WOMAN

THE BEATLES

EIGHT DAYS A WEEK

I DON'T WANT TO SPOIL THE PARTY

THE BEATLES

I DON'T WANT TO SPOIL THE PARTY

EIGHT DAYS A WEEK

the BEATLES
TICKET TO RIDE
YES IT IS
Capitol RECORDS
5407
PRINTED IN U.S.A.

THE BEATLES
HELP!/I'M DOWN
5476
Capitol
RECORDS

THE BEATLES

YESTERDAY

ACT NATURALLY

5498

Capitol RECORDS

FAN RECOLLECTIONS

Help! Yeah right, we needed help in the USSR in late 1980s and especially in early 1990s. In 1989, after watching the *Help!* film on video, the only thing more exciting was to rewind the tape over and over just to listen to the seven brand new songs which couldn't be found anywhere else in our country. Thanks to having the *Love Songs* album and the film, we were now familiar with ten songs from the British *Help!* album, which literally meant we were collecting the album piece by piece!

In 1992, a Russian independent label reissued an unofficial version of the *Help!* album with different front and back covers. It was sometimes sold with a pair of rare custom-made booklets. At the time, I was only able to get a copy. It was 25 years later that I found out those booklets were actually copied from the German promo booklets, which I now also have. Today, as Beatles collector, I own multiple versions of the *Help!* album from the U.K., Israel, Germany, U.S., Holland and more. I'm most proud of my 1969 U.K. mono version with one EMI box logo on the silver and black Parlophone label, which is one of the rarest versions.

Yaakov Edisherashvili

I was nine years old when *Beatles '65* was released. It's hard to imagine now, but in those days, one album could be so life changing. Thankfully, my young parents loved the Beatles as much as I did and encouraged my reading every fan magazine – 16 Magazine was my favorite – to learn more about the group. My father, in particular, shared his deep love for jazz, Broadway cast albums, movie soundtracks, traditional singers and classical music with me. So even at that tender age, I was musically curious and had developed opinions.

Beatles '65 was a brilliant John-centric LP, with him singing lead on seven of the album's 11 tracks, including all but one on Side One. I loved all the Beatles, but at that time, John was my favorite – clever, sarcastic, someone who didn't suffer fools lightly. His attitude appealed to my contrarian nature. The first three songs – "No Reply," "I'm A Loser," and "Baby's in Black" – had a plaintive quality that showcased another step in his growth as a songwriter. These songs felt more personal, as opposed to being strictly crowd pleasers. I also played Paul's ballad "I'll Follow the Sun" countless times, and rocked along with George and Ringo's rockabilly covers of Carl Perkins' "Everybody's Trying to Be My Baby" and "Honey Don't," but the Lennon songs really touched my young soul.

As with previous Beatles albums, I studied the cover to *Beatles '65* with the intensity of a Harvard Law student prepping for a final exam. Seeing the group seated indoors, wearing suits and ties, holding umbrellas over their heads, was yet another example of their slightly anarchistic and distinctly British humor which was so beguiling.

Like millions of young people first exposed to the Beatles on The Ed Sullivan Show and coming to know them "close-up" by watching *A Hard Day's Night*, I firmly imagined myself as the 5th Beatle – playing along to their records using my father's old tennis racket as a guitar and a metal Christmas tree stand as a microphone. The photo on this page shows me strumming a guitar and wearing a Beatles wig. With *Beatles '65*, I remember sitting on my bedroom floor, watching the Capitol rainbow label spin on my portable record player and just listening. I was growing up, and so were the Beatles.

Jay Landers, executive producer/A&R

In April 1965, I was a ninth grader in Maywood, New Jersey. Rather than eat in the cafeteria, a lot of us would walk a couple of blocks to the town's main drag for lunch. One day, heading out to lunch I saw a bunch of guys gathered around a transistor radio. Now this was smack in the middle of the 1960s, not that far after the assassination of President Kennedy and the Cuban Missile Crisis. Seeing kids huddled around a radio could not mean anything good. I walked up to one of the guys and asked what was going on. He said that WABC in New York had just premiered the new Beatles single, "Ticket To Ride." Along with the relief that we weren't in the middle of another national crisis, it was impressive to see teenage boys so caught up in the debut of a new Beatles record. It was an indication of just how massively popular the Beatles had become by the spring of 1965.

Al Sussman

When *Beatles For Sale* was released, I was 14 and at boarding school in Hastings, New Zealand, where you were either a Beatles or Rolling Stones fan and could not admit to liking both! I was a Beatles fan. During the Christmas holidays, I went into the local shop (which sold everything from light bulbs to washing machines to records) and asked if they had *Beatles For Sale,* to which the shop assistant replied: "We have lots of Beatles records for sale." It took some explaining to get the message through! This was the first LP I purchased and was therefore the first I was able to play at time of release and hear the new songs for the first time.

Back at boarding school January 1965, my *Beatles For Sale* disc was played near non-stop on a primitive portable record player with single lift-off speaker. Regardless, as 14 year olds we were absolutely engrossed in the music. Our music teacher was in his mid-twenties. We were able to take along our latest LP purchases for playing and hear his knowledgeable critiquing. *Beatles For Sale* was the catalyst for my life-long addiction to the Beatles.

Nigel Every

I was an American college sophomore in fall 1964 and couldn't wait for more of the Beatles. In those days, there was no internet. I had to find a British seller's address in a magazine and use the regular mail to request a catalog, place an order, and have the U.K. *Beatles For Sale* LP shipped to me in the States. I didn't know what songs would be on that LP, but it was the Beatles. It turned out that those songs were new to me (and everyone else). It would be quite a while before all of those tracks were released here in the U.S. I felt like a big-man-on-campus having those, as yet, unreleased songs. Eventually the *Beatles '65* and *Beatles VI* albums got those tracks out, but I still had the real thing and it was fab!

Glenn Kukla

My friend and I went to a high school record hop dance in Waltham, Massachusetts in late 1964. We stood behind the DJ and saw that he had a copy of a Beatles album neither of us had seen before lying on the table. My heart was pounding as I picked it up! It was titled *Beatles For Sale* and had a shiny gatefold cover which I opened. I wanted to take it, something I had never thought of in my life, but I had never been so excited. My friend kept begging me: "No, no you can't!" Well I didn't, but I will never forget the absolute thrill of seeing that album cover. It's still etched in my mind!

Francis 'Mac' McAvoy

My mother had a pen pal in England for years. Both my mother and the pen pal would send Christmas presents for the other's children. In 1964, when I was in the sixth grade, one of my brothers and I received the "I Feel Fine"/"She's A Woman" single direct from England on the Parlophone label. We got the single a bit before it was released in America. We felt on top of the world. The toppermost. We had in our possession an actual Beatles 45 sent from England. This meant a big deal at the time. Oh, and we played that record to death!

Martin E Horn

Like many from my generation (I was 11 when the Beatles came to the States), I became a fan almost instantly. The first single I bought was "I Feel Fine" b/w "She's A Woman," and the first Beatle albums I owned were *Beatles '65* and *The Beatles' Story.* The first thing that stood out to me was that on *Beatles '65*, with the umbrellas on the front cover, somehow they were also able to make the shrink wrap appear to be raindrops. I constantly played my copy. "I'm A Loser" was the big one for me. I still love that tune as well as the entire album.

Lew Karp

When I was 10 years old in 1976, the Beatles became my gateway into serious, life-long music fandom. One of the first albums I acquired was *Beatles '65*. I loved most of the songs on it, especially "I Feel Fine." At the time, I didn't understand why that track, along with "She's A Woman," sounded so different from the others on the record. Of course I had no idea who Dave Dexter, Jr. was and that Capitol often doctored the sound of the master tapes sent from EMI. All I knew was that the freakish fake stereo, distorted tornado of a mix of "I Feel Fine" sounded incredibly exciting. Although I now prefer the U.S. mono mix, the fake stereo version of "I Feel Fine" from *Beatles '65* always brings back fond memories of when I first discovered the Beatles. Well done, Mr. Dexter!

Guy Hankel

Upon first playing my mono *Beatles '65*, I noticed a difference in the Beatles newer tracks like "No Reply" and "I'm A Loser." "Baby's In Black" became my favorite Beatles song up to that point. Although these tracks were brilliant, I hated "Mr. Moonlight," mostly because of the organ. To my ears, "She's A Woman" and "I Feel Fine" were punchier on the 45. The most exciting part for me was getting a clean copy of a song (identified as "Back Again") that was being played on the radio from a poor-sounding source. "I'll Be Back" was a great finishing touch.

Michael Solomon

My first "grown up" LP was a cracking good start to my still growing record collection: *Beatles For Sale*. In 1974, my cousin was emigrating and held a family gathering to say goodbye. At 12, I was always rummaging through record collections in the same way people browse the bookshelves of their hosts. I had my usual nose around while the adults were talking. Amongst the Bert Kaempfert and Tijuana Brass albums that belonged to my Uncle and Aunt, I came across *Beatles For Sale*. "You can have that," my cousin said. I was thrilled at being given an LP, and it became the first of many.

Although *Beatles For Sale* was only ten years old at the time, it was like I'd been given the Dead Sea Scrolls– an ancient text that shaped my listening for years to come. The album's cover songs were the first time I'd heard songs written by Buddy Holly and Chuck Berry. To this day, their version of "Words of Love" is still one of my favorite Beatles recordings. I can play my *Beatles For Sale* CD in the car and still belt out each song with gusto, taking me back to being the 12 year old discovering the album for the very first time.

David Smith

An album jacket you could open and make double size. I had more to see. But the Beatles looked tired on their LP for the Christmas market 1964, *Beatles For Sale*. There were some great Lennon/McCartney songs like "No Reply" and "Eight Days A Week." But contrary to *A Hard Day's Night* where there were only Lennon/McCartney songs, this disc had six cover songs like the Beatles first two albums. Certainly not the best Beatles LP, but still it has some great songs.

Marcel Reichmuth

As an eight year old in 1964, I had no interest in rock 'n' roll or the Beatles. Although the group's media splash was hard to ignore, I did not buy records. In 1965, I went to see a movie that was part of a twin billing with *Help!*, forcing me to watch the Beatles film. This was my first real exposure to the Beatles–not so much the songs but their personalities. By middle school three years later, I began buying their records and developed a life-long passion.

Andrew Caldwell

"I Feel Fine" changed my life. My best friend's uncle took us to the 1974 Beatlefest. We were both ten years old. "I Feel Fine" was the first Beatles song I truly heard and at that moment I fell in love with a rock band! Any time I hear that feedback it takes me back to 1974, when everything was in front of me. Other than my family, John, Paul, George and Ringo are the most important people in my life, and it started on that day with that song.

Randy Straff

I became a Beatles fan in 1977. My parents had a copy of the *Abbey Road* LP that I devoured. Soon after, I asked them if they had any other Beatles records. The only other record they owned was the single of "Help!" b/w "I'm Down." As with *Abbey Road*, I played both sides of this single over and over and over before I obtained more songs from the record store. Shortly after, the movie *Help!* played on TV. I was already a fan of Monty Python, SCTV and SNL and I felt this movie totally fell along the same lines. We recorded it on our new Betamax video cassette recorder, and I played the movie again and again, virtually memorizing the entire script. Ah, the good times of discovery. Even though I was exposed to the Beatles out of order, every new discovery brought me hours, days, months and years of delight!

Mark Arnold

As a young boy in 1979, I asked my mom if "Yellow Submarine" was really sung by a group called the Beatles. She laughed and told me a little about them, and how big they were when she was younger. (I didn't get it). She then went to her room and came back with *Beatles '65* and told me to go play it. You can call that my "gateway album" to the Beatles because I walked out of my room and realized, even at that young age, that I had just listened to greatness, and immediately told my dad I wanted to be a drummer (and today I am). Looking back, I feel two strong emotional experiences. The first being how great I felt listening to that music for the first time. I can't really explain it, but it was a mix of surprise and jubilation. The other being my older self, thinking "Mom, how could you possibly let your ten-year-old son play that wonderful, original stereo, first pressing album on a kid's record player so many times??!!"

Donald Jack

When I got my first real stereo in the mid-seventies, it had an 8-track player. It replaced my cheap mono record player. To launch the new stereo, my folks included a *Beatles '65* 8-track tape. Even then, I realized what a lousy format 8-tracks were. I only purchased vinyl from that point on. My *Beatles '65* LP had the orange Capitol Records label from the late seventies. I loved "No Reply" and would hear "I'm A Loser" on the FM stations I listened to in Philadelphia – WMMR, WYSP, and WMGK.

I had heard the *Help!* tracks from *The Beatles 1962-1966*, but when I finally purchased the *Help!* Original Motion Picture Soundtrack on the orange Capitol label, I loved hearing the whole album. And yes, I like the incidental music from *Help!* Somewhere in that time period, I had also purchased *The Early Beatles* and *Beatles VI*. I loved my acquisition of each Beatles album and catching up with the 1960s Beatles fans.

Tom Drill

I wasn't familiar with the *Help!* soundtrack album or film until four years after its original release. I was taking time off from school due to the mumps and, much to my surprise, my folks surprised me with that nifty green label target version of the LP as a get well present! That really did the trick!

Mike Sarafian

I was in a teenage band that played a lot of Beatles covers. We were so excited to learn to play "I Feel Fine" as soon as we heard it on the radio. Our lead guitar player learned the riff and our singers learned the harmonies. But what was that sound at the start? We'd never heard feedback on a record. Someone suggested that it must be the sound of George plucking the string and then holding a coin against the vibrating string. So that's what we did. Who knew! We were just kids!

When we heard "Ticket To Ride" on the radio, we knew we had to learn it. We worked on the song all that week and played it at a teen dance that weekend. Many of the kids had just heard it on the radio, and some had not even heard it yet. The kids thought it was really cool that we were playing the new Beatles single so soon.

Michael McEntarfer

In 1965 South Dakota, the transistor radio was our window to the world. My best friend Steve came over to our summer cabin on the lake and brought over his Emenee Folk Singer and Tiger guitars so we could practice for our first major tour around the lake as the Marshall County Beatles. We were obsessed with their sound and waited patiently through songs by Perry Como and Roger Miller to maybe get a Beatle record we could pretend to play along with as we practiced our craft. Without warning, lightning struck with a jangle and thunderous drum fills that left us dazed. Crystal clear, the song "Ticket To Ride" jumped off the dial and positively sparkled on the lake that sunny afternoon. Paralyzed, we couldn't move as the song dissolved into the ether. The Beatles had somehow done it again–lighting our path forward. The music change was seismic now, and we welcomed the ride. The tour around the lake would have to be postponed that day. We needed to practice. A LOT.

Jon Erdahl

"Eight Days A Week" was always playing on our transistor radios when me and my Cub Scout buddies were camping. I remember thinking "that is a perfect song." I still feel the same. The harmonies, the intro, the ending.

Daniel Lawton

In December 1964, I bought *Beatles '65* during its first week of release. The lady at the store gave me a set of the four Nicholas Volpe drawings of each Beatle free with my purchase. I thought *Beatles '65* was a bit of a let down as it had too many cover songs. But it did have their latest single, "I Feel Fine" and "She's A Woman," which at the time I thought was their best. It also included one of my favorite early Beatles songs, "I'll Be Back."

In 1970, I discovered the U.K. pressings with different covers and more songs than the American albums. I immediately bought *Beatles For Sale* and *Help!*. As much as I liked the cover of *Beatles '65*, I had to admit that *Beatles For Sale* had a better cover. And it included six songs that Capitol had held back for *Beatles VI*. Of course, I would return to buy more of the U.K. albums because their sound quality was better, even though the British albums didn't always include the singles. But hey, we did get "Bad Boy" a year and a half before the Brits.

David R Rauh

Back in the fall of 1967 when I was nine years old, my dad took me to our local record shop on Devon Avenue in Chicago to buy me the Capitol *Help!* LP. The record store, Kenmac, had the practice of embossing the letter "K" on the back album cover to establish that the album was purchased there should someone try to return it. For me and former Kenmac customers, the "K" makes the album more authentic and valuable. Six decades later, it's still cool to pull out and look at while listening to *Help!*.

Harvey Greenberg

By 1965, the world was becoming more colorful. More than half of the prime-time shows broadcast in America were then in color, and color TV sets, although still expensive, were working their way into more households. The Beatles were no exception to the phenomenon. While their first movie was in black and white, *Help!* was in glorious color. As the film's poster said: "The Colorful Adventures of THE BEATLES are more colorful than ever...in COLOR!" My memories of the movie and album are intrinsically linked to one another. Leo McKern as Clang, Eleanor Bron as Ahme, and Patrick Cargill as the Superintendent all hold special memories. I would later collect their and other cast members' signatures. As for the music, the Beatles were maturing. The influence of Bob Dylan was apparent in "You've Got To Hide Your Love Away." John gave an early indicator of his insecurities with the title song.

That year, I got the idea of doing a Beatles skit at our elementary school. I, along with three other 10-year-old Cub Scouts, wore unsightly self-made Beatles wigs that were clearly not authorized by NEMS! (That's me on the left.) Although we weren't the only group of wanna-Beatles to hit the stage, we were the only kids who had the courage to sing along with the Beatles as "She Loves You" and "I'll Get You" played on a backstage 45 RPM record player. As no one left the auditorium, I assume we did OK! It was a magical year in which everything seemed to transition from color to black and white, and our culture was now coming of age. I miss those days!

John Bezzini

As a second-generation Beatles fan in the 1970s, I bought the import British *Help!* LP instead of the U.S. soundtrack album because it had more Beatles songs on it. I eventually acquired the Capitol record and had Victor Spinetti autograph it for me. When *Help!* was broadcast on Chicago's WLS TV, I recorded the audio with my cassette player. Years later, my movie-related dream came true when I stood in my *Help!* shirt on the same beach in the Bahamas where the movie's final scene was filmed. The great music and fun of *Help!* helped ignite my love of the Beatles even more and more in my heart.

Dr. Jennifer Sandi

No one dared bother me when I was listening to the singles "I Feel Fine" and "Ticket To Ride." The first was a celebration for me every time it came on the air and was number one for five weeks at WAKY in Louisville, Kentucky. The song knocked me out. Since the early 1980s, I've used my "Ticket To Ride" 45 to test every new stylus for my turntable. I hear those great vocal harmonies in mono like the first time back in 1965.

Allan McGuffey

What I remember the most about the "Ticket To Ride" single was the notation that the song was: "From The United Artists Release Eight Arms To Hold You."

Mick Pollack

I was 13 years old in the summer of 1965. I always looked forward to Saturday mornings when my Beatles record buddy and I would take the city bus to downtown Williamsport, Pennsylvania. Our first stop was always Central Music Store, where we scouted for the latest Beatles releases. On one Saturday in late July, we picked up the "Help!" b/w "I'm Down" 45. Back then, the single usually came out before the album, so we asked the record store owner when the new LP would be available. He told us that by mid-August both the *Help!* movie and soundtrack album would be out. We asked him to reserve copies of the *Help!* album for us, and the record store owner obliged.

A few weeks later, we picked up our reserved mono copies of the *Help!* movie soundtrack to play on our bedroom mono record players. I remember listening to the record dozens of times while looking at the photos on the album's gatefold cover, and anxiously awaiting for the movie to come to our town.

A week or two later, the movie came to the State Theater, which was right next to Central Music Store. The movie theater was full, packed with screaming girls. Despite the noise, we really enjoyed the Beatles performing the songs that we had been playing on our record players and coming to life on the big screen in living color. WOW! I remember the movie being "the buzz" for weeks to come with my friends and school mates. It seemed like everybody I talked with had seen it!

Rob Foust

A radio DJ in Chicago gave instructions on ordering *Beatles For Sale* from England via sea mail. From that point on, I bought most of my Beatles records direct from England. I was always the first of my classmates to have them!

David Straker

In July 1965 I was seven years old, living in Honolulu, Hawaii. "Help!" was the second single I ever bought with my own allowance money, the first being Sonny & Cher's "I Got You Babe." My friends would come over to listen to "Help!" and the flip side, "I'm Down," over and over.

We saw the movie in August, and my parents gave me the Random House *Help!* book, which had tons of cool pictures and the lyrics to all the songs. My friend Bob got the soundtrack album, which we played non-stop! But it got to the point where we just wanted to hear the Beatles songs and skip the instrumentals. So one day I picked up the tonearm to skip "Another Hard Day's Night" and go right to "Ticket To Ride," but I dropped the arm and scratched the record! "Another Girl" was irreparably damaged. Bob was really upset. I felt really bad. What could I do? I didn't have enough allowance to buy him a new album. Luckily, my Mom saved the day. She told Bob that we'd replace it, and I would keep the scratched one. She bought Bob a new "Help!" LP but accidentally purchased a stereo one, which cost an extra dollar. Bob was thrilled to get the upgrade, and I was happy to have Bob's mono copy, which I continued to play repeatedly until my parents gave me *Rubber Soul* for Christmas. To this day, "Another Girl" doesn't sound right to me unless the stylus skips and Paul sings "Nobody in all the world can do what shhhhhand so I'm telling you..."

The coolest thing about owning the "Help!" single was having "I'm Down." Because it was only released as a B-side, it became a rather obscure Beatles song. It's hard to believe, but only us lucky ones who owned the single really knew this great rocker. I can't tell you how many times I played it for someone who loved the Beatles yet had never heard it before. "I'm Down" remained a rarity for nearly 23 years until it appeared on 1988's *Past Masters* CD.

Mark Helfrich

I was a mere 11 years old in 1965 when *Help!*, the single, the album and the film were released. And just to put things into perspective, I didn't own a record player, but my family had radio, TV and a local cinema. My Beatles scrapbooks remind me that I had known about the film for some time, about six months in fact, as there are cuttings from national newspapers showing the boys on Salisbury Plain and in the Bahamas, especially pictures of them playing in the sea with bikini clad girls. All my cuttings came from friends and neighbors, as we only bought the local newspaper, and my girl friends provided many pictures from the girls magazines of the day.

The single, "Help!," came out at the end of July on Friday 23rd, at the start of the school summer holidays. I watched it being "performed" on Top Of The Pops, where they showed bits from the film a week later on 29th July. I loved it instantly, but only had the one chance to enjoy it as we had no way to record TV back then.

The following Sunday, 1 August, I listened to Pick Of The Pops on the BBC Light Programme, as I did every week, and taped it using my Dad's Grundig TK20 reel-to-reel tape recorder. By doing this I had the top 20 chart hits for a week, and I could listen to "Help!" again and again along with the other top hits. Also on Sunday, 1 August, the Beatles appeared live on TV on ABC's Blackpool Night Out. They sang "Help!" last, and I remember hearing Paul sing "Yesterday," which must have been the first time I heard it. We only had two TV channels so there was no contest as to what to watch that Sunday evening.

I saw the film *Help!* during that first week of August 1965 at our local Odeon Cinema in Hanley, Stoke on Trent, the one that I had been going to for some years, every Saturday morning. ("We come along on a Saturday morning greeting everybody with a smile.") I remember the long queue to get in, all the girls squealing, and not being able to get our usual seats! The pictures, as we called it, was packed out, and there was a constant noise throughout the film of those girls! The cinema screen in those days was massive compared to some of the ones today, being the only one in the place, and the Beatles on screen were truly giants. I remember well the Intermission, and Elias Howe of course. It had a great impact on my view of the Beatles, I loved them even more, but I had no real idea of who James Bond was!

During the summer holiday at Prestatyn Holiday Camp in North Wales, the Beatles songs, both new and old, were played around the fairgrounds non-stop. I had my Dad's transistor radio with me, and I listened to the pirate radio station Radio Caroline, which was always playing the top twenty and loads of Beatles tracks from the new album. The BBC Light Programme also played the top hits too, so it wasn't hard to hear some Beatles songs any time of the day back then.

Garry Marsh

I was only eight years old when *Help!* came out but luckily my Uncle David was 15 and already a big Beatles fan! He had *Meet The Beatles!* and *Beatles '65*, which we played incessantly. Upon his acquiring the great new *Help!* album, I noticed (and loved) that it had a gatefold cover with lots of pix and info. The picture of Paul's cordial smile was so captivating that I couldn't take my eyes off it. And while I already liked the Beatles a lot by then, when I heard "Another Girl" and "I Need You" they just blew me away and that feeling has never left me. Later, when we got to see the movie at the Strand Theater in Lowell, Massachusetts, the fun that they were having inspired me to learn to play many musical instruments and become a performer, which I still do to this day. Thank you so much, Bruce, for the opportunity to relive such a wonderful memory and all you do for this hobby.

David E. Stirk

When the movie *Help!* came out, I went to see it at the same theater in which I had seen *A Hard Day's Night* a year earlier in my hometown of Dover, New Hampshire. Although I was a rabid 10-year-old Beatle fan, I had been disgusted by all the girls screaming in the theater during *A Hard Day's Night* when I wanted to hear the movie! I was hoping that would not be repeated during the *Help!* screening. So, when the movie started, I was even more disgusted when I saw all these large, colorful spitballs appearing on the screen, and I was angry some kids were throwing them, ruining my movie experience yet again – until, of course, the camera pulled back and I realized the spitballs were actually darts being thrown by Leo McKern. Whew! And, even better, none of the girls in the theater screamed this time!

Susan Gagne

It was the summer of 1965. I, along with my friends and cousins, waited patiently (well, patiently for a ten-year-old) for the release of the next Beatles movie, having loved *A Hard Day's Night*. All we had heard was that it was going to be in color. We all piled into my cousin's Chevy station wagon and headed to the All Weather Drive-In in Copiague, Long Island, New York. At first, I thought we were watching a different movie. People of India about to sacrifice someone. People asking: "Why isn't he wearing the ring? Where is the ring? Who has the ring?" Then POW! "HELP! I need somebody!" There are the Beatles! On the huge screen! Even in the cars, girls were screaming! Car horns honking! But wait! The Beatles are in B&W singing "Help!" Very confusing! But then back to color after the song! Awesome! My favorite songs were "You're Going To Lose That Girl" and "Ticket To Ride." It was a great movie with great songs and many laughs—another happy Beatles memory. Thank you, boys!

Brian J. Moran

One of my older brothers liked taking me along on his out-of-town road trips. As I had been able to read maps since I was five, I was a good traveling companion. When given the chance, I would scan the AM radio dial for rock music. I remember a short trip we took in July 1965 into northern Indiana, where I could easily find WOWO out of Fort Wayne, which was one of the better stations that I could pick up at night! They were playing the world premiere of the Beatles new single "Help!" and were pretty gracious with it, too! WOWO played the song at least once an hour, along with the whispered phrase "world premiere." I don't recall anything else about that weekend. It was great being able to hear that new song pretty much constantly—at least in my own mind!

As for the *Help!* Soundtrack album, its inclusion of those instrumental songs opened my musical horizons to pretty much every kind of world music! In addition to all the wonderful songs by the Beatles, I received a bonus gift that I didn't realize until many years later! I am now a Music Director & DJ at a college radio station, WHFR in Dearborn, Michigan. I'm only supposed to play unknown artists, but occasionally I slip in a Beatles song!

Phil Maq

I was born about a decade after *Help!* was originally released. For Christmas 2020, my wife and kids got me a DVD copy of the film. I invited my 10-year-old daughter and 7-year-old son to watch it with me. My daughter liked the movie well enough, but my son, who says the Beatles are his favorite band, thought it was hilarious. He and I laughed together for days over our favorite jokes from the film. I can't think of a better example of the Beatles enduring appeal – a child born 50 years after Beatlemania first hit can still be enchanted not only by their music, but by their personalities and humor.

Matthew Turnage

The Capitol *Help!* Soundtrack is one of my favorite Beatles albums. It was the first Beatles record that borrowed the folksy and introspective Dylan style. The group was moving in leaps and bounds from their previous records—the progression was breathtaking. It paved the way into *Rubber Soul* and all that was cool in the mid-Sixties. I got my mono copy from the Capitol Record Club of Canada. My personal favorites were ALL of the tracks! I also loved the gatefold cover's color photos of the Bahamas and the Austrian Alps. The reference to Salisbury Plain created a very personal link for me because our family had lived there two years earlier. I have since visited Nassau and Austria and have experienced these special places. Most of all, the music contained on the *Help!* album was very personal music—music that made you think. That is what the Beatles were starting to make their fans do.

This album had the ability to take you somewhere interesting and private for half an hour or more. In those days, our record player did not have a cueing arm so I pretty much had to listen to the entire LP, including the Ken Thorne bits, which I grew to appreciate. Because I didn't see the film before receiving the album, Thorne's film soundtrack music—including new sounds of sitar, flute, and classical music—allowed me to imagine my own Beatles film!

Piers Hemmingsen

Growing up in Montreal, Canada, I was used to hearing my parents favorite songs such as Gilbert Bécaud's "Et Maintenant," Johnny Hallyday's "Retiens la nuit," Elvis Presley's "Are You Lonesome Tonight?" and the Everly Brothers' "Cathy's Clown," along with classical pieces by Bach and Mozart.

By the summer of 1965, I was ten years old. I often listened to my transistor radio while riding my bicycle, hearing great new songs like Roy Orbison's "Oh, Pretty Woman," the Beach Boys' "Help Me, Rhonda" and the Beatles "I Feel Fine." The sound of the guitar riff in the Rolling Stones' "Satisfaction" intrigued me but I found it a bit noisy.

Before classes started, a new song, "Help!," reached the top of the R.P.M. charts and became one of the very first 45 RPM records that I purchased. I listened carefully to the single on my father's hi-fi system. The B-side "I'm Down" attracted me more than "Help!" with its rock style and organ sound. When I bought the record, I saw the *Help!* soundtrack LP and realized that the Beatles were in a new movie. WOW! I had missed *A Hard Day's Night*, so now I had a chance to see them on the big screen.

I finally got to see the Beatles second movie in October 1965 at a two-screen cinema with two separate rooms: the blue room with an English soundtrack and the red room with a French soundtrack. As my English was very limited at the time, I saw the film in French with its Quebec title, *Au Secours!* I was very happy to see my favorite group singing great new songs but surprised to see them play in an adventure movie. I did not expect this. I thought I would see them in a studio or in concert but not in danger! This film allowed me to hear new music, and especially new sounds of instruments that I did not know, like the sitar. I really liked this style.

When I got the *Help!* album, another surprise was waiting for me. I could open the sleeve like a book with lots of photos and liner notes about the movie. I was also happy to hear the classical and other instrumental music from the movie as well. My father even pointed out to me that the album had a classical instrumental piece by Richard Wagner. Yes, really, it was at that very moment, thanks to the Beatles (and my parents, too), that I opened up to THE music.

Normand Tremblay

When I first saw *Help!* in 1965, I was 13 years old. It was playing at the Colony Theater in Chicago near my neighborhood. My dad was a mailman whose route included the theater. I spent a Saturday morning and afternoon watching the film. Since the management knew my dad, after he was clocked out at the post office for the day, they let him in to come find me in the theater to tell me when it was time to leave. By then, I had already seen the film several times. During those days, they didn't empty the theater after every showing and people would walk in after films already started and played catch up and would leave when "this is the part where I came in." I remember seeing the opening in color and then it switched to the black and white film of the Beatles performing the title song. I was so disappointed thinking the rest of the movie would be in black and white, kind of like a reverse of *The Wizard Of Oz*. As the film switched back to color, I was relieved.

When *Help!* and *A Hard Day's Night* came on TV for the first time, I recorded the entire films from the TV speaker via microphone to my 5" reel-to-reel recorder. (Home video systems were not available then.) I learned the entire dialog (what I could understand from their accents), even typing out the whole scripts. I later copied those tapes onto 8-tracks and again later onto cassettes to play in the car. Once VCRs were mass produced, I bought a Betamax only because *Help!* was being shown on TV again. As for the original LP, I didn't find out until many years later that the semaphore positions the Beatles used didn't even spell "HELP" and that their order was different between the U.S. and U.K. covers. When I play the Capitol soundtrack LP, I do not skip the instrumental tracks. Even now, when I see actors from *Help!* in other roles, I identify them first as being co-stars of the Beatles in *Help!*. To me, that is their claim to fame.

Robert Jakubiec

I was nine years old when my parents took me to the Woods Theater in downtown Chicago to see *Help!* the weekend it came out. This was a rare event for me and my parents to go downtown for a movie, dinner and a bit of shopping. The stores had Beatles merchandise, but my parents did not buy me any because they could not afford it. The movie gave me an opportunity to see the Beatles in color and hear their new songs. I remember being most impressed by the Beatles sunken beds in their home and John singing "You've Got To Hide Your Love Away." I also loved the parts where the Beatles played live or in the studio.

The next weekend, I got the Capitol *Help!* album at Sears. By then, I already had the previously released Beatles albums and singles. I would constantly play all of the Beatles records in my room – especially on weekends – while looking at the album covers. It was a very important part of my life then and now.

Lenny Samczyk

I was just about to turn 11 years old in the summer of 1965. I bought the "Help!" 45 RPM single with picture sleeve in early August. I remember being amazed at the wonderful B-side "I'm Down." My cousin and I attended a showing of the *Help!* movie at the Fox Redondo theater in Redondo Beach, California. It was paired with "Beach Blanket Bingo" – yikes! I remember all the girls screaming throughout the movie, especially when it looked like the boys were blown up on the Salisbury Plain. The scenes I loved the best were the staged studio session for "You're Going To Lose That Girl" and the performance of "Another Girl" out on the plain. I received the mono soundtrack LP on my birthday, August 27, and even liked the Ken Thorne instrumentals. Even though played many times, that record plays fine to this day.

Jon Roe

I became a Beatles fan back in 1964 when I bought the Swan single "She Loves You" at the local pharmacy. When *Help!* came to Chicago, a neighborhood friend and I walked to the State Theater on Madison Street. We pretended we were from England and spoke with our idea of what English accents sounded like. We really thought we were something, although I bet the only people who believed we were from England were me and my friend. Two silly ten-year-old boys struck by Beatlemania.

Gregory Link

The "Help!"/"I'm Down" single was the very first record I bought without hearing it first. I felt extremely fortunate to have a copy so fast. In Louisville, Kentucky, we had two radio stations, WAKY and WKLO, that played the Beatles continually, even playing some tracks before they were released in the U.S. I remember hearing "I'll Be Back" in July 1964 while riding around the Daniel Boone statue in Cherokee Park. I had complete faith in the Beatles. Still, it was almost an otherworldly experience to hear a Beatles song first on my mother's own stereo. Every note was brand new to my ears with no static and no DJ talk.

Allan McGuffey

In 1965, I was ten years old and living in a suburb of Cleveland, Ohio. The first time I saw *Help!* was right after its release when my parents took me to the drive-in to see the film. Seeing the Beatles in living color was mind-blowing! I loved it so much that I begged to see it again. After I got the "Yesterday" single, I started playing "Act Naturally" and singing to my mom, "I hope you'll come and see me in the movies" but no dice! I had to wait until it showed up on TV to see it again. Thank goodness for DVDs so we can see it anytime we want!

Nancy Riley

In 1965, there was a popular DJ, Bud Ballou, on WNDR in Syracuse, New York that we listened to every day. He also hosted a dance show on our local TV station that my brother and I watched every day after school, at 5:00 PM. He used to play new records on his TV show that were not yet being played on his radio show. One afternoon he was excited because he had just received a promo copy of the *Help!* LP and was going to preview some of the songs. When he held it up, I thought "how cool, a gatefold cover." I was even more excited hearing these new Beatle songs for the first time. I had to wait a few days until the LP was available to buy, but it was worth it! Like the American *A Hard Day's Night* soundtrack, even the instrumentals made for great listening. Since this was way before home videos, listening to these soundtracks was like reliving the movies over and over again.

Robert G. Robbins

I remember first hearing "Ticket To Ride" on my favorite radio station, Chicago's WLS. When I found the single in a local store, I was intrigued by the words under the title: "From the United Artists Release 'Eight Arms To Hold You.'" Later that year, I was immediately impressed with the Capitol *Help!* soundtrack album. It had a gatefold sleeve with color photos and the movie's title in bold letters. This was a stark contrast to the lack of graphics and black and white photos of the British Parlophone *Help!* LP that I would later see. Although the British album has twice as many Beatle songs, the Capitol record is a true soundtrack with only songs from the movie. Even the instrumental pieces on the album are nice. To this day, the song "Help!" doesn't sound right to me without the James Bond intro. Whenever I hear that, it takes me right back to being ten years old and listening to that album in my bedroom in Kewanee, Illinois.

Michael Rinella

I have vivid memories of watching the Beatles on the September 12, 1965 Ed Sullivan Show. The look was very different from 1964! Their hair was much longer, especially for John and George. The band's Vox amplifiers were in plain sight right behind them, rather than hidden off to the side as they had been the previous year. The Ludwig logo on Ringo's bass drum head was crooked. George's lead guitar and solos sounded great! Paul and George's backing vocals on "I Feel Fine" and "Help!" were spot on perfect, though John flubbed the lyrics on each! I had never seen John and Paul sing into the same microphone like they did on "Ticket To Ride." My dad thought the Beatles sounded even better than they had the year before. They seemed looser and more confident while having more fun, especially John!

About three weeks prior to this broadcast, my father took me to see the Beatles perform live at Metropolitan Stadium in Bloomington, Minnesota on August 21, 1965. Before the show, we were able to enter the Minnesota Twins clubhouse and meet the Fab Four! I was in heaven! An excellent year for a ten year old!

Bob Pratt

The anticipation for the Beatles September 1965 appearance on The Ed Sullivan Show was not as great as in February 1964. For adults, the novelty was gone. And by then, fans had seen them in two films. But with all the great music the group had released in the year and half following their first time on the show, there was plenty to look forward to. Of course, we expected them to be great. The only question was, "What songs will they play?"

Those tuning in that night would have to sit through Soupy Sales, Cilla Black and a magician before Ed finally introduced and shook hands with each Beatle. The group opened with "I Feel Fine." It was a solid performance, though John muffed the words at one point. Paul provided a powerful vocal for "I'm Down," but reversed the order of the first two verses. Towards the end of the song, John was shown playing an electric organ with his elbow. Next, Ringo introduced himself as "all nervous and out of tune, Ringo!" for a new number, "Act Naturally."

After more from Soupy and Cilla and a comedy bit by Allen & Rossi, the Beatles closed the show. A flawless "Ticket To Ride" had an extended opening to allow for side shots of each Beatles face. George then introduced a song featuring only Paul, who played acoustic guitar and sang "Yesterday" backed by pre-recorded strings. The group followed with a slightly sloppy "Help!" But overall, the Beatles showed why they were still top of the pops.

T.H. Spidell

In 1965, my friend Darlene and I attended the August 14, 1965 taping of the Beatles on The Ed Sullivan Show at CBS Studio 50 in New York City. The studio is not very large, and we had great seats downstairs on the left. When the Beatles were announced, we were stunned – they seemed to come from the audience just a few feet away as their names were called. It was so exciting seeing them so up close. I was surprised to see that John was playing the keyboard. On "I'm Down," Paul reversed the verses. He was sweating bullets while singing "Yesterday." I could see this with the binoculars I had around my neck. Some CBS executives in front of us wanted to see the sweat too and grabbed my binoculars to have a better look. The awkward part was that the binoculars were still around my neck!

Linda Bunson

[At my request, Linda sent me the full story of her 1965 trip to New York to see the Beatles on The Ed Sullivan Show. Her detailed account appears in the Supplement to this book, available in the digital edition of the book and separately as a free download at www.beatle.net.]

A Fan's Notes: *Help!* and the Summer of 1965

(an alternate version first published in Beatlefan #126, September 2000)

by Bill King

I have distinct memories of the first time I heard the Beatles song "Yesterday." It was late August 1965. I grew up in Athens, Georgia, about 66 miles from Atlanta — close enough that we got the Atlanta TV stations and some radio stations.

But none of the radios in our house (AM only, of course) could pick up Atlanta Top 40 giant WQXI, and I'd really been wanting to hear Quixie, which billed itself as Atlanta's "official" Beatles station.

The problem was solved when I bought myself a pocket transistor radio. I was thrilled to discover that it could pick up WQXI, and later that afternoon I tuned in just in time for a Quixie exclusive: the Atlanta premiere of "Yesterday."

The tune had been omitted from the $4.98-list-price U.S. *Help!* movie soundtrack album that I'd been spinning for the past week or so on my portable stereo, and the song wouldn't be issued as a single for another three weeks. To ensure "Yesterday" remained a Quixie exclusive, the deejay played the station's ID a couple of times in the middle of the song. That really irritated me, but at least I'd heard a new Beatles song that Athens radio didn't have yet!

That summer of 1965 easily was the height of Beatlemania, and that was especially true in the local media, because that was when the Beatles came to Atlanta Stadium. The Atlanta show was August 18, just three nights after their triumphant, record-breaking concert at New York's Shea Stadium. The Atlanta show was the first big event at the new stadium, which the next year would become home to baseball's Braves.

I wasn't at the show, but I followed the excitement via the morning Atlanta Constitution and afternoon Journal, which had been beating the Beatles drum-beat for weeks. There were features on mod fashions, Beatles hairstyles, a rich local girl who'd gotten her parents to take her to Nassau to meet the Beatles, and a five-day syndicated series, "The Beatles Let Their Hair Down," that began running on the front page of the combined Sunday paper on August 8. "It was the only time we ever had as much publicity for a show as we thought we should have," the promoter, Ralph Bridges, would joke to me 20 years later, when I was working for the Constitution, covering music.

It's not that there wasn't anything else going on. President Lyndon B. Johnson had announced a call-up of 340,000 additional troops as the Vietnam War escalated, and the Voting Rights Bill was passed. But the Beatles still were big news, especially in cities they were visiting.

A week before the concert, Bridges ran an ad saying: "Beware of Rumors! We are not sold out. Good tickets still available." Actually, that meant 8,000 of the upper deck $4.50 seats were available. All the $5.50 lower deck tickets were long gone. The show, which drew 34,000, ended up falling about 2,000 short of a complete sell-out. (A street poll saw some folks citing the "high cost" of tickets.)

Quixie deejay Paul Drew — Atlanta's "Fifth Beatle" because he'd traveled with the Fab Four on their '64 tour and visited them in the Bahamas during the filming of *Help!* — was in the entourage that greeted the Fab Four in New York when they landed on Friday, August 13, and he called in a breathless report to a local TV station and was interviewed in the Journal about "How to Get Along With The Beatles."

Amid news of race riots in Los Angeles' Watts area, Sunday's paper was full of the Beatles, with a photo of them arriving at JFK Airport in New York and tips for Atlanta parents, asking that they not drive directly to the stadium but let their kids use the special "Beatle Bus" shuttles.

The Monday paper had a report on the Shea Stadium show and noted that a 16-year-old runaway boy from Florida had been found in Atlanta Stadium Sunday night.

Wednesday morning's Constitution declared on the front page that "B Day" had arrived. (The first fans apparently got to the stadium at 4:30 AM) The Beatles landed that afternoon at a remote corner of Atlanta's airport — out of view of fans waiting at the terminal —and proceeded via three limos to the stadium, where a press conference was held. It consisted of about 15 minutes of nonsensical questions ("stupid," George Harrison called one) from a gathering heavy on high school newspaper editors and local deejays.

Asked about recent reports that he was engaged to actress Jane Asher, Paul McCartney replied, "I haven't said anything to anyone, but people keep writing about it and putting it in papers, so I'm getting to believe it." Did The Beatles have any Atlanta acquaintances? "Not yet," John Lennon replied dryly. Was George thrilled to have a nightclub named after his haircut (a reference to him calling it "Arthur" in *A Hard Day's Night*)? "Well, I was until I saw the nightclub," he said, drawing a big laugh. Ringo Starr said he didn't have a name yet for the child his wife was expecting. Where did John and Paul get the ideas for their songs? "Out of John and Paul's heads," Lennon said.

What did they think of Elvis? "We liked his early stuff," Paul said. "We liked it a lot more than the stuff he's doing now," which he called "middle-aged." A Journal report the next day attributed those remarks to Ringo. (Apparently, it was so hard to tell those Beatles apart!)

The gates opened at 6:00 PM, with showtime at 8:15. A fashion show, backed by a Beatles-type band called the Atlanta Vibrations, preceded the opening acts: The Discotheque Dancers, Brenda Holloway with King Curtis, Cannibal and the Headhunters and Sounds Incorporated. When the latter group took the stage, Beatles manager Brian Epstein, who'd been chatting with the Journal's TV editor, stopped to listen. "It's funny, this is my newest group, but I haven't heard them yet," he said.

The Beatles took the stage at 9:37 PM and did essentially the same show as at Shea, except "I Wanna Be Your Man" was substituted for "Act Naturally."

The Fab Four went straight from the show to the airport for their flight to Houston. Later, the Beatles praised the Atlanta sound system as the best they encountered on the tour — they actually could hear themselves!

The show was splashed all over the front pages of Thursday's newspapers, with four pages of pictures and stories in the Constitution and six pages in the Journal. Coverage was favorable, if somewhat condescending. Said the Journal: "Hearing one of their concerts is the most amazing and entertaining headache a person can get."

The next week, a Journal columnist who had been a notorious Beatles basher, wrote a mea culpa, admitting he liked the group. "I know a lot of very cynical newspaper men and women who went to Atlanta Stadium to scoff, but emerged enlightened, enriched and excited," he wrote. He added that Epstein had said the Shea show had been filmed for a TV special, and that, while in New York, the Beatles had taped the season-opening Ed Sullivan Show for broadcast September 12.

With summer vacation hurtling toward its traditional Labor Day end, I watched with rapt attention as Gemini V took off for a then-record eight days in space, and I took my brothers to see *Help!* at a local cinema a couple of days after reading in the paper that producer Walter Shenson expected the group's third film to be a western, *A Talent For Loving*. (He said the Beatles might do some songs in "folk music" style to fit in.)

Also in cinemas at the same time were Richard Burton and Liz Taylor in *The Sandpiper*, *Clarence The Cross-Eyed Lion* (the first movie my youngest brother got to go to), Jimmy Stewart in *Shenandoah*, Peter Sellers in *What's Up Pussycat?*, Jerry Lewis in *The Family Jewels*, Stephen Boyd in *Genghis Khan* and John Wayne and Dean Martin in *The Sons Of Katie Elder*.

Once school had started, there were declarations of undying love for Dino, Desi & Billy and Herman's Hermits emblazoned on some girls' notebooks in my eighth-grade class, but the title song from *Help!* was all over the radio, soon to give way to "Yesterday." Also getting airplay were Sonny & Cher's "I Got You Babe," Gary Lewis and the Playboys' "Save Your Heart For Me," the Righteous Brothers' "Unchained Melody," the Beach Boys' "California Girls," the Four Tops' "It's The Same Old Song," Babara Lewis' "Baby I'm Yours," James Brown's "Papa's Got A Brand New Bag," Barry McGuire's "Eve Of Destruction," We Five's "You Were On My Mind," the Turtles' "It Ain't Me Babe," the McCoys' "Hang On Sloopy," the Dave Clark 5's "Catch Us If You Can" and Freddy Cannon singing the theme song from Where The Action Is, the ABC pop music showcase that aired on weekday afternoons, along with The Lloyd Thaxton Show. American Bandstand remained a Saturday lunchtime staple, and in prime time we had Shindig! (now twice a week) and Hullabaloo.

The Beatles remained in the news. Ringo's son Zak was born on September 13, and the new father proved less than prophetic in a story in the next day's paper by declaring, "I won't let Zak be a drummer."

The night before, the show the Beatles had taped for Sullivan aired (the last one ever in black & white). Amid Soupy Sales, Cilla Black, Fantasio the magician and Allen & Rossi, the Fabs performed live in two segments, first doing "I Feel Fine," "I'm Down" (or "I Am Done," as one local columnist misheard it) and "Act Naturally," then later "Ticket To Ride," "Yesterday" and "Help!" They looked and sounded great, with "Yesterday" a real showstopper. (Cracked John after the number: "Thank you, Paul, that was just like him.") I think that show is my favorite of their Sullivan appearances, even topping the first one in February 1964.

Another high point that fall came at Sanford Stadium, as I watched our hometown Georgia Bulldogs upset defending national champion Alabama 18-17!

The other thing, besides college football, that Saturdays meant in those days was TV cartoons, and I still watched a few. I tuned in on September 25 when ABC grabbed the biggest share of the audience — better than 50 percent, outrating both other networks combined and every other show in daytime TV — with a departure from cute talking animals and super heroes. Instead, the new show offered four animated, singing moptops. Yeah, it was called The Beatles.

Bill King's Interview with Walter Shenson on *Help!*

(Originally appeared in Beatlefan #16, June 1981)

I first met Walter Shenson, the producer of the Beatles first two films, at a Beatlefest convention in early 1981, when he had gotten back the rights to *A Hard Day's Night* and was preparing to re-release the black-and-white classic. The 1964 film, a fictionalized look at the Beatles preparing for a TV performance, was acclaimed by critics, who hailed Alun Owen's witty script, Richard Lester's innovative direction, and the natural, winning performances by the Fab Four, who played themselves with considerable charm.

A year after the first film, Lester, Shenson and the Beatles teamed up again with a bigger budget for *Help!* — a more ambitious color production that spoofed the James Bond series (with a variation of the Bond theme even opening the U.S. soundtrack album). This time, portions of the film were shot on location in the Austrian Alps, the Bahamas and Britain's Salisbury Plain.

Help! had an over-the-top plot about an Eastern cult looking to reclaim a sacrificial ring that had gone missing and wound up being worn by Ringo Starr. A subplot involved a mad scientist who wanted the ring so he could "dare I say it? — rule the world."

The second film might not have matched the cinematic heights of its predecessor, but as Brad Hundt wrote in Beatlefan magazine, "it's splashy, absurd and still a great deal of fun."

Plus, of course, it had seven new Beatles songs, which saw the Beatles sound evolving, with keyboards, particularly electric piano, replacing harmonica as the key addition to the basic lineup of guitars and drums. Flutes and strings also had been added to their musical arsenal. And there were some country influences, along with obvious nods to Bob Dylan and the folk-rock movement. Lester's treatment of the songs in the film — as self-contained sequences — would be cited in later years as the template for the music videos of the MTV era.

The film *Help!* was a box office hit, but it didn't draw the rave reviews that *A Hard Day's Night* had garnered. Still, Shenson said he felt that *Help!* was underrated. "If there had never been an *A Hard Day's Night*, *Help!* would have been better received," Shenson said. "But people were always comparing the two. I think maybe we were taken to task by some of the critics because we were more ambitious in *Help!*."

As producer, Shenson cast both Beatles films along with Lester. "We got the best of British talent," he said. Starring alongside the Beatles in *Help!* were such standout British actors as Leo McKern (who later achieved TV stardom with Rumpole of the Bailey), Eleanor Bron, Roy Kinnear and Patrick Cargill, as well as Victor Spinetti, who also had appeared in *A Hard Day's Night* (and would later appear in *Magical Mystery Tour*).

Strangely, the strong supporting cast of *Help!* bothered the Beatles. "They felt, Paul in particular, and John, too, that they were merely puppets being pulled around on strings and that these very fine actors (such as Leo McKern) were actually the stars," Shenson said.

"I disagree totally. It was the Beatles who made it work. Their personalities were far stronger than any of the actors. But the Beatles felt that where *A Hard Day's Night* was their movie, *Help!* wasn't."

In comparing his two Beatles films, Shenson said: "There's a purity in *A Hard Day's Night*, and it's a tribute to Dick Lester that it doesn't look like a film made on a tight budget and schedule. But *Help!* was a more complete film. It works on more levels and it's a prettier picture. There are so many layers to it. I think that picture's a knockout."

While he preferred the first film, Shenson said that *Help!* was Lester's favorite "and I can see why."

People often wonder why, considering the success of the Beatles first two features, they never made a third. "It has a lot to do with the Beatles themselves and their development as artists and people," Shenson said. "The Beatles became impatient. They wanted to break out and do new things. After *Help!*, movies were no longer a challenge to them.

"We were looking for a story idea and John came to the office by himself one day. I asked him if he'd like to write the third movie. He said he didn't think he could. He said, 'Our next movie should be a story in which we don't play The Beatles.' I said I didn't think that was possible. I employed a few writers, and we had a couple of ideas the Beatles liked, but they didn't develop well."

One was hip playwright Joe Orton's *Up Against It*, a surrealistic story commissioned by Brian Epstein that Shenson said never was considered seriously — at least not by him. Another was *A Talent For Loving*, based on the Western novel by Richard Condon, which actually was announced as the Beatles third film at one point. "Bud Ornstein, the head of production for United Artists, was an old friend of Condon's and he had a personal love for that book," Shenson said. "He wanted that movie made. He suggested it to the Beatles and got Brian Epstein to buy the film rights. Condon wrote a screenplay that wasn't very good. I saw it later but had nothing to do with the production [writing] of that script." The idea was scrapped when Ornstein moved to Paramount; he later talked Shenson into making *A Talent For Loving* with Richard Widmark and Topol in 1969. "The Beatles still owned the property, so they had a profit participation in it," Shenson said.

Then it was announced that in September 1967 the Beatles would begin filming Owen Halder's *Shades Of A Personality*, a story of four sides of a man's personality, with the four sides played by the Beatles. "We all liked the original idea very much," Shenson said. "It was a super idea and still is. But the script didn't develop right, and everyone was very impatient. The Beatles finally decided to discharge the third film in their contract [with] *Let It Be*. They financed it with UA and gave me a small piece of the profit. I think if we'd had a sensational script of a great idea, we might have made a third film. But it just wasn't in the cards."

Shenson said that he had sent a script to Lennon a few years before John's death, and "he wrote back and said, 'Thanks but no thanks.'"

Shenson admitted that the Beatles films were: "the highlight of my career. I guess, in a way, the success of those pictures spoiled me. I wasn't hungry anymore. I made a lot of low-budget comedies that I financed myself, and a lot of pictures nobody else would have made." Those included: *30 Is A Dangerous Age*; *Cynthia* (Dudley Moore's first film); *Don't Raise The Bridge, Lower The River* with Jerry Lewis; *Welcome To The Club*; *Digby, The Biggest Dog In The World*; and Shenson's last film, *The Chicken Chronicles*, in 1977. "They didn't work," he said, "but I had fun making them."

After 18 years of living and working in London, Shenson and his photographer wife Gerry moved back to California in 1973, living in Bel Air. Shenson died on October 17, 2000, at age 81.

Beatles For Sale at a Record Store Near You

Robert Freeman, the photographer responsible for the eye-grabbing covers to *With The Beatles* and *A Hard Day's Night*, was once again given the assignment for designing and shooting the cover for *Beatles For Sale*. This project would be a bit more involved as the jacket would be a one-piece gatefold cover. In addition to providing concepts and images for a front and back cover, Freeman would need to design two interior flaps for the jacket. This was in keeping with the Beatles desire to give consumers good value for their money.

The jacket has a thin front side panel that when opened exposes a pocket that opens on the left side of the right inside panel. The vinyl album, packaged inside a generic EMI inner sleeve, slides into the pocket from the left. The front and back sides of the cover, as well as the interior upper and lower white flaps on the right side opened panel, are laminated. This was the first time a British pop or rock LP was packaged in such a cover.

The front cover features a color picture of the group taken in October 1964 at London's Hyde Park near the Albert Memorial. According to photographer Freeman, the concept was developed at a meeting with Brian Epstein and the Beatles during which it was decided to shoot a color photo at an outdoor location towards sunset. "Again the Beatles wore dark clothes–black scarves, jackets and coats, which they needed anyway because the weather was already getting cold. We were lucky to have sunshine for the shot since there was little chance of getting them back for another session." Freeman added that he used the same Pentax 180 mm telephoto lens used for the cover to *With The Beatles*, creating a soft-focus atmospheric background. The Beatles squeezed in the session on the way to a gig in Northern London.

As part of the concept, the group took on a serious look for the tight portrait–no smiles, as was the case for *With The Beatles*. But while that cover was praised for its innovation and viewed as a work of art, the jacket for *Beatles For Sale* was later viewed as evidence that the group was weary from too much time spent touring, which supposedly led to a sub-par album.

Paul recalls the photo session: "The photographer would always be able to say to us, 'Just show up,' because we all wore the same kind of gear all the time. It was easy. We showed up in Hyde Park by the Albert Memorial. I was quite impressed by George's hair there. He managed to create his little turnip top." Tony Bramwell claims responsibility for the orange blob in the picture's lower right corner. "I held the branches of the tree out of the way, but my hand got in the shots!"

By this time, EMI was confident that the British record-buying public would recognize the famous faces of George, John, Ringo and Paul without the cover showing the group's name in large print. The title *Beatles For Sale* is barely visible, appearing in small uppercase letters on three lines next to the Parlophone/EMI box logo in the jacket's upper left corner. The eyes of those viewing the cover focus solely on the Beatles faces.

The back cover (shown on page 207) has another Freeman color portrait from the same session. Freeman climbed into a tree and shot down, getting a picture of the Beatles looking upwards. The image of the group was superimposed over a background of autumn leaves. Capitol used this picture for its album *The Early Beatles*.

PARLOPHONE
TRADE MARK OF
THE PARLOPHONE CO LTD
EMI
– THE GREATEST RECORDING
ORGANISATION IN THE WORLD
BEATLES
FOR
SALE
mono

The left inside panel has a black background with white text. The upper portion is divided into three columns, with a list of the Side One songs, along with their composers and singers, on the left, and Side Two songs with the same information on the right. Derek Taylor's liner notes, followed by George Martin's production credit and Robert Freeman's photography credit, are in the center column. A rectangular box below the text contains the Parlophone logo, LP speed and EMI information. The bottom portion has a photo taken of the Beatles on stage at their first U.S. concert at the Washington Coliseum on February 11, 1964.

The right inside panel has Freeman's photograph of the group taken at Twickenham Film Studios in the lobby by the viewing theatre. The group posed in front of a wall covered with a collage of publicity pictures and film stills. The collage includes French actress Simone Signoret (above George), a male gypsy from the 1922 film *The Bohemian Girl*, Albert Finney in *Saturday Night And Sunday Morning*, silent era actress Theda Bara (wearing hat), Jayne Mansfield (right of Paul), Victor Mature (on horse with rifle), and Ian Charmichael (right of Ringo).

In his liner notes, Derek Taylor discusses the songs, stating that three of them were seriously considered for single release: "Eight Days A Week," "No Reply" and "I'm A Loser." He makes an odd reference to a "radio-active, cigar-smoking child, picnicking on Saturn" to make his point that hearing a few tracks from the album will enable such a person to understand what the Beatle affair was all about. More to the point, he predicts that "The kids of AD 2000 will draw from the music much the same sense of well being and warmth as we do today." Taylor goes on to say: "the magic of the Beatles is, I suspect, timeless and ageless. It has broken all frontiers and barriers. It has cut through differences of race, age and class. It is adored by the world."

Although *Beatles '65* has six songs from *Beatles For Sale*, Capitol's Dave Dexter decided not to use the British album's title, front cover photo or graphics. He did not think the subdued, earthy colors of Freeman's picture were suitable, wanting something more colorful and eye-catching. He also objected to the small print used for the album's title, which could barely be seen next to the Parlophone/EMI box logo. Dexter believed that an album's title should be at the top of cover in large letters so it would be easier to read by customers flipping through albums in record store bins. Dexter emphasized marketing over artistic considerations.

Capitol's art department, then led by George Osaki, designed the cover as per Dexter's guidelines. The text at the top of the front cover proclaims "GREAT NEW HITS BY JOHN • PAUL • GEORGE • RINGO." The album title appears below the text in thick red block letters, with the song titles listed below. The background color ranges from light gray to various shades of green.

The cover features four color pictures from an October 1964 photo session by Robert Whitaker in which the group holds various props. The pictures symbolize the four seasons. The main photo (Winter) shows each member of the group wearing a dark jacket and holding an umbrella for protection against winter showers. Ringo shows a hint of a smile, while the others look bored with the proceedings. The other three pictures appear in square boxes below the umbrella photo.

The left photo (Spring) has John seated in a chair holding a stemmed flower. To drive home the point that the photo represents spring, Paul, George and Ringo are holding large springs. The center photo (Summer) has John sitting in front of a beach table, complete with umbrella and beverage can. John and Ringo are wearing sunglasses and Paul has a pair of shades propped on his head. All four Beatles have removed their jackets. The right photo (Autumn) has the group back in their jackets for the cooler weather. Ringo, John and Paul are holding large brooms while George holds a basket. Small branches and autumn leaves are spread on the ground in front of the boys.

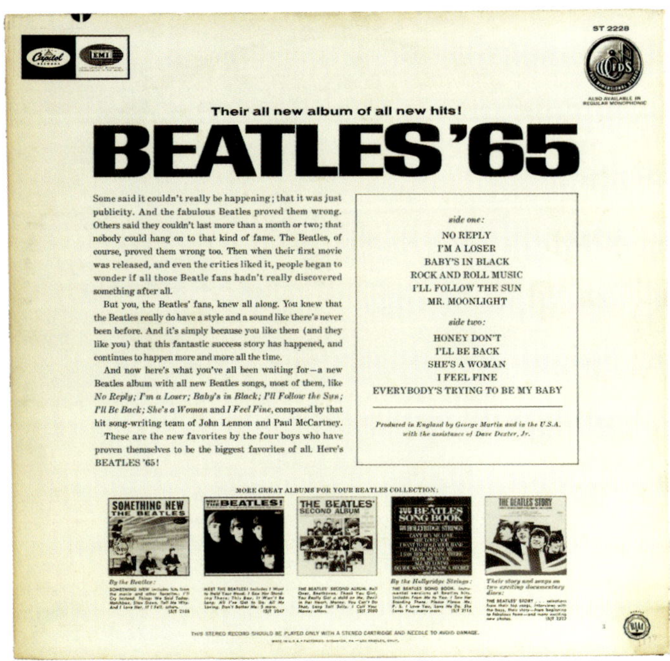

The back cover has the album title in the same font as the front cover. "Their all new album of all new hits!" is centered above the title. The left center area has text discussing how the Beatles have proven their skeptics wrong and congratulating the group's fans for knowing all along that "the Beatles really do have a style and a sound like there's never been before." The notes conclude with: "These are the new favorites by the boys who have proven themselves to be the biggest favorites of all. Here's BEATLES '65!" The right center has a box with the album's track listing along with a dubious production credit: "Produced in England by George Martin and in the U.S.A. by Dave Dexter, Jr."

File Under: The Beatles ST 2228

CAPITOL FULL DIMENSIONAL STEREO

GREAT NEW HITS BY JOHN • PAUL • GEORGE • RINGO

BEATLES '65

Capitol RECORDS

HIGH FIDELITY

I FEEL FINE • SHE'S A WOMAN • NO REPLY • I'M A LOSER • ROCK AND ROLL MUSIC • I'LL FOLLOW THE SUN • HONEY DON'T • I'LL BE BACK • BABY'S IN BLACK • EVERYBODY'S TRYING TO BE MY BABY • MR. MOONLIGHT

The front cover to *Beatles VI* features a color photo of the group wearing non-matching clothes. At that time, this was a departure from the usual matching suits. All four Beatles display toothy smiles. The boys are shown with their hands holding the top of a thin object. Because the picture on the cover is cropped slightly below their waists, the purpose of the photo is not clear. For years it was speculated that the group was holding either the handle to an upside-down umbrella, a microphone cord or a cake knife. The entire photo (shown on page 213) reveals that the boys are holding a long-handle cake knife above a traditional Christmas cake surrounded by red party crackers. The picture was taken by Bill Francis for Fabulous Magazine as part of a series of photos of pop stars celebrating Christmas and New Year's Eve.

Pictures from the Fabulous 1964 holiday photo session ran in the magazine's holiday season issues. These included Barry Markham shots of George with boxes of presents (December 12 cover) and Ringo and Paul holding parts of a separated Christmas party cracker (December 19 cover). Also included were Bill Francis' photos of an alternate shot of the boys around the Christmas cake (December 26 back cover) and the group celebrating New Year's Eve with George pouring champagne into glasses (January 2, 1965 cover). These Fabulous covers are shown on page 213.

The Beatles also appear in a few other places: John trying to push a box into a postal box mail slot (December 12 interior page picture by Barry Markham); an alternate Markham photo of Ringo and Paul with a party cracker, but this time frowning instead of smiling (December 19 back cover); and the group sitting in front of a Christmas tree opening presents (December 26 centerfold poster by Bill Francis).

According to an article in the December 12 issue, the photo session was set up by Beatles promotion man Tony Barrow. Fabulous staffers were sworn to secrecy about the photo shoot, which was dubbed "Operation Earwig." The group was cordial, with Paul telling everyone hello and assisting Barry Markham in setting up his equipment. According to the magazine, the boys declined to drink the champagne because they hated it, leaving more for everyone else. The session, which may have taken place on October 7, 1964, lasted over four hours and may have been followed by the Bob Whitaker session that produced the cover for *Beatles '65*.

Because Capitol was rush releasing its sixth Beatles album, the art department could not wait for new pictures of the group to be taken. Instead, a half-year-old Christmas photo was pressed into service by cropping out the cake and party crackers. The upper portion has a white rectangular box with the album's title in large red block letters. Below the title is the phrase "THE WORLD'S MOST POPULAR FOURSOME! JOHN • PAUL • GEORGE • RINGO" in black, along with the song titles, "RECORDED IN ENGLAND" and the Capitol logo.

The back cover has four black and white pictures, one of each Beatle in the studio: John in dark sun glasses; Paul sitting behind a piano; Ringo playing timpani drums; and George with a guitar. These photos are attributed to Robert Whitaker; however, the October 31, 1964 Record Mirror credits these pictures, most likely taken on September 30, 1964, to John Dove. To the left of the photographs is a box containing information about the album. "BEATLES" appears in the upper portion of the box in black block letters above a huge "VI" in gray. A list of the album's songs, along with the singer(s) for each song, appears in the bottom half of the box. The initial batch of back liners were printed before the album was programmed and state: "(See label for correct playing order)." Below the track list is the credit "Produced by GEORGE MARTIN" and the cover photo credit.

File Under: The Beatles

ST 2358

NEW IMPROVED FULL DIMENSIONAL STEREO

BEATLES VI

THE WORLD'S MOST POPULAR FOURSOME! JOHN • PAUL • GEORGE • RINGO

YOU LIKE ME TOO MUCH • TELL ME WHAT YOU SEE • BAD BOY • DIZZY MISS LIZZIE • EIGHT DAYS A WEEK • YES IT IS
WORDS OF LOVE • KANSAS CITY • I DON'T WANT TO SPOIL THE PARTY • EVERY LITTLE THING • WHAT YOU'RE DOING

RECORDED IN ENGLAND

Capitol RECORDS

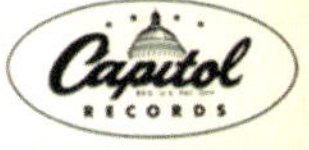

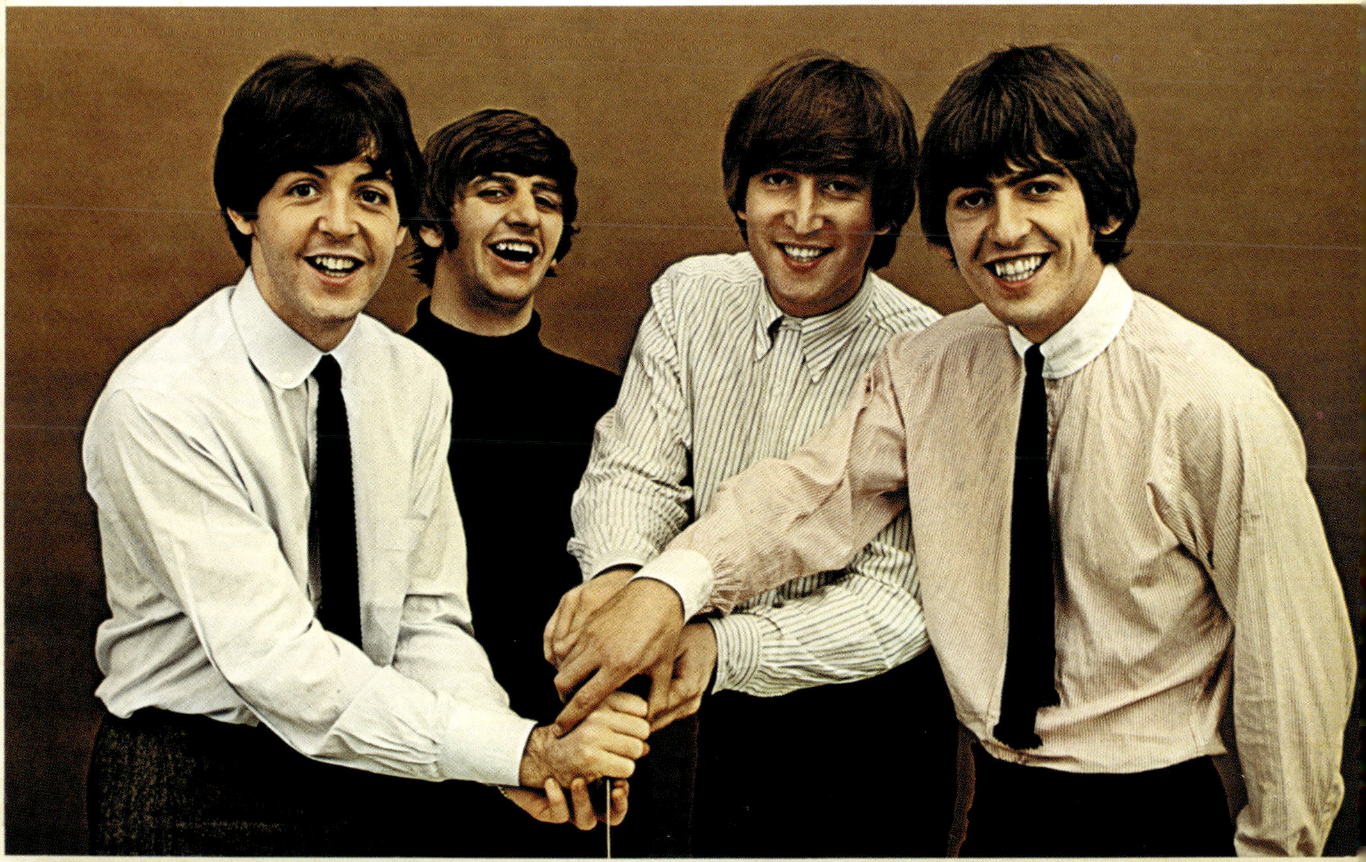

ST 2358

CAPITOL'S *NEW IMPROVED* FULL DIMENSIONAL STEREO SOUNDS BETTER THAN STEREO HAS EVER SOUNDED BEFORE!

...better, in fact, than it has ever been *possible* for stereo records to sound before. Now you can enjoy the results of the latest in our never-ending series of technical developments when you listen to Capitol's *new improved* Full Dimensional Stereo... ☐ new "presence" in the vocal passages ☐ new "impact" in the percussion ☐ new "transparency" in the strings and reeds ☐ new "bite" to the brass ☐ new crisp clarity such as you've thrilled to in a good live performance. Whether your stereo phonograph is modest or the finest that money can buy...you'll get better, more lifelike sound when you listen to Capitol's *new improved* Full Dimensional Stereo—better than stereo has ever sounded before!

MADE IN U.S.A. • FACTORIES: SCRANTON, PA.—LOS ANGELES, CALIF.—JACKSONVILLE, ILL.

THIS STEREO RECORD SHOULD BE PLAYED ONLY WITH A STEREO CARTRIDGE AND NEEDLE TO AVOID DAMAGE.

ALSO AVAILABLE IN REGULAR MONOPHONIC

BEATLES

SIDE ONE	SUNG BY
KANSAS CITY	Paul
EIGHT DAYS A WEEK	John, Paul & George
YOU LIKE ME TOO MUCH	George
BAD BOY	John
I DON'T WANT TO SPOIL THE PARTY	John & Paul
WORDS OF LOVE	John & Paul

SIDE TWO	
WHAT YOU'RE DOING	Paul
YES IT IS	John, Paul & George (solo by John)
DIZZY MISS LIZZIE	John
TELL ME WHAT YOU SEE	John & Paul
EVERY LITTLE THING	John & Paul

Produced by GEORGE MARTIN

Cover photo:
Fabulous Magazine—Fleetway Publications Ltd.

MORE GREAT ALBUMS FOR YOUR BEATLES COLLECTION:

SOMETHING NEW • Hits from their first movie and other favorites: *I'll Cry Instead; Things We Said Today; Matchbox; Slow Down; Tell Me Why; And I Love Her; If I Fell;* and others. (S)T 2108

THE BEATLES' SECOND ALBUM • *Roll Over, Beethoven; Thank You Girl; You Really Got A Hold On Me; Devil In Her Heart; Money; You Can't Do That; Long Tall Sally; I Call Your Name;* others. (S)T 2080

THE BEATLES' STORY • Two exciting documentary discs, presenting selections from their top songs, interviews with the boys, their story—from beginning to fabulous fame—and many exciting new photos. (S)T 2222

MEET THE BEATLES! • Includes *I Saw Her Standing There; I Want To Hold Your Hand; This Boy; All I've Got To Do; It Won't Be Long; All My Loving; Don't Bother Me;* five more hits. (S)T 2047

BEATLES '65 • *No Reply; I'm A Loser; Baby's In Black; She's A Woman; I Feel Fine; Rock And Roll Music; Mr. Moonlight; Everybody's Trying To Be My Baby; Honey Don't; I Feel Fine; I'll Follow The Sun.* (S)T 2228

WORLD'S POP STARS IN COLOUR COLOUR COLOUR
1/-
2nd JANUARY 1965
Fabulous
NEW YEAR'S HONOURS
10 KING SIZE FULL COLOUR PIN-UPS
CILLA PAUL DUSTY STONES PJONES PJSEAN

WORLD'S POP STARS IN COLOUR COLOUR COLOUR
Fabulo
XMAS SHOP
8 KING SIZE FULL COLOU
JOHNL. CLIFFB. POETS MOJOS

WORLD'S POP STARS IN COLOUR COLOUR COLOUR
1/-
19th DECEMBER 1964
Fabulous
PARTY TIME
9 KING SIZE FULL COLOUR PIN-UPS
BRIANJ. N.TEENS LULU GENEP. SUPREMES

For the fourth time in a row, the Beatles turned to Robert Freeman to design and photograph their album cover. As was the case with *A Hard Day's Night*, the jacket for *Help!* would need to tie in to the movie. Freeman got the idea for his shot after observing the Beatles being filmed as they stood in the snow waving their arms against a skyline background. He was in Austria during the filming to shoot publicity stills for the movie.

The white background front cover's color photo was taken at Twickenham Film Studios on a specially constructed platform. The Beatles dressed in the same black hats, coats and capes worn during the ski sequences filmed in the Austrian Alps. Freeman envisioned the group positioning their arms to spell "HELP" in letters from the semaphore alphabet, a visual signaling system that uses hand-held flags to convey letters and numbers by extending the arms in different positions. When the arm placements of the four members of the group spelling "HELP" looked awkward, he scrapped the idea and had them place their arms in a visually attractive manner.

For reasons unknown, the cover has the images of George, John and Ringo flipped, while Paul's image remains as it was shot. As with the *Beatles For Sale* front cover, the rectangular Parlophone/EMI logo is in the upper left corner. The album title is in hollow red letters directly below the logo. The group's name is in solid black letters to the right of the logo. The mono or stereo designation is in the upper right corner. Freeman thought that these graphics were not needed and lessened the impact of the image.

Some people have pointed out that the British cover appears to spell "NUJV." Others claim that if the cover image is reversed, it spells "LPUS" or "elp us." While such speculation is entertaining, it is meaningless. Freeman made it clear they are not spelling anything.

Unlike the first four albums, *Help!* does not contain any liner notes. By the time the album was released in August 1965, the Beatles had decided that no narrative about their music or accomplishments was needed. This trend actually started two months earlier with the June release of *Beatles For Sale (No. 2),* which was the first Beatles EP issued without liner notes.

The back cover features Freeman portraits of each of the Beatles along with the list of songs on each side. To compensate for the lack of liner notes, each song is followed by the names of the songwriters and, of even more interest, the names of the singers and, for some songs, limited information about the instruments played on the track. The usual back album cover information appears in a rectangle at the bottom.

Although Robert Freeman's idea of having a front cover without the usual graphics was not followed, he got his way with his next LP cover, *Rubber Soul*.

THE BEATLES

mono

HELP!

While Robert Freeman pushed EMI for artistic covers with limited graphics, that was not the Capitol way. Dave Dexter wanted something flashy with bold colors that emphasized the group's name and album title. He also liked listing the names of the album's songs on the front cover. George Osaki's design for the *Help!* soundtrack LP checks all the boxes.

The cover features the Beatles standing above a modified HELP! logo with the letters in a different font and the space between each letter and the exclamation point compressed. The colors of the logo are changed from red and gray to orange and yellow. These colors are more attention grabbing and are reminiscent of the orange and yellow Capitol swirl 45 RPM label. Although the Beatles are in a different order than on the British LP cover, they are in the same order as on the promotional posters. While the images of group members are in color on the U.K. album jacket, they are in black and white on the Capitol cover as on the movie posters. The posters have each Beatle standing over a letter, but the Capitol jacket has Paul moved slightly to the left to accommodate the placement of the Capitol logo. This leaves Paul's right foot suspended in open space rather than being grounded by the top of the letter P. The Capitol cover is based on the movie poster rather than the British album cover. The film credits Robert Freeman with "colour consultant & titles," so he may have designed the film's logo. (See page 41 to compare and contrast the modified logo created by Capitol to the original poster design.)

The cover has "Original Motion Picture Soundtrack" in dark blue uppercase letters at the top, with a small "THE" and large "BEATLES" in orange letters in a font similar to that of the Capitol HELP! logo. The bottom text, also in dark blue uppercase letters, lists the titles to the Beatles songs followed by the phrase "And Exclusive Instrumental Music From the Picture's Soundtrack."

The back cover (shown on page 219) features a cropped version of the color photograph of the Beatles used on the picture sleeve for Capitol's "Help!" single (see page 183). This photo was taken in the Bahamas by Robert Freeman during the filming of the movie. Information regarding the film and album appears above the picture in orange, green, brown and black print.

"THE BEATLES in 'HELP!'" appears at the top in the same font and shade of orange as on the front cover. The names of the other stars of the film are in green, while the movie's creative team appears in brown. "Eastmancolor" and "Released Thru United Artists" are also in green. The listing of the album's songs is in orange print. At the time the back cover was designed and printed, the instrumental selections had not been named. Thus, all five of the non-Beatles performances are identified as "(instrumental)" in the track listing. The production credit for the album is in black and reads: "Produced in England by George Martin and in the U.S.A. by Dave Dexter, Jr." Although Dexter did not produce the Beatles, he compiled the soundtrack album and named the instrumental selections (see page 262). As with previous back covers, Capitol plugged its other Beatles albums on the lower portion with the statement "More great albums for your Beatles collection" followed by images of the covers and track listings for each album.

Although United Artists issued its soundtrack LP for *A Hard Day's Night* in a conventional cover, Capitol opted for a gatefold jacket to house its "Original Motion Picture Soundtrack." The interior panels have three color and five black and white still pictures from the film along with text about the movie. Although uncredited, these photographs were most likely taken by Robert Freeman as he was on location in the Bahamas and Austria. The left panel has a large color photo of the Beatles standing in the snow sharing a red and white scarf.

NEW IMPROVED FULL DIMENSIONAL STEREO

ORIGINAL MOTION PICTURE SOUNDTRACK

THE BEATLES

Capitol RECORDS

HELP!

HELP! · THE NIGHT BEFORE · YOU'VE GOT TO HIDE YOUR LOVE AWAY · I NEED YOU
ANOTHER GIRL · TICKET TO RIDE · YOU'RE GONNA LOSE THAT GIRL

And Exclusive Instrumental Music From the Picture's Soundtrack

The left gatefold text starts with an error: Guess where the Beatles are now? Bermuda!! Austria!! And what are they doing there?" The Beatles, of course, were in the Bahamas, not Bermuda. This is followed by a slightly modified list of questions that were part of the United Artists press package (see page 34). After telling readers that Ringo is the cause of it all, Capitol advises: "And now...Hear Ringo, John, George and Paul sing their sensational 'Help!' songs in this very special movie soundtrack souvenir album!"

The text on the right panel opens with: "It's an established fact. Whatever the Beatles do, they do it big." The text then focuses on the film *Help!*, stating that the movie matches expectations for "the fun to be fast, frantic and totally unpredictable" with the group having "staged one of the wildest comedy chases ever." The text incorrectly indicates that the Beatles had shooting sessions in "the chill of February London" before heading to "the sweltering 90-degree heat of Nassau." Although London was no doubt cold, filming began in the Bahamas, where temperatures were warmer than London, but not in the 90s. The text erroneously states that "In the midst of filming, autographing and swimming," John and Paul "wrote the film's sensational musical score featuring seven new numbers." While those songs are sensational, most were written and then recorded in London before the Beatles left for the Bahamas. The text also states that Ringo was the only experienced skier in the group, but John had previously taken ski lessons during a vacation at the St. Moritz ski resort in the Swiss Alps. Walter Shenson was quoted as saying: "'Help!' is essentially a good-time picture. We traveled from calypso to yodel with a lot of scenery and yeah-yeah thrown in besides. The boys sincerely hope that what they've done will be fun for everyone." Capitol concludes: "No need to worry. Wherever they are, that's where the fun is."

"HELP!" *Guess where the Beatles are now? Bermuda!! Austria!! And what are they doing there?*

Why are the high priests of the terrible Goddess of Kaili interested in the Beatles?
Why is Ringo being pursued to the ends of the earth by a gang of Eastern thugs?
What do they want of him—they aren't fans.
Two leading scientists hope to rule the world.
Paul is threatened by a beetle.
An Eastern beauty saves the boys' lives time and time again.
A channel swimmer ends up in an Alpine lake and Buckingham Palace has a busy day.
When Scotland Yard arrives in the sunny Bahamas after unsuccessful maneuvers on Salisbury Plain they find four Ringos but only one George, one Paul and one John.
When the power crazy scientists arrive in the Alps the boys miraculously escape their deadly weapons.
Will John live to sleep in his pit again?
Will Paul ever get back to his electric organ?
Will George be re-united with his ticker-tape machine?
And Ringo—will he ever play the drums again?

(Just in case you haven't seen the movie yet we don't want to spoil the story for you but we will tell you that Ringo is the cause of it all.)

AND NOW... HEAR RINGO, JOHN, GEORGE AND PAUL SING ALL THEIR SENSATIONAL "HELP!" SONGS IN THIS VERY SPECIAL MOVIE SOUNDTRACK SOUVENIR ALBUM!

2386

"HELP!" It's an established fact. Whatever the Beatles do, they do it big. Take their latest film epic, "Help!" With a title like that you'd expect the fun to be fast, frantic and totally unpredictable. It is. What's more, you can be sure that John, Paul, George and Ringo have staged one of the wildest comedy chases ever — from the sunny shores of Nassau to the snowy Alps of Austria and back again.

The plot for the film-making of this full-color saga reads like a success story itself. Men-behind-the-scenes,' producer Walter Shenson and director Richard Lester, are the same team who made the fabulous first Beatles film, "A Hard Day's Night." That film, in the Beatles do-it-big tradition, went on to become as popular with adult audiences as with the younger set and won Academy Award nominations in two categories.

Locations play a vital role in every film and "Help!" is no exception. After shooting sessions in the chill of February London, a chartered jet deposited Beatles, cast, crew, luggage, and their special co-star the 40-ft. tall, ten-armed Goddess of Kaili, in the sweltering 90-degree heat of Nassau. In the midst of filming, autographing and swimming, Beatles John Lennon and Paul McCartney wrote the film's sensational musical score featuring seven new numbers in all. No sooner had the Bahama silver-white sands proved irresistible than the Beatles, cast, crew, luggage and co-star found themselves journeying to Austria's famous skiing paradise, Obertauern. Although Ringo is the only experienced skiier in the group, they all took to the slopes for semi-Olympic style capers. Winding up the shooting schedule were four days on England's Salisbury Plain for a bit of military maneuvering, with the cooperation of the British War Office which supplied troops and tanks for the occasion.

"As you can see, 'Help!' is essentially a good-time picture," comments producer Shenson. "We traveled from calypso to yodel with a lot of scenery and yeah-yeah thrown in besides. The boys sincerely hope that what they've done will be fun for everyone."

No need to worry. Wherever they are, that's where the fun is.

THE BEATLES in "HELP!"

ALSO STARRING LEO McKERN

ELEANOR BRON   VICTOR SPINETTI   ROY KINNEAR

Produced by WALTER SHENSON
Screenplay by MARC BEHM and CHARLES WOOD
Story by MARC BEHM
Directed by RICHARD LESTER
Musical Score by KEN THORNE
EASTMANCOLOR
A WALTER SHENSON-SUBAFILMS PRODUCTION
RELEASED THRU UNITED ARTISTS
(All performance rights are BMI)

side one: HELP! 2:35 • THE NIGHT BEFORE 2:33 • (instrumental) 2:03 • YOU'VE GOT TO HIDE YOUR LOVE AWAY 2:08
I NEED YOU 2:28 • (instrumental) 2:21 • **side two:** ANOTHER GIRL 2:02 • (instrumental) 2:28 • TICKET TO RIDE 3:03
(instrumental) 2:20 • YOU'RE GONNA LOSE THAT GIRL 2:18 • (instrumental) 2:24

Produced in England by George Martin and in the U.S.A. by Dave Dexter, Jr.

The *Beatles For Sale* and *Help!* Sessions

The sessions for the Beatles third single of 1964 and follow-up LP to *A Hard Day's Night* took place over eight days during August, September and October 1964. During the time when the group was not at EMI Studios in St. John's Wood, London (now known as Abbey Road Studios), John, Paul, George and Ringo were touring the United States, Canada, England and Scotland, recording songs for BBC radio, appearing on television and giving interviews.

The first session for the album that would later be named *Beatles For Sale* took place from 7:00 to 11:00 PM on August 11. The group recorded a new Lennon-McCartney song, "Baby's In Black." Three nights later on August 14, the Beatles were back at EMI Studios. From 7:00 to 9:00 PM, they recorded "I'm A Loser" and a cover of Dr. Feelgood and the Interns' "Mr. Moonlight." After an hour break, the group worked on a cover of Little Willie John's "Leave My Kitten Alone" from 10:00 to 11:15 PM.

After returning from their first North American tour, the boys were back at EMI Studios to resume recording tracks for their next album. During the 2:30 to 6:30 PM September 29 session, the group worked on "Every Little Thing" and "I Don't Want To Spoil The Party." After a dinner break, they returned to "I Don't Want To Spoil The Party" and started work on "What You're Doing." The next day, the band completed "Every Little Thing" during their 2:30 to 5:30 PM session and finished, for the time being, "What You're Doing" and recorded "No Reply." On October 6, the group taped "Eight Days A Week" during a 3:00 to 10:00 PM session. Two days later, from 2:30 to 6:00 PM, the Beatles recorded "She's A Woman."

On Sunday, October 18, the Beatles took a break from their British tour to work on the album from 2:30 to 11:30 PM. They recorded edit pieces for "Eight Days A Week," knocked out a cover of the Little Richard version of "Kansas City," did a remake of "Mr. Moonlight," and started and completed "I Feel Fine," "I'll Follow The Sun," Carl Perkins' "Everybody's Trying To Be My Baby," Chuck Berry's "Rock And Roll Music" and Buddy Holly's "Words Of Love."

The album's final session was held on October 26. After attending a three-hour mixing session (a first for the group), the Beatles recorded Carl Perkins' "Honey Don't" from 4:30 to 6:30 PM. During the final 7:30 to 10:00 PM session, the group did a remake of "What You're Doing." They also recorded their second fan club holiday disc, "Another Beatles Christmas Record."

Although *Beatles For Sale* was well received at the time of its release, revisionist rock critics do not hold the album in high esteem, arguing that the Beatles were too worn down from their brutal touring schedule to produce an album up to their usual standard. They point to the number of covers on the disc and claim the boys even look tired on the album's jacket. But such criticism ignores the brilliance of both the original compositions and cover versions on the LP.

The sessions for the Beatles second movie, first single of 1965, and fifth album began on Monday, February 15 at EMI Studios. For most of the songs recorded at this and future sessions, the group would no longer sing and play at the same time over multiple takes. Instead, they would record rehearsals, giving them the ability to fine tune the songs before taping over the rehearsals with proper takes of the basic instrumental track when they were ready to proceed. Once they had a satisfactory backing, they superimposed the vocals and additional instruments. On this, the first of six consecutive days in the studio, the group completed "Ticket To Ride" during a 2:30 to 5:45 PM session and did substantial work on "Another Girl" and "I Need You" in the 7:00 to 10:30 PM block.

The next day, the group completed those songs with superimpositions during a 2:30 to 5:00 PM session. They then recorded "Yes It Is" before calling it a night at 10:00 PM. On Wednesday, February 17, they completed "The Night Before" from 2:00 to 7:00 PM and "You Like Me Too Much" from 7:00 to 11:00 PM. Between mono mixing sessions on February 18, the group recorded "You've Got To Hide Your Love Away" from 3:30 to 5:15 PM. Then, from 6:00 to 10:30 PM, they taped "If You've Got Trouble" and completed "Tell Me What You See." That Friday, the Beatles recorded "You're Going To Lose That Girl" during a 3:30 to 6:20 PM session. Finally, on February 20, once again between mono mixing sessions, the group recorded "That Means A Lot" between 12 noon and 5:15 PM. In addition, Johnnie Scott superimposed his flute solo onto the end of "You've Got To Hide Your Love Away."

The Beatles flew to the Bahamas on February 22, bringing a tape of the mono mixes of the 11 songs recorded during the six-day session to Richard Lester and Walter Shenson for their consideration. Norman Smith supervised the stereo mixes on February 23. On March 30, the group attempted a re-make of "That Means A Lot" during a 7:00 to 10:00 PM session.

On April 13, the Beatles recorded the title song for their second film, *Help!*, during a 7:00 to 11:00 PM session. John, Paul and George would re-record their vocals for the mono version of "Help!" at C.T.S. Studios, London in late May. The mix incorporating those vocals would be used for the film, single and U.K. mono LP.

The Beatles were back at EMI Studios from 8:00 to 11:30 PM on May 10 to record a pair of Larry Williams songs, "Dizzy Miss Lizzy" and "Bad Boy," for Capitol's early summer album, *Beatles VI*.

The songs needed to fill out the non-film side of the group's *Help!* LP were recorded during three sessions held in mid-June. On June 14, Paul McCartney demonstrated his remarkable talents singing lead on three totally different styles of music. During a 2:30 to 5:30 PM session, the Beatles recorded the country-folk flavored tune "I've Just Seen A Face" and the Little Richard influenced rocker "I'm Down." The latter track was hard on Paul's throat, but that did not stop him from singing the beautiful ballad "Yesterday" during the evening session held from 7:00 to 10:00 PM. The following day, the band recorded John's "It's Only Love" during a 2:30 to 5:30 PM session. On the final day of rerecording, June 17, the band completed Ringo's vocal contribution to the album, "Act Naturally," and a not-ready-for-prime-time track, "Wait," which would have to wait for the next album, *Rubber Soul*, for its augmentation and release. The album's final mixing session took place on June 18.

Help! is a remarkable album that showcases what Record Mirror called "The Many Moods Of The Beatles." Their songs range from rock to folk to country & western to a ballad with a string quartet to pure rock 'n' roll. They expanded their sound by using new instruments such as John's Framus Hootenanny 12-string acoustic guitar, a Hohner Pianet electric piano, and a Vox Continental organ. Superimpositions allowed the group to add effective percussion. George used a volume pedal to alter tones. Paul played guitar on five of the album's songs (plus one that didn't make it). The Beatles spent more time fine-tuning their recordings. *Help!* is the product of a maturing band learning how to make new sounds in the studio.

No Reply

Recorded: September 30, 1964 (early taping on June 3, 1964)
Mixed: October 16 (mono); November 4 (stereo)

Producer: George Martin
Engineers: Norman Smith; Ken Scott & Mike Stone

John: Lead vocals; acoustic rhythm guitar (Jumbo); handclaps
Paul: Backing vocal; bass guitar (Hofner); handclaps
George: Guitar (Gretsch Country Gentleman); handclaps
Ringo: Drums (Ludwig kit); handclaps
George Martin: Piano (Steinway)

John began writing "No Reply" in May 1964 during a vacation in Tahiti with Cynthia, George, and Pattie Boyd. He recorded a demo of the song, which did not yet have a bridge, with the intent of giving it to Tommy Quickly. The demo, which was recorded in a bathroom, ends with a flushing toilet, perhaps indicating what John initially thought of song. The storyline was taken from "Silhouettes," a number three U.S. hit in late 1957 by the Rays, a black doo-wop group from Harlem, New York. The song was issued in the U.K. on London HL-U.8505 in November 1957 but did not chart.

John recalled: "I had that image of walking down the street and seeing her silhouetted in the window and not answering the phone, although I never called a girl on the phone in my life! Because phones weren't part of the English child's life." Paul also remembers the song being John's idea: "I think he pretty much had that one, but as usual, if he didn't have the third verse and the middle eight, then he'd play it to me pretty much formed, then we would shove a bit in the middle or I'd throw in an idea." According to John, music publisher Dick James told him: "You're getting better now–that was a complete story," meaning that the song resolves itself.

The Beatles first recorded the song on June 3, 1964, the last day of the sessions for *A Hard Day's Night*. As Ringo had taken ill that morning, he did not attend. The identity of the drummer remains a mystery. John sang lead and played guitar. Paul provided a backing vocal and most likely played bass. But if Paul filled in on drums, then George would have been on bass. Although announced as "Take 1," this version of "No Reply" was more like a run-through than a proper attempt to record the song. John and Paul laugh along with their accidental and later intentional vocal gaffes. The tape of this fun version of the song was unearthed in 1993 and is on *Anthology 1*.

The Beatles returned to "No Reply" towards the end of the September 30 evening session. The song was recorded "live" with John singing lead and strumming his Gibson J-160E acoustic-electric "Jumbo" guitar, Paul on his Hofner bass guitar, George strumming his Gretsch Country Gentleman electric guitar (with a reggae-sounding rhythm during the verses), Ringo on drums, and piano by George Martin, who accents the "I saw the light" and "I nearly died" lines, plays on the bridge, and ends the song with an ear-catching C 6/9 chord. John double-tracked his vocal, with Paul adding high harmonies. Ringo overdubbed bass drum and crash cymbal. Handclaps were added to the bridge. The song took eight takes to complete. Take 5 repeated the bridge and ran a minute longer than the master. John's coarse-sounding vocal was treated with echo during the mono (October 16) and stereo (November 4) mixing sessions.

Paul indicated in the November 14, 1964 Disc that the group "tried to give it different sounds, starting off quietly with sort of a vaguely bossa nova tempo, building up to a straight beat crescendo in the middle, and then tailing off quietly again." Take 2, which has more of a bluesy feeling than the finished master, is on *Anthology 1*. Although the take has vocal miscues, at its end, John says: "Well, we just found out what to do anyway—it's good!" Apparently George Martin agreed as "No Reply" was judged strong enough to be the opening track for *Beatles For Sale*.

I'm A Loser

Recorded: August 14, 1964
Mixed: October 26 (mono); November 4 (stereo)

Producer: George Martin
Engineers: Norman Smith; Ron Pender

John: Lead vocals; acoustic rhythm guitar (Jumbo); harmonica
Paul: Backing vocals; bass guitar (Hofner)
George: Rhythm and lead guitar (Gretsch Tennessean)
Ringo: Drums (Ludwig kit); tambourine

"I'm A Loser" is another Lennon-McCartney original written primarily by John. He probably began work on the song in July 1964 after the Beatles returned to England from their world tour. John's admission about being a loser in love was quite bold for a rock 'n' roller, although such themes were common in country music. While musically and lyrically the tune appears to be a country-western knock-off, a more careful listening of the song reveals more depth. Particularly telling is the line "And I'm not what I appear to be."

John may have already worked personal experiences into his lyrics in songs such as "Tell Me Why," but this was not apparent to most listeners at the time. Prior to interviewing John about his book *In His Own Write* for the BBC on March 23, 1964, British journalist Kenneth Allsop was openly critical to John about his songwriting, suggesting that he move away from the abstract imagery of his love songs and write lyrics that were autobiographical based on personal experience. By that time, John and the Beatles had become Dylan enthusiasts after listening to the album *The Freewheelin' Bob Dylan* while in Paris in January 1964.

John later indicated: "'I'm A Loser' is me in my Dylan period, because the word 'clown' is in it. I objected to the word 'clown,' because that was always artsy-fartsy, but Dylan had used it so I thought it was all right, and it rhymed with whatever I was doing. I started thinking about my own emotions–instead of projecting myself into a situation I would just try to express what I felt. Part of me suspects I'm a loser and part of me thinks I'm god almighty."

Paul observed: "We used to listen to a lot of country and western songs and they were all about sadness and 'I lost my truck,' so it was quite acceptable to sing 'I'm a loser.' You really didn't think about it at the time, it was only later that you'd think, god, that was pretty brave of John. I reckon the best way to describe this one is a folk song gone pop. 'I'm A Loser' was pretty much John's song and there may have been a dabble or two from me."

"I'm A Loser" was recorded on August 14 with John on lead vocals and his Gibson J-160E acoustic-electric "Jumbo" guitar, Paul on backing vocals and providing a walking bass part on his Hofner, George on his Gretsch Chet Atkins Tennessean and Ringo on drums. Take 1 was a false start, while Take 2 was complete. At this stage, the song started with a brief instrumental opening and John singing "I'm a loser" before the first verse. Paul sings with John on all lines of the chorus, and he and John sing "I'm a loser" multiple times in falsetto voices over the song's ending. On this take only, John sings "behind this mask" instead of "beneath this mask." By Take 3, the group worked out the song's opening featuring John and Paul twice singing "I'm a loser" over John slowly picking and strumming chords. Paul continues to sing on all lines of the chorus. The instrumental break leaves a place for John's harmonica solo, followed by George working on his guitar solo (which would be overdubbed).

John has his harmonica ready for Take 4, but it breaks down when John messes up the lyrics. After a false start on Take 5, Take 6 is complete. For this performance only, John sings "I should have known I would lose in the end" rather than "...she would win in the end." John now sings solo on the last line of each verse and plays his harmonica during the first part of the instrumental break and at the end of the song. After another false start, Take 8 becomes the best performance, with John and George forgoing their live instrumental solos. Then John and Paul double-tracked their vocals, John added his harmonica solo and end bit, George added his solo and guitar fills, and Ringo played tambourine on the chorus. The song was mixed for mono on October 26 and for stereo on November 4. George Martin had high regard for the song, which was considered a potential single and initially chosen to be the LP's opening track.

Prior to the album's release, the Beatles performed "I'm A Loser" live before lucky members of the Beatles Fan Club at Granville Studio in London on October 3 for broadcast four days later on the American TV show Shindig! (see pages 66-67).

The song also made its British debut before the album was issued. The group lip-synced the song on November 14 for broadcast the next week on Thank Your Lucky Stars. A November 17 BBC recording of "I'm A Loser" aired on Top Gear on November 26, and is on the 1994 album *Live At The BBC*. The song was also recorded for the group's final session for the BBC, broadcast on June 7, 1965.

"I'm A Loser" was part of the band's concerts from December 1964 through mid-1965. The *Anthology* video contains the group's June 20, 1965 performance of "I'm A Loser" in Paris, France.

Gibson

Baby's In Black

Recorded: August 11, 1964
Mixed: October 26 (mono); November 4 (stereo)

Producer: George Martin
Engineers: Norman Smith; Ron Pender

John: Lead harmony vocal; rhythm acoustic guitar (Jumbo)
Paul: Lead harmony vocal; bass guitar (Hofner)
George: Lead guitar (Gretsch Tennessean)
Ringo: Drums (Ludwig kit); tambourine

"Baby's In Black" was the first song recorded for the Beatles fourth album and one of the last songs that was a full collaboration between John and Paul, written, as John would say, while they were sitting "nose to nose." It was started from scratch and finished by the duo in July 1964 at John's Kenwood home. The lyrics were a departure from the Beatles usual fare. Paul explained that after writing songs like "From Me To You" and "Thank You Girl" to "please the girls and make money," he and John "wanted to write something a little bit darker, bluesy, the title's dark anyway...more grown up rather than just straight pop." Paul told Disc: "The story is about a girl who's wearing black because the bloke she loves has gone away forever. The feller singing the song fancies her, too, but he's getting nowhere. We wrote it originally in a waltz style, but it finished as a mixture of waltz and beat."

They got the waltz idea from James Ray's "If You Gotta Make A Fool Of Somebody," a number 22 hit in America that was issued in the U.K. on Pye International 7N.25126 in February 1962. Although the British disc did not chart, George had a copy, and the Beatles soon added the tune, described by Paul as a "wacky...R&B waltz" and a "cool three-four blues thing," to their set list. Paul indicated that "Baby's In Black" was "one of the first waltzes we wrote, which was interesting for us because most of our stuff's in 4/4." Although Paul has said the song is in 3/4 time, it is actually in 6/8 time.

"Baby's In Black" was recorded on August 11 (see page 2) with John and Paul "nose to nose" at a single microphone singing Everly Brothers influenced harmony backed by John on his Jumbo acoustic-electric guitar, George on his Gretsch Tennessean, Paul on his Hofner bass and Ringo on drums. John's intricate rhythm guitar part keeps the song moving forward despite its slow tempo, while George adds a complimentary rhythm when he is not playing lead guitar riffs. The song opens with George's attention-grabbing riff during which he hits his guitar's Bigsby vibrato bar towards the end.

The group took 14 takes to achieve a satisfactory performance. Five takes failed to get beyond George's unsuccessful attempt to get the opening riff right. Only five of the 14 were complete. After Take 14, John asked: "Can we hear that rubbish back?" The song has a change of pace where the strumming is replaced by straight power chording during the last verse before resuming during the following chorus. John and Paul double-tracked their vocals on the bridge and last chorus. Other overdubs included additional guitar strumming by John, George's double-tracked lead guitar and Ringo's tambourine. During Harrison's overdubs, John sat on a chair in front of him and turned the guitar's volume knob to vary the sound (see picture below). 13 edits pieces of the song's opening were recorded, but none were used. The song was mixed for mono on October 26 and for stereo on November 4.

While neither a rocker nor a classic ballad, the tune appealed to the group and was part of their stage show from December 1964 through 1966, including the band's final concert. According to Paul, "We used to put ["Baby's In Black"] in there, and think, 'Well, they won't know what to make of this, but it's cool.'" Although not on the 1977 album *The Beatles At The Hollywood Bowl*, the band's August 30, 1965 performance of "Baby's In Black" is on the "Real Love" maxi-single issued concurrently with *Anthology 2* in 1996 and as a bonus track on the 2016 reissue of the *Hollywood Bowl* album. The group performs the song in the film *The Beatles At Shea Stadium*.

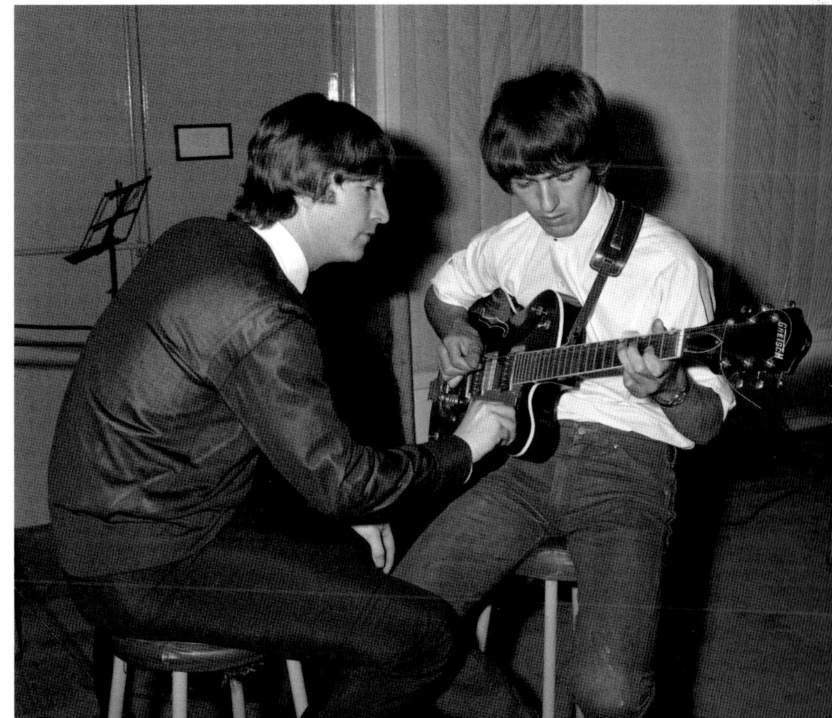

Rock And Roll Music

Recorded: October 18, 1964
Mixed: October 26 (mono); November 4 (stereo)

Producer: George Martin
Engineers: Norman Smith; Geoff Emerick

John: Lead vocal; rhythm guitar (Rickenbacker Capri); piano
Paul: Bass guitar (Hofner); piano
George: Lead guitar (Gretsch Tennessean)
Ringo: Drums (Ludwig kit)
George Martin: Piano (joined by John and Paul)

After three somber Lennon-McCartney originals, the LP shifts gears with an upbeat cover of "Rock And Roll Music," written and originally recorded by Chuck Berry. The song received considerable airplay in the U.S. upon its 1957 release. It remained in the Billboard Hot 100 for 19 weeks, peaking at number eight. It also appeared on Billboard's Rhythm & Blues charts for nine weeks, peaking at number six. The song peaked at 14 in Cash Box and 11 in Music Vendor. It was issued in the U.K. on London 45-HLU 8868 but did not chart.

Recorded by the Beatles on October 18, 1964, "Rock And Roll Music" is another incredible one-take rocker with John on lead vocal and his Rickenbacker Capri electric guitar, George on his Gretsch Tennessean guitar, Paul on his Hofner bass and Ringo on drums, embellished with an exciting piano overdub featuring George Martin, John and Paul playing on a single Steinway piano. In the November 14, 1964 Disc, McCartney described it as the three of them "on the keyboard all at once!," meaning that this had to be superimposed over Take 1. He added that the group "tried for that old-type clipped down-in-the-valley echo on it." The echo on John's vocal was achieved by STEED (single tape echo and echo delay), a technique developed by Abbey Road engineers that adds both a delayed signal and tape loop to create an echo effect. The song was mixed for mono on October 26 and stereo on November 4.

The Beatles EMI recording of the song made its debut prior to the release of the album, being one of four songs the group lip-synced on November 14, 1964, for the November 21 broadcast of Thank Your Lucky Stars. The band's sole BBC recording of the song took place on November 25, 1964, at the Playhouse Theatre in London. It was broadcast a month later on the December 26 Saturday Club and is on *Live At The BBC*.

"Rock And Roll Music," which had been part of the group's stage show in their formative years, was inserted into the lineup for the 1964 Christmas concerts and remained part of the live act for the 1965 European tour. The song was not performed in America during 1965, but was added back into the set list as the opening selection for the 1966 world and North American tours.

The Beatles were filmed performing the song at their Munich concert on June 24, 1966, and at two of their 1966 concerts in Japan. The group's June 30 evening performance appears on the Japanese laserdisc *The Beatles Concert At Budokan 1966*. The *Anthology* video contains the July 1 afternoon performance, which, like the show from the day before, was video taped in color by Nippon Television.

I'll Follow The Sun

Recorded: October 18, 1964
Mixed: October 21 (mono); November 4 (stereo)

Producer: George Martin
Engineers: Norman Smith; Geoff Emerick

Paul: Lead vocals; bass guitar (Hofner)
John: Backing harmony vocal; acoustic rhythm guitar (Jumbo)
George: Lead guitar (Gretsch Tennessean)
Ringo: Tapping the beat on his knees

Paul recalls writing "I'll Follow The Sun" at age 16 in the front living room of his family home on Forthlin Road, Liverpool in 1958. The tune originally had a swing arrangement, as evidenced by a tape from April 1960 of the Quarrymen performing the song at Paul's house. Being short on new material for the LP, the Beatles recorded "I'll Follow The Sun" on October 18, 1964. As for the delay in recording the song, Paul explained: "We had this R&B image in Liverpool, a rock and roll, R&B, hardish image with the leather. So I think that songs like 'I'll Follow The Sun,' ballads like that, got pushed back." McCartney told Disc that he and John "changed the middle eight bars before [the group] actually recorded it."

The song was completed in eight takes. It features Paul on lead vocals and bass, John adding a harmony vocal on the bridge (scored by George Martin) and playing an intricate rhythm part on his Jumbo acoustic, George providing effective lead guitar on his Gretsch Tennessean, and Ringo tapping the beat on his knees (after his drumming on early takes sounded out of place on the up-tempo ballad). Paul double-tracked his vocal in a few places and George overdubbed a short simple solo. The Beatles November 17 BBC recording of the song aired on the November 26 Top Gear and is on *On Air-Live At The BBC Volume 2* (and the *Baby It's You* EP).

Mr. Moonlight

Recorded: August 14 & October 18, 1964
Mixed: October 27 (mono); November 4 (stereo)

Producer: George Martin
Engineers: Norman Smith; Ron Pender (Aug); Geoff Emerick (Oct)

John: Lead vocals; rhythm guitar (Rickenbacker Capri)
Paul: Harmony vocals; bass (Hofner); organ (Hammond RT3 organ)
George: Harmony vocals; Gretsch Tennessean; African drum
Ringo: Conga drum

"Mister Moonlight" (credited on the LP jacket and label of *Beatles For Sale* as "Mr. Moonlight") was originally recorded by Dr. Feelgood and the Interns and released in the U.S. as the B-side to "Doctor Feel-Good" on OKeh 4-7144 in early 1962. Dr. Feelgood was Willie Perryman, who had previously recorded as Piano Red. Although the original issue of the American single gave songwriter's credit to "R. Stevens-R.C. Stephens," "Mister Moonlight" was written by the band's guitarist, Roy Lee Johnson, Jr., who also sang the tune. The record's A-side, "Doctor Feel-Good," reached number 66 on the Billboard Hot 100. The disc was issued in the U.K. on Columbia 45-DB4838 in May 1962 but did not chart.

The Beatles first attempted to record "Mr. Moonlight" on August 14, with John on lead vocal and his Rickenbacker Capri, Paul on backing vocal and his Hofner bass, George on backing vocal and his Gretsch Tennessean, and Ringo on conga drum. Take 1 ended quickly, with John muffing the song's shouted introduction. The best performance was Take 4, which starts with John nailing his opening vocal and has George's guitar solo given a tremelo effect through his Vox amplifier. *Anthology 1* contains the first and fourth takes.

The Beatles did a re-make of "Mr. Moonlight" on October 18, recording four more takes with the same instruments. Takes 5 and 7 were false starts, and Take 8 was considered the best. John and Paul then double-tracked their vocals, and Paul superimposed the song's solo on a Hammond RT3 organ. The song's unique percussion sound was achieved by Ringo on a horn-shaped conga drum and George overdubbing his accent strikes on an old African drum. The percussion gives the song a Latin flavor.

On October 27, John's "Mister Moonlight" vocal introduction from Take 4 was mixed for mono (RM-1) as was Take 8 (RM-2). The mono master is an edit of John's opening vocal from RM-1 and the rest of the song from RM-2. The stereo master was created the same way on November 4.

Kansas City

Recorded: October 18, 1964
Mixed: October 26 (mono and stereo)

Producer: George Martin
Engineers: Norman Smith; Geoff Emerick

Paul: Lead vocal; bass guitar (Hofner); piano; handclaps
John: Backing vocal; rhythm guitar (Rickenbacker Capri); handclaps
George: Backing vocal; lead guitar (Gretsch Tennessean); handclaps
Ringo: Drums (Ludwig kit); backing vocal; handclaps
George Martin: Piano

Side One closes with a dynamic performance of Little Richard's arrangement of "Kansas City," which had been in the Beatles stage act since at least 1961. Although the song comes across as a simple rocker, its recording and publishing history is quite complex.

"Kansas City" was written in 1952 by Jerry Leiber and Mike Stoller, who at the time were both only 19 years old. The pair had met in Los Angeles and soon became friends due to their shared love of rhythm and blues music. Their first hit was "Hard Times" by Charles Brown, which was a top ten R&B single in early 1952. They specifically wrote "Kansas City" for R&B singer Little Willie Littlefield, who recorded the song on August 12, 1952. When issued that year on Federal 12110 (78 RPM) and 12351 (45 RPM), the song was titled on the label as "K.C. Loving" because Federal's Ralph Bass thought it sounded "hipper." Although the record did not chart, the song would later become a huge hit. As for Leiber and Stoller, they would soon write "Hound Dog" for Big Mama Thornton, whose recording of the song topped the R&B charts for seven weeks in 1953. They would later write songs for Elvis Presley, as well as the Coasters, an R&B vocal group that the duo also produced. The Beatles added several Coasters songs to their repertoire including "Searchin'," "Youngblood," "Three Cool Cats,"Yakety Yak" and "Besame Mucho."

Little Richard recorded two completely different versions of "Kansas City" in 1955, with the second one recorded on November 29, 1955, at Radio Recorders in Los Angeles, California. For this session, he was backed by Guitar Slim's band, the vocal group the Chimes and probably female vocalist Barbara Salisbury. His spirited R&B recording, with its added call and response section towards the end, remained unreleased until 1959, when it first appeared on the album *The Fabulous Little Richard*, issued in the U.S. on Specialty SP 2104 and in the U.K. on London HA-U 2193.

American R&B singer Wilbert Harrison had been performing "Kansas City" as part of his stage show for several years before recording the song in 1959 at a New York session for Fury Records. His version had an infectious shuffle groove and great guitar work by Wild Jimmy Spruill. Shortly after its release on Fury 1023, other versions quickly hit the market in late March 1959, including singles by Hank Ballard and the Midnighters, Rocky Olson, Rockin' Ronald & the Rebels, and the reissue of Little Willie Littlefield's original recording. Specialty rushed out Little Richard's second recording of the song in April on Specialty 664. In America, Harrison's single crushed the competition, topping the Billboard Hot 100 for two weeks and the magazine's Hot R&B Sides chart for seven weeks.

In England, the Little Richard single was issued on London HLU 8868. It entered the charts on June 6, 1959, peaking at number 26 during its five-week run. The Wilbert Harrison disc was released on Top Rank 45-JAR 132 in May 1959 but did not chart.

The Beatles recorded "Kansas City" in two takes on October 18, 1964, with Paul's powerful lead vocal on Track 3, his Hofner bass, John's Rickenbacker Capri and Ringo's drums on Track 1, and George's Gretsch Tennessean guitar on Track 2. Overdubs onto Track 4 included John, George and Ringo contributing the "bye, bye" and "so long" vocal refrains during the later part of the song, handclaps by all towards the end of the song, and piano by George Martin and Paul. [Engineer Geoff Emerick recalls Ringo adding backing vocals, and Paul told Disc that he did some "piano playing on the song."] Take 1, which was selected for the master, has an exciting guitar solo improvised by George. Take 2, later issued on *Anthology 1*, is also an excellent performance, though George's guitar solo is clearly superior on the first take. Take 2 has a proper ending, while the Take 1 master fades out at the end. As Take 2 has superimposed backing vocals and handclaps, the decision to make Take 1 the master was made after hearing the playback of Take 2 with the additions.

A decade or so after the release of the Beatles recording, Little Richard's last name, Penniman, was added to the songwriter's credit because the call and response vocals in Little Richard's arrangement of the song bore a strong resemblance to his song "Hey-Hey-Hey-Hey." That song, which was recorded on May 9, 1956, at J&M Studio in New Orleans, Louisiana, nearly a half-year after he recorded "Kansas City," has similarities with "Kansas City" in its "Goin' Back To Birmingham" lyrics. The song "Hey-Hey-Hey-Hey" was later released as the B-side to the hit "Good Golly Miss Molly" on Specialty 624 in early 1958. [And that's the simplified story!]

Prior to recording "Kansas City" for *Beatles For Sale*, the band performed the song three times for the BBC. The July 16, 1963 recording broadcast on the August 6 Pop Go The Beatles is on *Live At The BBC*. The group's fourth BBC recording on November 25 for the December 26 Saturday Club is on *On Air-Live At The BBC Volume 2*..

"Kansas City" was a staple in the group's stage act from the early days. Volume 1 of the *Anthology* video has a brief portion of the song taped on September 5, 1962, at the Cavern Club. The tune is on *Live At The Star Club*. The Beatles performed the song before a live audience at Granville Studio, London, on October 3, 1964, for broadcast in the United States on Shindig! A portion of this spirited performance appears on Volume 4 of the *Anthology* video. During the *Get Back/Let It Be* project, the group sang a few verses of the song as part of a rock 'n' roll warm-up medley that included Little Richard's "Miss Ann" and Lloyd Price's "Lawdy Miss Clawdy." This performance was recorded by the cameras on January 26, 1969.

Eight Days A Week

Recorded: October 6 & 18, 1964
Mixed: October 27 (mono and stereo)

Producer: George Martin
Engineers: Norman Smith; Ken Scott & Mike Stone (October 6); Geoff Emerick (October 18)

John: Lead vocals; acoustic rhythm guitar (Jumbo); handclaps
Paul: Lead/harmony vocals; bass guitar (Hofner); handclaps
George: Lead guitar (Gretsch & Rickenbacker 12-string); handclaps
Ringo: Drums (Ludwig kit); handclaps

Side Two of *Beatles For Sale* opens with another song once given consideration for release as a single, "Eight Days A Week." Paul told Disc in 1964: "I got the title for this one when I was being driven over to visit John. The chauffeur was talking away to me, saying how hard his boss worked the staff, so hard that they seemed to do eight days a week. We've altered the plot a bit for the song, of course. The bloke loves the girl for eight days a week." In Barry Miles' *Many Years From Now*, Paul further explained: "Neither of us had heard that expression before so we had that chauffeur to credit for that. It was like a little blessing from the gods. I didn't have any idea for it other than the title, and we just knocked it off together, just filling in from the title. So that one came quickly."

In his book *Ticket To Ride*, disc jockey/radio journalist Larry Kane recalls hearing the group working on the song on a flight during the 1964 tour. "As three of The Beatles worked on guitar, Ringo tapped his knees and all four sang as they tested the tune for a song that would later become 'Eight Days A Week.' On the plane, they were just humming the song and jamming with each other." If Kane's recollection is correct, the song would have been written at John's house shortly before the Beatles left for America on August 18.

Although "Eight Days A Week" would become a number one hit in America, John's negative view of the song dates back to 1965 (see page 52). In 1980, he told journalist David Sheff: "'Eight Days A Week' was never a good song. We struggled to record it and struggled to make it into a song. It was [Paul's] initial effort, but I think we both worked on it. I'm not sure. But it was lousy anyway." He further said: "'Eight Days A Week' was the running title for *Help!* before they came up with *Help!* It was Paul's effort at getting a single for the movie." This, of course, is not correct as the film's working title was *Eight Arms To Hold You* and the song in question was recorded several months before the Beatles began work on their second film.

"Eight Days A Week" was recorded on October 6 during a seven-hour session. Mark Lewisohn's *The Beatles Recording Sessions* describes the song as a landmark recording as it marks the first time the group brought an unfinished idea to the studio and experimented with different approaches. The basic track has John and Paul singing over a backing track of John's driving rhythm on his Gibson Jumbo acoustic-electric guitar, Paul's melodic bass on his trusty Hofner, George on his Gretsch Tennessean, and Ringo on drums.

Anthology 1 contains an edit of Takes 1, 2 and 4 that give the flavor of how the song's intro was initially conceived—John and Paul singing a sequence of harmonized "Ooohs" over hand claps and acoustic guitar, with Paul's walking bass and Ringo's drums falling into place. This edit is followed on *Anthology 1* by the complete Take 5, which also begins with "Ooohs" and acoustic guitar before Paul, Ringo and George add their instruments to the tune. The vocals on this run-through vary considerably from the vocals on the master take, with different emphasis, phrasing and harmonies on the "hold me" and "love me" lines and on the word "week" on which John and Paul break into two syllables going falsetto on the second. The song finishes with harmonized "Ooohs" similar to those that start the recording. While Take 5 is charming, the revamped version that was ultimately released is clearly superior. The group would perform six more takes, including two false starts, before obtaining a suitable track with Take 13. John and Paul then double-tracked their vocals and all added handclaps to Take 13. George also overdubbed his introduction bit on his Rickenbacker 360-12 electric 12-string.

Although the track was finished, the group wasn't completely satisfied. At the start of the October 18 session, they listened carefully to the playback. According to Geoff Emerick, "we all excitedly agreed that the high-energy performance captured on tape was a definite 'keeper,'" but that the beginning was ragged and the end too abrupt. Edit pieces were recorded for the intro (Take 14), which was not used, and the ending featuring George's 12-string Rickenbacker (Take 15). During the mono and stereo mixing sessions held on October 27, Norman Smith mixed Take 13, executing his idea of starting the song with a fade-in (RM 2 & RS 1), and the Take 15 ending (RM 3 & RS 2). These mixes were then edited for the masters.

The song has all the ingredients of a hit single: a hum-along melody over a steady and swinging beat, clever lyrics, top-notch vocals and hooks galore. The track is also memorable for Paul's walking bass line, stop and go pacing and tight harmonies on the bridge, hand claps and superb drumming throughout by Ringo.

Words Of Love

Recorded: October 18, 1964
Mixed: October 26 (mono); November 4 (stereo)

Producer: George Martin
Engineers: Norman Smith; Geoff Emerick

John: Harmony vocals; rhythm (Rickenbacker Capri); handclaps
Paul: Harmony vocals; bass guitar (Hofner); handclaps
George: Harmony vocals; lead guitar (Tennessean); handclaps
Ringo: Drums (Ludwig kit); packing case

"Words Of Love" had been part of the Beatles repertoire prior to the group taking on its name in 1960. It was written by Buddy Holly, who recorded the song with his backing band, the Crickets, at Norman Petty's Clovis, New Mexico studio on April 8, 1957. It was released in America on June 20, 1957, as a "Buddy Holly" single on Coral 61852. Unfortunately for Holly, radio stations in the U.S. jumped on a cover version of his song by the Diamonds on Mercury 71128. As the Diamonds previous single, "Little Darling," spent eight weeks at the number two spot on the Billboard charts, disc jockeys pushed the homogenized version of the song by the Diamonds over the recording by the boy from Lubbock, Texas. While Holly's single failed to chart, the Diamonds were blessed with a number 13 ranking on the Billboard Most Played By Jockeys chart. The Buddy Holly single was issued in the U.K. on Coral 72449 in 1957 but did not chart.

"Words Of Love" was the last song recorded by the Beatles during a long and productive session held on Sunday, October 18. It was one of five cover tunes performed that day as the group was on a mission to complete the needed tracks for their 1964 Christmas season LP. As the group idolized Holly, it is no surprise that they gave his composition loving treatment. The Beatles recorded three takes of the song, with the third being the best. It consists of John, Paul and George singing harmony vocals (into one microphone as recalled by Geoff Emerick), backed by John on his Rickenbacker Capri, George playing lead on his Gretsch Tennessean, Paul on his Hofner bass, and Ringo softly on drums. John, Paul and George double-tracked their vocals, and George expertly double-tracked his guitar ("sounding almost like bells" according to Paul), and Ringo tapped a packing case. The group also superimposed handclaps. The song was mixed for mono on October 26 and for stereo on November 4.

Prior to recording the LP, the Beatles taped "Words Of Love" for the BBC on July 16, 1963, for broadcast on the August 20 Pop Go The Beatles. This performance is on *On Air-Live At The BBC Volume 2*.

Honey Don't

Recorded: October 26, 1964
Mixed: October 27 (mono and stereo)

Producer: George Martin
Engineers: Norman Smith; Tony Clark & Anthony Bridge

Ringo: Lead vocal; drums (Ludwig kit)
George: Lead guitar (Gretsch Tennessean)
John: Rhythm acoustic guitar (Jumbo)
Paul: Bass guitar (Hofner)

"Honey Don't" had been part of the Beatles stage act since at least 1962. The song, written and recorded by American singer/guitarist Carl Perkins, was issued as the flip side to Perkins' most famous composition, "Blue Suede Shoes," on Sun 234 in January 1956. While "Honey Don't" didn't chart, Billboard reported "Blue Suede Shoes" at number four in The Top 100, at two in its Juke Boxes chart, and at one in its Country & Western Juke Boxes chart. The same single was issued in the U.K. on London 45-HL-U 8271 and charted at ten. "Honey Don't" is on *Dance Album Of Carl Perkins*, issued in the U.S. in 1957 on Sun LP-1225 and in the U.K. in 1959 on London HA-S 2202, as are "Everybody's Trying To Be My Baby" and "Matchbox."

Following the format of the Beatles first two albums, Ringo was to have a lead vocal spot. Initially, John and Paul planned on giving the drummer their newly-written country & western song, "I Don't Want To Spoil The Party," but ended up singing it themselves. On the final day of the sessions, October 26, Ringo had his vocal spotlight on "Honey Don't." Prior to then, the song's lead vocal was handled by John. The song was recorded in five takes, with Take 5 being the best. Ringo delivers his usual charming vocal, backed by his steady drums, George perfectly copying Perkins' lead guitar work on his Tennessean, John on his Jumbo acoustic, and Paul on his Hofner bass. Ringo overdubbed tambourine. Just before George's first solo, Ringo shouts out: "Ah, rock on, George, one time for me." Afterwards, he ad-libs "I Feel Fine," perhaps a nod to the new single. Before the second solo, he shouts: "Ah, rock on, George, for Ringo one time." The song was mixed for mono and stereo on October 27.

The group recorded the song four times for the BBC. The first, with John on lead vocal, was taped on August 1, 1963, for broadcast on the September 3 Pop Go The Beatles. It is on *Live At The BBC*. The third BBC performance, with Ringo on lead and timed to promote the new LP, was taped on November 17, 1964, for broadcast on the November 26 Top Gear. It is on *On Air-Live At The BBC Volume 2*.

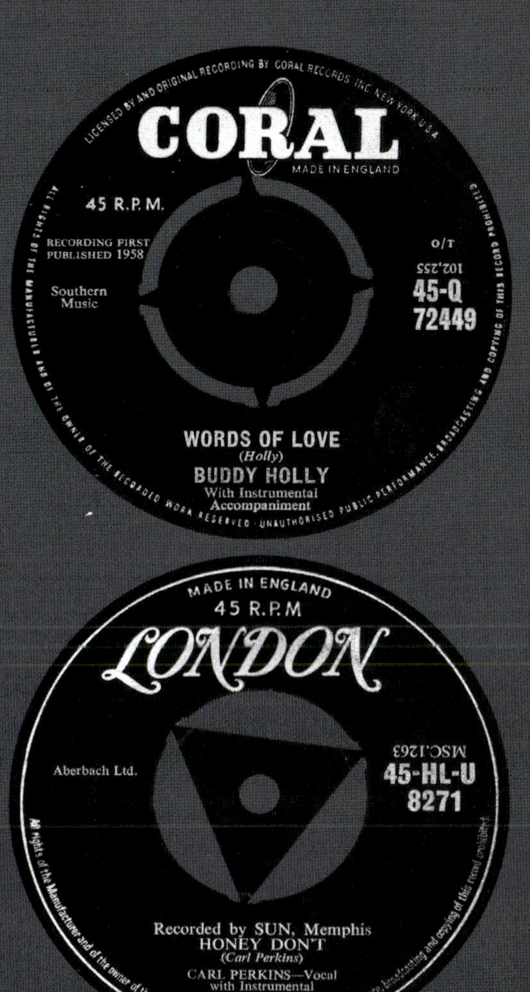
CORAL
MADE IN ENGLAND
45 R.P.M.
RECORDING FIRST PUBLISHED 1958
Southern Music
O/T
102,255
45-Q
72449
WORDS OF LOVE
(Holly)
BUDDY HOLLY
With Instrumental Accompaniment
MADE IN ENGLAND
45 R.P.M
LONDON
Aberbach Ltd.
MSC.1263
45-HL-U
8271
Recorded by SUN, Memphis
HONEY DON'T
(Carl Perkins)
CARL PERKINS—Vocal
with Instrumental Accompaniment

Dance Album of
CARL PERKINS
LONDON
HA-S 2202

Every Little Thing

Recorded: September 29 & 30, 1964
Mixed: October 27 (mono and stereo)

Producer: George Martin
Engineers: Norman Smith; Ken Scott; Mike Stone

John: Lead vocal; lead guitar (Rickenbacker 325-12 electric guitar)
Paul: Harmony vocal on chorus; bass guitar (Hofner); piano
George: Rhythm guitar (Jumbo)
Ringo: Drums (Ludwig kit); timpani drums

Every little thing about "Every Little Thing" seems to be a contradiction. In the November 14, 1964 Disc, Paul says he and John wrote the song in Atlantic City during the group's first North American tour (see page 15), but Barry Miles' 1997 biography on Paul, *Many Years From Now*, says the song was written alone by Paul in the Asher's home. Paul further recalled hoping that the song would be the next Beatles single, but it became an album track because "It didn't have quite what was required." However, comments from 1964 imply that Paul's "What You're Doing" was the one in the running for the follow-up to "A Hard Day's Night" (see next page). As Paul's contemporaneous comments are more reliable than recollections of events from three decades in the past, the song was most likely written in Atlantic City and not in the running for being the next single.

The recording of the song provides additional contradictions. Although "Every Little Thing" was written primarily by Paul, John sings lead. And while photos from the day of the session show George on his 12-string Rickenbacker, Paul told Disc in 1964 that John plays the guitar riff and George is on acoustic guitar.

The Beatles recorded four takes of "Every Little Thing" on September 29, 1964, before moving on to other original compositions. The following day, they returned to the song, completing it with Take 9. Taking Paul's comments into consideration, the song features John on lead vocals, with Paul singing harmony on the chorus and during the fade out ending. George plays his Gibson Jumbo acoustic-electric guitar, Paul is on his Hofner bass, and Ringo on drums. John overdubbed his custom-made Rickenbacker 325-12 electric 12-string for the song's opening and closing riffs, solo, and fills during the chorus. This guitar, which was ordered from Rickenbacker representatives during the Beatles February 1964 U.S. visit, is the same shape and size of his Rickenbacker 325 Capri. It has a shorter neck and thus a more limited scale than George's Rickenbacker 360-12 electric 12-string. It also has a different tone.

Paul superimposed four sustained low piano notes on every third line of each verse and at the end of the solo. Ringo added accenting timpani drum beats during the chorus (described by Paul as "the big noise you'll hear.") Paul also overdubbed four ascending bass notes in two places during the instrumental break–first at the start of the break preceding the first line of John's 12-string guitar solo, and again between the first and remaining lines of the solo. He also added some thumping bass notes over the song's ending.

"Every Little Thing" was mixed for both mono and stereo on October 27. The mono mix fades during the third "Every little thing" vocal line, while on the stereo mix it is complete. If you listen closely to the left channel at the start of the song, you can hear Ringo hitting his bass drum four times to fill in the measure where John would add his opening guitar riff during overdubs. In earlier takes, John most likely sang and played guitar before determining that it was too hard to do both at the same time. Although "Every Little Thing" was not worthy of being issued as a single, it is an excellent track that demonstrates how the Beatles were being sure that every little thing about each of their recordings was given careful attention.

I Don't Want To Spoil The Party

Recorded: September 29, 1964
Mixed: October 26 (mono); November 4 (stereo)

Producer: George Martin
Engineers: Norman Smith; Ken Scott; Mike Stone

John: Lead vocals; acoustic rhythm guitar (Jumbo)
Paul: Harmony backing vocal; bass guitar (Hofner)
George: Limited backing vocal; lead guitar (Gretsch Tennessean)
Ringo: Drums (Ludwig kit); tambourine

"I Don't Want To Spoil The Party" was written primarily by John, who called it one of his favorites, adding: "That was a very personal one of mine." In the November 14, 1964 Disc, Paul stated: "We went after a real country and western flavour when we wrote this one. John and I do the singing in that style and George takes a real country solo on guitar." The song was written during the 1964 North American tour with Ringo in mind. In Miles' *Many Years From Now*, Paul said: "Ringo had a great style and great delivery. He had a lot of fans, so we liked to write something for him on each album. 'I Don't Want To Spoil The Party' is a quite nice little song co-written by John and I. It sounds more like John than me so 80-20 to him, sitting down doing a job. Certain songs were inspirational and certain songs were work, it didn't mean they were any less fun to write, it was just a craft, and this was a job to order really, which Ringo did a good job on." [Apparently, Paul's recollection of writing the song with Ringo in mind was so strong that Paul forgot that John's personal attachment to the song caused John to sing the song himself instead of handing it off to Ringo.]

"I Don't Want To Spoil The Party" was recorded in 19 takes (only five were complete) on September 29, with the band playing and singing live. The track has John singing lead and strumming his Gibson Jumbo acoustic-electric, Paul singing harmony on the bridge and playing his Hofner bass, George playing lead guitar on his Gretsch Tennessean, and Ringo on drums. Overdubs included vocals by John, Paul and George, and tambourine played by Ringo during the bridge.

The song opens with a guitar introduction by George and John before Paul and Ringo come in leading to the first verse. During the verses, John sings the high harmony part live and overdubs a low harmony on the first, second and fourth lines. John, Paul and George add backing harmony "ooh"s behind John's solo voice on the third line. During the bridge, John sings the low harmony part joined by Paul handling the high harmony. George's excellent guitar playing is reminiscent of that of Carl Perkins and Chet Atkins. His solo fits perfectly into the song's country and western style. Ringo's drumming completes the effect. He is on his hi-hat and mounted tom for most of the song, but effectively shifts to his floor tom for the "I still love her" second and fourth lines of the bridge.

The song was mixed for mono on October 26 and for stereo on November 4.

What You're Doing

Recorded: September 29 & 30, 1964; October 26, 1964
Mixed: October 27 (mono and stereo)

Producer: George Martin
Engineers: Norman Smith; Ken Scott; Mike Stone

Paul: Lead vocals; bass guitar (Hofner); piano
John: Backing vocals; acoustic rhythm guitar (Jumbo)
George: Backing vocals; lead guitar (Rickenbacker 12-string)
Ringo: Drums (Ludwig kit)

"What You're Doing" is another Lennon-McCartney song that Paul traces to Atlantic City in his November 14, 1964 Disc interview. "It's not that Atlantic City is particularly inspiring, it's just that we happened to have a day off the tour there." In the October 24 Disc, Paul said that the song, described but not named, might be issued as the Beatles next single. After stating that the band had already recorded five or six tracks, he thought they would select a song with a "big and really distinctive intro." He explained: "We wanted to do a number which had a start as distinctive as the chord at the beginning of 'A Hard Day's Night' and we decided to do a fast drum roll with a guitar phrase over it. When we did it in the studio, we kept doing the roll wrong and we'll probably re-record this one before the disc comes out." Although Paul later recalled in 1997 that he had hopes that "Every Little Thing" would have been a single (see previous page), he most likely confused the two songs as "What You're Doing" opens with a memorable drum pattern and George's 12-string guitar riff, and was later re-recorded during the sessions.

The first attempt at the song took place on September 29, with the group recording seven takes of instrumental backings. This may have been where Ringo had difficulty with the drum roll. The next day, four more takes were recorded, with Take 11 being the best. At this stage, the song was a ragged countrified rocker with the jangle sound of two Rickenbacker 12-string electric guitars. George played the lead on his 360-12, while John strummed his 325-12. Paul and John sang harmony vocals throughout the verses. The problematic drum roll was dropped, perhaps with the intention to later record it as an edit piece if the song was not re-recorded.

The group completely remade the song on October 26, the final day of the sessions. After seven takes, perfection was achieved. The song opens with Ringo borrowing from the classic drum introduction (played by Hal Blaine) to the Ronettes' "Be My Baby," which was produced by Phil Spector and was a favorite of the band. The rest of the group then joins in with George playing the lead guitar riff on his Rickenbacker 12-string, John strumming his Gibson Jumbo acoustic guitar and Paul on his Hofner bass. The song's instrumental break is an overdubbed duet featuring Paul's rollicking piano and George on his Rickenbacker 12-string. The piano is also heard during the song's coda following a reprise of Ringo's "Be My Baby"-style drum part augmented by Paul's exuberant bass notes. "What You're Doing" is sung primarily by Paul (double-tracked), with John adding his voice to emphasize the first word of the first two lines of each verse. John and George provide "ooh" background vocals during the later lines of the verses. On the first word of the second line of the third verse, John accidentally sings "I" while Paul sings "You." Take 19 was mixed for mono and stereo on October 27.

Everybody's Trying To Be My Baby

Recorded: October 18, 1964
Mixed: October 21 (mono); November 4 (stereo)

Producer: George Martin
Engineers: Norman Smith; Geoff Emerick

George: Lead vocals; lead guitar (Gretsch Tennessean)
John: Acoustic rhythm guitar (Jumbo)
Paul: Bass guitar (Hofner)
Ringo: Drums (Ludwig kit); tambourine

The album closes with an exciting performance of "Everybody's Trying To Be My Baby." The tune came to the group's attention by its inclusion on *Dance Album Of Carl Perkins* (see pages 230-231). (An earlier take has a straight boogie beat and two different verses.) Although credited to Carl Perkins, the chorus and two of Perkins' three verses are essentially the same as the chorus and two of the six verses in Rex Griffin's song "Everybody's Tryin' To Be My Baby" recorded in 1936 at the Roosevelt Hotel in New Orleans as a vocal and guitar song in the style of Jimmie Rodgers and issued on Decca 5294. Perkins apparently was familiar with the recording of the song by Jimmy Short and the Silver Saddle Ranch Boys released on 4 Star 1538 in 1951.

The Beatles, with George on lead vocal, recorded the song in one take on October 18. The instrumental backing features George on his Gretsch Tennessean, John on his Gibson Jumbo acoustic, Paul on his Hofner bass and Ringo on drums. George then double-tracked his vocal, which was treated with a heavy dose of STEED (single tape echo and echo delay), and Ringo overdubbed tambourine.

The Beatles *Live At The Star Club* album includes the group's late December 1962 performance of the song in Hamburg, Germany. The group performed the song four times for the BBC, with the first two taking place prior to the EMI session. *Live At The BBC* includes the November 17, 1964 recording which aired first on the November 26 Top Gear and then on the day after Christmas on Saturday Club.

After the release of *Beatles For Sale*, "Everybody's Trying To Be My Baby" returned to the group's stage show before being dropped after the 1965 American tour. The group's June 20 Paris performance is on the *Anthology* video. Although performed at the 1965 Shea Stadium and Hollywood Bowl concerts, the song was not included in *The Beatles At Shea Stadium* film or on the 1977 *The Beatles At The Hollywood Bowl* LP. It was added as a bonus track on the 2016 remixed and remastered version of the LP titled *Live At The Hollywood Bowl*. The audio of the Shea performance is on *Anthology 2*.

Banding, Mixing & Mastering

The original running order for *Beatles For Sale* varied from the final product. According to a hand-written sheet by George Martin, his initial order for Side One was: (1) I'm A Loser; (2) Every Little Thing; (3) Baby's In Black; (4) Rock And Roll Music; (5) What You're Doing; (6) I'll Follow The Sun; and (7) Kansas City. After considering "Mr. Moonlight" for the Side Two opener, Martin changed his mind, crossed out the title and wrote down the following titles in this order: (1) No Reply; (2) Eight Days A Week; (3) Mr. Moonlight; (4) Everybody's Trying To Be My Baby; and (5) Words Of Love. His notes further show he was thinking of moving "Honey Don't" to the third slot. Before coming up for a spot for "I Don't Want To Spoil The Party," he apparently got the idea to open the album with "No Reply." Martin started over with a fresh sheet of paper and came up with the running order used on the album.

George Martin prepared different mono mixes of the songs on the single recorded during the *Beatles For Sale* sessions for England and America. The British disc uses RM 3 (Remix Mono 3) for "I Feel Fine" and RM 1 for "She's A Woman." Martin provided Capitol with RM 4 for "I Feel Fine" and RM 2 for "She's A Woman." He added more reverb to the U.S. mixes, perhaps hoping that Capitol would use these mixes without adding reverb as the company had often done with previous Beatles recordings. Capitol, however, added its own reverb, giving these songs an echo-drenched effect.

Beatles '65 was mastered at the Capitol Tower in Los Angeles by Maurice Long. He first mastered the stereo version of the album on November 9, 1964. The eight songs from *Beatles For Sale* have the same stereo mixes found on the U.K. disc. "I'll Be Back," which first appeared on the British *A Hard Day's Night* LP, has the same stereo mix as on that album. Although George Martin made preliminary stereo mixes for "I Feel Fine" and "She's A Woman," he apparently did not send them to Capitol because the songs were only intended for single release in the U.K.. Capitol created duophonic (fake stereo) mixes for these songs with disastrous results due in part to reverb added by Capitol.

Long mastered the mono LP the following day. The songs from *Beatles For Sale* have the same mono mixes found on the U.K. disc. For "I'll Be Back," Capitol used RM 3, which was prepared by Martin for the American market. (The British *A Hard Day's Night* LP has RM 2.) "I Feel Fine" and "She's A Woman" have the same mono mixes found on the Capitol single, RM 4 and RM 2, respectively.

I Feel Fine

Recorded: October 18, 1964
Mixed: October 21 (mono); November 4 (stereo)

Producer: George Martin
Engineers: Norman Smith; Geoff Emerick

John: Lead vocal; acoustic guitar (Jumbo)
Paul: Backing vocal; bass guitar (Hofner)
George: Backing vocal; lead guitar (Gretsch Tennessean)
Ringo: Drums (Ludwig kit)

Although there are contradicting accounts as to when "I Feel Fine" was written, there is no uncertainty as to the song's inspiration. The tune was influenced by "Watch Your Step" by Bobby Parker, an American blues singer/guitarist born in Lafayette, Louisiana. The 1961 single was released in the U.S. on V-Tone 223, reaching number 51 in the Billboard Hot 100. The record, a favorite of John's, was first issued in the U.K. on London 45-HLU 9393 but did not chart. By coincidence, it was reissued in Britain in 1964 shortly before the release of "I Feel Fine" (see pages 4-5). George described the guitar part he and John play in "I Feel Fine" as a bastardized version of the lead riff from "Watch Your Step."

John came up with the riff shortly before or during the October 6 session for "Eight Days A Week." He can be heard playing the riff between takes. John indicated that he wrote the song "around that riff going on in the background." According to Derek Taylor, John and Paul wrote the bridge in the studio the day the song was recorded.

As for the song's distinctive feedback opening, it was at first created by accident. During a break, John leaned his Gibson Jumbo acoustic-electric guitar against his Vox amplifier without turning down the volume knob on the guitar. At that moment, Paul hit a low "A" note on his bass, sending out sound waves that caused a howling feedback sound. They were so fascinated with the effect that they asked George Martin if it could be recorded. Geoff Emerick recalls being told this happened at the session for "Eight Days A Week."

When "I Feel Fine" was recorded on October 18, the unique accidental sound was recreated by Paul hitting an open bass string and John intentionally causing feedback distortion with his Jumbo guitar and amplifier. This is followed by a catchy guitar riff played by John on his Jumbo and George on his Gretsch Tennessean, soon joined by Ringo's exciting drumming and Paul's bass. John plays three variations of the same riff. George plays in tandem with John in most places, often with the exact same riff, but not always. Ringo's playing takes on a Latin flavor, influenced by Milt Turner's drumming on Ray Charles' "What'd I Say" (and parts of Parker's "Watch Your Step.")

Take 1, played in the key of A, proved difficult for John to sing and broke down shortly after the instrumental section. As the riff is a variation off of a bar chord, it was easy to drop the key to G for all remaining takes. Take 2 ended at about the same place as Take 1. After two false starts, Take 5 was complete. Then, between takes, George worked out his solo. Take 6, with a longer feedback opening and extended ending, is complete, but this time John does not sing, allowing him to concentrate on his guitar part. After two more false starts, Take 9 is the keeper. Afterwards, John double-tracked his vocal, Paul and George overdubbed their backing vocals, and George added his solo. This marked the first time since "Love Me Do" where a Beatles lead vocal was not recorded live with the instruments. The song was mixed for mono on October 21 (RM 3 for the U.K. and RM 4 for the U.S.) and for stereo on November 4 (RS 1). The stereo mix is preceded by whispers. Apparently, it was not sent to Capitol.

The Beatles recorded "I Feel Fine" and its flip side "She's A Woman" for the BBC on November 17 for broadcast on the November 26 Top Gear. These performances are on *Live At The BBC*. The BBC session tape for "I Feel Fine" is on *On Air-Live At The BBC Volume 2*. Both songs were fixtures in the Beatles concert program for 1965 and 1966. The group's performances of the songs at the New Musical Express 1964-65 Annual Poll-Winners' All-Star Concert on April 11, 1965, was video-taped for broadcast. The group can be seen performing the songs in *The Beatles At Shea Stadium* and on the Japanese laserdisc *The Beatles Concert At Budokan 1966*. The audio to the Budokan performance of "She's A Woman" is on *Anthology 2*. Although Capitol included "She's A Woman" on *The Beatles At The Hollywood Bowl* album, "I Feel Fine" did not make the cut.

She's A Woman

Recorded: October 8, 1964
Mixed: October 12 (mono & stereo); October 21 (mono for U.S.)

Producer: George Martin
Engineers: Norman Smith; Ken Scott; Mike Stone

Paul: Lead vocals; bass guitar (Hofner); piano
John: Rhythm guitar (Rickenbacker 325 Capri)
George: Lead guitar (overdub on Gretsch Tennessean)
Ringo: Drums (Ludwig kit); chocalho

"She's A Woman" was written primarily by Paul on the same day as the October 8 session during which it was recorded. John, who helped finish the song, claims they added the words "turn me on" as an expression about marijuana. The rocker features a blues shouter vocal from Paul with simple, but effective, instrumental backing with Paul on his Hofner bass, John on his Rickenbacker 325 Capri playing chords on the up-beat, and Ringo on drums. The finished master, Take 6, contains George's superimposed guitar solo on his Gretsch Tennessean, piano by Paul and Ringo's percussion on a metal shaker chocalho. Take 7 showcases the band cutting loose in the studio. It extends well beyond the length of a standard early sixties pop tune with Paul's bluesy gravel voice whooping it up for three extra minutes. Upon completion of the take, Ringo observes "We got a song and an instrumental there." The song was mixed for mono and stereo on October 12, with a mono mix made for the U.S. on October 21. Although George only played the solo on the studio version of the song, in concert he mimicked Paul's piano part on guitar.

Leave My Kitten Alone

Recorded: August 14, 1964
Mixed: 1995 in stereo for *Anthology 1*

Producer: George Martin
Engineers: Norman Smith; Ron Pender

John: Lead vocals; rhythm guitar (Rickenbacker Capri)
Paul: Bass guitar (Hofner); piano (Steinway grand)
George: Lead guitar (Gretsch Tennessean)
Ringo: Drums (Ludwig kit); tambourine

"Leave My Kitten Alone" is a high-spirited rocker originally recorded by American R&B singer Little Willie John, who co-wrote the song with Titus Turner and James McDougal. It was issued on King 5219 in the summer of 1959. The song charted for nine weeks in the Billboard Hot 100, peaking at number 60, and for nine weeks in the Billboard Hot R&B Sides chart, peaking at 13. When Johnny Preston released a cover version of the song in 1961, King reissued the single. Preston's version only got to 73, while Little Willie John once again reached 60. It was released in the U.K. on Parlophone 45-R 4571 in July 1959 but did not chart. Little Willie John is best known for recording the first released version of "Fever," which topped the Billboard Most Played R&B By Jockeys chart for five weeks and peaked at 24 in the Billboard Hot 100 in 1956.

The Beatles recorded five takes of "Leave My Kitten Alone" on August 14. The track has John on lead vocal and rhythm guitar on his Rickenbacker 325 Capri, Paul on his Hofner bass, George on his Tennessean and Ringo on drums. The following overdubs were added onto Take 5: John's double-tracked vocal; George's guitar solo; Paul on piano; and Ringo on tambourine. The Beatles arrangement drops the "meow" backing vocals heard on the original recording.

The song was recorded at the same session as the first version of "Mr. Moonlight." But while "Mr. Moonlight" was later recorded as a remake on October 18 and subsequently mixed for inclusion on *Beatles For Sale*, "Leave My Kitten Alone" was left alone and not considered for the album. The song was scheduled to appear on the canceled *Sessions* album in 1984 and would have been the lead single from the LP (picture sleeve shown above). It was finally released on *Anthology 1* on November 21, 1995.

Help!

Recorded: April 13, 1965
Mixed: June 18 (mono and stereo)(April 18 mixes not used)

Producer: George Martin
Engineers: Norman Smith; Ken Scott

John: Lead vocals; acoustic 12-string guitar (Framus Hootenanny)
Paul: Backing vocals; bass guitar (Hofner)
George: Backing vocals; guitar (Tennessean & lead on Stratocaster)
Ringo: Drums (Ludwig kit); tambourine

"Help!" is the opening and title track to the Beatles fifth Parlophone album. As the title song to the Beatles second film, the song is heard twice in the movie. Shortly after the film opens, the Beatles are seen performing the song for what looks like a black and white television appearance. As darts begin flying onto the screen, the camera pulls back to reveal the religious cult leader Clang and his clan, who are watching the performance as it is being projected onto a home movie screen. Clang is shown throwing darts at the band while some of his female followers swoon. During much of the performance, the Beatles are shown full screen. When the song ends, Clang describes the performance as "shocking." His assistant, Bhuta, adds: "Monstrous." Clang's symbolic throwing of darts at the Beatles cleverly pokes fun at the group's detractors. The title song also appears at the end of the film during the beach fight scene. The band's lip-synced performance of the title song was filmed on April 22, 1965, at Twickenham Film Studios in South West London.

"Help!" was written by John, with an assist from Paul, to serve as the title song to the group's second film, initially known as *Beatles Production 2*. Director Richard Lester wanted the motion picture to be named *Beatles 2*, but this was opposed by the Beatles, who not only thought it was unimaginative, but also were concerned about the problem of coming up with a title song. According to Beatles press agent Tony Barrow, Lennon asked, "How can we write a song called 'Beatles 2'?" For a while the film was named *Eight Arms To Hold You*, which had been suggested by Ringo (even though the giant idol shown in the film had ten arms). This new title appeared on film production documents, in the press and on the label to Capitol's "Ticket To Ride" single. Realizing that it would be difficult for John and Paul to write a song titled "Eight Arms To Hold You," Lester came up with *Help, Help*, but was told that the title was already registered with the Writer's Guild of America. A lawyer advised Lester that naming the film *Help!* (with an explanation point) would solve the problem, so *Help!* it was. A relieved Lennon told Barrow he was glad they ditched Ringo's title because it would have been a difficult song to write. "Help!" was most likely written at John's house on April 11, with John adapting another song he had been working on.

Once again, John and Paul were asked to write a made to order song incorporating the title of a movie. Once again, time was of the essence. Once again, John (with a little help from Paul) delivered. Once again, the Beatles took an evening off from their film schedule to enter the studio and record a perfect title song/hit single. In his 1980 interview for Playboy, Lennon recalled: "I just wrote the song because I was commissioned to write it for the movie. But later, I knew I was really crying out for help. It was my fat Elvis period."

"Help!" was recorded during a three-hour evening session on April 13. The instrumental backing features John on his Framus Hootenanny 12-string acoustic guitar and George on his Gretsch Tennessean on one of the four tracks, and Paul on his Hofner bass and Ringo on drums on another. The first two takes broke down early, and the third take stopped after the second verse. After discussion, George agreed not to play the trickier guitar parts during the initial instrumental backing, but would leave them to an overdub. John said he would keep time in the gap by tapping his guitar (which can be heard in the mix). Although Take 4 was announced, there was none. Take 5 was the first complete performance. The next three takes were incomplete, with Takes 6 and 8 breaking down early. Take 9 produced an acceptable instrumental backing over which doubled-tracked vocals and a tambourine part were superimposed over the two remaining tracks. The two vocal tracks were mixed down to a single track and transferred with the two instrumental tracks to another four track tape leaving one empty track. This took three attempts, with Take 12 proving satisfactory. One of John's double-tracked vocals on the song's introduction was mixed out as his timing was off (as heard on Take 11). George superimposed his Stratocaster guitar to the intro and added the descending low guitar notes on the first part and intricate cascading riff at the end of the choruses. Although mono and stereo mixes were made on April 18, neither was used.

The mono mix appearing on the single and on the mono Parlophone LP has different vocals than the stereo mix, which was generated from Take 12. During the first verse of the stereo version John sings "but now these days are gone," while on the mono version he sings "and now these days are gone." John's phrasing of "changed my mind" differs between the two. In addition, tambourine is heard on the stereo version, but not on the mono one.

THE
BEATLES

Although documentation is incomplete, it appears that the vocals heard on the mono single and album were recorded during the fourth week of May 1965, at C.T.S. Studios in London, a facility often used for post-sync sound production work for film and television. EMI documents show that a twin-track tape, apparently with vocals on one track and the other track having instruments (minus the tambourine which had been recorded on a vocal track), was made on April 18 and delivered to the film company. The instrumental track may have been transferred to one track on C.T.S. Studio's three-track recorder, with a fresh set of vocals double-tracked over the other two tracks. The reason why the vocals were re-recorded is not known with certainty, but perhaps it was done to improve the syncing between the film of the Beatles performing the song and the soundtrack. This would have been necessary had the Beatles done a poor job of lip-syncing along with the original recording of the song. A mono mix was probably made at C.T.S. for use in the film.

When the song was mixed for mono at Abbey Road on June 18, it was decided that the vocals during the song's introduction on the re-recorded vocal version were not satisfactory. The single and Parlophone mono album version of "Help!" is an edit of the first 11 seconds of Take 12 with the remaining portion of the song being the re-recorded vocal version. The stereo mix found on the Parlophone and Capitol stereo albums was made on April 18. As the Capitol mono album was mastered entirely with stereo fold-down mixes, the mono mix on the Capitol album differs from the single.

George told Disc that the song was "a bit more involved than others we've done because it has a counter-melody [sung by Paul and George] as well as the main melody [sung by John]."

The title sequence (without the darts being thrown at the screen) was used as a promotional clip for the "Help!" single. This performance film was broadcast in the U.K. on July 17, 1965, a week ahead of the disc's July 23 release, as part of the 200th anniversary edition of the ABC TV show Thank Your Lucky Stars (titled Lucky Stars Anniversary Show). It also aired twice on the BBC's Top Of The Pops, first on July 29, and then three weeks later on August 19.

The Beatles performed "Help!" twice on TV, first on the August 1, 1965 British show Blackpool Night Out. This is on *Anthology 2* and the *Anthology* video. The group also taped the song on August 14 for the September 12 Ed Sullivan Show. "Help!" was a played during the Beatles 1965 North American Tour. The band is shown performing the song in *The Beatles At Shea Stadium*. The Capitol LP *Live At The Hollywood Bowl* contains the group's August 29, 1965 performance.

The Night Before

Recorded: February 17, 1965
Mixed: February 18 (mono); February 23 (stereo)

Producer: George Martin
Engineers: Norman Smith; Ken Scott

Paul: Lead vocals; bass guitar (Hofner); lead guitar (Casino)
John: Backing vocals; electric piano (Hohner Pianet C)
George: Backing vocals; guitar (Tennessean); solo (Stratocaster)
Ringo: Drums (Ludwig kit); maracas

In *Help!*, the Beatles are shown recording "The Night Before" outdoors on Salisbury Plain surrounded by tanks, military vehicles and soldiers protecting the group from Clang and his henchmen. The song starts without its instrumental introduction and runs for about 1:25 before cutting midway through the solo for 18 seconds of Clang planting T.N.T. and lighting a fuse as "She's A Woman" plays on a tape recorder hidden by Ahme. This is followed by a 54-second edit of "The Night Before" that ends in an explosion.

Paul most likely wrote "The Night Before" at the Asher home on 57 Wimpole Street in London in early 1965. It was recorded during the initial sessions for the film and LP in two takes on February 17. The backing instrumental track consists of John on a Hohner Pianet C electric piano, George on his Gretsch Tennessean, Paul on his Hofner bass and Ringo on drums.

The song's backing vocals were superimposed onto Take 2. Paul's lead vocal is double-tracked. Each of the first two lines of the verses sung by Paul are followed by John and George singing "Aah, the night before." They also provide four extended "Aah"s behind Paul's vocal during the third and fourth lines of the verses. Paul sings solo on the bridge, where the backing track has Ringo effectively tapping the bell of his cymbal and pounding his floor tom.

Other overdubs include Ringo playing maracas, and Paul and George adding guitar during the instrumental break and at the end of the song. According to John, "George and Paul are playing the same break exactly, both playing but in different octaves." Paul does the lower part on his Epiphone Casino, while George handles the higher octave on his Fender Stratocaster. McCartney thought the dual guitar break was one of the best instrumental sounds that the band had gotten on record.

The Beatles performed "The Night Before" on their last BBC radio show, The Beatles Invite You To Take A Ticket To Ride, which was recorded on May 26 and aired on June 7 prior to the LP's release.

ODEON
THE
MEO 105
YESTERDAY / THE NIGHT BEFORE / ACT NATURALLY / IT'S ONLY LOVE
BEATLES
MEO 105 · THE BEATLES
Ludwig
THE BEATLES
Photo X...

You've Got To Hide Your Love Away

Recorded: February 18, 1965 (flute added February 20)
Mixed: February 20 (mono); February 23 (stereo)

Producer: George Martin
Engineers: Norman Smith; Ken Scott

John: Lead vocal; acoustic 12-string guitar (Framus Hootenanny)
Paul: Bass guitar (Hofner)
George: Nylon-string acoustic guitar; 12-string acoustic guitar
Ringo: Snare drum (Ludwig) with brushes; tambourine

Outside musician: Johnnie Scott (tenor flute & alto flute)

"You've Got To Hide Your Love Away" makes its appearance in the film during a scene in the boys' communal apartment as they entertain the beautiful Ahme. During the tune, Paul and George compete for the girl with eye-contact while Ringo taps a tambourine.

John wrote the song at his Kenwood home, saying that he wrote it specifically for the film and freely admitted his lyrics were Bob Dylan-influenced. The song's phrasing borrows from Dylan's "I Don't Believe You (She Acts Like We Never Have Met)" from his 1964 album *Another Side Of Bob Dylan*.

The song was recorded in less than two hours on February 18. Although there were nine takes, only Takes 5 and 9 (the master) are complete. The ballad features John as solo vocalist. The initial backing track has John on his Framus Hootenanny 5/024 acoustic 12-string guitar, George on his José Ramirez nylon-stringed acoustic guitar, Paul on his Hofner bass and Ringo playing his snare drum with brushes, all on Track 1. Overdubs include John re-recording his lead vocal (Track 2), and George adding 12-string acoustic guitar on the chorus (matching notes with John's vocal and strumming the next four measures), Paul on maracas during the chorus and at the end, and Ringo on tambourine (Track 3). Two days later, Johnnie Scott added a flute solo to the song's end. Scott's solo was separately recorded on tenor flute and alto flute (with one part on Track 2 and the other on Track 4). This was the first time the Beatles used a non-band member other than George Martin to embellish one of their songs with a non-percussion instrument. (Andy White played drums on "Love Me Do" and "P.S. I Love You" and Norman Smith added bongos to "A Hard Day's Night.") The unplugged tune is in 6/8 time. It was mixed for mono on February 20 and for stereo on February 23.

Anthology 2 contains John's studio banter before and after Take 1's false start, including his announcement that "Paul's broken a glass." This is followed by Take 5, which is a complete performance.

I Need You

Recorded: February 15 & 16, 1965
Mixed: February 18 (mono); February 23 (stereo)

Producer: George Martin
Engineers: Norman Smith; Ken Scott & Jerry Boys

George: Lead vocals; nylon-string acoustic; electric 12-string guitar
John: Backing vocal; snare drum (on the off beat)
Paul: Backing vocal; bass guitar (Hofner)
Ringo: Keeping time on back of Jumbo acoustic guitar; cowbell

In the film, the group is shown recording "I Need You" at the start of the same military-protected outdoor recording session as "The Night Before." The segment opens with the barrel of a tank and contains a brief but effective image of Stonehenge in the background. Although George is shown on his Gibson Jumbo during the film sequence, he played his nylon-string acoustic guitar on the song.

"I Need You" was written by George Harrison. Although it is not known exactly when he started and finished the song, he may have come up with its basic idea while the Beatles were in London for their December 1964 Christmas Show. The song may have been finished with an assist from John at Lennon's Kenwood house on February 11 before they attended Ringo's wedding to Maureen Cox.

The mid-tempo pop tune was the last song recorded during the group's first session of the year on February 15, 1965, with the basic tracks completed in five takes. The initial recording consisted of George's vocal on Track 2, backed by George on his nylon-stringed acoustic guitar, Paul on bass, John playing the snare drum on the offbeat and Ringo keeping time on the back of a Gibson Jumbo guitar, all on Track 1. After the band and George Martin determined that Take 5 was a keeper, Harrison recorded his lead vocal, and Paul provided occasional harmony vocals on the last phrase of each verse ("I need you" on all but the second verse where they sing "you told me") onto Track 3. Track 4 was filled with more vocals by George and Paul, and Ringo's cowbell.

The following day, Track 4 was wiped with the recording of a new lead vocal by George, backed by Paul and John's vocal "aahs." George's original vocal on Track 2 was wiped with the recording of more backing vocals "aahs" from Paul and John, Ringo's cowbell (which needed to be re-recorded after being wiped from Track 4) and George's 12-string Rickenbacker played through a foot-controlled volume pedal. As Harrison was a novice on the device, for the most part he limited his playing to the open strumming of chords. The song was mixed for mono on February 18 and stereo on February 23.

Another Girl

Recorded: February 15 & 16, 1965
Mixed: February 18 (mono); February 23 (stereo)

Producer: George Martin
Engineers: Norman Smith; Ken Scott & Jerry Boys

Paul: Lead vocals; bass guitar (Hofner); lead guitar solo (Casino)
John: Backing vocals; rhythm guitar (Stratocaster)
George: Backing vocals; acoustic guitar (Jumbo)
Ringo: Drums (Ludwig kit); finger clicks

The performance sequence of "Another Girl" was filmed on February 27 on a coral reef on Balmoral Island in the Bahamas. During parts of the lip-syncing, Paul's Hofner bass is replaced by a girl in a white bikini. While John is normally shown on his Jumbo acoustic guitar as Ringo plays drums, sometimes it is reversed with John on drums and Ringo on acoustic guitar. George can also be seen playing John's Rickenbacker Capri and Paul's Hofner bass.

The song was written entirely by Paul while on vacation in early February 1965 in Hammamet, a seaside resort in Tunisia. According to Barry Miles' *Many Years From Now*, the house Paul was staying at had "a magnificent bathroom with a sunken bath." The isolated room had ideal acoustics for songwriting.

The basic tracks for the rocker, completed in one take on February 15, have Paul's Hofner bass and Ringo's drums on Track 1, and George's strumming Gibson Jumbo acoustic-electric guitar part and John's Fender Stratocaster on Track 2. During the verses, John hits the chords on the off-beats, similar to his playing on "She's A Woman." For the bridge, he mostly picks notes of the chords. Paul's lead vocal, joined by John and George singing "another girl" and on the bridge, was recorded onto Track 3. Overdubs added to Track 4 include Paul's double-tracked lead vocal, John's occasional backing vocal and Ringo on tom tom. George then recorded ten edit pieces of a guitar flourish on his Gretsch Tennessean electric guitar using his tremelo bar to add to the end of the song. Edit No. 7 was marked as the best, but it would not be used.

The following day, Paul superimposed lead guitar fills on his Epiphone Casino during the introduction and at various other places in the song. He also played the guitar bit at the end, eliminating the need for George's edit piece. Apparently, this overdub was on Track 2, wiping out what was there before, meaning George and John re-recorded their rhythm guitar parts as Paul played lead. The song was mixed for mono on February 18 and for stereo on February 23.

You're Going To Lose That Girl

Recorded: February 19 and March 30, 1965
Mixed: April 2 (mono and stereo)

Producer: George Martin
Engineers: Norman Smith; Ken Scott

John: Lead vocals; rhythm guitar (Gretsch Tennessean)
Paul: Backing vocals; bass guitar (Hofner); piano
George: Backing vocals; guitar solo (Stratocaster)
Ringo: Drums (Ludwig kit); bongo drums

The motion picture contains a clever and effective sequence of the group recording "You're Going To Lose That Girl" (sung as "You're Gonna Lose That Girl") on a set designed to mimic EMI Studios. The lip-synced performance was filmed at Twickenham Film Studios on April 30. It incorporates many of the elements from the performance scenes in *A Hard Day's Night*, including close-up shots of the band members. For the most part, the song is treated as a straightforward live-in-the-studio performance. But, because Paul's piano and Ringo's bongos are clearly audible, the film sometimes shows Ringo on bongos and contains a shot of Ringo glancing into the corner of the studio and spotting Paul on piano. At the conclusion of the song, the men in the booth complain that the group will have to record the song again due to a mysterious buzzing sound on the tape. The buzzing is revealed to be a chain saw cutting a huge circle in the floor around Ringo's drum kit. Ringo, still seated behind his drums, then crashes through the floor into a lower level storeroom and into the hands of Clang's henchmen. John, Paul and George are shown peering down into the hole in the studio's floor.

"You're Going To Lose That Girl" was written by John and Paul at John's Kenwood house in Weybridge, most likely in close proximity to the February 19 evening session during which it was recorded. After rehearsing the tune, the group was ready to tape a proper take, misidentified as Take 2. The next attempt, Take 3, was the only complete performance of the song. According to George Martin's notes, the basic instrumental backing had John on a Gretsch (most likely George's Tennessean), bass (Paul on his Hofner) and drums (Ringo) on Track 1. John's lead vocal, backed by Paul and George, were then superimposed onto Track 3. Martin further notes solo guitar (George) and electric piano (Paul) were recorded onto Track 2. John double-tracked his vocal onto Track 4. The next day, the song was mixed for mono. An acetate of this mix has the keyboard barely audible. George's solo starts strong, but is a bit off.

VISA N° 1814
LES BEATLES dans Au secours!
TECHNICOLOR
(HELP!)
Produit par
WALTER SHENSON
Réalisé par
RICHARD LESTER
Une Production WALTER SHENSON-SUBAFILMS
UNITED ARTISTS

On March 30, Track 2 was wiped and recorded over with a new and improved solo from George on his Fender Stratocaster, Paul on piano and Ringo on bongos. The finished master has John's double-tracked vocal answered by Paul and George in harmony for the verses. All three sing harmony on most of the bridge, though the line "Watch what you do" is sung only by Paul and George. John adds some nice falsetto touches. The song ends effectively with the three singing "lose that girl" in harmony. The song was remixed for mono and stereo, utilizing the new overdubs, on April 2.

Ticket To Ride

Recorded: February 15, 1965
Mixed: February 18 (mono); February 23 (stereo)

Producer: George Martin
Engineers: Norman Smith; Ken Scott & Jerry Boys

John: Lead vocals; rhythm guitar (Stratocaster)
Paul: Backing vocals; bass guitar (Hofner); lead guitar (Casino)
George: Lead guitar (Rickenbacker 12-string); guitar (Stratocaster)
Ringo: Drums; tambourine

The "Ticket To Ride" sequence is one of the highlights of *Help!* Beautifully filmed in the Alps, the Beatles are shown riding snow bikes, pretending to ski, actually skiing, falling down, rolling in the snow, crawling in the snow, having a picnic in the snow and hanging around a piano brought up the mountain. Paul rides a horse, and the boys ride in a horse-drawn sleigh. There are clever shots with each Beatles turning a ski pole aimed at the camera and one where the scored notes of the song appear on electrical lines. Several of its shots were copied in The Monkees TV show, but with a sunny, sandy California beach replacing the snowy Austrian mountain.

"Ticket To Ride," which closes the film side of the album, was written by John with an assist from Paul at John's Kenwood house during a three-hour songwriting session most likely held the day before the song was recorded on February 15. According to Paul, "at the end of it all we had all the words, we had the harmonies, and we had all the little bits." Music publisher Dick James claims that John told him during rehearsals for the Beatles 1964 Christmas Show that he had a title called "She's Got A Ticket To Ride." George Martin recalls John playing him the tune when they went skiing in early February 1965 (see page 34). "I liked it straightaway. John said he would get together with Paul as soon as he got back to London and finish it off." The title is a pun referring to the town of Ryde, located on the Isle of Wight off the coast of England.

The track was the first song recorded at the Beatles initial session of 1965 on February 15. After an immediate false start on Take 1, the group turned in a perfect performance of the backing track on Take 2. According to George Martin's notes, it was recorded with Paul's bass (Hofner) and Ringo's drums on Track 1; and the song's guitar riff played by George on his 12-string Rickenbacker and John's rhythm part on his new Fender Stratocaster on Track 2. John's lead vocal and Paul's occasional harmony vocal were then recorded on Track 3. The remaining track was used for overdubs, which included John's double-tracked lead vocal, Ringo on tambourine, Paul's lead guitar played on his Epiphone Casino (at the end of the bridge and during the ending coda), and George playing single low accent notes (A, B or E) on his Fender Stratocaster over the riff. The song's distinctive drum pattern was conceived by Paul (perhaps inspired by Arabic rhythms he heard in Tunisia) and expertly executed by Ringo.

"Ticket To Ride" contains an innovative and unexpected coda. The song comes to a sudden halt, only to have the vocals and music start again for an ear-grabbing end bit containing a different melody and tempo. The fast-paced ending has the group singing the line "My baby don't care" over churning music dominated by a sizzling lead guitar played by Paul on his Epiphone Casino. This type of ending was later used by the Beatles on their single "Hello Goodbye," with its so-called "Maori finale" tagged on the end. "Ticket To Ride" was mixed for mono on February 18 and for stereo on February 23.

The Beatles taped "Ticket To Ride" on May 26, 1965, for their last BBC radio program, The Beatles Invite You To Take A Ticket To Ride, broadcast on June 7. This performance is on *Live At The BBC*.

The Beatles performed "Ticket To Ride" on Blackpool Night Out, broadcast live on August 1, 1965. The audio is on *Anthology 2*. The *Anthology* video switches between the Blackpool performance and the song's promotional video. The group also taped the song on August 14 for broadcast on the September 12 Ed Sullivan Show. This version has an extended beginning. A clip of the Beatles doing "Ticket To Ride" was shown on an episode of the British science fiction TV show Doctor Who. The 30-second video is all that remains from the group miming their single on the April 10 Top Of The Pops.

"Ticket To Ride" was added to the Beatles set list for the 1965 European and American tours. Thus, there are several live versions of the song on both legitimate and illegitimate releases. Their August 15 concert performance was filmed for the TV special *The Beatles At Shea Stadium*. Capitol's *The Beatles At The Hollywood Bowl* includes their August 29 Hollywood Bowl performance.

LES BEATLES dans **Au secours!**

TECHNICOLOR (HELP!)

Produit par WALTER SHENSON

Réalisé par RICHARD LESTER

Une Production WALTER SHENSON-SUBAFILMS

UNITED ARTISTS

VISA N°1814

Act Naturally

Recorded: June 17, 1965
Mixed: June 18 (mono and stereo)

Producer: George Martin
Engineers: Norman Smith; Phil McDonald

Ringo: Lead vocal; drums (Ludwig kit)
Paul: Backing vocals; bass guitar (Hofner)
John: Rhythm acoustic guitar (Jumbo)
George: Lead guitar (Gretsch Tennessean)

The non-film side of the *Help!* album opens with the group's fabulous cover of "Act Naturally," a charming country & western tune selected by Ringo as his vocal spotlight on the album. This move was necessitated by the group's dissatisfaction with "If You've Got Trouble" (see page 260). "Act Naturally" was written by Johnny Russell and Voni Morrison, and originally recorded by singer/guitarist Buck Owens at Capitol Recording Studios in Hollywood on February 12, 1963. It was released in America as Capitol 4937 on March 11, 1963. The song became Owens' first number one hit, topping the Billboard Hot Country Singles chart for four weeks. "Act Naturally" was included on the U.S. and U.K. album *The Best Of Buck Owens*.

The tune was the perfect vehicle for Ringo, who had a fondness for country music. Its opening lines ("They're gonna put me in the movies/They're gonna make a big star out of me") seemed as if they were written with Ringo in mind. The Beatles recorded the song on June 17, 1965, the last day of the *Help!* sessions. The group recorded a dozen backing tracks featuring John on his Gibson Jumbo acoustic-electric, George on his Gretsch Tennessean, Paul on bass and Ringo on drums. Take 13, the finished master, added Ringo's lead vocal, Paul's backing vocal, and drum sticks hitting the rim of a snare drum. The song was mixed for mono and stereo on June 18.

With the exception of the numerous oldies performed by the band during the *Get Back* project, "Act Naturally" was the last song recorded by the Beatles that was not written by a member of the group. (Ringo later recorded a duet of the song with Buck Owens.)

The Beatles performed "Act Naturally" on the August 1965 Blackpool Night Out and Ed Sullivan television shows. The song was added to the band's set list for the August 15, 1965, Shea Stadium concert and performed by the Beatles at some of their 1965 American and British shows. Although the song appears in *The Beatles At Shea Stadium* concert film, the studio recording was dubbed to the soundtrack in place of the ragged live version.

It's Only Love

Recorded: June 15, 1965
Mixed: June 18 (mono and stereo)

Producer: George Martin
Engineers: Norman Smith; Phil McDonald

John: Lead vocals; acoustic guitar (Jumbo); Rickenbacker Capri
Paul: Bass guitar (Hofner)
George: 12-string acoustic; 6-string electric (Gretsch Tennessean)
Ringo: Drums (Ludwig kit); tambourine

"It's Only Love" was one of the songs for the non-film side of the album written by John and Paul in late May/early June at John's Weybridge home. Although based on John's original idea, he didn't like the song, telling David Sheff: "I always thought it was a lousy song. The lyrics were abysmal." Paul, in Miles' *Many Years From Now*, provided the following justification: "Sometimes we didn't fight it if the lyric came out rather bland on some of those filler songs like 'It's Only Love.' If a lyric was really bad we'd edit it, but we weren't that fussy about it, because it's only a rock 'n' roll song. I mean, it's not literature." Fans were less critical of the track, which holds the distinction of being the first Beatles song that refers, somewhat innocently, to getting high ("I get high when I see you go by, my oh my").

"It's Only Love" was recorded towards the end of the *Help!* sessions on June 15, 1965, and was completed in six takes. The initial backing has John strumming his Gibson Jumbo acoustic guitar, George strumming a similar pattern on John's Framus Hootenanny 12-string acoustic guitar, Paul on his Hofner bass, and Ringo on drums, all on Track 1. John and George have a capo on the fifth fret of the guitars. Ringo plays the same simple but effective drum part utilizing his hi-hat throughout the song. John's lead vocal, recorded live during the early takes, is on Track 3. *Anthology 2* contains the brief false start from Take 3 edited to the beginning of Take 2, which is presented in its entirety, complete with John's vocal. For Take 6, John concentrated on his guitar, so he did not sing along. His lead vocal was superimposed onto Track 3. John, on his Rickenbacker Capri, and George, on his Gretsch Tennessean, overdubbed additional guitar parts onto Track 2. The song's opening and recurring low note riff is played by George backed by John adding a pair of notes with the vibrato tremolo effect of his Vox amplifier activated by foot pedal. When the riff is not being played, John hits accent chords (with the tremolo off) and George supplies guitar fills. John double-tracked his vocal, and Ringo added tambourine, both on the chorus, onto Track 4. The song was mixed for mono and stereo on June 18. When George Martin recorded the song for his instrumental *Help!* LP, it was titled "That's A Nice Hat (Cap)."

You Like Me Too Much

Recorded: February 17, 1965
Mixed: February 18 (mono); February 23 (stereo)

Producer: George Martin
Engineers: Norman Smith; Ken Scott

George: Lead vocals; acoustic guitar (Jumbo); lead guitar (Gretsch)
Paul: Backing vocal; bass guitar (Hofner); piano (Steinway grand)
John: Tambourine; electric piano (Hohner Pianet C)
Ringo: Drums (Ludwig kit)
George Martin: Piano (Steinway grand)

While George only contributed one self-written song to *With The Beatles* and had none on the group's other three albums, he had two compositions ready for the *Help!* sessions. Both were offered for inclusion in the film, but only "I Need You" made the cut.

"You Like Me Too Much" was recorded in eight takes on February 17, 1965. The instrumental backing on Track 1 consists of George on his Jumbo acoustic guitar, Paul on his Hofner bass, Ringo on drums, and John on tambourine (on the bridge and at the end). George Martin provides the rollicking yet graceful piano introduction. George Harrison's lead vocal was superimposed onto Track 3, and then double-tracked and joined by Paul's harmony backing vocal (reinforcing the line "'Cause you like me too much and I like you" throughout the song and on the first and third lines of the bridge) on Track 4. Final overdubs were added to Track 2. This included John on the Hohner Pianet C electric piano, which was set in its vibrato mode for the song's introduction. During the song's instrumental break, George's lead guitar riffs (played on either his Gretsch Tennessean or Fender Stratocaster) are echoed by Martin's barrelhouse-style piano, aided by Paul on the same Steinway Model B Grand Piano, in an effective call and response pattern played six times. The rollicking piano of Martin and McCartney returns for the ending. The song was mixed for mono on February 18 and for stereo on February 23.

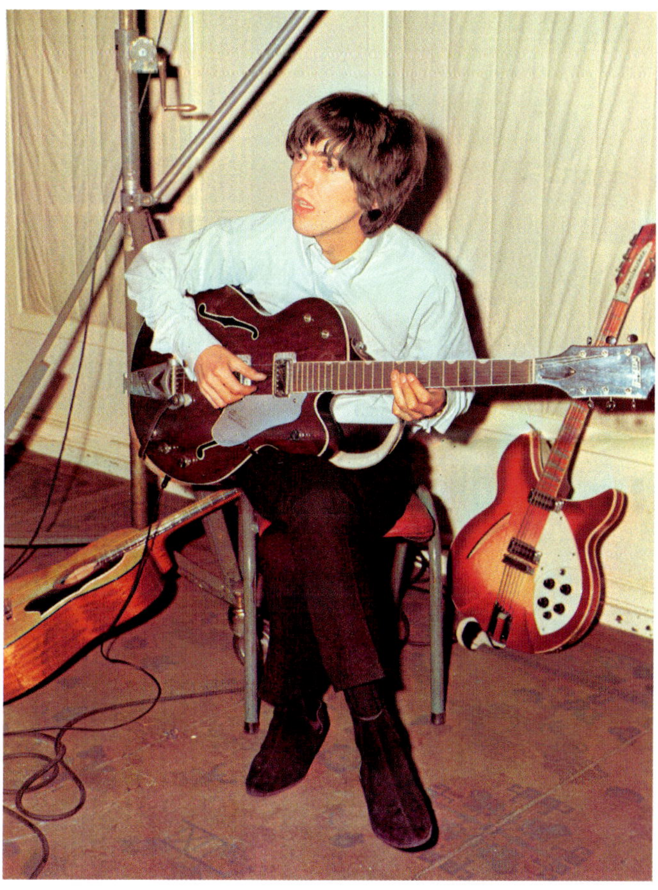

Tell Me What You See

Recorded: February 18, 1965
Mixed: February 20 (mono); February 23 (stereo)

Producer: George Martin
Engineers: Norman Smith; Ken Scott

Paul: Lead vocals; bass guitar; electric piano (Hohner Pianet C)
John: Lead vocals; electric guitar (Fender Stratocaster)
George: Güiro
Ringo: Drums (Ludwig kit)
Percussion: Tambourine (Ringo or John); claves (George or Ringo)

"Tell Me What You See" was written primarily by Paul, most likely in early 1965, but John apparently reached back to a childhood memory for part of the lyrics. Mark Lewisohn writes that John was fascinated by a religious motto that was framed and hung on the wall of his Aunt Mimi's Mendips home: "However black the clouds may be/In time they'll pass away/Have faith and trust and you will see/God's light make bright your day." This was modified to form a verse of the song: "Big and black the clouds may be/Time will pass away/If you put your trust in me/I'll make bright your day."

The song was recorded in four takes on February 18, 1965. It was presented to Richard Lester for inclusion in the film, but the director chose not to use the song. Although viewed by Paul as little more than album filler, it is a pleasant pop tune. The initial backing features John on his new Fender Stratocaster, Paul on his Hofner bass, Ringo on drums, and George on a güiro, a Latin American/Caribbean percussion instrument (an open-ended hallow gourd with parallel notches on one side played by rubbing a stick over the notches), all on Track 1. After the one-line "Tell me what you see" chorus that follows the second and third verses, there is a pause leading into a Ringo drum fill. Paul and John superimposed their harmony vocals onto Track 3. Track 4 has double-tracked vocals on the first and third lines of the verses, the chorus and the end bit, along with tambourine and claves (two short thick pieces of wood frequently used in Latin American music). Paul added an effective Hohner Pianet part to fill the gap after the chorus and also at the end. Journalist Ray Coleman, who was at the session, reported that John shook a tambourine and Ringo played maracas (clearly misidentified as claves are heard on the recording). George Martin's notes have Ringo on tambourine and George on claves. John said güiro and claves were added because the group wanted "the Mexican effect." The song was mixed for mono on February 20 and stereo on February 23.

I've Just Seen A Face

Recorded: June 14, 1965
Mixed: June 18 (mono and stereo)

Producer: George Martin
Engineers: Norman Smith; Phil McDonald

Paul: Lead vocals; acoustic guitar (Epiphone Texan)
John: Acoustic guitar (Gibson Jumbo)
George: Lead guitar (Framus Hootenanny acoustic 12-string)
Ringo: Drums (Ludwig kit); maracas

"I've Just Seen A Face" started out as a piano instrumental written by Paul, who would play the tune at family gatherings. He began calling it "Auntie Gin's Theme" due to his aunt's fondness of the song, which may date back to the early sixties or even before. Paul added lyrics to the tune while residing at the Asher family home on Wimpole Street. Based on the lyric's upbeat love theme, it was most likely written with Jane Asher in mind.

The Beatles recorded "I've Just Seen A Face" in six takes on June 14, 1965–a day on which Paul later sang lead on "I'm Down" and "Yesterday." It was the first all-acoustic track by the band as previous ballads such as "And I Love Her" had Paul on his Hofner electric bass. The up-tempo song has a slight country sound.

The initial instrumental backing features Paul on his Epiphone Texan acoustic guitar, George on John's Framus Hootenanny acoustic 12-string guitar (mostly playing bass patterns as a substitute for Paul's bass except for strumming during the chorus), John on his Gibson Jumbo acoustic guitar, and Ringo playing with brushes on his snare drum. The first sound heard in the song is George's three notes on the 12-string with Paul quickly joining in with attention-grabbing triplets of variations of an F# minor chord played in four ascending positions up the neck of his guitar followed by triplets of other chords. This intricate introduction is followed by Paul's churning rhythm for the rest of the song. John strums along on his Gibson Jumbo, probably with a capo on the second fret (buried in the mix), while Ringo adds his brushes. These parts are all on Track 1. Paul's vocal, which probably was performed live, is on Track 3. Paul overdubbed guitar on the introduction, with a harmony part over the F# minor triplets segment and duplicating the triplets for the remaining part, while George superimposed his guitar solo on the Framus, both on Track 4. Paul added harmony vocals during the chorus, while Ringo played maracas during the chorus and solo on Track 2. The song was mixed for mono and stereo on June 18.

THIS MONTH—COMPLETE GUITAR PRICE LIST
BEAT
MONTHLY
INSTRUMENTAL
2/-
JULY 1965
No. 27

Yesterday

Recorded: June 14, 1965 (strings added June 17)
Mixed: June 18 (mono and stereo)

Producer: George Martin
Engineers: Norman Smith; Phil McDonald

Paul: Lead vocal; acoustic guitar (Epiphone Texan)
Outside musicians: Violins (Tony Gilbert and Sidney Sax); Viola (Kenneth Essex); and Cello (Francisco Gabarro)

"Yesterday" literally came to Paul in a dream. At the time, he was living at the Ashers' house in a tiny attic room that had a small sawn-off piano by his bed. Paul recalls waking up one morning with the lovely melody in his head. He got out of bed, sat at the piano and began playing the tune. Concerned that the melody was a song he had previously heard, Paul played it for John and George Martin, neither of whom recognized it. He performed the tune for singer Alma Cogan on the green art deco Eavestaff piano at her mother's house, asking if she had heard the tune. Alma told him that she did not know what it was and that it was beautiful. After people kept telling Paul it was lovely and previously unheard, he claimed it as his own.

Prior to coming up with any serious lyrics, the song was called "Scrambled Eggs." In Barry Miles' *Many Years From Now*, Paul tells of his early performances of the tune: "The lyrics used to go, 'Scrambled eggs, oh, my baby, how I love your legs....' There was generally a laugh at that point, you didn't need to do any more lyrics."

Chris Dreja of the Yardbirds recalls Paul playing the song on acoustic guitar for the group in their dressing room during the Brian Epstein production Another Beatles Christmas Show, which ran from December 24, 1964, through January 16, 1965. Dreja said Paul hadn't got the lyrics, only the melody, and called it "Scrambled Eggs."

During the filming of *Help!*, Paul would often sit at the piano and refine the song by perfecting the melody and adding a middle eight. While on vacation in late May, Paul finally wrote the words. In his 2023 book *The Lyrics*, Paul said he wrote the lyrics to "Yesterday" during a three-hour drive [on May 27] from Lisbon to Albufeira, Portugal, where he was to stay at the home of Bruce Welch, guitarist with the Shadows. Two weeks later, he was ready to record the song.

On the evening of June 14, after singing "I've Just Seen A Face" and "I'm Down" that afternoon, Paul auditioned "Yesterday" before George Martin and the band. None of the members could think of anything they could add to the number, with John telling Paul he should do it by himself as it was really a solo song.

Although Paul had written the song in the key of G, he realized that it would sound better in the key of F. Paul re-tuned all six strings of his guitar a whole tone lower so he could play the chords as written, but musically be in the key of F. He then recorded two takes of "Yesterday," singing by himself, accompanied only by his acoustic guitar. Take 2 was selected as the best performance.

After the song was completed, Martin suggested adding a string quartet. Although Paul was initially against the idea, he agreed to the plan and assisted Martin with his score. On June 17, four musicians from the London Symphony Orchestra (Tony Gilbert and Sidney Sax on violin, Kenneth Essex on viola and Francisco Gabarro on cello) entered EMI Studios to add their contribution to the song. The George Martin-conducted string quartet was overdubbed onto Take Two. Paul double-tracked "something wrong, now I long for yesterday" during the bridge (heard only on the first one). Upon hearing the finished master, Paul was pleased with the result, thinking it was "smashing." The first take of the song, to which strings were never added, is on *Anthology 2*.

Although "Yesterday" was a beautiful recording with widespread appeal, the group was against the song being issued as a single in the U.K. In addition to their concern that the ballad would harm their image as a rock 'n' roll band, the group did not want to issue a single that featured only one member. According to Paul, "'Yesterday' would have meant that the spotlight would go on me, so we never did that." Matt Monro's cover version of the song on Parlophone got to number eight on the U.K. charts. When Capitol released "Yesterday" as a single in the U.S., the song topped the Billboard Hot 100 for four weeks and sold over a million copies.

"Yesterday" was first performed before a live audience on the August 1, 1965 TV show Blackpool Night Out (rehearsal shown previous page). This performance is included on the *Anthology* video and on the *Anthology 2* album. The song made its American debut on the September 12 Ed Sullivan Show. On both performances, Paul takes center stage without the other members of the band, accompanied by his acoustic guitar and a taped backing of string musicians.

When "Yesterday" was added to the group's set list for its 1965 British tour, the song was played with Paul accompanying himself on electric organ. For the 1966 tours, the song was played by the entire group, with two electric guitars, bass and drums. The Japanese laserdisc *The Beatles Concert At Budokan 1966* contains the June 30 performance of the song. The Beatles played the electric version of "Yesterday" at their final concert at Candlestick Park.

Dizzy Miss Lizzy

Recorded: May 10, 1965
Mixed: May 10 (mono and stereo)

Producer: George Martin
Engineers: Norman Smith; Ken Scott

John: Lead vocal; guitar (Rickenbacker Capri); organ (Hammond)
Paul: Bass guitar (Hofner)
George: Lead guitar (Gretsch Tennessean)
Ringo: Drums (Ludwig kit); cowbell

"Dizzy Miss Lizzy" was recorded on May 10, 1965, specifically for Capitol Records, which had requested two additional Beatles songs to flesh out its next Beatles album, *Beatles VI*. As time was of the essence, the group knocked out a pair of Larry Williams rockers, "Dizzy Miss Lizzy" and "Bad Boy," that had been part of their stage show from 1960-1962. The former song was written and originally recorded by Williams at Master Recorders in Hollywood on February 19, 1958. "Dizzy Miss Lizzy" was paired with "Slow Down" (which was recorded by the Beatles in 1964) and released in the U.S. on Specialty 626 (picture sleeve from the Specialty single shown on the following page). The song peaked at number 69. The same single was released in the U.K. on London 45-HL-U 8604 but did not chart.

"Dizzy Miss Lizzy" was the first song the group attempted at the session. John sang live backed by his Rickenbacker Capri, Paul on his Hofner bass, George playing lead on his Gretsch Tennessean, and Ringo on drums. After a false start, Take 2 was complete and considered acceptable. However, after the band recorded "Bad Boy," George Martin directed the Beatles to see if they could improve upon their performance of "Dizzy Miss Lizzy." Take 3 was complete, but not quite right. Apparently, Martin did not think it was exciting enough. After three false starts, Take 7 became the keeper. Overdubs were then added. George double-tracked his stinging (but at times imprecise) lead guitar riff heard throughout the song, while John played the studio's Hammond RT-3 organ, and Ringo added cowbell. The finished master has a scorching lead vocal from John. As time was of the essence for Capitol, the song was mixed for mono and stereo the same night as the session. Although not originally intended for the *Help!* LP, "Dizzy Miss Lizzy" was chosen to be the album's last track.

The Beatles taped "Dizzy Liss Lizzy" on May 26 for the BBC radio program, The Beatles Invite You To Take A Ticket To Ride, broadcast on June 7. This recording is on *Live At The BBC*. "Dizzy Miss Lizzy"was part of the band's set list for its 1965 North American tour. The group is shown performing the song in the film *The Beatles At Shea Stadium*. Capitol's *Live At The Hollywood Bowl* contains an edit of the August 29 and 30, 1965 performances of the rocker. The group ran through the song during the *Get Back* sessions on January 6, 1969.

Banding, Mixing & Mastering

A June 22, 1965 EMI memo from George Martin has the full label copy information for the *Help!* LP. This indicates that George Martin had little time to decide on the running order of the songs as songs were still being mixed on June 18. Six of the songs recorded during the *Help!* sessions were mixed for mono on February 18, with five additional mono mixes made on February 20. These 11 songs were brought to the film's producer and director, Walter Shenson and Richard Lester, for review. Six of these songs were selected for the film, with the title track later added to the lineup. While George Martin produced the mono mixing sessions, he was not present when engineer Norman Smith mixed all 11 songs for stereo during a three hour session on February 23. The April 18 mono mix of "Help!" was used for the single, the film and the mono LP, while the stereo album uses a June 18 mix.

The Larry Williams rockers recorded for Capitol were mixed for mono and stereo at the end of the May 10 session and sent to Capitol the next day. "Yesterday" was mixed for mono on June 17. The remaining songs were mixed for mono and stereo on June 18. As "Wait" was mixed for mono but not stereo, it may have remained in the running for inclusion on the album until that time. After ruling out "If You've Got Trouble," "That Means A Lot" and "Wait" (see pages 260-261), and not wanting to include either of the B-sides "Yes It Is" and "I'm Down," only 13 of the songs recorded for the album were available, leaving the disc one short of the standard 14. Martin solved this problem by selecting "Dizzy Miss Lizzy" to close the album. This was a throwback to the group's first two albums, which both end with a rousing John Lennon vocal on a high-energy cover of a song originally recorded by an American artist.

The Capitol album ***Beatles VI*** includes the six songs from *Beatles For Sale* that were not included on the label's *Beatles '65* LP. Two of those songs, "Eight Days A Week" and "I Don't Want To Spoil The Party," were previously released on a Capitol single. Only five more songs were needed to get to 11 tracks, which had become the standard for the label's Beatles albums. After adding the B-side "Yes It Is" to the line-up, Capitol was still four short. After asking EMI

if any additional Beatles recordings were available, the company was told that two songs recorded back in February, "You Like Me Too Much" and "Tell Me What You See," could be used. Apparently, George Martin had by then determined that "If You've Got Trouble" and "That Means A Lot" were not suitable for release. To accommodate Capitol's need for two more tracks, Martin had the Beatles record two songs intended exclusively for the Capitol LP, "Dizzy Miss Lizzy" (mistitled "Dizzy Miss Lizzie" by Capitol) and "Bad Boy."

The mono *Beatles VI* was mastered by Wally Traugott on May 14 using the mono mixes sent to Capitol by EMI. The stereo version of the album was also mastered on May 14, but by Maurice Long and Wally Traugott. All of the tracks are true stereo mixes provided by EMI except for the mono B-side "Yes It Is," which is a Capitol duophonic fake stereo mix.

Bad Boy

Recorded: May 10, 1965
Mixed: May 10 (mono and stereo)

Producer: George Martin
Engineers: Norman Smith; Ken Scott

John: Lead vocal; guitar (Rickenbacker); organ (Vox Continental)
Paul: Bass guitar (Hofner); electric piano (Hohner Pianet C)
George: Lead guitar (Gretsch Tennessean)
Ringo: Drums (Ludwig kit); cowbell

"Bad Boy" was one of two Larry Williams songs recorded on May 10, 1965, specifically for Capitol's *Beatles VI* album, the other being "Dizzy Miss Lizzy." Larry Williams recorded "Bad Boy" at Radio Recorders in Hollywood, California, on August 14, 1958. The song was paired with "She Said Yeah" (later recorded by the Rolling Stones) on Specialty 658, which was released on January 19, 1959. The disc failed to make either the American pop or R&B charts. The single was released in the U.K. on London 45-HLU 8844 but did not chart. "Bad Boy" was part of the Beatles stage show from 1960-1962.

The group completed the song in four takes. John provided a guide vocal backed by his Rickenbacker 325 Capri, Paul on his Hofner bass, George's lead on his Gretsch Tennessean, and Ringo on drums. After a false start on the first try, Take 2 was complete, but not good enough. After another false start, Take 4 proved satisfactory. John then superimposed his lead vocal, while Ringo added tambourine. Other overdubs included George double-tracking his lead guitar, Paul on the Hohner Pianet C electric piano, and John on a Vox Continental organ. The song was mixed for mono and stereo immediately after the session ended. "Bad Boy" was first issued in the U.K. in December 1966 on the album *A Collection Of Beatles Oldies*.

Williams' version of the song contains a "He's a bad boy" refrain after each line of the verses. The Beatles increased the beat and wisely dropped the corny vocal response, relying strictly on John's powerhouse lead vocal to carry the song. In addition to his excellent guitar solo, George provides guitar fills after each of the lines in the verses, in effect replacing "He's a bad boy." George plays different riffs throughout the song, with half enhanced at the end by his use of the guitar's Bigsby B6G vibrato bar . The rocker concludes with John shouting "Now junior, behave yourself, woooo!" While Larry Williams' song is about a juvenile delinquent, John and the Beatles turn him into a rock 'n' roll rebel.

Yes It Is

Recorded: February 16, 1965
Mixed: February 18 (mono); February 23 (stereo)

Producer: George Martin
Engineers: Norman Smith; Ken Scott & Jerry Boys

John: Lead vocals; rhythm guitar (José Ramirez nylon-string)
Paul: Harmony vocal; Bass guitar (Hofner); cymbals
George: Harmony vocal; lead guitar (Tennessean & volume pedal)
Ringo: Drums (Ludwig kit); tambourine
George Martin: Hammond RT-3 organ (inaudible)

"Yes It Is" was written primarily by John, with an assist from Paul. They completed the song at John's Kenwood home some time in January or February 1965. In Miles' *Many Years From Now*, Paul recalled: "I was there writing it with John, but it was his inspiration that I helped him finish off. 'Yes It Is' is a very fine song of John's, a ballad, unusual for John. He wrote some beautiful ballads." John, who was often dismissive of his work, was less complementary of the song in his 1980 Playboy interview with David Sheff. "That's me trying a re-write of 'This Boy,' but it didn't quite work."

Many people disagreed with John, believing that the number worked quite well. It was selected by the Beatles to be the B-side of their first single of the year, "Ticket To Ride." In fact, George Harrison preferred "Yes It Is" and thought it should have been the A-side. John's wife Cynthia told music writer Ray Coleman that it was her favorite Beatles track so far. It was not issued on the British *Help!* LP, although Capitol did include the song on the album *Beatles VI*.

"Yes It Is" was recorded on February 16. While the backing track for the A-side "Ticket To Ride" was completed in two takes, it took the band 14 takes over two hours to obtain a satisfactory backing. John provided a guide vocal to help the band follow along. The initial instruments were John on George's nylon-stringed acoustic guitar, George on his Gretsch Tennessean augmented by a volume pedal, Paul on bass and Ringo on drums. The session tape, nearly all of which has been bootlegged, reveals that most takes were false starts and breakdowns.

Take 1 is complete. John's guide vocal is timid-sounding and at times shows him having difficulty with the words; however, the rhythm guitar strumming is strong as ever on this and subsequent takes. Paul, whose bass starts the song, provides a simple but effective backing. George plays his guitar through a volume foot pedal connected to his amplifier. When the pedal is fully open, no volume goes to the amp. As he pushes down on the pedal, the volume increases, creating a swelling sound. For most of the song, he plays a single chord per measure. Ringo keeps time with his hi-hat. At this stage, the first verse end with a single "yes it is" and goes directly into the second verse without a measure that would later be added to accommodate the words "it's true, yes it is." The song's ending has yet to be worked out. When done, John says: "We loused it up." Take 2 stops during the bridge (on which John sings "die-de-de-die"), with John explaining: "A string broke, didn't you hear?" And yes, you can clearly hear the broken string striking his guitar. Takes 3-6 are false starts. Before Take 5, John talks about adding a measure between the first and second verses. Take 7 breaks down during the bridge and Take 8 is yet another false start.

Take 9 is complete. The band has worked out chord changes for the song's ending, with George adding four notes played with his volume pedal. John's singing is weak, giving the impression he is saving his voice for the real deal. Takes 10 and 11 are also false starts, while Take 14 is near perfection, marred only by George accidentally playing a B minor chord instead of an F# minor during the first bridge. He begins his part on the song with two single notes and a harmonic tone, all played with the volume pedal, giving the song a distinctive opening.

Overdubs were then added onto Take 14. After rehearsing under George Martin's supervision, John, Paul and George superimposed a beautiful three-part harmony for the verses. John sings solo on the bridges, backed on the last two lines only by Paul and George singing four sustained "aah"s in harmony. Martin commented: "They always experimented with close harmony singing. All I did was change the odd note." Whatever recommend changes he made paid off. Although some have reported that the three-part harmony was sung by John, Paul and George around a single microphone, the picture from the session shown right shows John on a separate mike. George added more volume pedal guitar, doubling his opening and ending riffs and adding a mixture of single notes and harmonics during the verses. John double-tracked his vocal on the bridge, while Ringo added tambourine and Paul hit cymbals. The session tape reveals a series of chords played on a Hammond RT-3 organ through a Leslie speaker cabinet prior to the start of the song. It is likely that the organ was played by George Martin. It is not heard in the mix. The song was mixed for mono on February 18 and for stereo on February 23. *Anthology 2* has an edit of Takes 2 and 14.

VOX

I'm Down

Recorded: June 14, 1965
Mixed: June 18 (mono and stereo)

Producer: George Martin
Engineers: Norman Smith; Phil McDonald

Paul: Lead and backing vocals; bass guitar (Hofner)
John: Backing vocals; electric organ (Vox Continental V301J)
George: Backing vocals; lead guitar (Gretsch Tennessean)
Ringo: Drums (Ludwig kit); bongo drums

"I'm Down" was written almost entirely by Paul sometime during April through early June 1965 while he was residing at the Asher's home at 57 Wimpole Street in London. The Little Richard influenced rocker was the type of song the Beatles had been wanting to write for years. In the October 17, 1964 Melody Maker, Paul told Ray Coleman: "We spend a lot of time trying to write a real rocker, something like 'Long Tall Sally.' It's very difficult. 'I Saw Her Standing There' was the nearest we got to it. We're still trying to compose a Little Richard sort of song...I'd liken it to abstract painting. People think of 'Long Tall Sally' and say it sounds so easy to write. It's the most difficult thing we've attempted....Writing a three-chord song that's clever is not easy." Coleman added that Paul and John "carried on for some time about their yearning to write a real rocker," with John telling him that Paul visited his house some evenings trying to do it, but so far they were dissatisfied.

Apparently, Paul was further motivated by his desire to find a homegrown replacement for the Beatles then-current closing number, "Long Tall Sally." In Miles' *Many Years From Now*, Paul explained: "A lot of people were fans of Little Richard, but there came a point when I wanted one of my own, so I wrote 'I'm Down.'" He added that the song was: "my rock 'n' roll shouter...a good stage song, and inasmuch as they are hard to write, I'm proud of it. Those kind of songs with hardly any melody, rock 'n' roll songs, are much harder to write than ballads, because there's nothing to them."

In Paul's 2021 book *The Lyrics*, he discussed the songwriting process for such a song: "In the course of writing that first verse, you've pretty much established everything that's going on. You just elaborate on that. Also, when you're shouting a rock and roll song, you want to be immediate; you don't want to get too fancy. Your natural rhyming pattern is trying to find the two rhymes. 'Man buys ring/Woman throws it away/Same old thing/Happens every day.' It's like a telegram." McCartney elaborated: "One of the great things about rock and roll and blues is that it's very economical. In the first verse you find your little rhyming pattern, and then normally you stick to that in successive verses. It's going to be a three-minute song; there's no time to be too fancy. We have to bang this out and get it said, powerfully and quickly, in two and a half or three minutes."

Paul also described his singing on "I'm Down": "It's a rock and roll screamer, and the voice belongs to Little Richard... With the Little Richard thing, you just have to give yourself over to it."

The Beatles recorded "I'm Down" on June 14. Paul sang live backed by his Hofner bass, George on his Gretsch Tennessean, John on a Vox Continental V301J organ, and Ringo on drums. *Anthology 2* contains Take 1. Prior to the start of the song, Paul announces: "Let's hope this one turns out pretty darn good, huh." With Paul singing, hollering, barking and whooping it up, it does turn out pretty darn good. At the 1:40 mark, he encourages the band to "keep going," and all respond by rocking out until the track ends after 2:36 of pure excitement. After completion of the song, Paul can be heard muttering "plastic soul, man, plastic soul." Apparently Paul was observing that the song wasn't a real soul shouter, but rather was a plastic imitation of soul music. This phrase may have inspired the title to the group's next album, *Rubber Soul*.

After recording three more complete takes, a false start and a breakdown, the group perfected the backing, complete with Paul's lead vocal, with Take 7. Paul, John and George then superimposed their backing vocals, along with additional Vox organ by John and bongos played by Ringo, onto Take 7. The vocal trio double-tracked their backing vocals. George overdubbed additional guitar. Although not used, the extra guitar can be heard due to microphone leakage.

The Beatles performed "I'm Down" twice on television during 1965, first on the August 1 British show Blackpool Night Out (part of which is on the *Anthology* video), and then on August 14 Ed Sullivan Show taping (broadcast on September 12) that features an energetic performance from Paul, who switches the first and second verses.

Paul's goal of writing a Little Richard-style rocker to close the Beatles concerts was achieved with "I'm Down." Beginning with the Beatles 1965 North American tour, the song closed out nearly all of the group's concerts, including the Shea Stadium performance and the Capitol-recorded Hollywood Bowl concerts of August 29 and 30, 1965. The frantic Shea version of "I'm Down" (shown on next page), highlighted with John smiling and playing Vox organ with his elbows, appears on the *Anthology* video. Neither of the Hollywood Bowl performances was included on Capitol's *Live At The Hollywood Bowl* LP.

VOX Continental
VOX Continental

If You've Got Trouble

Recorded: February 18, 1965
Mixed: February 20 (mono); February 23 (stereo)

Producer: George Martin
Engineers: Norman Smith; Ken Scott

Ringo: Lead vocals; drums (Ludwig kit)
Paul: Backing vocal; bass guitar (Hofner); guitar (Casino)
John: Backing vocal; guitar (Fender Stratocaster)
George: Guitar (Gretsch Tennessean; Fender Stratocaster for solo)

"If You've Got Trouble" was written for Ringo's solo spot on the album. It was recorded at a February 18, 1965 evening session attended by Ray Coleman, who wrote about his experience in the February 27 Melody Maker. John told Coleman: "I wrote it. It's the funniest thing I've ever done–listen to the words." Coleman said that Ringo sang something like "You've gone soft in the head." [He actually sings "You think I'm soft in the head."] John joked: "I didn't expect anybody to want to record it." George Martin's notes state "Routine 5:30," meaning the group worked on the arrangement of the song at that time, and that recording began at 6:00 PM. This started with the taping of rehearsals. According to Coleman, before the actual recording of the song began, Martin announced: "Right Ringo. That sounded okay. Let's try it for taping properly now."

The initial backing had George playing a low note riff on his Gretsch Tennessean, Paul on his Hofner bass, and Ringo, who starts the song, on drums, all on Track 1. This was accomplished in one take. Overdubs began at 6:40, with Ringo superimposing his vocal onto Track 3 with a trio of guitars recorded onto Track 2. This consisted of: John on his Fender Stratocaster with tremolo effect, hitting accent chords during the verses and a rock 'n' roll boogie rhythm on the bridge; Paul on his Epiphone Casino matching John's accent chords on the verses; and George double-tracking his riff on the Tennessean. At 7:15, Ringo's double-tracked lead vocal, John and Paul's background "Aah"s (not heard in the mix), and George's very rough guitar solo on his Stratocaster were dubbed onto Track 4. Ringo, perhaps sensing the song was in trouble, shouted out "Aah, rock on, anybody" prior to the solo. The recording was finished at 7:30. Martin noted: "Have to do George's solo again." Coleman, who described the song as having "a slight Bo Diddley beat," wrote that Martin joked: "Okay, John and Paul played awfully but Ringo was very good." The song was mixed for mono on February 20 and for stereo on February 23. It was finally released in 1996 on *Anthology 2*.

That Means A Lot

Recorded: February 20 & March 30, 1965
Mixed: February 20 (mono); February 23 (stereo)

Producer: George Martin
Engineers: Norman Smith; Ken Scott (February 20); Ron Pendeer/ Vic Gann (March 30)

Paul: Lead vocals; bass guitar (Hofner)
John: Backing vocals; guitar (Fender Stratocaster)
George: Backing vocals; nylon string acoustic guitar (February 20); Fender Stratocaster & Rickenbacker 12-string electric (March 30)
Ringo: Drums (Ludwig kit); maracas
George Martin: Piano (Steinway "Music Room" Model B Grand)

"That Means A Lot" was finished by Paul towards the end of the initial *Help!* session. Ray Coleman wrote in the February 27 Melody Maker that at the end of a session he attended [on February 18], Paul told George Martin he wanted to record a song he thought he'd finished writing a few hours earlier [being "That Means A Lot"].

Paul apparently had high hopes for the song as much effort was put into its recording on February 20. The initial backing consisted of Paul on his Hofner bass, John on his Stratocaster, George on his José Ramirez nylon-stringed acoustic guitar, and Ringo on drums. This was all recorded onto Track 1 in one take. Superimpositions of additional bass from Paul, John's double-tracked lead guitar introduction, and Ringo's echoed tom tom fills were then added onto an open track. A reduction mix of the two instrumental tracks was made to one track to form Take 2. With three open tracks, Paul added his lead vocal on one track, while John and George put down backing vocals on another. The remaining open track was filled with Paul, John and George double-tracking their vocals, George Martin's piano and Ringo on maracas. The song was mixed for mono at the end of the session and for stereo on February 23. The finished master, reminiscent of Phil Spector's "Wall of Sound" girl group recordings, is on *Anthology 2*.

As no one involved was particularly satisfied with the track, the Beatles attempted a re-make on March 30, this time with George playing his Stratocaster and Rickenbacker 12-string guitars. Take 20 was played at a slower tempo and sounded totally different than the earlier version, with George adding bluesy guitar fills between vocal lines. Take 22 was a return to the initial arrangement. Takes 23 and 24 broke down, while a final "test" take mercifully ended quickly. These later takes have been bootlegged. Giving up, the Beatles gave the song to P.J. Proby, whose recording was issued in September 1965, stalling at number 30 on the Record Retailer chart.

Wait [pre-*Rubber Soul* version]

Recorded: June 17, 1965
Mixed: June 18 (mono)

Producer: George Martin
Engineers: Norman Smith; Phil McDonald

John: Lead vocal; rhythm guitar (Rickenbacker Capri)
Paul: Lead (on bridge) and backing vocal; bass guitar (Hofner)
George: Lead guitar (Fender Stratocaster with volume pedal)
Ringo: Drums (Ludwig kit)

"Wait" was written primarily by Paul while the Beatles were in the Bahamas filming *Help!* In Miles' *Many Years From Now*, Paul said: "I think it was my song. I don't remember John collaborating too much on it, although he could have." McCartney had memories of writing the song in the presence of actor Brandon deWilde, who was "interested to see it being written." As Paul wrote the song while he was away from his girlfriend Jane Asher, it is possible that he wrote it with her in mind.

Apparently, the song was viewed as little more than filler as it was the last song recorded during the *Help!* album session on the evening of June 17. The instrumental backing track includes George on his Fender Stratocaster with a volume pedal, John on his Rickenbacker Capri, Paul on his Hofner bass, and Ringo on drums. John and Paul then overdubbed their vocals. Although McCartney's composition, John opens the song with "It's been a" before being joined by Paul in harmony for the rest of the first line ("long time") and all of the next line ("Now I'm coming back home"). This pattern is followed for the next two lines and for all of the remaining verses. Paul and John sing harmony on the chorus, and Paul sings solo on the bridge. The song was mixed for mono on June 18, indicating that the track was under consideration for the album. But after listening to the mix, George Martin decided that the song was not strong enough in its present state to be on the album. No stereo mix was made at that time.

When the Beatles were one song short for their next album, *Rubber Soul*, "Wait" was resurrected and given a series of overdubs. George's Stratocaster (with volume pedal) and Ringo's tambourine were superimposed on one track. John and Paul double-tracked their vocals, and Ringo added maracas, to the other open track. In the stereo mix made for the *Rubber Soul* LP, the instruments recorded on June 17 are in the left channel, while the added guitar and percussion from November 11 are in the right channel.

About the Instruments

The listings of the instruments played by each Beatle in this chapter were determined by listening to the song and utilizing the best available information. In some cases, this was fairly straightforward (some sessions were photographed), while in others, the instrument listed is the one most likely played on the recording. When in doubt, I consulted with Anthony Robustelli, author of *I Want To Tell You - The Definitive Guide To The Music Of The Beatles Volume 1:1962/1963*, and Andy Babiuk, author of *Beatles Gear: All the Fab Four's Instruments From Stage To Studio*. I also referred to *The Beatles Recording Reference Manual*, Volumes 1 and 2, by Jerry Hammack, and *Playback* by George Martin, which contains Martin's notes on many of the songs recorded during the *Help!* album sessions.

While Martin's contemporaneous notations on songs were a great deal of help, sometimes they were not specific enough. For example, George's guitar is listed as Gretsch or Fender. While Fender clearly refers to George's sonic blue Stratocaster, George had two different Gretsch guitars available, his Country Gentleman and his Chet Atkins Tennessean. Because the Tennessean had become George's preferred guitar by the *Beatles For Sale* sessions, I list it as the Gretsch played on most songs even though it could be the other. Andy Bubiuk indicated that it can be difficult to distinguish between the two Gretsch guitars as tone adjustments on the amplifiers and the guitars themselves can make one sound like the other.

There were also a few occasions where I was uncertain as to whether John was playing his Gibson J-160E "Jumbo" acoustic guitar or a 12-string acoustic guitar. This was not an issue for the *Help!* sessions as John purchased a Framus Hootenanny 12-string acoustic guitar prior to the sessions and definitely used this guitar on "Help!" and "You've Got To Hide Your Love Away." But as John did not own an acoustic 12-string during the *Beatles For Sale* sessions, it can be tricky to determine if John is playing a 6-string or 12-string acoustic on songs such as "I'm A Loser" or "Honey Don't." While one would assume that would not be a problem, that is not the case as John's Gibson Jumbo can produce a ringing-type sound similar to that of a 12-string. Because John did not own a 12-string acoustic guitar during those sessions, I believe he is playing his 6-string Jumbo.

But please keep in mind that while I am extremely confident on the instruments played on most of the songs, there are some instances where my listing may not be completely accurate. After all, life always has some mysteries, and that keeps things interesting.

The Capitol *Help!* Soundtrack Album

In his 1976 book *Playback*, Capitol's Dave Dexter recalls asking George Martin if there were plans for a *Help!* soundtrack LP, with Martin replying: "No. We plan no *Help!* album because the boys won't be featuring sufficient songs to fill an LP, and it's a pity, really. United Artists doesn't have the American rights to the package as they did with *A Hard Day's Night*." For that film, UA had issued an album with eight Beatles recordings plus four instrumentals by the George Martin Orchestra, but Capitol could not do that because director Richard Lester replaced Martin with Ken Thorne as the film's musical director, and Martin had an exclusive recording contract with UA. Dexter would need to compile his own film soundtrack LP.

It took Dexter over two months to obtain "two tape reels of the film's soundtrack scraps." Assisted by engineer John Kraus, Dexter played the tapes in one of the Capitol Tower's studios, timing and taking notes on the various music cues. There were 36 of them, most of which were brief. He did not have a print of the film, but was told the film had Ringo being chased in the Bahamas, Austria and England's Salisbury Plain, and a 10-armed, 40 foot tall goddess, Kaili.

Dexter described his job: "Working around the seven original [Beatles] songs..., by adventurous editing and by employing a number of mechanical tricks, I ended up with enough tracks to fill two 12-inch microgroove sides and justify the album's production as a 'complete original soundtrack' package." He was forced to repeat snippets of music and use a "bombastic" bit of Richard Wagner's *Lohengrin*. He created names for the tracks such as "From Me To You Fantasy" and "Another Hard Day's Night." After his own hard day's night at the Tower, he played the finished product to Capitol president Alan Livingston the following morning. Livingston asked: "Is that all there is?" Although not impressed with the album, he approved the package for release, "well aware of the demand for Beatles product."

The Capitol soundtrack album opens with an uncredited 15-second variation of the "James Bond Theme" from the film's Harrods truck "chase scene." The orchestrated opening adds sitar to the guitar-dominated tune. The actual "James Bond Theme" made its debut in the master spy's first film, *Dr. No* (a United Artists film released in the U.K. on the same day, October 5, 1962, as the Beatles first single, "Love Me Do"). Although Monty Norman received sole writer's credit for the theme, it was arranged by John Barry, who went on to score several Bond films. In the movie *Help!*, this sound cue is about 42 seconds long.

The uncredited James Bond intro leads directly into the film's title song, "Help!," as a single track. This is followed by another Beatles recording, "The Night Before." The album's third selection is titled "From Me To You Fantasy." Because this orchestrated background music briefly lapses into a few of the melody lines from "From Me To You," John and Paul are given composer's credit for the selection, which otherwise bears little resemblance to the Beatles third British single. The song is full of stop and start rhythms and mixes a hodgepodge of sounds, including brass, strings and Indian instruments, before fading out over a solo snare drum. This 2:03 cue is heard shortly after the start of "Part 3" of the film, which takes place in the Beatles shared apartment as Clang and his henchmen, along with the mad scientists, prepare to invade the premises. Inside, Paul is accidentally injected with a juice "distilled from the essence of orchids," which causes him to shrink to the size of a gum wrapper, which he wraps around himself.

After two more Beatles tracks, "You've Got To Hide Your Love Away" and "I Need You," Side One closes with an instrumental named "In The Tyrol (Introducing Wagner's Overture to Act III Of 'Lohengrin' Beatles Style)." The track is an edit taken from two different cues in the film. It opens with a snare drum roll and a brass band playing a march. This runs for about 34 seconds. This cue is an expansion of a 22-second bit that plays as Clang is picked up from the snowy ground and led to a medal stand where he is honored for having the longest jump in a ski competition he unintentionally took part in. The Beatles are shown as part of the brass band playing the tune. George takes a bite out of his cymbal. Tyrol is a region split between Italy and Austria. Its Austrian section is in the heart of the Alps. Although Tyrol has ski resorts, Obertauern, where the Beatles filmed *Help!*, is not "in the Tyrol" but it is not that far away.

The next section of the track is a 1:27 section of Richard Wagner's *Lohengrin-Prelude to Act III*. The joyous, dramatic orchestral piece features bold brass fanfares and pulsating rhythms from the strings. In the movie, this cue accompanies the battle between the Beatles and Clang's henchmen, who have broken into the boys' communal apartment. After the Wagner selection is faded out, the march heard at the start of the track fades in and runs for about 19 seconds, bringing an end to the 2:21 selection.

Wagner's *Lohengrin-Prelude to Act III* is a popular symphonic number that is frequently performed. In addition, it is the only bit of music that appears in both a Beatles movie, *Help!*, and a Marx Brothers movie, *At The Circus* (about 79 minutes into the film).

Side Two opens with another Beatles recording, "Another Girl," which is followed by another instrumental, "Another Hard Day's Night." The track is a medley of songs from the first Beatles movie played on Indian instruments. Guitars, piano, bass and drums are replaced by sitar, sarod, tabla and tamboura. In addition to turning "A Hard Day's Night" into a raga, the musicians play parts of the melody lines from "Can't Buy Me Love" and "I Should Have Known Better" towards the end. This medley appears in the Indian restaurant scene, where a group of four Indian musicians are playing. They are attacked and replaced one by one by members of Clang's gang, who then play the Beatles tunes. While this music is clearly audible at the start, its volume is soon lowered in the film's soundtrack to enable the audience to hear the conversations between the Beatles and Clang and his followers, who have also replaced the restaurant's staff. The album contains this entire musical cue at full volume.

The Beatles "Ticket To Ride" is followed by a track titled "The Bitter End"/"You Can't Do That." This is another edit of two cues from different parts of the film. The first 1:15 is a slow and dreamy instrumental containing many of the suspense elements present in John Barry's James Bond scores. This music is from the scene early in the film where Ahme attempts to remove the sacrificial ring from Ringo's finger with a long-poled device when he is asleep in his bed.

The track then segues into a jazz-flavored, barely recognizable version of "You Can't Do That." The music starts with ominous tones before breaking into an upbeat tempo. Its melody lines are played by alternating brass and woodwind sections, accented by lead guitar lines ala Vic Flick's playing on the "James Bond Theme." This 1:07 cue is taken from the Alps scene where the Beatles are riding on a sled and Ringo's leg is snared by a rope, dangling him from a ski-lift until the rope breaks, dropping him to the ground. The total track has a running time of 2:22.

After the Beatles recording of "You're Gonna Lose That Girl" (as titled on the Capitol LP), the album closes with an instrumental titled "The Chase." This Ken Thorne number, 2.25 in length, is dominated by Indian instruments. The fast-paced selection is a raga containing many of the elements that would later turn up on George's Indian music selections. This number does not appear in the film.

Not all of the musical cues heard in the film are on the album. During one of the ski scenes, there is a classical cue incorporating bits of "She's A Woman." At the end of the Salisbury Plain battle, we hear Tchaikovsky's *1812 Overture*. The Beatles ride bikes to a march arrangement of "I'm Happy Just To Dance With You." The music accompanying "The Very Famous Plan" alternates between slow, deliberate notes from "A Hard Day's Night" and a whimsical cue that incorporates elements of "She's A Woman" and the vibe of Henry Mancini's "Baby Elephant Walk." The film's ending credits are backed by the Beatles impromptu vocalizations over Rossini's overture to "The Barber Of Seville," complete with George adding "'I Need You' by George Harrison," and an ending cough.

The liner notes to George Martin's orchestral album of *Help!* songs indicate that the songs appearing in the film are published by "Maclen Music, Inc. [American publisher for Lennon-McCartney] & Unart Music Corp. [United Artist's publishing subsidiary]." For legal publishing reasons, the three songs on the album that had yet to be issued in America were given different names: "Scrambled Egg" for "Yesterday;" "Auntie Gin's Theme" for "I've Just Seen A Face;" and "That's A Nice Hat (Cap)" for "It's Only Love." The latter substitution was most likely random and was not a working title of the song.

"HELP!" Guess where the Beatles are now?
Bermuda!! Austria!! And what are they doing there?
Why are the high priests of the terrible Goddess of Kaili interested in the Beatles?
Why is Ringo being pursued to the ends of the earth by a gang of Eastern thugs?
What do they want of him—they aren't fans.
Two leading scientists hope to rule the world.
Paul is threatened by a beetle.
An Eastern beauty saves the boys' lives time and time again.
A channel swimmer ends up in an Alpine lake and Buckingham Palace has a busy day.
When Scotland Yard arrives in the sunny Bahamas after unsuccessful maneuvers on Salisbury Plain they find four Ringos but only one George, one Paul and one John.
When the power crazy scientists arrive in the Alps the boys miraculously escape their deadly weapons.
Will John live to sleep in his pit again?
Will Paul ever get back to his electric organ?
Will George be re-united with his ticker-tape machine?
And Ringo—will he ever play the drums again?
(Just in case you haven't seen the movie yet we don't want to spoil the story for you but we will tell you that Ringo is the cause of it all.)
AND NOW... HEAR RINGO, JOHN, GEORGE AND PAUL SING ALL THEIR SENSATIONAL "HELP!" SONGS IN THIS VERY SPECIAL MOVIE SOUNDTRACK SOUVENIR ALBUM!